Part-Time Soldiers

STUDIES IN **CMR**
CIVIL-MILITARY RELATIONS

William A. Taylor, Series Editor

Part-Time Soldiers

Reserve Readiness Challenges in Modern Military History

Andrew Lewis Chadwick

 University Press of Kansas

Published by the University Press of Kansas (Lawrence, Kansas 66045), which was
organized by the Kansas Board of Regents and is operated and funded by Emporia State
University, Fort Hays State University, Kansas State University, Pittsburg State University,
the University of Kansas, and Wichita State University.

Library of Congress Cataloging-in-Publication Data

Names: Chadwick, Andrew Lewis, author.
Title: Part-time soldiers : reserve readiness challenges in modern military
  history / Andrew Lewis Chadwick.
Other titles: Reserve readiness challenges in modern military history
Description: Lawrence, Kansas : University Press of Kansas, 2023. | Series:
  Studies in civil-military relations | Includes bibliographical references and index.
Identifiers: LCCN 2023008280 (print) | LCCN 2023008281 (ebook)
  ISBN 9780700635870 (cloth)
  ISBN 9780700635887 (ebook)
Subjects: LCSH: Armed Forces—Reserves—History. | United States. National
  Guard—History. | United States—Armed Forces—Reserves—History. | United
  States. Army—Reserves—History. | United States—Military policy. | Israel. Tseva
  haganah le-Yiśra'el—Reserves—History. | Israel—Military policy. | BISAC:
  HISTORY / Military / General | HISTORY / Military / United States
Classification: LCC UA15 .C47 2024 (print) | LCC UA15 (ebook) | DDC
  355.00973—dc23/eng/20230802
LC record available at https://lccn.loc.gov/2023008280.
LC ebook record available at https://lccn.loc.gov/2023008281.

British Library Cataloguing-in-Publication Data is available.

Printed in the United States of America

10 9 8 7 6 5 4 3 2 1

The paper used in this publication is acid free and meets the minimum requirements of
the American National Standard for Permanence of Paper for Printed Library Materials
Z39.48–1992

Contents

List of Tables   *vii*

Series Editor's Foreword   *ix*

Preface   *xi*

1. The Reserve Dilemma   1

2. The United States Confronts the Reserve Dilemma   38

3. The National Guard as an Operational Reserve   77

4. The Heights of Israeli Reserve Performance   113

5. The Decline of the Israel Defense Forces Army Reserve   151

Conclusion   191

Notes   *201*

Bibliography   *273*

Index   *297*

Tables

1.1 Prussian Force Generation Model   7
1.2 Military Personnel of Major European Powers   11
1.3 Prewar Reserve and Active Army Strength, 1914   18
2.1 National Guard World War I Deployment Timeline   46
2.2 National Guard World War I Campaigns and Losses   48
2.3 National Guard Mobilization and Composition, 1940–41   58
2.4 National Guard World War II Deployment Timeline   64
2.5 Army National Guard Maneuver Units Deployed during
     the Korean War   72
3.1 Rising Costs of the All-Volunteer Force   96
4.1 Demographics of Palestine during the British Mandate   115
4.2 IDF Size and Order of Battle, 1948–67   133
4.3 Expansion of IDF Weapons Systems, 1967–73   143
5.1 IDF Army Growth, 1973–84   153
5.2 IDF Personnel Costs (Civilian and Military), 1972–84   153
5.3 Expansion of IDF Combat Systems, 1986–90   161
5.4 IDF Personnel Costs and Defense Imports, 1990–2015   184
5.5 Israeli Defense Spending, 2005–18   185
6.1 Historical Examples of Policy Responses to the Reserve
     Dilemma   194

Series Editor's Foreword

William A. Taylor

The nature, purpose, and history of reserve forces are critically important topics that are often understudied and underappreciated. Andrew Chadwick's compelling and comparative study, *Part-Time Soldiers*, goes a long way toward rectifying this imbalance. The book is an innovative, detailed, and sound contribution to the existing literature, as the author advances our understanding of how the reserve dilemma has developed over time and why it matters today and moving forward.

Chadwick introduces myriad factors that have influenced and shaped reserve forces in different contexts, including military, political, and socioeconomic ones. With the general shift away from conscription during the last quarter of the twentieth century, the rising costs of maintaining full-time, highly trained active forces led to increased reliance on reserves. As a result, reserve forces have undertaken new roles and missions, further altering how states wage war. Chadwick leverages the instructive examples of the United States and Israel to illustrate the unique ways these powerful dynamics emerged in each country and the consequences wrought by this metamorphosis. By examining the development of the US Army National Guard (ARNG) and the Israel Defense Forces (IDF), the author interrogates the two primary contemporary models for reserve forces and provides many useful points of contrast. As this engaging story unfolds, one lesson becomes clear: finding the appropriate balance between reduced costs and sufficient training has proved difficult for leaders, civilian and military alike, to achieve.

John McAuley Palmer, a longtime advocate of reserve forces and principal adviser to George C. Marshall on universal military training, often used the metaphor of steel and concrete to describe the relationship between active and reserve forces.[1] "While nothing can be proved by analogy alone, we can get a reasonable conception of the interrelations between the professional military establishments and civilian components by considering the relation between steel and concrete in a reinforced concrete building," Palmer contended. "With too little steel there would be a deficiency in tensile strength throughout the structure; with too much it would be unnecessarily expensive."[2] Indeed, as Chadwick persuasively shows in

Part-Time Soldiers, additional developments well after World War II only exacerbated the dilemma so eloquently described by Palmer.

A more informed understanding of the reserve dilemma relates to civil-military relations in three important ways. First, the missions undertaken by military forces are perennial facets of the field. Chadwick illuminates the roles reserves have filled in both the United States and Israel. He adroitly demonstrates how those tasks have morphed over time and the implications of such weighty changes. Second, this novel study illuminates the importance of who serves in the military, in this case, through the long-standing notion of the citizen-soldier. Third, operational challenges and military effectiveness are essential to civil-military relations. Chadwick does an excellent job outlining both of these crucial areas vis-à-vis reserve forces. As a result, he achieves a balance between outlining the theoretical and historical context of the reserve dilemma and detailing how and why these issues matter to operational effectiveness.

Part-Time Soldiers is a welcome addition to military history, policy analysis, and civil-military relations writ large. It advances our understanding of how reserve forces have developed over time and reinforces why they matter to military effectiveness, including opportunities and challenges in the past, present, and future. Anyone interested in reserve forces, force structure, and the vital lessons they reveal about civil-military relations will find much to ponder in this deeply researched, persuasively argued, and lucidly conveyed book.

In the past it was sufficient that the reservist was motivated and
proficient in basic fighting skills. Today . . . this is no longer enough
in view of the great complexity of modern warfare.
—Lieutenant General Mordechai Gur[1]

On 1 November 2019 US Central Command (CENTCOM) deployed elements of a mechanized infantry battalion from the South Carolina Army National Guard (ARNG) to the al-Omar oil fields in northeastern Syria. Its two-part mission was an extremely sensitive and highly controversial one: prevent Russian, Iranian, and Syrian forces from seizing the oil fields and help US Special Forces and their Kurdish allies defeat the remnants of the terrorist Islamic State in eastern Syria.[2] In 2018, at the same location, US Special Forces had repulsed an assault by upward of five hundred Russian mercenaries and Syrian soldiers.[3] Given such dangers and sensitivities, one US defense expert questioned why a guard unit was assigned to carry out such a significant and complex mission.[4] Similar questions would arise among leaders of the US Eighty-Second Airborne Division when—to their surprise—Minnesota guardsmen arrived at Kabul International Airport in 2021 to help with the evacuation of noncombatants as the Afghan government and military collapsed under the weight of a Taliban onslaught.[5]

For most of modern history, reserve forces—part-time soldiers who reinforce or augment full-time professionals or conscripts in wartime—played largely supporting roles in conflicts outside of their countries' borders. Rarely did nations, including the United States, deploy reserve combat units to take part in strategically significant missions like the ones the South Carolina guardsmen faced in 2019 or the Minnesotans confronted two years later.[6] But those who questioned their participation in these missions overlooked the fact that a confluence of military, political, and socioeconomic processes and decisions led to a situation in which the United States had little choice but to send guardsmen to these and other battlefronts because it lacked sufficient active-duty units. And as this book shows, in the past century, many other states have had to rely on reserve units for missions that historically were carried out by full-time soldiers, be they conscripts, volunteers, or mercenaries.

This book examines the underlying historical developments and decisions that led to an increased reliance on reserve units for critical and routine security tasks. In doing so, it identifies two important yet seemingly paradoxical historical trends. First, states preparing for major war have confronted rising personnel and equipment costs as their armed forces embraced increasingly high-tech and high-skilled means and methods of waging war. This change in the character of war occurred in the context of a general decline in societies' tolerance of industrial-era conscription practices mandating near-universal military service. As a result, states have had to depend on higher-paid volunteers and reserve soldiers whose part-time service makes them relatively cost-effective compared to full-timers.

Second, over the past century, reservists have struggled to keep up with the changing character of war, given their limited time to train. In most cases, industrial-era policies are still in place, requiring reservists to train for ten to thirty days a year—or sometimes not at all—to maintain proficiency in their respective occupations and to stay abreast of the latest tactical and technological developments. This was generally sufficient in the context of the relatively simple mass infantry tactics of the late nineteenth and early twentieth centuries, but it has proved inadequate in the mechanized and highly dynamic battlefields of the past century. Consequently, reservists have often performed poorly in battle compared to active-duty soldiers, as evidenced by their widespread struggles in the world wars and in more recent conflicts such as the 2006 Lebanon War and the ongoing Russia-Ukraine war.

These two trends—the growing need for reservists and their general inability to meet the standards of contemporary war-fighting practices—presented defense policymakers with a dilemma. At the heart of that dilemma was the age-old question of how to build a military force capable of meeting its strategic and tactical requirements at an affordable cost in blood and treasure. Some, like the Soviet Union, chose to utilize their reserves for routine combat support tasks, leaving more complicated assignments to full-time professionals or conscripts. Others, such as the United States since the 1960s, greatly expanded the training requirements for reserve units, bringing them closer to the standards of the active-duty army. Each choice carried its own risk and was often possible only because of special historical circumstances. And failure to understand or address this dilemma risked, and in several cases led to, tactical and even strategic disaster, as the French learned in World War II.

This book's examination of the historical developments and dilemmas that led to contemporary challenges in reserve policy is significant for three reasons. First, there are no systematic historical studies of the development and evolution of army reservists. That said, several works address the capability and performance of certain reserve forces over time or during a particular conflict. For instance, Eugenia Kiesling provides a comprehensive analysis of the capabilities of the interwar French army reserve in *Arming against Hitler*.[7] Similarly, in his study of the interwar British army, David French shows how British reservists struggled to keep up with technical and tactical changes in the character of war in the 1930s and 1940s.[8] Michael Doubler's *Civilian in Peace, Soldier in War* examines the history of the ARNG—the main combat reserve component of the US Army.[9] And Ute Frevert's *A Nation in Barracks* is the definitive history of the German reserve and conscript system.[10] These works reveal how the technical demands of soldiering challenged reservists' ability to maintain a state of readiness for war, but they do not fully explore the broader historical processes and decisions that helped create and sustain these challenges.

Second, this book identifies an unintended and important second-order effect resulting from the mid-twentieth-century shift away from mass conscript armies to armies staffed by long-service professionals and specially trained technicians. That shift, which has been explored by other historians such as Michael Howard, John Keegan, and Antulio Echevarria, created major stresses on the nineteenth-century reserve training and personnel models that are still in use today.[11] In short, this book takes a well-explored theme in military history—the development and adoption of high-skilled and high-tech approaches to warfare over the past century—and examines how it shaped the role, capability, and performance of army reservists.

Finally, by documenting and explaining the development and significance of the dependence on reserve forces, this book provides a historical context for ongoing policy debates in the United States and elsewhere on how best to structure and employ reserve units. Such debates, as one US policy analyst noted, often lack a rigorous historical context that explains how and why armies are dependent on reservists and what reservists have proved capable or incapable of doing.[12] In short, this book enriches the historiography of modern warfare while providing a valuable context for policy analysis.

This book cannot—and does not—account for the experiences of all reservists in the past century. Instead, it concentrates on a new type of reservist: the kind that armies use to replace or augment active units for offensive and defensive operations inside or outside national borders. Such reservists emerged during the French Revolution but did not become a standard form of military organization until the Prussians developed and demonstrated the ability to field highly effective reservists during the wars of German unification in the mid-nineteenth century. Since then, nearly every state preparing for major war has developed Prussian-style reserve systems or variations of them. Such reservists are the focus of this book. Therefore, it does not examine the experience of militias and other reservists serving almost exclusively as homeland defense forces with little or no expeditionary capability (e.g., the territorial militias of Estonia, Poland, and other states).

I narrow my focus even further to the experience of reserve maneuver units: armor and infantry, including mechanized, motorized, and airborne infantry. I center my analysis on these units because, historically, armies have primarily utilized their reserve components as trained or semitrained maneuver units to replace or augment their standing forces. Of course, reservists also perform a host of combat support functions, including medical, intelligence, and transportation services, but because these reservists have unique training and technical requirements, they fall outside the scope of this book. Such personnel also have the advantage of being able to practice their professions in the civilian world. For example, a military nurse can practice nursing outside the military, but the combat arms have no equivalent civilian profession.

In exploring contemporary reservists, this book relies primarily on two case studies: the US ARNG and the Israel Defense Forces (IDF) army reserve. They were selected because they represent the two main types of reserve models. The ARNG uses the Anglo-American model built around volunteers, many of whom have no prior active-duty experience.[13] In contrast, the Israelis employ a Prussian-style model in which all reservists have served as full-time conscripts for at least two to three years.[14] Additionally, for unique geopolitical reasons, the US and Israeli reserves have had to go to war more frequently than other reserve armies since World War II, providing insights into how their capabilities and performance have changed over time.

To analyze the history of reserve forces in general and the experiences of the ARNG and IDF reserve in particular, this book relies on a variety of primary and secondary sources. Field manuals, biographies, annual reports, press reports, and recently declassified US national security documents provide an appreciation of how the changing character of war has affected reserve forces. Secondary sources often ignore reservists or conflate their experiences with active-duty units; however, they allow an understanding of broad trends in military history and the experiences of reserves within that history. Additionally, the ARNG case study uses rarely cited primary source documents, including the personal papers of senior guard leaders, which provide firsthand accounts of readiness issues.[15]

Strict classification rules governing Israeli military documents limit the information available about the IDF's capabilities and intentions, especially in more recent wars. Thus, the analysis of the IDF draws more heavily on secondary sources, biographies, press reports, and declassified US intelligence reports. In addition, articles written by Israeli officers—many of whom are reservists—in the IDF's professional journal *Maarachot* (Hebrew for "systems") provide direct insights into some of the personnel, training, and equipment challenges facing the Israeli reserves since the early 1950s.[16]

There is also a fieldwork-type component to this book. Since 2009, I have served in the Maryland Army National Guard, first as an enlisted soldier and then as an officer.[17] During my service in the ARNG, I have worked as a squad member in a combat engineer company, a staff officer with a cavalry squadron and at an infantry division headquarters, and an analyst at the National Guard Bureau. While writing this book, I also had the privilege of serving with guardsmen and reservists while deployed to Afghanistan and Kuwait and during multiple disaster and civil response missions in the United States. These experiences at the tactical, operational, and strategic levels alerted me to the growing challenge of building and maintaining readiness in a reserve unit during an era of high-tech and high-skilled warfare. In addition, my education in military history at the University of Maryland–College Park helped me understand the historical processes, decisions, and events that produced and sustained these challenges.

Ultimately, this book does not provide any solutions to the readiness issues my fellow guardsmen and I have confronted and will almost certainly continue to face. However, I hope it provides readers with an understanding of how and why the reserve readiness issues described in the following chapters emerged, why they persist, and their tactical and strategic significance. To accomplish this, chapter 1 provides a broad examination of the history of the trained reserves from their emergence as a crucial military organization in the nineteenth century to contemporary challenges facing reserve forces, including the constraints and compulsions shaping how states have developed, trained, and employed their reserves in modern military history. With its core themes established, the book then turns to case studies of a volunteer reserve (the ARNG) and a reserve composed of discharged conscripts (the IDF army reserve). A summary of my findings and key judgments is presented in the conclusion.

I could not have completed this book without the loving support, encouragement, and editorial advice of my wife, Gretchen. Without her, I might have given up on this project long ago. My parents also provided me the confidence, mentorship, and support to embark on my long college career and subsequent professional and military pursuits. I am also thankful for my sister, Ashley, who taught me how to write my first college paper and made sure I stayed motivated during my early days as a college student. And I am forever grateful to the faculty of the Political Science and History Departments at the University of Saint Mary, who gave me the confidence and tools to pursue graduate studies. I could not have succeeded as a graduate student without the support, mentorship, and sage wisdom of Professor Jon Sumida at the University of Maryland–College Park, who guided me through the writing of my dissertation, which eventually turned into this book. I also want to thank the Joseph and Alma Gildenhorn Institute for Israel Studies at the University of Maryland–College Park—especially Professors Paul Scham and Yoram Peri, who taught me the history and politics of Israel—which graciously provided funding for my Ph.D. studies. I am extremely grateful to the University Press of Kansas for giving this new author an opportunity to publish and share this work. Finally, this book owes a tremendous debt to the soldiers and officers of the Maryland Army National Guard, who consistently demonstrate how citizen-soldiers can excel in an era of high-tech and high-skilled warfare.

Part-Time Soldiers

Chapter One

The Reserve Dilemma

Technology, which in the nineteenth century had made mass participation in warfare both possible and necessary, was in the twentieth century to place increasing power in the hands of highly qualified technicians.
—Michael Howard[1]

Since World War I, armies preparing for major war have struggled to reconcile their nineteenth-century reserve systems with the increasingly high-tech and high-skilled character of modern warfare. Such systems, developed by Prussia in the mid-nineteenth century, generally consisted of two elements: a small standing army composed primarily of short-service conscripts and a larger reserve of part-time soldiers. After two or three years of service as a conscript or longer service as a professional, reservists were nearly as effective as active soldiers. The Prussian reserve system addressed the need for an affordable army that was numerically and qualitatively comparable to a larger army composed of long-service professionals. Other Great Powers followed Prussia's example after its decisive victories over Austria-Hungry and France in the German wars of unification. Some, like Great Britain and the United States, attempted to imitate the Prussian system by boosting reserve training standards for their volunteer reserve and militia systems.

However, both the Prussian and the Anglo-American reserve models—and their variations—proved inadequate in the wars of the twentieth and twenty-first centuries, as reservists struggled to keep up with the rising technical demands of soldiering with only thirty days or less of annual training. This situation presented defense policymakers with a dilemma: they could not afford to fight without their reserves because a host of military, financial, political, and socioeconomic constraints denied them sufficient active-duty soldiers to meet strategic and tactical requirements. Each policy approach to address the dilemma, such as increasing reserve training standards or keeping reserve forces in supporting roles,

1

carried its own risks and drawbacks. And failure to recognize and resolve the problem could lead to tactical and strategic disaster, as the French and others experienced in the world wars and as Russia was learning in Ukraine as of mid-2023.

Three Revolutions and the Emergence of Trained Reserves

In the eighteenth and nineteenth centuries, states developed two types of reserve models to reinforce their standing armies with trained or semi-trained part-time soldiers: a reserve composed of discharged short-service conscripts and one composed of volunteers who may have had active-duty experience. The former is most strongly associated with the Prussian armed forces, whose mass army of conscripts and recalled reservists revolutionized how war was waged in the second half of the nineteenth century. The latter was primarily employed by the armies of Great Britain and the United States, which made incremental improvements to their citizens' militias and reserves in the forty years leading up to World War I to ensure that they were better prepared to succeed on an industrial-era battlefield.

Prior to the late eighteenth century, citizen-soldiers—be they militiamen or reservists—had little tactical and strategic value due to various political, administrative, and military constraints. From a political perspective, rulers and the military elite were hesitant to arm their subjects, fearing that such a policy would risk instability or revolution.[2] And even if they had wanted to, early states lacked the administrative capabilities and financial means to train, equip, and deploy mass armies.[3] Moreover, part-time soldiers were poor substitutes for full-timers because medieval and early modern tactics required considerable physical stamina and practiced skill.[4] A civilian thrust into battle with little to no formal training or experience was no match for a seasoned professional. Thus, rulers relied primarily on small armies of long-service professionals and mercenaries who possessed the physical and mental skills necessary to survive and thrive on the battlefield. Keeping a small, long-service army also enabled rulers to maintain control when confronted by revolutionaries or other internal threats.[5]

The constraints that restricted the development and employment of militarily effective part-time soldiers loosened during the American and French Revolutions. Revolutionaries in those countries demonstrated that nationalistic societies facing the threat of annihilation could field a militia or reserve with tactical and strategic value. When the Americans rebelled against Britain in 1775, they lacked a standing army, but they had local militias that helped secure their communities from internal and external threats for more than a century. Although unprofessional by European standards, these militias provided a semitrained reserve of soldiers who reinforced the small standing army the Americans hastily formed in 1775.[6]

Despite early defeats by a much more experienced and better-trained British army, the Americans' sense of divine purpose, support from France, and British logistical shortfalls enabled the United States to secure independence in 1783.[7] Without the militias, the Americans likely would have had too few soldiers to pressure Britain to end the war. Afterward, the United States formalized its commitment to citizen-soldiers for national defense with passage of the Militia Act of 1792, which required all free, able-bodied white male citizens between the ages of eighteen and forty-five to join a local militia.[8] But, as the next chapter shows, the American militia remained highly unprofessional and militarily insignificant for much of the nineteenth century.

Six years after the American Revolution, French revolutionaries developed their own militia: the National Guard (NG). The NG was a part-time military organization consisting primarily of middle-class Frenchmen who, together with other citizen-volunteers, defeated an invading Prussian army in 1792 and saved the revolution.[9] However, members of the French NG had little will or ability to leave their homes for training or campaigns abroad.[10] Thus, the NG was unable to meet the standards of regular soldiers, and its amateur officer corps was, in the words of Napoleon Bonaparte, a "laughingstock" among the men.[11]

Although weak from a tactical perspective, the NG was strategically important because it helped garrison France. This freed the active army, which had grown through the mass conscription of patriotic French youth, for expeditionary operations.[12] Nevertheless, Napoleon's disastrous 1812 Russian campaign destroyed a large portion of his army, forcing him to retreat to France, where he had to deploy the NG to intercept an invading coalition army in 1814. Despite a vigorous defense, the French NG was no match for the large standing armies of its adversaries, which seized Paris and forced Napoleon to abdicate power.[13]

To defeat the massive armies of France, the nations allied against it had to develop or improve their existing militias and reserve-like organizations. The Prussians were particularly dependent on reservists and their *Landwehr* militia. Like the rest of its allies, Prussia initially attempted to defeat France with its standing army of long-service professionals. But after its defeat by Napoleon at Jena-Auerstedt in 1806, Prussia began to examine how to maximize the military potential of its citizenry, as France had done through mass conscription and establishment of the NG.[14] One way it did so was by building a reserve of part-time soldiers through the *Krumper* system.[15] Under this system, each active-duty infantry company released twenty of its most senior soldiers every year to serve in the reserves on a part-time basis; twenty new recruits replaced those veterans in active units.[16] This system allowed Prussia to build a reserve of trained personnel that it could recall in wartime, and it could do so without violating treaty restrictions put in place by France that limited the Prussian army to forty-two thousand active soldiers.[17]

Once war with France resumed, Prussia refined its conscription and reserve system. Under new regulations laid out in September 1814, conscripts would serve three years in the active army, two in the reserve, six in the first line of the *Landwehr*, seven in the second-line *Landwehr*, and ten years in the *Landstrum*.[18] At the same time, Prussia infused its reserve and militia ranks with veteran leadership by placing each reserve infantry battalion under the command of an active regiment. To grow its reserve battalions, Prussia used a mixture of new recruits and demobilized soldiers.[19] By mixing veteran soldiers and leaders with inexperienced ones, Prussia ensured that its reserve and, to a lesser extent, the *Landwehr* performed well during two years of campaigning.[20]

In short, the American and French Revolutions demonstrated that, under certain circumstances, reservists and militiamen had tactical and strategic value. Those circumstances included the presence of an existential threat that compelled rulers or revolutionaries to maximize the military potential of their citizenry through conscription and the deployment of reservists and militiamen. For this to occur, a significant number of individuals had to be willing to serve. Early forms of nationalism in Europe and North America made it easier for states to activate their militias and implement conscription. And, in the case of Prussia, the presence of veteran leaders in the ranks of militia and reserve formations demonstrated that part-time soldiers could face—and even defeat—long-service professionals and conscripts when they were well led. Yet, for the most part, reservists and militiamen remained poor substitutes for active soldiers, given their relative lack of training and experience, as evidenced by the struggles of the American and French militias. This widespread use of citizen-soldiers as conscripts, reservists, and militiamen did not survive the French Revolution, as the victors sought to reimpose the old aristocratic order in Europe.

Smaller professional armies were better suited for the military requirements of the first half of the nineteenth century. During that period, European armies generally had two missions: defend against domestic revolutionaries and serve in the colonies. For domestic missions, states needed to ensure that their armies were loyal and willing to suppress revolutionary movements, not join them. To guarantee loyalty, states kept armies small and segregated from the civilian population, enabling them to maintain better oversight of the armies' activities while walling them off from outside political influences.[21] For missions abroad, states needed soldiers who served on long contracts and had few obligations outside the barracks. Short-service conscripts or part-time reservists—who had families and civilian work commitments—were ill-suited for such duties.[22] In addition, recruiting, housing, and supplying armies of professionals, short-term conscripts, recalled reservists, or mobilized national guardsmen were simply too expensive at the time.

Part-time soldiers lacked the training time to develop the tactical and physical skills necessary to fight according to the military standards of the first half of the nineteenth century. Armies at the time retained eighteenth-century close-order infantry tactics that required soldiers to march in step in columnar or linear formations and to load and shoot their firearms in unison.[23] Because firearms were highly inaccurate, infantrymen needed to fire in unison on a concentrated front to shock opponents into submission both physically and psychologically. Learning how to fight in this manner required practice and experience, which was difficult for part-time or short-service soldiers to obtain.

Soldiers also needed time to develop the physical fitness necessary to perform their jobs effectively. Preindustrial armies did not have reliable overland transportation for personnel and equipment. Thus, when moving to and from battle, soldiers had to carry all their personal equipment on their backs, marching dozens of miles a day with little or no protection from the elements. Militiamen who were civilians most of the time lacked the physical training of professional soldiers and were unlikely to endure such conditions.[24]

Despite these limitations, Prussia continued to rely on part-time reservists and short-service conscripts, given its tiny economy and small population relative to its larger allies and adversaries.[25] Yet, in the first half of the nineteenth century, Prussia struggled to maintain an effective reserve due to a variety of fiscal, political, and military constraints. From a fiscal perspective, Prussia's economy could not sustain its conscription system, and it frequently had to discharge conscripts early to save money.

Cost-cutting measures also forced Prussia to reduce the length of conscript service from three years to two in 1833.[26] In addition, because of fiscal and recruiting constraints, the army had to send many eligible conscripts directly into the *Landwehr* without the benefit of active-duty service; once in the *Landwehr*, men received little training or subpar instruction from amateur militia leaders.[27] By 1832, up to 50 percent of militiamen entered the *Landwehr* under such circumstances.[28]

Political pressure was also a factor. Prussian elites worried that militiamen posed a threat to internal stability, and the middle class questioned the purpose of universal military service during peacetime.[29] These concerns helped justify cuts to reserve and militia training.[30] Consequently, the *Landwehr* and the reserves fell into disrepair. When they were activated to suppress revolutionaries and rioters in the 1840s, it was no surprise that they demonstrated poor discipline; some even participated in the unrest.[31]

Despite these flaws, the Prussian military system had many benefits, some of which were not fully realized until later in the century. For instance, keeping a significant percentage of soldiers in the reserves and the militia could save money, as the state did not have to feed or house them during peacetime. Second, Prussia's regional recruitment practices allowed the formation of cohesive units that were relatively easy to mobilize in wartime or for training, given that most soldiers lived near local training depots.[32] But the most important benefit of having a trained reserve was the greater number of soldiers available in the event of war, compensating in part for the scale and lethality of industrial-era warfare.

Wars of the mid-nineteenth century, such as the Crimean War (1853–56), the Franco-Austrian War (1859), and the US Civil War (1861–65), demonstrated that new firearms and artillery could rapidly render small professional armies combat ineffective.[33] New rifled muskets that used percussion caps instead of flintlocks and fired conical bullets had much higher rates of fire and were more accurate and more reliable than older models.[34] And new breech-loading artillery that fired exploding shells had twice the rate of fire compared to muzzleloaders and about 33 percent greater range.[35] Armies equipped with these weapons could inflict devastating losses on opposing forces that still fought in close-order formations.[36]

Such losses were problematic because few armies had trained reserves to replace dead or wounded active soldiers. As one British historian wrote of the Crimean War, "There were no reserves to take the place of those dauntless legions which melted in the crucible of battle and left a void which time alone could fill."[37] As predicted by nineteenth-century military theorist Antoine-Henri Jomini in 1838, these developments "threatened a great revolution in army organization, armament, and tactics."[38] The Prussian reserve system was a major part of that coming revolution. In the 1850s and 1860s the Prussians took steps to modernize that system, aiming to improve their ability to deter foreign adversaries in general and the increasingly aggressive French in particular.

As Great Power competition again turned violent, the Prussian army consisted of three elements: the active army, the reserve, and the *Landwehr*. Prussian soldiers served in the active army for three years, followed by four years in the reserves and then five years in the *Landwehr*.[39] Three-year terms were reestablished by the early 1860s as part of a reform effort led by William I, who took over for his ailing brother in 1858.[40] In theory, this system meant that Prussia could rapidly expand its wartime army with trained and semitrained soldiers; these additional soldiers would help Prussia compete with France's larger standing army and give it depth in terms of replacement personnel to compensate for heavy battlefield losses. For example, if Prussia conscripted ten thousand men every three years starting in 1860, it would be able to field an army four times that size by 1869, as shown in table 1.1.

To improve the viability of their conscript and reserve army, the Prussians made several important technical and tactical changes. Perhaps the most important development was the advent of the breech-loading rifle, which the Prussians had secretly started to stockpile in the 1840s.[41] Known as the Dreyse needle rifle (named after inventor Johann Nicholas von Dreyse), this Prussian weapon simplified and accelerated the loading process. Soldiers could just insert a paper cartridge consisting of the black powder charge and the bullet into the breech, rather than having to drop the bullet and the gunpowder down the barrel separately. This was an important development because it was difficult to teach short-service or part-time soldiers how to master the multistep process of loading and

Table 1.1 Prussian Force Generation Model

Year	Active Duty (3-Year Conscripts)	Reserve (Discharged Conscripts, 4-Year Terms)	*Landwehr* (Former Reservists, 5-Year Terms)
1860	10,000	0	0
1863	10,000	10,000	0
1866	10,000	20,000	0
1869	10,000	30,000	10,000

firing muzzle-loading rifles, especially amid the chaos of battle. A faster loading and firing process also meant that relatively unskilled soldiers could generate a higher volume of fire. In fact, the Prussians discovered that a soldier armed with a breechloader had a six-to-one advantage in shots fired per minute compared to one equipped with a muzzleloader.[42] This increased rate of fire also improved reservists' confidence in their ability to compete in battle with long-service professionals.[43]

But Prussia could produce only about ten thousand Dreyse rifles a year using the preindustrial manufacturing techniques of the late 1840s. At that rate, it would have taken more than thirty years to reequip the Prussian army's 320,000 soldiers with new rifles. However, production increased markedly in the 1850s and 1860s, when mass production technologies developed in the United States were introduced in Europe.[44] With these new methods of production, the Prussians were able to equip reservists and members of the *Landwehr* with the Dreyse breech-loading rifles in the early 1860s.[45]

The railway, meanwhile, provided a new means of transporting hundreds of thousands of Prussian reservists—and their equipment—from mobilization depots to battle, reducing the need for long marches that left the out-of-shape reservists exhausted before the fighting even started.[46] Prussian officers had recognized the railroads' potential for the rapid mobilization of reservists and conscripts as early as the mid-1830s.[47] Over the next three decades, the Prussians expanded their rail networks and conducted exercises demonstrating the feasibility of moving men and equipment from the interior to the frontier by rail.[48]

Overseeing the mobilization and deployment of reservists was the Prussian General Staff. By the 1860s, the General Staff consisted of about sixty highly trained and experienced officers who managed plans, operations, logistics, administration, and intelligence for the entire Prussian army.[49] At the time, other armies generally improvised these increasingly important functions, but the Prussians did not have that luxury because they depended on the speedy and efficient mobilization of hundreds of thousands of reservists. Failure to mobilize quickly could allow France's large standing army to strike first and overwhelm Prussia's small conscript army. But this mobilization process required careful planning; otherwise, reservists and conscripts might arrive at the front too late, looking like a "ragged assembly . . . of disorderly armed men," as Prussian chief of staff Helmuth von Moltke later explained.[50] To prevent such disorder, the General Staff conducted detailed studies and exercises in peacetime that refined and tested Prussia's ability to mobilize and deploy its army. The staff, for instance, produced rail timetables to ensure that men and material arrived at the right place at the right time.[51] They also produced studies of opposing armies and created detailed maps of potential battlegrounds so that subordinate commands understood the operating environment and their adversaries.[52]

Helping the General Staff coordinate these functions and processes was a revolutionary communications technology: the telegraph. Invented in the 1840s, the telegraph gave the General Staff the means to instantly pass orders to its field armies and subordinate corps. Without such a capability, the General Staff almost certainly would have been unable to coordinate the movement of separate army commands moving across a broad front.[53]

As Prussia expanded its rail networks and developed contingency plans for war, it also reformed how it trained and organized its army. In doing so, it greatly increased the readiness of its reserve forces. The decision to return conscript service to three years was particularly important. King William I and his advisers considered three years of service essential to instill discipline, a martial spirit, and military skills in conscripts. In their estimation, it took that long for conscripts to master marksmanship skills and develop the confidence and ability to take the initiative if required.[54] Longer service also provided discharged conscripts with a more substantial base of training and experience to draw on when they were reactivated for reserve service.

The ability to take the initiative and fight with minimal supervision was important because of changes to Prussian tactics in the early 1860s. At the time, Prussian leaders understood that even the best-trained short-service conscripts and recalled reservists might not have the discipline and marksmanship skills to prevail in a protracted firefight with long-service professionals. Thus, in 1861 they decided to increase the intervals within and between their tactical formations, moving from battalion column formations to smaller company columns and skirmish lines that could maneuver rapidly to an enemy flank or rear while taking advantage of cover and concealment.[55] Doing so reduced the likelihood of conscripts and reservists engaging in prolonged firefights because smaller and more dispersed formations could move faster and through more restricted terrain than larger, more cumbersome units. Additionally, the company formation presented a smaller target that would be harder to detect and concentrate fire against.

Prussia's ability to fight in company-sized formations was made possible by several factors. First, nearly all Prussian men were literate, having attended Prussia's robust public school system, which was unmatched in Europe.[56] Literate soldiers could be trusted to read and understand maps, orders, and manuals explaining the tactics they needed to employ in battle. Second, Prussian soldiers and the society from which they emerged were highly nationalistic; once in the army, conscripts and reservists underwent further indoctrination in Prussian national myths and ideals.[57] Such indoctrination likely enhanced the soldiers' willingness to fight with reduced supervision from officers and noncommissioned officers (NCOs), as they would be more inclined to believe their actions and sacrifices served a higher purpose. But most important, Prussia had a robust professional officer and NCO corps that operated under a military command culture known as *Auftragstaktik* (mission tactics), which gave subordinates leeway on how to accomplish their assigned tasks.[58] In other words, junior and mid-ranking Prussian officers and NCOs almost certainly had the training, expertise, and motivation to fight with minimal supervision in company columns or skirmish lines.

During the 1850s and 1860s the Prussians ensured that reservists and militias benefited from this highly professional officer and NCO corps. Starting in 1859, Prussia replaced many reserve officers with retired veterans and provided additional opportunities for reservists to train alongside active soldiers.[59] A decade later, the Prussians reorganized the *Landwehr* to mirror the structure and capabilities of the active army, likely making it easier for militiamen to work with active units in peacetime exercises and in battle.[60] This training alongside active units and the training they received as three-year conscripts also meant that reservists needed to be recalled only four or five days a year to maintain their soldiering skills.[61]

Conscript training in the Prussian army was particularly advanced. Prussian conscripts completed more marksmanship training than those in other armies in the 1860s. And they conducted realistic small-unit exercises that included hands-on tutorials. The French, in comparison, allowed most soldiers to drink away their days, assuming that previous experience would make up for limited peacetime training. After exercises, Prussian conscripts continued to receive training in the evenings from veteran NCOs who gave lectures on discipline and tactics.[62]

These reforms were expensive. In fact, in 1859 Prussia estimated that it would have to increase defense spending by 25 percent to fund them. Fortunately for Prussia, its economy had grown significantly between 1830 and 1860, providing it with a larger tax base to support increased military spending.[63] Such growth resulted from the industrialization of Europe, which led to the emergence of a vibrant urban middle class that

Table 1.2 Military Personnel of Major European Powers

State	Number of Military Personnel	
	1830	1860
Great Britain	140,000	347,000
France	259,000	608,000
Russia	826,000	862,000
Prussia	130,000	201,000
Austro-Hungarian Empire	273,000	306,000

Source: Kennedy, *Rise and Fall of Great Powers*, 154.

produced additional wealth. Prussia and other European states were able to tap into that wealth by adopting representative government systems throughout the first half of the nineteenth century to placate liberals and revolutionaries who threatened to upend the existing social order.[64] In doing so, they gave new capitalist elites and the middle class greater oversight on government spending. This allowed states to borrow more funds with lower interest rates, as the citizenry was able to ensure that the state would repay these loans on time.[65] With lower-interest loans, states gained the financial means to support massive increases in the size of their armies, as shown in table 1.2.

In short, Prussia's technological, financial, socioeconomic, and political circumstances gave it the motivation, means, and methods to field an effective combat reserve. Prussia was motivated to develop an effective reserve because of its precarious geostrategic situation and its inability to fund and staff a large professional army. It had preexisting models for reserve service developed in the eighteenth century and refined during the Napoleonic Wars that it could use to train and deploy effective combat reservists. It improved on those methods during the 1850s and 1860s by intensifying reservist training and developing new tactics to enhance the survivability and maneuverability of reservist and conscript infantry units. Technological changes provided the means to arm reservists with new breech-loading rifles that allowed them to generate as much firepower as well-drilled active soldiers. Railroads and the telegraph enabled the Prussian high command to mobilize and deploy a massive reserve and conscript army in a timely and efficient manner, while reducing the physical demands on recalled reservists and militiamen.

Ultimately, this reserve system gave Prussia a major advantage over its rivals. As one Prussian officer explained to a French counterpart in 1869, just one year before the outbreak of the Franco-Prussian War: "You may win in the morning, but we will win in the evening with our reserves."[66]

Indeed, by the outset of the war in 1870, the French could amass around 400,000 professional troops, but the Prussians could field more than a million by recalling reservists and activating their militia.[67]

The first real test for the reformed Prussian military system came against the Austrians in 1866. On paper, Austria had a clear military advantage; its standing army was larger and filled with long-service veterans.[68] But technological and organizational advantages gave Prussia a qualitative edge. For instance, the Prussian General Staff utilized five railways to mobilize and concentrate three armies, supported by 180,000 *Landwehr* militiamen, inside the Austrian province of Bohemia, catching the Austrians by surprise.[69] And the Austrians were unable to bring their full strength to bear against the Prussian advance because they had to keep about a quarter of their forces deployed in Italy to suppress an uprising. Making matters worse, those available to meet the Prussians lacked the support of a general staff and suffered from decades of underfunding, low morale, poor leadership, and inadequate rail and logistics networks.[70]

In battle, the Prussians had the advantage of nimbler company formations and rapid-shooting breech-loading rifles and artillery. They inflicted devastating losses on the Austrian infantry, which fought in densely packed battalion formations.[71] The Prussians' company columns could penetrate and exploit gaps in the Austrian defenses, as occurred during the Battle of Königgrätz on 3 July 1866.[72] Prussia's victory in that battle set the conditions for a political settlement three months later, which granted Prussia virtual sovereignty over the North German states and control over the military and foreign policy of the southern states.[73] It also put Prussia and France on a collision course.

At the time, France's army was generally thought to be the best in Europe. Its professional soldiers—who served on seven-year contracts—had extensive combat experience gained from counterinsurgency operations in North Africa and conventional wars against Russia and Austria.[74] And, unlike Austria, France had taken substantive steps to prepare its army for the changing technical and tactical realities of industrial-era war. French military officials, for instance, identified breech-loading rifles as the key to Prussia's victory over Austria in 1866. Thus, between 1866 and 1870, the French developed and produced more than a million of their own breech-loading rifles known as the *chassepot*. The *chassepot* was superior to the Dreyse because it had a rubber ring that sealed gases within the breech when a rifleman fired a round. This increased the velocity of the round, allowing it to fire accurately up to 1,460 meters, compared to the 548-meter effective range of the Dreyse.[75]

To compete with the enlarged Prussian army, France worked to grow its own armed forces. Political pressures and legal challenges, however, prevented the emperor from initiating mass conscription, as he would have preferred.[76] Instead, France reduced the time soldiers served on active duty from seven to five years, after which they were inducted into the newly formed army reserve. Those not conscripted served four years in the reserve—after receiving minimal military training—followed by five years in the NG.[77] These reforms enabled the French army to expand from 288,000 active soldiers to 490,000 active and reserve soldiers, backed by about 400,000 national guardsmen, by 1870.[78]

French reservists, however, were poorly trained compared to their Prussian adversaries. By regulation, French reservists trained three weeks a year after completing five years of conscription service. Those requirements were reduced to just two weeks by 1870, and reservists could avoid training altogether by claiming they already had adequate expertise. Reservists who did participate in training were not permitted to stay overnight in military housing, due to legal restrictions that aimed to prevent the corruption of French youth by barracks life.[79] Thus, training time was wasted as the men traveled to and from the barracks.

France also lacked efficient methods of mobilizing and deploying reservists. Unlike the Prussians, French reservists and active soldiers were scattered across France, not located in consolidated mobilization zones. Once mobilized, many reservists had to travel hundreds of miles to regimental depots, delaying France's ability to bring its army up to full strength. In addition, France lacked an efficient General Staff to manage the movement of soldiers and supplies to the front.[80] Consequently, less than 50 percent of reservists were available to reinforce the army at the outset of the war with the Prussian-led North German Confederation in late July and early August 1870.[81]

Using its superior mobilization system, Prussia concentrated sixteen army corps against France by early to mid-August 1870, giving them a near two-to-one advantage in personnel at the front.[82] Included in these sixteen corps were thousands of reservists and militiamen, who would see extensive service during the war. In fact, 121 of the 147 *Landwehr* battalions eventually served in France; in some cases, they helped spearhead attacks and hold territory, freeing the rest of the army to push deeper into France.[83] Such extensive use of part-time reservists and militiamen in operations beyond their homeland was unprecedented.

Prussia used its advantages in personnel to overwhelm and destroy the standing French army by September 1870.[84] For its part, France was able to inflict heavy losses on the Prussians, using the highly accurate and long-range *chassepot* rifles. During the Battle of Gravelotte on 18 August 1870, approximately eight thousand Prussian soldiers were killed in twenty minutes as they charged into French rifle fire.[85] But the Prussian army—reinforced by thousands of reservists and militiamen—absorbed the losses and breached the French defenses with the aid of accurate artillery fire.[86]

The destruction of the French army sparked a revolution in Paris and the formation of the Third Republic on 4 September. Like their ancestors in 1789, the revolutionaries sought to defend France with a people's army. Yet, unlike their forefathers, they lacked a cadre of professional officers and NCOs to train and lead such a force, given that the majority of France's professional soldiers were dead, wounded, or captured.[87] Thus, once it was committed to battle in December, the newly formed French army—which numbered around 200,000—was defeated by a Prussian corps of just 60,000.[88] Following that defeat, France agreed to an armistice in January 1871, paving the way for a formal peace treaty with Prussia four months later.

Prussia defeated France for a variety of reasons, including its superior staff system that mobilized and concentrated forces more quickly and in a far more organized manner than the French. But one key reason for Prussia's victory was its large, reliable, battle-tested reserve—something the French lacked. A viable reserve gave the Prussians the manpower to maintain their army's strength, despite high battlefield attrition rates. And the Prussians could commit their reservists to battle knowing they had the leadership, training, and equipment to succeed, even when pitted against long-service professionals.

The rest of the Great Powers of Europe took note of the Prussian successes and developed or enhanced their own reserve systems and general staffs.[89] Russia, for instance, established a Prussian-style conscript and reserve system in 1874.[90] France did the same in 1889, reducing its long-service army to three-year terms.[91] As armies embraced this conscript and reserve system, the character of modern war was transformed. In the words of Helmuth von Moltke, the architect of Prussia's victory in the Franco-Prussian War, "The days [were] gone by when, for dynastical ends, small armies of professional soldiers went to war to conquer a city, or a province . . . the wars of the present day call whole nations to arms."[92]

Not all the Great Powers adopted a Prussian-style reserve. The Americans and the British clung to their volunteer reserve models due to a host of political, economic, and military constraints and their unique geographic situations. As the next chapter shows, the United States had little choice but to rely on a poorly trained volunteer militia for national defense because the American people and their representatives in Congress had no stomach for conscription and feared that a large standing army could lead to the rise of a tyrannical federal government.[93] But based in part on observations of Prussia's successes in the 1870s, the Americans moved to reform their reserve system in the forty years preceding World War I.[94] For instance, they boosted militia training to twenty-four days a year and ensured that militia training, personnel, and equipment standards more closely mirrored those of the active army.[95] Despite these reforms, a wide qualitative gap remained between the active army and the militia, as described in the next chapter.

The British army also retained its volunteer reserve force, but unlike the Americans, many of its reservists had active-duty experience. For most of its history, Britain relied on local militias and a small reserve (starting in the Napoleonic Wars) to reinforce the active army in a crisis, but most militiamen and reservists were amateurs with little to no ability to deploy abroad, unless they volunteered to do so.[96] And Britain's long-service model meant that when active soldiers completed their enlistment obligations, they were almost certainly too old to fight.

This changed in the 1870s, when Britain began modernizing its armed forces based on lessons learned from the Crimean War and observations of Prussia's successes against Austria and France. One of the most important reforms during this period was the introduction of short service in 1870, which enabled Britain to build a trained reserve. Enlistment in the army was still voluntary and consisted of twelve-year contracts—three to seven years with the active army and the rest in the reserves. At the same time, Britain started linking militia battalions to active regiments, providing them with closer supervision by experienced soldiers. Later, in 1906, it converted much of the militia into the Special Reserve, which could be sent abroad to reinforce the active army in wartime.[97] Rather than fighting as independent units, special reservists filled vacancies in active battalions, working under the supervision of veterans.[98] Militiamen who were not converted to special reservists formed the Territorial Army, which served primarily as a homeland defense force.

The benefit of the British reserve system was that many reservists had extensive active-duty experience. However, because service was voluntary, the British reserve remained minuscule compared to those of the other Great Powers. And the militiamen of the Territorial Army were unavailable for overseas service unless they volunteered. But Britain, like the

United States, would discover that its geographic advantages provided the time and space to retrain and reorganize militiamen prior to deployment.

With few exceptions, the development of a trained reserve, whether along Prussian or Anglo-American lines, was a European and North American affair.[99] Through centuries of near-continuous warfare, European states were able—and willing—to develop the administrative, financial, and military methods and capabilities needed to field and maintain mass armies of conscripts and reservists, as historian William McNeill details in *The Pursuit of Power*.[100] Nations outside of Europe simply lacked the need or the political will to develop such massive and expensive organizations.

The conditions that enabled a part-time soldier to closely approximate the capabilities of a professional were transitory. In the late nineteenth and early twentieth centuries, armies developed more complex tactical organizations and concepts to ensure that their forces could function effectively on the modern battlefield. For instance, between 1870 and 1914, armies subdivided their units into smaller semi-independent formations to improve their ability to survive on battlefields increasingly dominated by highly lethal industrial weapons.[101]

By 1914, most armies embraced the Prussian method of using the company (around 250 riflemen) as the basic maneuver unit on the battlefield, as opposed to larger battalions.[102] At the same time, armies abandoned columnar infantry formations in battle, opting to organize riflemen in lines of one or two ranks that walked quickly or ran when under fire.[103] Soldiers could also use cover and concealment while moving, but they had to keep pushing forward to stay in contact with the main effort and avoid being run over by friendly forces advancing from behind.[104]

Armies adopted these tactics in response to rapid improvements in the range and accuracy of firearms during this period. The advent of metal cartridges and magazines simplified and accelerated the loading process, as an infantryman no longer had to load and chamber each round manually.[105] The US model 1866 Winchester repeater rifle was the first to incorporate some of these technologies; European armies fielded similar rifles, such as the French Lebel, by the 1880s.[106] These newer models also included smokeless powders that reduced fouling and therefore enhanced the rifle's reliability. This also improved the stealth of riflemen, as the decrease in smoke emitted when firing a round made them harder to detect. Less smoke had the added advantage of improving a rifleman's ability to take aimed shots by clearing his field of vision.[107]

As armies improved the reliability and lethality of rifles, they also developed the first machine guns and better artillery designs that increased the depth, breadth, and lethality of the battlefield. In 1885 Hiram Maxim introduced the Maxim machine gun, which fired six hundred rounds per minute, giving its four-man crew the ability to annihilate entire platoons or even companies of infantry in short order.[108] Meanwhile, the invention of high explosives in the late nineteenth century increased the blast power and deadliness of artillery rounds.[109] Artillery's rate of fire also increased as the rest of Europe adopted breech-loading guns by the end of the century. Guns were further improved by mountings that largely eliminated the recoil effects after firing an artillery piece.[110] This meant that crews did not have to move guns back into firing position after each shot, which increased the rate of fire and accuracy.[111] Better accuracy also enabled gunners to fire effectively at targets beyond their line of sight (indirect fire), using maps and mathematical calculations. The first and most famous of these new model guns—the French 75—entered service in the late 1890s; comparable guns were adopted by foreign armies in the next decade.[112]

The increasing lethality of the battlefield had two important implications for the trained reserve. First, armies became more dependent on reservists as it became more likely that active-duty units would suffer heavy losses due to these new weapons. For example, in World War I, 23 percent of the active German officer corps and 14 percent of German enlisted men died in combat, and many more were grievously wounded.[113] Such losses reflected the fact that by 1914, a single infantry brigade (three thousand men) could expel the same amount of firepower in one minute that the entire British army (sixty thousand men) discharged during the Battle of Waterloo.[114]

Second, the greater dispersal and flexibility of tactical formations in response to these developments drove up the intellectual demands of soldiering for the enlisted ranks and officers alike. This widened the qualitative gap between active soldiers and reservists because the latter generally lacked the time to meet more rigorous standards. In other words, technological change in the late nineteenth and early twentieth centuries made reservists more necessary, but at the same time it made them less capable than their active counterparts, as became evident during the world wars.

Failures of the Industrial-Era Reserve Models

The world wars revealed how technological change significantly reduced the tactical efficacy of nineteenth-century reserve models. During both

Table 1.3 Prewar Reserve and Active Army Strength, 1914

Country	Active Army Strength	Reserve and Militia Strength
Austria-Hungary	415,000	2,935,000
France	600,000	2,400,000
Germany	800,000	2,200,000
Italy	265,340	3,127,881
Russia	1,400,000	3,500,000
Serbia	180,000	170,000
United Kingdom	156,110	461,667

Sources: Statesman's Yearbook 1914, 55, 880; Keegan, *First World War*, 21; Herwig, *First World War*, 79; Strachan, *First World War*, 18; Showalter, *Tannenberg*, 71; Wawro, *Mad Catastrophe*, 55, 66; Stone, *Russian Army in the Great War*, 33.

wars, most reservists performed poorly relative to their active counterparts; this poor performance sometimes led to major tactical and strategic setbacks. These struggles resulted from the fact that armies failed to make substantial changes to their reserve training and personnel policies, despite the increasing intellectual and physical demands of soldiering. These demands arose because of the increasingly sophisticated technologies and tactics developed to restore battlefield mobility after the bloody stalemates of the first two years of World War I. And reservists who received only thirty days of training a year or less simply lacked the time and the resources to learn how to execute those tactics effectively. They would have required either substantial predeployment training, which most armies were unable or unwilling to provide, or direct supervision from veteran leaders.

World War I revealed the extent to which the armies of Europe relied on reservists. As shown in table 1.3, most of the main belligerents' combat power resided in their reserve components. But, with the exception of Germany, none maintained high levels of reserve readiness in peacetime. So when war erupted in 1914, there was little to no time to resolve any reserve personnel, equipment, or training deficiencies.

France, Austria-Hungary, Russia, and Italy went to war in 1914 and 1915 with reserves of discharged conscripts that were neither well trained nor well equipped. Changes to the character of war required armies to adopt more flexible infantry tactics and to integrate specialized equipment, such as machine guns and grenades, into infantry formations, which necessitated more training days for reservists to develop and maintain proficiency in their respective military occupations.[115] But budgetary, political, and operational considerations prevented many armies, including those of Italy, Russia, and Austria-Hungary, from increasing reservists' training or providing them with satisfactory equipment.[116] Additionally, recalling men from their civilian lives for intensive peacetime exercises was risky. They often resented such disruptions, and this resentment sometimes resulted in domestic political troubles.[117]

Operational demands and immigration practices also restricted reserve training. In Italy, for instance, reservists lost training time when they had to respond to civil strife or instability in the colonies.[118] Millions of Italians had immigrated to the United States, Canada, and South America in pursuit of employment opportunities, and although many returned to Italy in 1915 and 1916 to serve in the war, they had missed years, if not decades, of refresher training.[119]

Due to these problems, reservists often struggled to meet the standards expected of them in 1914 and 1915; consequently, they suffered heavy losses that in some cases led to significant tactical and strategic setbacks. Poorly trained Austro-Hungarian reservists, for instance, broke down when forced to march carrying sixty-pound packs during a failed campaign to conquer Serbia in the summer and fall of 1914. One Austrian officer commanding reservists recalled that he had to halt his advance during a key battle "because of the poor physical conditioning of my men." Worse, most Austro-Hungarian reservists did not know how to fight in open-order skirmish lines, forcing commanders to pack them into dense columns, which the Serbians decimated with artillery and machine gun fire.[120] Because of these issues—and many other readiness and leadership problems—the Austro-Hungarian army suffered a string of major defeats at the hands of the Serbians and Russians in 1914 and early 1915.[121]

Similarly, Russian and French reservists were packed into dense formations because military leaders had little confidence in their ability to fight without close supervision from active-duty officers.[122] Such tactics, however, almost certainly led to higher battlefield attrition, which contributed to both powers' inability to meet their tactical and strategic objectives in 1914.

Anglo-American reserve models also proved inadequate. Like the other major belligerents in World War I, Britain was highly dependent on reservists. In fact, more than 50 percent of the British Expeditionary Force (BEF) that deployed to France in August 1914 consisted of reservists.[123] Yet even though many British reservists were experienced veterans, they were not at a high state of readiness when mobilized on 4 August 1914. There were two reasons for this. First, in the words of one British officer, many reservists had "grown soft . . . working as civilians" and were not physically prepared for the challenge of carrying kits that weighed up to sixty pounds in the "terrific [summer] heat" of northern France.[124]

Second, most had little training and no experience in fighting an adversary as powerful as Germany; they were better suited for combat against guerrillas in the colonies.[125] The hasty mobilization in August provided few opportunities for additional training before the reservists were rushed into combat. Instead, the short mobilization period focused on routine administrative tasks, such as receiving equipment and moving to ports of embarkation. Some units even wasted precious time organizing and participating in parades and other festivities.[126]

It is difficult to determine how well British reservists performed in battle, given that the BEF's seven divisions mixed reservists with active battalions.[127] On the positive side, British reservists who had served in the Boer War a decade earlier as active-duty soldiers demonstrated superior marksmanship skills that helped them inflict heavy losses on the German First Army when it stumbled into BEF lines near Mons on 23 August.[128] But these reservists—and their active army counterparts—were unpracticed and underequipped for collective tactical actions against the army of a European Great Power.[129] Such deficiencies enabled the Germans to outgun and outmaneuver them in combat in August and September 1914. Several months later, after gaining battlefield experience, the BEF performed better, helping defeat a German attack at Ypres, albeit against an exhausted and depleted force whose ranks included university students rushed to combat with minimal training.[130]

The fight at Ypres and the engagements leading up to it essentially destroyed the BEF, forcing Britain to call on volunteers, militiamen (the Territorial Army), colonial troops, and eventually conscripts to replenish the army's ranks.[131] However, it took a year to train, equip, and deploy these replacements, forcing the French to shoulder the burden of defending the western front until late 1915.[132] In short, British reservists helped slow the German invasion of France—an important operational and strategic contribution. But tactically, they were outmatched by their German adversaries due to their small size, limited prewar training in conventional military operations, and hasty mobilization.

The Americans had unique challenges—and advantages—when it came to their reserves. As discussed in detail in the next chapter, the Americans were unable to maintain a high level of reserve readiness in peacetime because their combat reserve—the National Guard—consisted of inexperienced soldiers led by amateur officers. Unsurprisingly, when the National Guard was mobilized in 1917, it was in a poor state of readiness. But the Americans had the advantage of time and space, which allowed them to train and reorganize guard divisions for almost a year prior to deployment. By the time they entered combat in mid-1918, guard units were nearly identical to formations composed of draftees and volunteers, and for the most part, they performed their missions adequately.

The German case was different. At the start of the war, Germany placed great trust in its reserves and militia, assigning them key missions on both the eastern and western fronts.[133] It did so for two reasons. First, it had no other choice but to use them. Although it maintained a large standing army, Germany was outnumbered because it was fighting a two-front war against France and Britain in the west and a massive Russian army in the east. German military planners, therefore, had to maximize all available military manpower—active, reserve, *Landwehr*, and even the *Landstrum* (militiamen with little or no formal training)—to have a realistic chance of success.[134]

Second, Germany could expect its reservists to perform well because it maintained high leadership and training standards. In terms of leadership, veteran active-duty officers were installed in many key command and staff positions at the company level and above.[135] Some reserve officers underwent a rigorous selection process by which they volunteered to undergo a year of active-duty training.[136] During that year, volunteers focused almost exclusively on combat and leadership training, while avoiding the administrative tasks that consumed much of a conscript's time and energy. Afterward, they took exams to determine how they would be used; those who scored highest were eligible for reserve commissions, while others became reserve NCOs.[137]

German reserve units also underwent intensive peacetime training, assembling twice during their four or five years of service to refresh or build on previous training received as conscripts. Training periods varied in length, ranging from one month to eight weeks (far more than the four or five days a year devoted to training in the 1860s and 1870s).[138] Additionally, once they were discharged into the *Landwehr*, reservists completed two more training sessions—each lasting between eight and fourteen days—over a ten-year period.[139] Thus, discharged conscripts likely retained at least some of the skills and experience necessary for front-line service until they were about thirty years old. German reserve units also received extra training in the weeks and months leading up to the first battles of August and September 1914.[140] Some units completed four weeks of field exercises that summer. Others conducted refresher training in the initial weeks of the war under the supervision of active and reserve officers.[141]

Such high training and leadership standards almost certainly contributed to the German reserves' tactical successes in the opening months of the war. For instance, in October 1914 a German reserve corps composed mostly of *Landwehr* and recalled reservists captured the critical fortress city of Antwerp from Belgian and British defenders. A German reserve corps also defeated French and Belgian forces during other engagements.[142] On the eastern front, the Third Reserve Division and a *Landwehr* division played critical roles in the German victory against the Russians at Tannenberg and subsequent operations that fall.[143]

That said, the German reserves did confront some readiness challenges in the early months of the war. Unlike their youthful counterparts in the active army, older reservists were often apprehensive about the prospect of war, many weeping in fear as they reported for duty in July and August 1914.[144] Physical fitness levels were also uneven. One reserve officer recalled in his memoirs that many older men in his unit "groaned under the burden of their heavy packs" and collapsed on the roadside during marches to the front, likely slowing Germany's failed attempt to encircle and destroy the French army.[145] Second-line German reserve troops from the *Landstrum* performed poorly during the First Battle of Ypres, and some hastily assembled reserve units struggled on the eastern front in the late fall.[146]

Still, for the most part, the German reserves performed in the manner expected of them in 1914. Germany, however, simply lacked sufficient numbers of them to defeat the French and British armies on the western front. Such shortages were exacerbated by battles on the eastern front that consumed multiple reserve and *Landwehr* divisions.[147] As a result, the war stalemated in the west.

At this point, the traditional reservist—the part-time soldier activated and sent into battle within weeks of mobilization—essentially disappeared from the battlefield. In the case of the Austro-Hungarians, nearly their entire first- and second-line reserves were destroyed; BEF losses were also quite high. For the rest of the Allies and, to a lesser extent, the Germans, most of their reserves had been committed to battle, and those who survived became hardened combat veterans. Meanwhile, thousands more were in the training pipeline, so by the time they reached the front, there was little difference between them and the new, untested volunteers and active-duty soldiers.[148] In other words, the line separating reservists from active-duty soldiers blurred and eventually disappeared by 1916 and 1917, the lone exception being the Americans.[149]

After 1914, the Central Powers and the Allies experimented with new tactics to break the stalemate; in doing so, they set the stage for the contemporary reserve dilemma.[150] This tactical change was a response to the fact that the established close-order infantry and supporting artillery tactics of 1914 and 1915 proved incapable of producing operational or strategic breakthroughs. Infantry advancing in long skirmish lines suffered too many casualties when attempting to breach prepared enemy positions defended by machine guns and artillery.[151] And even if they were able to breach and seize forward defenses, they generally lacked sufficient mass to overcome a counterattack from enemy reserves positioned in rear trenches. A basic change in tactics was necessary.

The German army was the first to innovate by developing more flexible open-order infantry tactics. Germany had military traditions dating back to the nineteenth century that encouraged and enabled such innovations, such as the concept called *Auftragstaktik*.[152] This approach allowed German commanders to make independent tactical and operational decisions based on their understanding of the situation at hand.[153] By allowing subordinates to execute what present US Army doctrine calls "disciplined initiative," the German military encouraged commanders to develop and experiment with new tactics.[154] For instance, middle- and junior-level officers were allowed to train and fight based on the unique needs and preferences of their units, thereby creating space for experimentation and innovation.[155] In fact, as early as 1914, some units were allowing infantry companies to divide into smaller platoon- and squad-sized elements for reconnaissance and attack missions, not just during drills.[156] Those smaller elements could make greater use of cover and concealment while crossing the fire-swept zone, reducing their exposure to observation and fire.[157]

Such experimentation drove the development of German assault troop detachments.[158] These specialized units—initially formed from cohorts of specially selected volunteers—advanced ahead of the main body to raid, seize, or destroy key positions such as machine gun emplacements.[159] To ensure they could survive the journey across no-man's-land, the Germans organized these detachments into small, nimble squad-sized elements (ten to twelve men) equipped with specialized equipment such as light machine guns and hand grenades.[160] These weapons provided squads and platoons the firepower to destroy or suppress fortified positions, enabling them to become self-contained fighting units.[161] When successful, assault detachments could clear the way for the main attack by reducing and confusing opposing forces. By the end of the war, the Germans and some Allied armies were widely employing these tactics.[162]

During the interwar years, armies refined their tactical and technical capabilities to restore mobility to the battlefield. Despite experimentation with more fluid infantry tactics, the war had stalemated on the western front for three reasons. First, armies could not accurately strike and degrade opposing forces beyond the first several lines of trenches.[163] This inability to attack in depth allowed opposing forces to husband reserves beyond the range of visual observation and carry out counterattacks that often reversed the gains of any offensives. It also meant that armies could not reliably and accurately strike and degrade the division-, corps-, and army-level headquarters and logistics nodes that controlled and sustained front-line forces and reserves. Second, armies could not adequately protect their infantry so that it maintained combat effectiveness as it approached enemy forward lines. Finally, armies lacked effective means to communicate with forces that managed to advance beyond the line of sight.

To resolve these three challenges, military professionals such as Heinz Guderian proposed building highly professional mechanized forces that could fight as combined-arms teams—that is, integrating infantry, artillery, armored vehicles, and even aircraft and airborne infantry.[164] With these capabilities, armies gained the potential to create what military theorist B. H. Liddell Hart called the "expanding torrent" to improve the survivability of front-line forces and enable attacks in depth against numerically stronger forces. As Liddell Hart explained in influential articles penned in the 1920s, armies could reduce infantry losses by the "intelligent maneuver of firepower" that concentrated mobile forces on narrow fronts—as opposed to advancing in long skirmish lines—to identify and breach gaps in enemy lines.[165] Once gaps were created using infantry supported by combat engineers and antitank forces, mechanized and motorized units could exploit the breach to execute attacks in depth, targeting opposing command and control hubs, logistics centers, and reserves.

Technological advances made such tactics feasible by the 1920s and 1930s. More powerful internal combustion engines, for instance, allowed tanks and other armored vehicles to carry heavier payloads and move faster and more reliably over greater distances. And portable radios permitted commanders to coordinate these forces beyond the line of sight or in areas where wired communications were unavailable.[166] Meanwhile, improvements in aircraft design and targeting methodologies and technologies gave armies the ability to locate and strike high-value targets, such as command centers, in support zones behind the front lines. Warfare was no longer a "linear affair," as armies could now strike rapidly and accurately in depth.[167]

To fight and survive in this nonlinear battle space, soldiers needed to develop "skills of an order of difficulty beyond the comprehension of most soldiers outside this [the twentieth] century," according to historian John Keegan.[168] Leaders from the battalion level down to individual soldiers needed the ability to "think and act on their own" and "analyze any situation and exploit it decisively and boldly," in the words of a 1920s German field manual.[169]

They needed such skills for two reasons. First, to survive in an extremely lethal combat environment, units often had to disperse, reducing officers' ability to provide direct supervision to their soldiers and NCOs. Second, threats and opportunities arose much faster in this new battle space, requiring junior and midlevel leaders to take the initiative. Lieutenants and captains and their NCOs would have to find gaps in opposing lines and make the initial breaches needed for an attack to unfold.[170] In other words, the days when soldiers and junior officers were essentially well-drilled automatons were over. Now they needed to memorize key tactical procedures—such as loading and firing their assigned weapons—and exercise independent judgment to seize and retain the initiative, exploit opportunities, and respond to threats across a rapidly changing battlefield.

Soldiers also needed greater technical skills. The mechanization and motorization of armies created new technical requirements, as soldiers had to operate and maintain trucks and armored vehicles.[171] In addition, they had to understand how to use critical support technologies, such as field radios, and new weapons, such as antitank rockets and light machine guns. All these technologies, moreover, created administrative distractions—what historian Eugenia Kiesling terms "the tyranny of the mundane"—as units had to allocate time to inventory and maintain new equipment and attend to other matters "tangential to fighting."[172]

Reservists—be they volunteers or discharged conscripts—found it difficult to keep up with these new administrative and training requirements. Although armies were becoming more technically advanced, they generally failed to provide reservists with the additional time and resources needed to compensate for these changes. For the most part, armies retained nineteenth-century training models, despite significant tactical and technological changes. Thus, in the words of historian Michael Howard, "technology, which in the nineteenth century had made mass participation in warfare both possible and necessary, was in the twentieth century to place increasing power in the hands of highly qualified technicians."[173]

The problem was that armies remained dependent on reservists because they lacked sufficient technicians and professional soldiers, given the increasing size and lethality of the modern battlefield. As Keegan describes in *The Face of Battle*, the extended battlefields of the post–World War I era greatly increased the dangers of soldiering. In addition to the possibility of death or injury from hostile fire along the front lines, soldiers now faced attacks from airplanes, long-range artillery, and airborne infantry, even while located in once safe rear support areas.[174] And because battles were becoming longer and more intense, the likelihood of psychological trauma also increased. In fact, an estimated one in four combatants in World War I suffered from shell shock and other psychological conditions.[175] Armies therefore needed trained reserves to replace such casualties— whether resulting from psychological or physical trauma. They also needed the extra manpower provided by their reserves to seize and secure territory across an extended battlefield. This demand for reservists—and reservists' struggles to keep up with the changing character of war—was evident in the performance of the Allied armies in World War II.

France was particularly dependent on reservists in World War II. But its reserve forces proved unable to keep up with the new tactical and technical requirements of France's interwar military doctrine. And the inability to do so contributed to France's defeat by Germany in 1940.[176]

France modernized its army in the 1920s and 1930s, developing a combined-arms capability by incorporating tanks, aircraft, motor vehicles, and antitank weaponry into its forces.[177] Its doctrine was revised in the 1930s to place a greater emphasis on mobile offensive operations. The objective was to ensure that the French army could respond to a German attack on the move inside Belgian territory while remaining on the defense farther south along the French-German border, where it had erected an impressive line of fortifications—known as the Maginot Line—to block a German invasion into the heart of France.[178] That said, France's main combat doctrine by 1940—methodical battle—focused on an initial defense and centralized control of operations, unlike the Germans' more mobile and flexible doctrine. French officers downplayed these differences because they were preparing their army to wage a more deliberate strategic defense; in addition, the Germans had yet to prove the viability of their doctrine.[179]

In reality, the French could not adopt a German-style approach to warfare because they relied on an army of one-year conscripts and reservists for national defense.[180] During the interwar years, France maintained conscription, requiring military service by every male citizen, except for those with an "established physical incapacity."[181] Under this system— formalized by laws enacted in 1927 and 1928—conscripts served on active duty for one year, after which they entered the reserve. A cadre of around

100,000 professionals provided leadership to prepare the active army and reserves for mobilization.[182] French officials preferred this system because it ensured that all Frenchmen, regardless of class, shared the burden of national defense. In addition, most officials believed that national mobilization was essential for modern warfare, given the high casualty rates of World War I.[183]

The French reserve consisted of three organizations. Following active service, a soldier was discharged into the ready reserve, where he served for three years and drilled with a formation linked to his former active unit. After service in the ready reserve, the soldier entered the first-line reserve for sixteen years, during which time he completed two three-week training periods. Finally, the soldier passed into the second-line reserve for eight years, which required participation in one seven-day training exercise.[184]

In practice, the French reserve system did not function as planned. Ready reservists did not begin training until 1933, and it totaled only three weeks.[185] Some men who had served in World War I were excused from training altogether, which meant they were not exposed to changes in French doctrine and new equipment.[186] Budgetary constraints caused in part by the high cost of constructing and maintaining the fortresses of the Maginot Line deprived reservists of access to ranges for tank maneuvers and other specialized training.[187] The French had no system to ensure that reservists trained with the unit they would be assigned to in wartime, which denied units the opportunity to become cohesive and learn the strengths and weaknesses of individual members.[188] In short, the French reserve system was broken. Reservists did not have sufficient opportunities to build and improve on their individual skills; nor were there sufficient opportunities for reserve units to maneuver collectively.

Some French officers recognized these problems but, for a variety of reasons, were unwilling or unable to do much about them.[189] During the late 1920s, for instance, political infighting, antimilitarist attitudes, and an economic downturn severely restricted France's ability to fund reserve training.[190] Even when training resumed in the mid-1930s, the administrative demands of managing a unit and its personnel often consumed precious training time. Senior French officers also ignored reserve readiness problems or explained them away, assuming they could muddle through in a crisis.[191]

France had an opportunity to provide its reservists with about eight months of training during the so-called phony war that unfolded between the German invasion of Poland in September 1939 and the battle for France the following May. During this period, France activated its reserves to deter a German attack, but this generated a host of problems. The mobilization of thousands of skilled industrial workers for reserve service seriously disrupted the economy, forcing the government to release many reservists and send them back to civilian life. This deprived reserve units of key leaders and technicians who were critical for planning and supervising training and operational activities.[192] Some reserve divisions were short by up to 50 percent of their officers and NCOs because of the partial demobilization.[193]

Additionally, the reserve officers who remained demonstrated poor leadership capabilities and struggled to maintain discipline and unit cohesion. Reserve discipline and morale plummeted even further because the army lacked sufficient cold-weather clothing and equipment for the unusually frigid winter of 1939–40. Boredom was another factor, as most missions, such as patrolling the German border, went to active-duty units or select groups of reservists.[194] In short, France squandered the eight-month period between mobilization and war from a reserve training perspective. This was a critical error because the entire French military system depended on the readiness of these part-time soldiers. In fact, reservists made up about 50 percent of active units, and about 85 percent of the French officer and NCO corps came from the reserves.[195]

Although they were unprepared for war, French reservists and their comrades fought doggedly against the German invasion in May 1940. They performed particularly well when they were able to fight from prepared battle positions, but once they were pushed into the open, they were simply outfought by the more thoroughly trained Germans.[196] With these advantages, the Germans were able to shatter French forces and those of its Belgian, Dutch, and British allies, which compelled the French government to surrender. Thus, as Kiesling argues, "France fell, not because its troops were outnumbered by the Germans, but because they were outfought—and outfought because of a failure to create the cohesive, well-trained, and well-officered reserve units upon which [their] combat power relied."[197]

The British reserve component was equally unprepared for war in 1940. As war with Germany became more likely in the late 1930s, the British government scrambled to improve its military readiness. One way it did this was by reintroducing conscription in 1939, allowing the military to bring the militia—the Territorial Army (TA)—into active service. At the same time, the government authorized an expansion of the TA to deter Hitler. Thus, on the eve of the battle for France, the British army consisted of around 224,000 active soldiers, 131,000 reservists, and 440,000 territorials. With many of these active soldiers abroad protecting colonial interests, Britain had to draw on its reserves and the TA to build the BEF that deployed to France in 1939, much like it had in 1914. Ultimately, the BEF consisted of five active divisions and five TA divisions, plus three lower-quality territorial divisions assigned to basic labor duties.[198]

During the interwar years, the qualitative gap between the active army and the TA widened. One reason was that the British army updated its doctrine during this period to emphasize mobile operations mounted by an army of professional soldiers. In the late 1930s it started providing its army with more advanced vehicles and equipment to make this doctrine work, but it neglected to train the TA on this new doctrine and its associated equipment. During the interwar years, the TA was supposed to train four weekends a year and two weeks in the summer (twenty-two days total), while maintaining the same fighting standards as active soldiers.[199] Few, however, completed this training, due in part to limited funding and resources. For instance, the TA lacked the funds and personnel to fully staff its units in the 1930s, thereby limiting opportunities for collective training, and its facilities were not large enough to train with modern military equipment such as the tank. Furthermore, the active army had limited time to supervise the TA and provide mentorship in the late 1930s, as it was engaged in learning how to operate new equipment, which generally did not make it to the TA. Consequently, much of the British reserve component required extensive retraining when it was mobilized in 1939.[200] That retraining period, however, was highly constrained because the army had to spend considerable time and energy reorganizing TA units to compensate for the fact that many territorials were medically unfit for service or could not deploy due to family, work, or legal restrictions.[201] Moving TA soldiers from their armories to ports of embarkation and onward to France consumed even more time.

The TA also suffered from deep leadership problems. Throughout the 1920s and 1930s it was chronically short of officers, and those officers it did have were often not trained to the same standards as their active-duty counterparts. For instance, many TA officers were unable to attend professional development courses due to civilian work and family commitments, meaning they were not up to date on changes in doctrine.[202] Others— especially those with combat experience in World War I—proved unwilling or unable to understand these new concepts.[203]

In short, in the summer of 1940, more than half the BEF was ill prepared to fight a battle-hardened and well-trained German army. Yet, unlike in 1914, the BEF deployed to France six months before the outbreak of hostilities, providing a relatively lengthy precombat training period. However, like France, it squandered much of that time building fortifications; in addition, the shortage of ranges and the bitterly cold winter made it difficult to train.[204] This lack of training almost certainly contributed to Britain's struggles against the Germans. Fortunately for the BEF, most of its personnel were able to escape from France, but at the cost of some 67,000 dead, wounded, or missing soldiers out of a force of about 390,000.[205]

The other Allies also confronted a host of reserve readiness challenges. As the next chapter shows, the US Army had to restructure and retrain its primary combat reserve—the National Guard—prior to deployment in 1943 and 1944. Meanwhile, the Soviet reserves—and the army in general—were unprepared for war in 1941. The Soviets' fourteen million reservists were plagued by low morale and inadequate training.[206] Enhanced training programs for reservists implemented in 1941 helped address these deficiencies, but only after the outbreak of war.[207] Unsurprisingly, the Soviet army was decimated during the opening phases of the German invasion in June 1941, and reservists suffered heavy attrition attempting to launch poorly coordinated counterattacks.[208] Still, their attacks likely helped Moscow buy time to reorganize its forces and resist the German advance on the city.[209]

Axis reserves suffered from similar readiness challenges. The Japanese, who developed a Prussian-style reserve system in the late nineteenth century, found that their reserve component had widespread disciplinary problems and lacked the same level of professionalism as active units.[210] And the Italians failed to maintain a ready reserve during the interwar years and during the war itself.[211]

Initially, reserve readiness was not a major issue for Germany, as it did not depend on reservists at the start of the war. Treaty restrictions following World War I limited the German army to 100,000 long-service soldiers (twelve years for enlisted men; twenty-five for officers) and no trained reserve.[212] Given these constraints, the German army, under the command of Colonel-General Hans von Seeckt, decided to compensate for its lack of mass by developing a highly skilled mobile force to defend itself against much larger conscript armies.[213] It developed this force through intensive peacetime training and long service terms. Seeckt, moreover, envisioned that this small professional army could one day serve as a cadre for an expanded force if Germany reintroduced conscription and reserve service.[214] With that in mind, he retained only the best officers and NCOs—nearly all of whom were hand-selected volunteers—and ensured that they were capable of commanding one or two levels above their rank.[215] Seeckt and his predecessors also found innovative ways to train this small army in mechanized and armored tactics; they used modified cars as dummy tanks and sent personnel to train in Russia, despite the Treaty of Versailles' restrictions on such activities.[216] Thus, when Hitler reintroduced conscription and reserve service in the latter half of the 1930s, the German army was able to maintain its high standards despite the influx of hundreds of thousands of untrained men into its ranks. It also placed long-service professionals trained in the 1920s and early 1930s in charge of new conscripts and reservists, and it generally kept more demanding jobs, such as those in the panzer divisions, in the hands of professionals.[217]

Heinz Guderian, who helped oversee the development of German armored forces in the 1930s, wanted professionals to staff and lead the panzer divisions for two reasons. First, he wanted those divisions to be ready "to take the field without having to recall reserves on a large scale, or resort to untrained recruits." Such delays could give Germany's larger French or Soviet adversaries an opportunity to strike the first critical blows in a war. Additionally, Guderian believed that only long-service professionals could master panzer tactics because tanks and their associated equipment were, in his words, "expensive and rather complicated" and required extensive technical training and experience.[218]

Germany's ability to field a highly skilled army in 1939 and 1940 helped it achieve decisive tactical victories against Poland and France. And because those campaigns came to such a rapid conclusion, Germany was able to preserve manpower and limit its reliance on unskilled reservists or new conscripts.[219] But the Germans lost these advantages when Hitler decided to invade the Soviet Union in June 1941. Securing such a massive amount of territory required a greater use of Germany's entire armed forces, including its underdeveloped reserve component.[220] The Germans suffered heavy casualties in the failed invasion and subsequent operations; many of their best and brightest soldiers and officers were killed or wounded, eventually forcing the Germans to rely on children, the elderly, the infirm, and slave labor to fight. Allied offensives in North Africa, Italy, and France between 1942 and 1944 further degraded Germany's tactical advantages.

During this time, the Allies slowly improved their technical and tactical capabilities through battlefield experience and a massive infusion of financial and material support from the United States. The British, for instance, rebuilt and improved their army as Hitler's attention turned to the Soviet Union in mid-1941. And the Soviets traded space for time to improve their military. The United States, meanwhile, used its geographic advantages to retrain and rebuild its army prior to deployment to North Africa and Europe. In short, the failure to develop effective reservists during the interwar years did not doom the Allies because, except for France, they had the time and resources to recover. This was possible because the Germans and the Japanese posed an existential threat to the Allies, giving them the will to mobilize an unprecedented amount of personnel, material, and capital to destroy the Axis.

The Contemporary Reserve Dilemma

A combination of factors—personnel and budgetary shortfalls, training constraints, and the rising technical and tactical demands of soldiering and officership—eroded the readiness and combat effectiveness of reservists during the interwar years and the initial phases of World War II.[221] Paradoxically, these same factors deepened armies' dependence on reservists, as active-duty units became more expensive and the likelihood of heavy battlefield attrition increased. These trends have persisted for eighty years, forcing some armies to become even more dependent on reservists—while the qualitative gap between the active soldier and the reservist widened. The risks associated with this dependence, in turn, compelled military leaders to make difficult—and sometimes risky—choices regarding how best to structure, resource, and employ their reservists.

This situation arose for several reasons. Following World War II, standing armies shrank as states curtailed or abandoned conscription—due in part to political pressures—and as the cost of the average soldier and all the associated equipment rose exponentially. To fill the resulting gap between mission requirements and personnel, states called on reservists, as they had in the past. However, armies generally lacked the ability to provide reservists with the necessary time and resources to keep up with the technical and tactical complexities of modern warfare. Making matters worse, active-duty units faced rapid attrition due to the increasing lethality of modern weaponry.[222] Consequently, there was no guarantee that reservists would undergo substantial periods of training before deployment.[223] Nor could states presume that reservists had developed and retained proficiency in their military occupations, even though the time allotted for training—thirty days a year or less—was the same as in the late nineteenth century. In short, nineteenth-century reserve models, which had already proved somewhat untenable during the world wars, risked becoming totally inadequate in the post–World War II era.

Over the past half century, armies have fielded longer-range weapons systems with higher rates of fire, while greatly increasing the number of systems managed by midlevel and junior-ranking leaders. For instance, after World War II, riflemen started carrying new rifles such as the M-16 and AK-47, which could fire three-round bursts or automatically. Additionally, armies faced a growing threat from the air, as helicopters became standard in the 1960s, and a new generation of aircraft and ground systems entered battle armed with precision-guided munitions.

Militaries had experimented with precision guidance capabilities in the early twentieth century by using radio controllers. However, the impact of such technology on ground forces was relatively minimal until the Cold War, which witnessed the development of fire-control computers, laser and infrared guidance technologies, and GPS. During World War II, tanks and other ground systems often had to rely on manual calculations and optics for magnification, which meant that tanks could effectively engage targets at ranges of only one to two kilometers.[224] By the 1970s, tanks could accurately engage targets at twice that distance with the assistance of laser range designators and gun stabilizers.[225] Meanwhile, the United States introduced GPS in the late 1970s, and the Russians introduced their equivalent, GLONASS, in the 1980s. This technology enabled the development of munitions that could strike targets with a high degree of accuracy by using satellites and onboard computers to navigate to specific geographic coordinates.[226] And GPS-guided munitions work in all weather conditions, unlike laser-guided munitions, which can be disrupted by clouds, smoke, or fog.[227]

The introduction of precision-guided munitions was accompanied by a rapid improvement in command, control, and communications (C3) and intelligence, surveillance, and reconnaissance (ISR) technologies. These technological developments, which both benefited from and drove the computer revolution of the latter half of the twentieth century, provided armed forces with enhanced battlefield awareness, improving and accelerating the target identification and acquisition process.[228] For instance, advances in ground radar systems in the late 1960s and early 1970s gave armies the means to detect the movement of tanks and infantrymen kilometers behind the front—even when those movements were concealed by dense foliage.[229] Improvements in data collection, processing, storage, and transfer technologies in the 1970s and 1980s enabled the rapid dissemination of imagery and signals intelligence gathered by aircraft and satellites in space.[230] This meant that armies could quickly locate, acquire, and strike targets across and beyond an active battlefield with highly accurate and long-range munitions.

In this new technological context, armies had to increase their dispersion, mobility, armored protection, and tempo of operations to avoid detection and destruction. For instance, the frontage covered by an infantry battalion nearly doubled between World War II and the 1991 Persian Gulf War, while the number of vehicles and weapons assigned to a battalion expanded by a factor of three or four.[231] Two factors made this greater dispersion possible. First, the range of weapons increased, allowing battalion commanders to disperse their companies. Second, armies' infantry and support systems became mechanized and motorized during the Cold War, providing the necessary transportation capabilities to disperse and concentrate rapidly.

The mass mechanization of infantry began in the Soviet Union. In the 1960s the Soviet Union introduced the BMP-1 infantry fighting vehicle (IFV), while the United States introduced the M-113 armored personnel carrier (APC). These tracked or wheeled armored vehicles gave armies the ability to transport team- to squad-sized infantry elements into battle while providing direct fire support and enhanced protection, in contrast to the unarmored trucks of the worlds wars, which generally unloaded soldiers near engagement areas and then quickly moved to the rear.[232] By the late 1970s, the Soviet armed forces had fully embraced these technologies to improve their ability to breach NATO antitank defenses.[233] Consequently, by the mid-1980s, the two main types of Soviet maneuver divisions—tank and motorized rifle—had integrated tanks, IFVs, or APCs to transport infantry and supplies.[234] The United States mirrored these trends in the 1970s and early 1980s, as it expanded its use of the M-113 APCs and developed the M2 Bradley IFV. Around the same time, the Chinese fielded their own APC—the YW 531A—while the West Germans developed the Marder IFV. Others followed later with their own models, such as the British Warrior IFV, introduced in 1988.

Because of these new technologies and tactical concepts, armies had to raise their technical training standards. Soldiers needed to understand how to operate and maintain the increasingly advanced equipment assigned to them, and they needed to be able to think and act independently as combat formations dispersed to avoid detection or destruction. Thus, the US Army overhauled its recruitment and training practices in the 1970s and 1980s to attract, develop, and retain highly skilled volunteer soldiers capable of mastering the intricacies of contemporary combat tactics and technologies. This revolution extended across all three components of the US Army: active, reserve, and National Guard.

Around the same time, the Soviet Union took steps to improve the quality of its military personnel, as it believed that conventional war was much more likely once NATO revealed its flexible response doctrine in the 1960s (see chapter 3).[235] Similar trends unfolded outside of Europe. China, for instance, initiated a program to modernize and improve the quality of its armed forces following their poor performance in a conflict with Vietnam in 1979.

Improving personnel and equipment standards raised overhead costs. Units had to expend more funds and resources on the recruitment, training, and retention of skilled soldiers. Equipment itself became more expensive. New armored vehicles introduced between the early 1960s and the mid-1980s incorporated sophisticated—and expensive—composite and reactive armor to counter increasingly lethal antitank munitions.[236] Communications and navigational systems were added to armored vehicles around the same time, raising costs even further.[237] And the increased mechanization of the battlefield added more and more vehicles to unit inventories—all of which generated additional costs for fuel and maintenance. The Soviet Union, for instance, doubled its inventory of IFVs, tanks, self-propelled howitzers, and attack helicopters between 1966 and 1986 as it sought to maintain an edge over NATO in ground forces.[238] Similar developments occurred in the armies of the Middle East during this period (see chapter 5).

The overhead costs of the armed forces also rose sharply in the latter half of the twentieth century because states largely abandoned or curtailed conscription, focusing instead on recruiting more expensive volunteers. This shift in recruitment practices reflected war wariness and antimilitarist attitudes throughout Europe and parts of Asia, as well as the conclusion by many military professionals that conscripts were ill equipped to understand and master the complex technologies and tactics of post–World War II warfare.[239] Thus, Great Britain phased out conscription between 1957 and 1963.[240] A decade later, the United States abandoned peacetime conscription, leading to a rapid decline in the size of the active-duty army; this decline accelerated amid budget cuts in the 1990s, after the end of the Cold War. More recently, Russia moved to professionalize its armed forces, continuing to reduce its dependence on conscripts in favor of professionals following the Cold War.[241] By 2014, the number of contract soldiers in the Russian army exceeded the number of conscripts for the first time.[242]

Volunteers with technical backgrounds need some incentive to join the military, such as payment of college tuition, the promise of a generous pension, or training in technical fields that could lead to a civilian career.

And providing those incentives drove up personnel costs. Take the case of the US Army. In 1949 a new, unmarried private in the US Army earned $737 a month in pay and $442 for living expenses, for a total of $1,179 per month (in 2016 dollars). In 2016 that same private earned almost twice as much, taking in $1,567 a month in pay and $532 for living expenses, or a total of $2,099 per month.[243] Similarly, Russia has seen a rise in personnel costs as it attempted to attract and retain more contract soldiers, who earn more than conscripts.[244]

The rising costs of modern armies and the political pressure to reduce the military burden on society have caused many states to slash the size of their armies over the past half century, turning to reservists to fulfill mission requirements. Late in the Cold War, many NATO countries such as the United Kingdom, the Netherlands, West Germany, and Norway increased the use of reservists in front-line roles as the size of their active-duty forces declined.[245] More recently, in 2010, Sweden abandoned conscription—due in part to its unpopularity—and increased its reliance on volunteers and part-time reservists.[246] Similarly, Poland, which gave up conscription in 2009, has attempted to boost reserve readiness in recent years due to the rising threats from Russia. To do so, it intensified peacetime training standards for reservists, while increasing their integration with the active-duty army.[247] Meanwhile, in 2018 the South Korean government announced plans to cut the size of its active-duty force by reducing conscription terms from twenty-one to eighteen months, due in part to societal demands to reduce the burden of military service on the country's youth. To compensate for the anticipated decline in the size of the conscript force, the South Korean army announced plans to boost reserve readiness through improved training and equipment standards.[248] That said, as of 2022, South Korean reservists trained only three days a year and were still using some World War II–era equipment. These readiness issues are problematic because, in wartime, the South Korean army depends on mobilized reservists to bring its active-duty divisions to full strength and to defend rear areas against North Korean commandos and guerrillas.[249]

Battlefield requirements have forced some states to deepen their reliance on reservists. The United States, for instance, made extensive use of the National Guard when the protracted wars in Iraq and Afghanistan exhausted the army's active component (see chapter 3). Likewise, the Israelis deployed reservists for lengthy tours in the Palestinian territories during the First and Second Intifadas, which overtaxed its small conscript army (see chapter 5). More recently, the Syrian armed forces had to recall reservists and establish militias to support ongoing attempts to suppress the Syrian revolution.[250] Since mid-2022 Russia has mobilized hundreds of thousands of reservists to bolster its highly depleted active-duty army following its botched invasion of Ukraine.[251]

Relying on reservists is risky, as they often struggle to master the intricacies of modern combat due to a host of constraints, leading to higher casualties and tactical setbacks. These setbacks can also lead to strategic defeat, as the Israelis learned during the 2006 Lebanon war (see chapter 5). What is more, taking citizen-soldiers away from their civilian lives for many months or longer can generate political backlash, as the United States experienced during the height of the Second Iraq War (see chapters 2 and 3) and the Israelis experienced during the war in Lebanon in the 1980s (see chapter 5). And sometimes, such as in Syria, many reservists just fail to report for duty when activated for unpopular or dangerous wars.[252] Thus, the tactical competence and motivations of reservists can be of great strategic and political import.

Reservists have struggled to keep up with the changing character of warfare since World War II largely because of insufficient time to train. Most train for only thirty days a year or less. This may have been sufficient in the nineteenth and early twentieth centuries, when a soldier's main duty was to maintain and fire his rifle as part of a battalion-sized tactical formation. However, since the interwar years, a reservist has needed to fight independently, assume a leadership position in a squad or team-level formation, fire and maintain a number of new weapons, and master new support technologies such as field radios, vehicles, various C3 and battlefield management systems, and, more recently, unmanned air and ground systems. Consequently, in the post–World War II period, armies could not easily substitute a reservist for a professional soldier or a conscript. In other words, the situation that existed prior to the mid-nineteenth century, when reservists were poor substitutes for professional soldiers, reemerged.

This situation presented a particular challenge to the United States and Israel. For unique geopolitical and cultural reasons, both countries were—and still are—highly dependent on army reservists for national defense, although they employed different types of reserve forces: the United States an all-volunteer reserve composed of soldiers who may or may not have had active-duty experience, and Israel a Prussian-style reserve of discharged conscripts. Despite these differences and very distinct strategic, political, and socioeconomic contexts, each country faced similar reserve readiness challenges over the past half century. How they responded to these challenges is explored in depth in the chapters that follow.

Chapter Two

The United States Confronts the Reserve Dilemma

It takes a long while to teach the average untrained man how to
shoot, to ride, to march, to take care of himself in the open, to
be alert, resourceful, cool, daring, and resolute, to obey quickly,
as well as to be willing, and to fit himself, to act on his own
responsibility.
—Theodore Roosevelt[1]

The United States had to confront the reserve dilemma during the world wars and the Korean War when it expanded its tiny peacetime army by activating and deploying its primary combat reserve: the National Guard (NG). The active-duty US Army had long disparaged and distrusted the NG, a state militia force led for most of its history by amateur officers. But political pressures from guard supporters in Congress, fear of a large standing army, and successful lobbying by NG officers and their political allies forced army leaders and defense policymakers to accept a force composed largely of untrained civilians as the US Army's combat reserve, rather than a European-style reserve of discharged conscripts, as many preferred. Thus, in 1917, 1942, and 1950 the citizen-soldiers of the NG went to war, and despite significant struggles during mobilization—and after bruising combat experience—they succeeded in closely approximating the tactical capabilities of their active-duty counterparts.

The US Army was able to achieve these successes because its geographic separation from the battlefields afforded it the luxury of time and space to reorganize and retrain guard divisions prior to deployment. During that time, the army infused guard divisions with veteran leadership while replacing many soldiers with conscripts and wartime volunteers. In short, the US Army resolved the reserve dilemma during the world wars and, to a lesser extent, in Korea by essentially transforming NG divisions into active army units before they were deployed. This chapter tells the story of how and why it was able to do so.

The Birth of the National Guard

The United States relied on state militias, as well as wartime volunteers, to reinforce the small active-duty US Army during the nineteenth century. However, the militias were poor substitutes for active-duty soldiers due to infrequent training, amateur leadership, and legal constraints that prevented the federal government from mobilizing them for more than three months a year. In addition, the federal government could not set standards for militia personnel, training, or equipment.[2] That said, the United States' inability to maintain a well-trained reserve had a negligible impact on national security. Protected from Great Power adversaries by two vast oceans, the United States could rely almost exclusively on its small volunteer army and the US Navy to deter and respond to domestic and foreign threats.[3]

Following the Spanish-American War, President Theodore Roosevelt sought to improve federal control over state militias and enhance their readiness for overseas service as the United States became a global power. To lead this effort, he turned to Secretary of War Elihu Root. Root initially advocated for replacing the militia with a federally controlled reserve of discharged conscripts.[4] However, he soon learned that this was unrealistic, as state governments and Congress opposed attempts to replace or marginalize militiamen.[5] Most importantly, the American public vehemently opposed conscription.[6] Root therefore had to maintain the militia in some form and work with its leaders, its allies in Congress, and the militia's powerful lobbying wing—the National Guard Association (NGA).[7]

For the most part, Root succeeded in enlisting the support of militia leaders, including Ohio representative Charles Dick, who was chairman of the Committee of the Militia, a senior officer in the Ohio militia, and president of the NGA.[8] Dick agreed with Root's assessment that the Militia Act of 1792 was obsolete and that the militia needed to improve its training and personnel standards.[9] With support from Secretary Root, Dick sponsored a new militia act—known as the Dick Act—which Congress passed in 1903.[10] That act improved militia (officially renamed the National Guard) readiness in two ways. First, it improved its accessibility by granting the president the authority to activate the guard for up to nine months a year, as opposed to the previous three-month limit.[11] Guardsmen who refused to comply with federal orders faced court-martial.[12] Second, the Dick Act forced the NG to adopt the organizational, equipment, and disciplinary standards of the active-duty army.[13] To help it do so, all guard units were required to train at least twenty-four days a year, with five or more of those days in the field.[14] Guard officers could also start attending US Army schools to learn the latest tactics and administrative practices employed by the active-duty army.[15]

The Dick Act faced pockets of opposition in both the active-duty army and the NG. Some worried that because of its dual status as a state and federal force, the NG could not be counted on in wartime because legally, it could not deploy abroad.[16] Some guard officers also worried that their units would be dismantled to provide individual replacements for the active army.[17] To address these concerns, Dick worked with the War Department to pass new legislation in May 1908.[18] This legislation, which faced no opposition in Congress, better defined the structure of the reserve component of the US Army by dividing it into two organizations: the Organized Militia (the NG), which served as the army's first-line reserve in wartime, and the Reserve Militia, which included all able-bodied men between the ages of eighteen and forty-five who could be mobilized in wartime to serve as a second-line reserve or to fill vacancies in the active army or NG.[19] Thus, guard units were less likely to be broken up if the active army could draw on the Reserve Militia to fill vacancies. To alleviate concerns about accessibility, the 1908 legislation granted the president the authority to deploy guardsmen overseas.[20]

The legislative victory was short-lived. Members of the William Howard Taft administration opposed the revisions to the Dick Act. In 1912 Secretary of War Henry L. Stimson argued that the new law was unconstitutional because it required state militias to serve abroad.[21] US attorney general George W. Wickersham agreed, effectively barring the NG from involuntary overseas deployment.[22]

Four years later, during the Woodrow Wilson administration, the War Department worked to devise a new reserve organization that would provide the army with more accessible and better-trained reservists. Those efforts culminated in a 1916 policy paper that called for the expansion of the active army from 108,000 soldiers to 230,000. To reinforce the army, the paper recommended expanding the reserves from 129,000 to 379,000 members.[23] To achieve this growth, the army planned to recruit soldiers on two-year contracts, after which they would enter the reserves and drill on a part-time basis for six years under federal command.[24] In other words, the War Department was aiming to establish a European-style reserve system, albeit with volunteers rather than conscripts.

The War Department believed that this system of reserves—which it called the Continental Army—would significantly improve reserve readiness through enhanced training. The NG, the War Department calculated, needed 150 training hours a month to meet the standards of a modern reservist—about ten times more hours than a typical guard unit trained.[25] The NG was almost certainly incapable of meeting those standards, as guardsmen would have to be away from home for eighteen days a month (assuming eight hours of training per day), severely interfering with civilian life. The Continental Army could overcome that obstacle by ensuring that reservists first served on active duty for two years or longer.

The NG rejected the Continental Army plan and took its case to Congress, which held hearings on the matter in early 1916. The NG found support in the House of Representatives, where James Hay, the influential head of the Military Affairs Committee, mounted a vigorous defense.[26] Hay was concerned that marginalization of the NG and growth of the active army would give the federal government too much power.[27] Other House members questioned whether the United States could afford an expanded army.[28]

In early February 1916, as opposition mounted in Congress, President Wilson withdrew his support for the Continental Army plan, perhaps fearing a backlash during an election year.[29] Frustrated, Secretary of War Lindley Garrison resigned in protest.[30] Before doing so, he wrote to Wilson and warned that relying on the NG was "a betrayal of the public trust . . . [as] the nation will be forced to depend on a military force for which it cannot recruit, it cannot name officers, it cannot train and over which it has no authority."[31]

With the Continental Army plan defeated, the War Department scrambled to find an alternative course of action. The result was the National Defense Act of 1916, which reaffirmed the NG's role as the first-line reserve for a small, all-volunteer active army. To ensure the NG's accessibility, the act mandated that guardsmen take federal and state oaths of enlistment, requiring them to deploy abroad in a national emergency for an unlimited period.[32] Guard training also doubled to forty-eight evening sessions a year—paid for by additional federal funds—and a two-week field exercise.[33] Training standards were enforced by the War Department, which gained the authority to screen guard officers for physical and mental fitness.[34]

The NG did not have time to adapt to these new standards before mobilizing in 1916 for its first federal mission since the Spanish-American War. That summer, President Wilson mobilized 125,000 guardsmen to assist the active army in the campaign along the US-Mexico border to capture or kill Pancho Villa.[35] However, the active army discovered that as many as 20 percent of guardsmen were ineligible for service due to a variety of physical or psychological ailments.[36] Others refused to serve, citing difficulties supporting their families while deployed and their erroneous belief that federal mobilization was voluntary.[37] In the end, these issues had a negligible impact on US security. But in less than a year, the readiness of the NG would become a matter of utmost importance.

World War I

The US Army and the NG were at a low state of readiness when they were mobilized for World War I in April 1917. Both organizations were designed for defensive operations inside the United States against irregular, insurgent-like forces or along the coastline against naval raids.[38] Its senior commanders and staff officers had no experience and little training in large-scale combined-arms operations against a Great Power army like Germany's.[39] Perhaps the biggest challenge facing the US military was its small size. Unlike the other Great Powers, the United States relied on an all-volunteer army backed by a volunteer reserve of guardsmen. Thus, in 1917 the US Army had only around 100,000 active soldiers—about one-sixteenth the strength of the German army.[40] To meet the challenge of fighting against the best army in the world, General John J. Pershing— overall commander of the nascent American Expeditionary Force (AEF)— calculated that the US Army had to rapidly expand to a million-man force.[41] To build such a force, the United States recruited wartime volunteers and—for the first time—implemented mass conscription.[42]

The War Department organized the conscripts, volunteers, guardsmen, and active soldiers into three types of divisions: active army divisions (numbered 1 to 25), divisions formed from the NG (numbered 26 to 75), and the National Army, formed of new conscripts and volunteers (numbered 76 and above).[43]

NG activations began in mid-July 1917. That summer, guard divisions and regiments from across the United States reported to hastily assembled training camps, where active-duty trainers determined that many guardsmen were ineligible or unprepared for federal service, as many were unable to meet basic physical fitness standards.[44] Training standards also remained low. In some states, as many as 50 percent of guardsmen had never fired a rifle or attended a full drill.[45] Meanwhile, guard officers had struggled to keep up with the higher standards imposed on them, as civilian work and family commitments interfered with their ability to attend US Army schools.[46] French liaison officers who visited the training camps in the summer and fall of 1917 rated most guard units as "poor," noting that they lacked discipline under the leadership of "bankers and business types, who are political appointees with poor physical conditioning."[47]

Perhaps a bigger challenge than a lack of readiness, which could be mitigated through training programs, was that the NG divisions were understrength. Some members refused to report for federal service, as they had not yet taken the dual federal and state oaths of enlistment, as mandated by the 1916 National Defense Act.[48] Others were exempted from service by the War Department so they could take care of family members at home.[49] Another 40,000 guardsmen could not report for duty because they were still engaged in the Mexican border mission or were held up by a host of administrative or medical problems.[50] Given these issues, the NG could muster only about 174,000 personnel—far fewer than its nominal strength of 433,000.[51]

To address these shortfalls, the NG turned to draftees, volunteers, and active-duty soldiers. Between April and August 1917, around 180,000 volunteers and draftees joined the NG, many of whom were offered the opportunity to serve with their local units.[52] Thousands more would join their ranks after the guard arrived in France.[53] This blending of personnel—guardsmen, active-duty soldiers, volunteers, and draftees—essentially eliminated the differences between an NG division and an active army or National Army division.

Distinctions were blurred even further with the mass discharge and replacement of guard officers. In the summer of 1917 the War Department replaced underperforming or unfit guard officers with active-duty or new officers who had attended an abbreviated three-month commissioning program.[54] The department could do this—despite guard protests—because NG units mobilized for federal service no longer had the protection of their respective state governors and adjutants general.[55] The War Department replaced or fired guard officers for a variety of reasons. The most common reason was age: General Pershing had established forty-five as the maximum age for an officer serving in combat.[56] Others—about 500 in total—were discharged because they could not pass physical fitness tests.[57] Around 350 were dismissed by efficacy boards chaired by active-duty officers who examined whether guardsmen were prepared to serve in mid- and senior-level command and staff positions.[58] Ultimately, the War Department discharged 10 percent of the NG officer corps in the first year of the war. Many others were removed from their positions and reassigned to support units or administrative posts.[59]

While its senior and midlevel leaders came under intense scrutiny, guard divisions underwent a major reorganization. The NG transitioned from a triangular model based on three infantry regiments to a rectangular model consisting of four regiments. Pershing and other senior US Army officers instituted this change to ensure that infantry divisions had sufficient manpower and material to execute independent operations and to withstand the heavy attrition rates of the World War I battlefield.[60] To align with the square division structure, the NG had to consolidate many units and shift personnel to other positions or separate units.[61] States like Missouri protested these changes, fearing that guard officers would be stripped of command and units would lose their local identities.[62] Despite these concerns, the War Department proceeded with the restructuring in the summer and fall of 1917.

The reorganization into square divisions left some units without a parent division. The army, in turn, created two new NG divisions: the Forty-Second and the Ninety-Third. The Forty-Second, nicknamed the Rainbow Division, was established with guard units from twenty-seven different states—an idea proposed by Major Douglas MacArthur and approved by the War Department.[63] MacArthur would go on to serve as the division's commander.[64] The Ninety-Third was made up of African American guard units from seven different states. This reorganization transformed the NG's character from an organization composed of mostly independent regimental units into a more cohesive force that integrated men from multiple states.

As the reorganization proceeded, NG divisions underwent extensive training for service in France. Initially, the US Army intended such training to last a year, but French and British commanders demanded that the Americans arrive sooner to boost sagging Allied morale and provide much-needed manpower ahead of a feared German offensive in 1918.[65] The War Department agreed to cut training time to as little as two months, with the goal of getting some divisions to France by the end of 1917.[66] That goal proved unrealistic, considering the poor state of readiness of both the active army and the NG and the time required to draft, train, and integrate raw recruits. Thus, by the end of the summer, the War Department decreased the training timeline to sixteen weeks, with the expectation that additional training would take place in France. During this period, units would conduct progressively complex exercises, starting with individual-level soldier training and ending with collective maneuvers at the battalion level and above.[67]

Stateside training almost certainly helped build unit preparedness and cohesion before deployment, but these efforts faced several obstacles.

Equipment shortages associated with the massive growth of the army meant some soldiers had to train without rifles or other essential equipment.[68] Low literacy rates among recruits also forced units to devote precious time to teaching soldiers basic reading and writing skills.[69] Training also suffered because experienced officers and noncommissioned officers (NCOs) were pulled away from their units and sent to US Army schools to enhance their understanding of tactics and administrative procedures.[70]

One of the more problematic aspects of training was that it was not preparing units to fight according to updated army doctrine. Pershing and other senior officers had devised an open-warfare doctrine in 1917 that aimed to restore mobility to the battlefield through aggressive, offensive infantry operations supported by artillery.[71] But each training camp taught doctrine according to the preferences of its respective cadres, which were not always aware of—or well versed in—open-warfare concepts. The War Department belatedly identified this problem and appointed an officer to supervise and standardize training in January 1918, but by then, some units had already deployed (table 2.1).[72] Unsurprisingly, then, some guard units performed poorly in training exercises in France because of their unfamiliarity with some of the key concepts of open warfare.[73]

The Twenty-Sixth (Yankee) and Forty-Second (Rainbow) Divisions were the first guard divisions to arrive in France in the early fall of 1917, joining two active-duty divisions—the First and Second—that had deployed three months earlier. Pershing's staff considered the Twenty-Sixth and Forty-Second the best guard divisions, as they had recently taken part in the Pancho Villa campaign.[74] Over the next year, another sixteen NG divisions arrived. Pershing, however, dismantled six of them to bring other undermanned divisions to full strength.[75]

Upon arriving in France, NG divisions completed additional training, which took place in relatively quiet sectors under the supervision of active-duty officers and Allied advisers.[76] Over the next three to six months, they progressed to more complex tasks as they moved closer to the front.[77] The Americans even had a chance to experience combat as German raiding parties attacked or shelled their training areas.[78] Those experiences certainly boosted the Americans' experience levels, but some of them ended in disaster. On 20 April 1918, near the village of Seicheprey, German raiders surprised and overran forward elements of the Twenty-Sixth Division, whose commander and staff were completely unprepared for the ensuing battle, which left eighty-six American soldiers dead.[79]

Not all divisions had the opportunity to gain experience before being sent to the battlefield. Those arriving later in the spring or summer of 1918

Table 2.1. National Guard World War I Deployment Timeline

Division	States	Activated	Date Deployed	Date Entered Battle	Time from Activation to Combat
26th	CT, MA, ME, NH, RI, VT	25 Jul 1917	6 Sep 1917	5 Feb 1918	6 months
27th	NY	15 Jul 1917	28 Apr 1918	19 Aug 1918	13 months
28th	PA	15 Jul 1917	21 Apr 1918	15 Jul 1918	12 months
29th	NJ, VA, MD, NE, DC	18 Jul 1917	14 Jun 1918	25 Jul 1918	12 months
30th	NC, SC, TN	18 Jul 1917	7 May 1918	16 Jul 1918	12 months
31st	GA, AL, FL	5 Aug 1917	15 Sep 1918	17 Oct 1918—Split to fill other units	
32nd	MI, WI	15 Jul 1917	2 Jan 1917	20 May 1918	10 months
33rd	IL	25 Jul 1917	8 May 1918	17 Jul 1918	12 months
34th	MN, IA, NE	15 Jul 1917	9 Sep 1918	17 Oct 1918—Split to fill other units	
35th	MO, KS	5 Aug 1917	16 Apr 1918	20 Jun 1918	11 months
36th	TX, OK	5 Aug 1917	15 Jul 1918	26 Sep 1918	14 months
37th	OH	15 Jul 1917	6 Jun 1918	4 Aug 1918	13 months
38th	IN, KY, WV	5 Aug 1917	15 Sep 1918	17 Oct 1918 — Split to fill other units	
39th	LA, MS, AR	5 Aug 1917	5 Aug 1918	29 Oct 1918—Split to fill other units	
40th	CA, NV, UT, CO, AZ, NM	5 Aug 1917	26 Jul 1918	24 Oct 1918—Becomes a replacement unit	
41st	WA, OR, MT, WY	25 Jul 1917	26 Nov 1917	20 Dec 1918—Becomes a replacement unit	
42nd	DC and 26 states contribute	1 Aug 1917	18 Oct 1917	21 Feb 1918	6 months
93rd	NY, IL, OH, DC, MD, TN, MA	24 Oct 1917	29 May 1918	23 Aug 1918	10 months

Sources: War Department, *Order of Battle of the United States Land Forces in the World War*, 113–228; War Department Annual Report (1918), 1, 1103–1104; Doubler, *Civilian in Peace, Soldier in War*, 179.

had to compress their training into a month or two so they could help contain the German offensives. In some cases, replacements had little or no time to train. As one officer recalled, "There were cases of soldiers dead in the field of France who had been civilians only days, rather than weeks or months before."[80]

While training in France, guardsmen came under the direct supervision and scrutiny of General Pershing. Judging from his diaries and postwar writings, he had mixed—and often negative—opinions about the NG. At times, Pershing questioned whether senior guard officers were overly politicized, given their state appointments and their tendency to use political connections back home to shield themselves from his rebukes.[81] Yet,

at several points in his diaries, Pershing cited the high quality of guardsmen, including the soldiers of the Thirty-Fifth Infantry Division, and the
notable leadership of Major General John O'Ryan, a guard officer who
commanded New York's Twenty-Seventh Infantry Division.[82] Despite
his praise, Pershing referred to the Twenty-Seventh as "a typical militia
organization . . . [with] great possibilities," suggesting that he viewed it
as less capable than an active-duty division.[83] Pershing's views were likely
validated by reports he received from Allied advisers, who maintained in
the spring of 1918 that guard division and regimental-level leaders were of
questionable quality.[84] Pershing's own inspection teams expressed similar
opinions about guard officers.[85]

Pershing was quick to fire and replace underperforming officers—both
NG and active duty—who did not meet his high standards. Most often,
though, he relieved officers who failed to meet physical fitness or age
requirements.[86] For instance, he sacked Major General William Mann,
commander of the Forty-Second Infantry Division, for demonstrating
poor physical fitness and low energy.[87] Other division commanders were
relieved for more obscure reasons. Brigadier General Charles Martin of
Kansas recalled in 1919 that an active-duty officer relieved him of command because he "lacked force," even though that same officer had once
considered Martin a capable commander.[88] Only O'Ryan of the Twenty-
Seventh, whom Pershing thought highly of, remained in command of his
division for the entire war.[89]

Many guard officers believed that Pershing and his staff targeted them
unfairly. Captain Evan Edwards from the Thirty-Fifth Infantry Division
complained, "We are told that no word should be spoken that criticizes
the individual Regular Army officer. But the National Guard officer was
criticized—stamped by an efficiency board as incompetent or not fully
efficient, and the reasons named. Sometimes they were not even named."[90]
In some cases, active-duty officers had predetermined opinions of NG
officers' incompetence. One officer, for instance, revealed his prejudice
while assessing First Lieutenant Evan Ridgley. In that officer's opinion,
Ridgley was "a typical NG Officer of the undesirable type, lacks leadership and the power of discipline."[91] Pershing himself would later admit
in congressional testimony that there "was always more or less prejudice
against" guardsmen during the war.[92] He passed on his negative views of
the NG to his protégé Major Lesley McNair, who would clash with NG
leaders during World War II.[93]

Despite Pershing's concerns, some NG divisions distinguished themselves in combat, suffering heavy attrition in several key campaigns (ta-

Table 2.2 National Guard World War I Campaigns and Losses

Division	Campaigns	Killed in Action	Wounded in Action	Total Casualties
26th	Champagne-Marne; Aisne-Marne; St. Mihiel; Meuse–Argonne	2,281	11,383	13,664
27th	Somme offensive; Ypres-Lys; Meuse–Argonne (field artillery only)	1,829	6,505	8,334
28th	Champagne-Marne; Aisne-Marne; Oise–Aisne; Ypres-Lys (field artillery only); Meuse–Argonne	2,874	11,265	14,139
29th	Meuse–Argonne	1,053	4,517	5,570
30th	Somme offensive; Ypres-Lys; St. Mihiel; Meuse–Argonne	1,641	6,774	8,415
31st	No campaigns; broken up for replacements	—	—	—
32nd	Aisne-Marne; Oise–Aisne; Meuse–Argonne	3,028	10,233	13,261
33rd	Somme offensive; St. Mihiel (field artillery only); Meuse–Argonne	993	5,871	6,864
34th	No campaigns; broken up for replacements	—	—	—
35th	Meuse–Argonne	1,298	5,998	7,296
36th	Meuse–Argonne	591	1,993	2,584
37th	Ypres-Lys; Meuse–Argonne	1,066	4,321	5,387
38th	No campaigns; broken up for replacements	—	—	—
39th	No campaigns; broken up for replacements	—	—	—
40th	No campaigns; broken up for replacements	—	—	—
41st	No campaigns; broken up for replacements	—	—	—
42nd	Champagne-Marne; Aisne-Marne; St. Mihiel; Meuse–Argonne	2,810	11,873	14,683
93rd	Oise–Aisne; St. Mihiel; Meuse–Argonne	591	2,943	3,534
Total NG Casualties				103,731

Source: Data from Hill, *Minute Man in Peace and War*, 285.

ble 2.2). During its ten months of near-continuous service at the front, the Twenty-Seventh Infantry earned high praise from active-duty officers and the French.[94] The Forty-Second Infantry became one of the most decorated US divisions in the war.[95] Even the Germans recognized the quality of some NG divisions. Of the eight US divisions the Germans deemed highly effective, six were NG.[96]

Yet, in some cases, guard divisions struggled in combat. In July 1918, during the Aisne-Marne offensive, the Twenty-Sixth performed disastrously near Épieds when its inexperienced officers failed to conduct proper preparatory artillery strikes on German lines. In the assault that followed, one of the division's infantry regiments was "practically wiped out"; some of its sister regiments lost cohesion, becoming unresponsive to orders. Afterward, the I Corps commander, who oversaw the Twenty-Sixth, recommended replacing all the regimental and battalion commanders in one of the division's brigades. Two months later, during the Meuse-Argonne offensive, two NG divisions—the Twenty-Eighth and Thirty-Fifth—exhibited extremely poor discipline. Hundreds of men in the Thirty-Fifth discarded their rifles and helmets and fled the battlefield, as reported by members of US First Infantry Division. I Corps was unsurprised by the performance, noting, "This is exactly what one expects of a National Guard division."[97]

The combat record of non-NG divisions was by no means beyond reproach. Nearly all these units experienced difficulties coordinating division-level operations. US Army officers crafted rigid plans, due in part to Pershing's distrust in their ability to take the initiative and to fight effectively without direct supervision from higher headquarters.[98] Despite these defects, the US Army—of which the NG was an important component—helped stem the tide of German offensives and went on the attack in an Allied operation that brought an end to the war in November 1918.[99]

The NG contributed to these successes by providing nearly 200,000 semitrained soldiers who added to the US Army and helped train and mentor new soldiers.[100] Even though nearly all senior guard officers were purged from combat commands, they served in vital supporting roles. This work lacked the glamor of operational leadership, but it helped create and sustain a powerful expeditionary force that played a critical role in defeating Germany.

In contrast, the NG's organizational and tactical shortcomings partially confirmed prewar suspicions about its ability to serve as a front-line reserve. As critics had predicted, the guard was unprepared for serious fighting when activated in the spring of 1917. And even after a year of training and reorganization, multiple guard divisions nearly collapsed in combat.

Blaming only the NG for these struggles is unfair.[101] Guard divisions deployed to France in 1918 were hybrid organizations that, in many cases, were led by active-duty officers and staffed by a mixture of guardsmen, wartime volunteers, and conscripts. As the commander of the Twenty-Seventh Infantry noted after the war, his division "was not a Regular Army division, it was not a National Guard division, nor was it a National Army division; it was a division of the army of the United States."[102] And the guard as a whole made up only about 10 percent of the AEF.[103] In other words, the entire US Army was responsible for the guard's failures and successes during the war.

The Interwar Years

After the war, the War Department demobilized guardsmen by releasing them from all military service, which meant they did not have to return to their state units.[104] And after more than a year of federal service, many guardsmen gladly seized the opportunity to end their military careers. Consequently, the NG essentially ceased to exist by 1920. In fact, fourteen states could not fully staff a single unit that year, forcing guard leadership to spend the next three years focused almost completely on recruitment.[105]

As it rebuilt, the NG confronted a renewed effort by the War Department and active-duty officers to replace it. In January 1919 the War Department and US Army chief of staff Peyton March revealed their vision—known as the Army Reorganization Plan—for the postwar US Army. As part of this plan, the army aimed to expand to around 500,000 active soldiers backed by 500,000 reservists. Those reservists would be a federally controlled force raised through universal military training of all eligible nineteen-year-old males.[106]

Despite its weakened position following demobilization, the NG and its supporters launched a campaign to block the plan. They wrote letters to prominent businessmen, sponsored pro-guard newspaper articles, and enlisted the support of the National Guard Association of the United States (NGAUS; formerly the NGA) to rally support in Congress.[107] They touted the guard's accomplishments in World War I and countered charges of incompetence by claiming such criticisms reflected anti-NG biases.[108] Ultimately, these efforts succeeded. Sympathetic members of Congress rejected compulsory universal military service, citing fears of militarism and the financial costs of such a program.[109] Without universal and compulsory service, the War Department had no way to raise a large federal reserve force.

The 1920 National Defense Act (NDA) emerged from the ashes of the Army Reorganization Plan. Passed by Congress and signed by the president on 4 June 1920, the NDA expanded the active army to 288,000 soldiers—far smaller than the War Department's ideal force.[110] The NG, meanwhile, would continue to serve as the "first reinforcement of the regular army" in a crisis.[111] The Organized Reserve—composed of demobilized National Army divisions—provided a pool of officers and NCOs who could serve as trainers and leaders for wartime conscripts and volunteers.[112] Today, the US Army retains this three-component structure: the active army, the NG, and the Organized Reserve (now called the US Army Reserve).

The 1920 NDA improved NG readiness while boosting its influence in national security policy. It enhanced readiness by mandating that guardsmen maintain the same equipment and organizational standards as active soldiers.[113] In theory, this decreased the time required to mobilize and deploy a unit, as it no longer had to be reorganized prior to deployment. And to ensure that the NG would survive a future demobilization process, the NDA required all guardsmen to return to their units after being discharged from federal service.[114] To increase the NG's influence over its own affairs, the act required that the position of chief of the Militia Bureau (CMB), the senior NG administrative position, be filled by a guard officer rather than an active-duty officer.[115] The NG also gained more positions on the US Army General Staff, giving it greater oversight and influence over US Army and War Department policies.[116]

Following passage of the 1920 NDA, the US Army reorganized to meet its new requirements and address lessons learned from World War I. To do so, it divided its forces into nine corps, each of which controlled one active, two guard, and three reserve divisions.[117] However, most divisions, except for those deployed along the Mexican border, were understrength and would reach full strength in wartime via the draft and calls for volunteers. The army also reorganized divisions to ensure they were nimbler and had a greater combined-arms capability. It did this by eliminating cavalry and some support personnel, reducing the size of a division from 28,105 to 19,385 personnel, and adding a light tank company.[118]

At the same time, the army introduced new doctrine—Field Service Regulation (FSR) 1923—which significantly increased the complexity of its tactics.[119] As historian Edward Coffman explains, previous US Army doctrine asked soldiers to perform only basic tasks: "shoot, march, and live in the field."[120] FSR 1923, in contrast, envisioned an army of infantrymen capable of integrating machine guns, mortars, gas, tanks, and artillery into these tasks.[121] FSR 1923 also increased the demands of soldiering below the battalion level, such as expecting infantrymen to use cover and concealment to cross the fire-swept battle zone in more flexible formations to evade and defeat enemy machine guns, as opposed to advancing upright in linear formations.[122] To ensure that the infantry could advance more fluidly, while taking advantage of cover and concealment, the army had to place more power in the hands of its junior leadership at the squad to company level.[123]

To train and educate its officers and soldiers on new doctrine and equipment, the US Army expanded its school system and training programs.[124] By the end of the 1920s, the army was sending fifty-three officers to civilian schools for training in the technical fields each year.[125] Pershing, now serving as chief of staff of the army (CSA), also enhanced army education by consolidating officer training at the corps level and below at the Command and General Staff School at Fort Leavenworth, Kansas.

These changes in army organization and training challenged the NG. Recruitment and equipment shortfalls limited its ability to maintain fully staffed units. Such shortfalls were particularly problematic in the early 1920s due to the War Department's decision to release demobilizing guard units from state and federal service in 1919. However, all but twenty states were able to meet recruiting quotas by the mid-1920s.[126] That said, states struggled throughout the 1920s and 1930s to acquire and maintain trucks and armored vehicles due to funding shortfalls.[127]

Perhaps the biggest challenge facing the guard in the interwar years was its limited training time. The 1920 NDA required guard units to train sixty days a year, but that fell to just forty-eight days because of budgetary constraints in the mid-1920s.[128] Thus, the average guardsman serving a three-year enlistment (assuming he did not reenlist or have prior active experience) trained only 144 days—most of which were evening sessions. And much of that time was consumed by administrative tasks and individual skills training rather than collective maneuvers.

Collective training was particularly challenging for guard units, as guard divisions were scattered throughout their respective states and sometimes across state lines.[129] To ensure that units had large recruiting pools, the NG placed armories in as many communities as possible. This made it difficult for divisions or brigades to assemble for collective maneuvers because their subordinate units would have to travel many miles to link up. Consequently, guard regiments or divisions could train collectively only during their two-week summer maneuvers.[130]

Other obstacles hindered collective training in the summer. Some units spent about 25 percent of that time—three or four days out of fifteen—on individual soldier-level tasks such as marksmanship, which they had failed to complete earlier.[131] Traveling to and from annual training sites likely consumed several days as well.[132] Ultimately, this meant that guard officers had few opportunities to command entire units above the company in the field, as the CMB explained in his 1924 annual report.[133]

In addition to the lack of collective training, the NG's limited access to army schools made it hard to stay abreast of the changing tactical and technical requirements of army doctrine. In 1921 the NG sent sixty-eight officers to the Infantry School at Fort Benning, but seventy-six other qualified applicants were unable to attend due to insufficient funding.[134] This was a recurring problem for the NG throughout the 1920s, and the CMB often highlighted it in the Militia Bureau's annual reports.[135] Guard officers had to learn new doctrine on their own, through peers who were fortunate enough to attend the army schools, or through active officers and NCOs assigned to mentor and train NG units.

The Militia Bureau and the states wanted to assign one or two active-duty officers and NCOs per NG battalion to provide mentorship and training support, but the active army was unable to provide these mentors due to personnel shortages.[136] Some active officers sought to avoid service with the guard, fearing it would undermine the progression of their careers.[137] One senior active-duty officer later conceded that it took "a high order of salesmanship" to convince officers to take assignments with the guard.[138]

Despite these challenges, the NG made modest gains in readiness during the 1920s. In 1919 the Militia Bureau mandated that all NG officers pass physical, moral, and professional exams to earn and maintain commissions.[139] Within five years, nearly all guard officers met these standards.[140] Additionally, guard units conducted more training than they had prior to World War I.[141] In fact, five guard divisions completed division-level field maneuvers in the summer of 1928—a rarity for guard and active units alike.[142]

The NG's political fortunes also brightened in the 1920s. Following the defeat of the Army Reorganization Plan, relations between the NG and the active army improved, as both institutions aligned to pressure Congress and the president to increase defense spending. The guard also gained greater influence in state politics when it started building armories outside of urban centers and in smaller rural communities, where prominent local businessmen and politicians joined units and promoted guard interests in state legislatures.[143]

The Great Depression reversed some of these gains. Faced with an unprecedented economic crisis, Congress cut spending for federal programs. For instance, it temporarily reduced annual guard training from forty-eight to thirty-six training sessions between 1934 and 1935.[144] Funding for army schools, and thus attendance, also declined.[145] That said, the Great Depression had some positive second-order effects. Guard recruitment increased as men sought additional sources of income.[146] Drill attendance rates improved from around 75 percent in 1930 to an all-time high of 91.5 percent by 1934.[147] With higher attendance rates, units could conduct more realistic training and ensure that soldiers' military skills were not being allowed to atrophy.[148]

The NG also benefited from legislation passed in 1933. That year, NGAUS successfully lobbied Congress to amend the NDA to reduce confusion regarding the NG's dual nature as a state and federal force. It did so by clarifying that the NG had two distinct roles: when guardsmen were at their home stations or supporting state missions, they fell under the "National Guard of Several States"; when they were on federal orders for missions or training, guardsmen were part of the "National Guard of the United States."[149] It was hoped that making this distinction in the law would ensure the NG's smooth transition to federal service when mobilized.[150] In addition, the amended act changed the name of the Militia Bureau to the National Guard Bureau (NGB), as it is known today.[151]

As its roles became clearer, the NG worked to keep up with other changes in army doctrine resulting from a larger CSA-led modernization effort. General Douglas MacArthur, who served as CSA from 1930 to 1935, prioritized modernization and training, with the goal of increasing the speed of army mobilization and deployment.[152] To achieve this, MacArthur focused on motorization, mechanization, and improvement in unit staffing levels.[153]

The NG, like the active army, had to scrounge for money to meet MacArthur's goals. One way it did so was by characterizing motorization as a cost-saving measure. In 1933 the chief of the National Guard Bureau (CNGB) argued that replacing horses with trucks and tracked vehicles could save money because horses "were eating their heads off" every day, whereas vehicles required fuel only during drills.[154] Budgetary constraints, however, prevented the full motorization or mechanization of the guard, which remained a light infantry force throughout the interwar years.[155]

The second half of the 1930s witnessed major changes to the active army and NG alike as the German and Japanese threat to US interests grew. A key architect of these changes was General Malin Craig, who succeeded MacArthur as CSA in 1935. Like MacArthur, Craig hoped to develop doctrine and capabilities that would improve the speed and efficacy of army mobilization and avoid some of the issues encountered during World War I.[156] During Craig's term as CSA, the NG made small readiness gains, and its end strength rose to meet its target of 210,000 guardsmen.[157] The NG also added to its fleet of trucks and armored vehicles, which increased from 6,192 in 1934 to more than 16,000 by the end of the decade.[158] In 1940, 819 guardsmen attended army schools, compared with only 398 a decade earlier.[159] Additionally, in 1935, 58,000 guardsmen and active-duty soldiers participated in the largest peacetime maneuvers to date, which were part of a wider effort by the War Department to increase active-duty and guard integration and interoperability.[160] These training events continued into the late 1930s.[161]

During the latter half of the 1930s the US Army also underwent a major reorganization as it transitioned to the triangular infantry division structure. The triangular division was the product of years of debate about how to reorganize combat divisions based on lessons learned during World War I and subsequent technological and tactical developments.[162] CSA Craig's solution was to increase the mobility and firepower of the army division by reducing the number of regiments in a division from four to three. At the same time, divisions could move faster by replacing horses with trucks and armored vehicles, and they could hit harder by adding tanks and arming infantrymen with the new semiautomatic M1 Garand rifle. General George Marshall, who succeeded Craig as CSA in 1939, authorized these changes for the active army and guard in 1940.[163]

In addition to reorganizing its divisions, the army updated its tactics when it published a revised FSR in September 1939. The new regulation built on the combined-arms tactics introduced in the 1923 version by adding new sections on the use of airpower, air defense artillery, trucks, and antitank tactics.[164] It also introduced modern armor tactics by explaining how commanders could use tanks to break through enemy lines and "penetrate deeply into the hostile position and attack the enemy's reserves and artillery."[165] And, borrowing from German doctrinal concepts, FSR 1939 called for greater initiative by individual soldiers on an increasingly complex and lethal battlefield.[166]

The soldiers and officers of the NG were unable to keep up with these changes. In the late 1930s widespread equipment shortages persisted, making it impossible to train in the newer fields of antitank and antiair-craft tactics.[167] Of particular concern to the CNGB was the shortage of radios, which severely restricted units' ability to practice combined-arms maneuvers integrating tanks, infantry, and artillery.[168] Furthermore, NG divisions generally lacked access to training ranges large enough to al-low realistic maneuvers.[169] And the time available for collective training was restricted by a growing need to focus on individual skills during annual training periods. Because of the increased ranges and calibers of army munitions, about 50 percent of guard units were unable to com-plete marksmanship training at or near their local armories due to safety concerns.[170]

Perhaps the biggest problem facing guard units during the 1930s was that its officer and NCO corps lacked the experience and schooling to manage internal training programs. During weekly drills, guard train-ers often just read manuals to their soldiers, rather than running them through dynamic exercises. And since most training took place on week-nights, many soldiers were tired after working all day at their civilian jobs, reducing their ability to grasp and retain instructions.[171] Guard officers, meanwhile, were often unable to attend midlevel and senior staff courses due to their civilian work commitments, undermining their ability to learn how to plan and execute training programs.[172]

War Department efforts to appoint senior officers from the active army as trainers for guard units mitigated some of these problems. While serving as a senior trainer for the NG, Colonel George Marshall planned and evaluated command post and field exercises for the Illinois National Guard between 1933 and 1936.[173] One guard officer was so pleased with the training he received that he wrote to Marshall in August 1934, "We have been attending [annual training] for eleven years and it is the honest opinion of all concerned that we got more this year than in any previ-ous camp."[174] Many others did not receive such support due to personnel shortages and budgetary constraints.[175]

In short, NG units simply lacked the time and the resources to learn—let alone master—the intricacies of the US Army's rapidly changing tac-tical doctrine and the new technologies it was fielding in the latter half of the 1930s. The effects of these shortcomings became apparent during mobilization for World War II.

World War II

The entire US Army was unprepared for World War II. For instance, no US officer—active or guard—had experience commanding a division-sized formation or above in combat.[176] Worse, as the secretary of war reported in 1941, "Total [US] military forces [amounted] only to a slightly larger number of soldiers than were contained in the armies of Belgium and Holland at the time when they were overthrown in a few days by the might of Germany." And the tiny active-duty army was already stretched thin garrisoning bases and outposts around the globe.[177]

Although its forces were inexperienced and outnumbered, the United States had a solid foundation on which to build an effective military. US industrial might and national income dwarfed that of Germany and Japan, enabling it to quickly raise a large and well-equipped army.[178] Plus, it had a generation of active-duty officers—as well as some guardsmen—who had benefited from a robust military education at the army's burgeoning school system. These officers, as other historians have shown, used that training and education to build and deploy an effective expeditionary army out of a collection of undertrained active-duty soldiers, guardsmen, reservists, and draftees.[179]

Efforts to build such a force accelerated in 1939 with President Franklin D. Roosevelt's limited readiness campaign, as hopes for peace were dashed by German expansionism and growing Japanese threats to US interests. Thus, between 1939 and 1941, the United States increased annual defense spending from $500 million to $3.7 billion.[180] Roosevelt and Congress also authorized the first peacetime draft in September 1940, enabling the army to expand to 1.2 million soldiers by the summer of 1941.[181] With additional funding and more personnel, the US Army established new division-, corps-, and army-level commands and began more extensive peacetime exercises to test and refine new concepts and equipment.[182]

The NG also underwent significant changes as it prepared for war between 1939 and 1941. Those changes began with the president's signing of Executive Order 8244, authorizing "the increase, as quickly as possible, in the enlisted strength of the existing active units of the National Guard to 235,000 men."[183] As defense spending rose, the NG could afford to increase its training sessions from forty-eight to sixty days per year, plus seven days of supplementary training.[184] More funding also enabled the NG to nearly double the number of guardsmen attending army schools by 1941.[185] Select officers were able to embed with active units in corps- and army-level exercises, likely improving their understanding of higher-level

Table 2.3 National Guard Mobilization and Composition, 1940–41

Division	Month Mobilized	Percent Selective Service (Draftees)
26th	Jan 1941	56
27th	Oct 1940	40
28th	Feb 1941	—
29th	Feb 1941	56
30th	Sep 1940	33
31st	Nov 1940	40
32nd	Oct 1940	46
33rd	Mar 1941	34
34th	Feb 1941	39
35th	Dec1940	39
36th	Nov 1940	39
37th	Oct 1940	58
38th	Jan 1941	57
40th	Mar 1941	37
41st	Sep 1940	38
43rd	Feb 1941	43
44th	Sep 1940	36
45th	Sep 1940	37

Source: National Guard Bureau Annual Report (1946), 26–27.

tactical concepts and their familiarity with changing army doctrine and technology.[186]

The fall of France in the summer of 1940 prompted President Roosevelt to mobilize the NG.[187] In total, around 300,000 guardsmen were activated in increments between 16 September 1940 and 23 June 1941 (table 2.3).[188] The War Department could not bring all units into federal service at once because of insufficient housing and training facilities.[189]

During that first year of federal service, the NG faced multiple challenges. Many guardsmen resented the yearlong activation, which eroded morale.[190] One Pennsylvania guardsman, for example, complained to a Pittsburgh newspaper, "Why should we give up our civilian jobs while the rest of the country stays home and reaps the harvest of good wages?" The War Department's internal surveys also found that morale was extremely low. [191]

Even though they were on full-time orders, guard units struggled with collective training. Constrained by the one-year limit on active service, the army could not advance guard units to large-scale maneuvers at the brigade and division levels.[192] The quality of training below the brigade level was uneven because few guard officers and NCOs "had adequate previous experience and training" to organize and supervise such events.[193] It was, as one senior officer noted, like "the blind leading the blind."[194] The situation improved slightly after August 1941, when President Roosevelt extended mobilization by six months, enabling guard divisions to participate in maneuvers supervised by active-duty officers in Louisiana and the Carolinas.[195]

The year and a half of federal service gave the NG an opportunity to reorganize. This was important because many guard units were in "bad shape" due to equipment shortages, as the CNGB observed in April 1941.[196] Beginning in the fall of 1940, guard divisions began to receive shipments of equipment, such as the M1 Garand rifle.[197] And on 6 December 1940 the NG received orders from the War Department to reorganize its divisions to align with the triangular concept.[198] This reorganization, which downsized the division from four to three regiments, produced eighteen separate infantry regiments that lacked a parent division. The army eventually assigned these excess regiments to active or draftee divisions, while others performed routine security missions around the world.[199]

The composition of the guard changed considerably during mobilization. To bring guard divisions to full strength, the War Department infused their ranks with thousands of draftees and new volunteers. Thousands of guardsmen also left the military because of the Selective Service Act of 1940, which called for the drafting of men over the age of twenty-one who did not have dependents or critical jobs in agriculture or industry.[200] This meant that the NG was unable to force soldiers who did not meet these requirements to remain on federal orders, resulting in the loss of around sixty thousand men—about 25 percent of the NG's prewar strength—because they were younger than twenty-one, had physical fitness issues, or had to care for dependents.[201]

Given these losses, NG divisions were transformed into hybrid organizations with a nearly even balance of guardsmen and brand-new soldiers. In some cases, draftees vastly outnumbered guardsmen. For instance, in the 175th Infantry Regiment of the Maryland National Guard, draftees filled two thousand of its thirty-five hundred billets.[202] Distinctions blurred even more in September 1941 when Secretary of War Henry Stimson issued the "One Army" policy, authorizing the War Department to transfer guardsmen to any unit, including to units outside their home states or to active formations.[203]

The One Army policy also authorized the army to replace guard officers with active ones, setting the stage for a bitter conflict. Leading the charge to replace guard officers was Lesley McNair, who had been promoted to lieutenant general. He commanded US Army Ground Forces and was responsible for training all army units in the United States during mobilization.[204] McNair, who placed a heavy emphasis on developing high-quality soldiers and officers who could master the intricacies of modern warfare, detested the NG due to its poor state of readiness.[205] He later wrote, "One of the great lessons of the present war is that the National Guard, as organized before the war, contributed nothing to national defense."[206]

Although he wanted to abolish the guard, McNair had no authority to do so.[207] Instead, he focused on replacing underperforming guard officers from brigade- and division-level commands. McNair's low opinion of guard officers was shared by many other senior officers at the time, including George Marshall.[208] McNair's opinions were based in part on his prewar experiences working with the guard, as well as his observations of guard units that struggled during field exercises in 1940 and 1941.[209] Such poor performances prompted McNair to write to Marshall that, in his estimation, the NG was "built on an unsound foundation in that its officers have had little or no training." He recommended that "it would be better to ease Guard units out of the picture as fast as others can be created in their places."[210] As evidence of the guard's poor leadership, McNair provided his assessments of each of the NG's twelve remaining division commanders (by October 1941, six had already been replaced by active officers):

- 26th—Eckfeldt, Mass.—[age] 50—Live but green; may learn; one of the few promising ones.
- 27th—Haskell [N.Y.]—63—Should go out for more than age.
- 28th—Martin, Pa.—62—No question but that he should go.
- 29th—Reckord, Md.—62—Good administrator but should go.
- 30th—Russell, Ga.—52—Pleasing; leader of a sort; but not a military comdr. Should go sooner or later.
- 31st—Persons, Ala.—53—Comds effectively; question is whether he has sufficient military background; one of the most promising ones.
- 32d—Fish, Wis.—62—Fine man; experienced in Nat. Gd., but believed lacking in military knowledge; should go sooner or later, preferably sooner.
- 33d—Lawton, Ill.—57—Dubious; performance thus far shows force, but not well directed; military knowledge too limited.
- 37th—Beightler, Ohio—49—One of the best Nat. Gd. comdrs if he stays with the job.
- 41st—White, Ore.—61—Strong comdr, but military knowledge none too full. However, one of the best.
- 44th—Powell, N.J.—48—Incompetent; Frendenall said would be reclassified.

• 45th—Key, Okla.—52—Forceful; impressive; and that's about all. Dubious for the long pull.[211]

In short, McNair had little confidence in the NG's remaining division commanders, with the exception of Robert Beightler of Ohio. Unlike most of his contemporaries, Beightler had the advantage of more extensive active-duty experience during World War I, a tour on the General Staff, and studies at the staff and war colleges.[212] And at forty-nine, Beightler was one of the youngest commanders, which was an advantage, given that Marshall and McNair sought young, physically fit officers.[213]

That said, Beightler did not have an easy path to battlefield command. In fact, army evaluators initially gave him and his division a low rating in mid-1940, during the early mobilization period. The unit's performance improved markedly in the next year and a half, as Beightler was determined to demonstrate that a guard unit could, in his words, "render equally good service to that of a division whose key officers were largely regular army." Thus, by the spring of 1941, evaluators rated his division "good," even though McNair still questioned its readiness.[214]

Despite McNair's criticisms, Marshall resisted calls to scrap the NG or remove all guardsmen from key leadership positions. Marshall had served as a senior trainer for the Illinois National Guard in the mid-1930s. He admired guardsmen for their service to their country and hoped they could meet the army's higher standards if given the opportunity to train properly.[215] He also understood that it was impractical to sideline the guard, given the army's lack of replacement personnel and the political storm it would generate in Congress.[216]

Even so, reports of low readiness levels and poor professionalism angered Marshall.[217] In July 1941 he wrote a letter to guard division commanders warning that their units' standards were "too low." The reason for this, in his estimation, was that "in the less advanced divisions [of the NG] . . . younger officers have not had enough tactical training or general education to enable them to conduct instruction in an efficient or at least in an interesting manner." Additionally, according to McNair, "the basic training of some units had been carried out so ineffectively as to necessitate repetition." These deficiencies, Marshall warned, had to be remedied immediately, even if it meant replacing guard officers.[218]

Empowered to remove poor-performing guard officers, McNair purged the leaders of guard divisions and regiments. In fact, only two of the eighteen NG division commanders—Persons and Beightler— led their units into combat.[219] And only three NG officers would rise to division command during the war.[220] The purge also extended below the division level. Rarely did an NG officer raise above the rank of colonel or command a unit above the battalion level.[221] In some cases, the active army may have decided to replace regimental commanders without evaluating them. Upon assuming command of the Thirty-Sixth Infantry Division of the Texas National Guard, Fred Walker, an active-duty officer, received orders from the War Department to remove all guard officers from regimental command positions. Walker reluctantly complied and allowed his three subordinate regimental commanders and chief of staff to resign to avoid embarrassment.[222] Another unit may have received a directive from higher headquarters to replace all NG officers with active-duty personnel, as reported by one senior guard officer after the war.[223]

Guardsmen believed they were unfairly targeted by McNair, even though he ruthlessly removed active-duty officers from command as well.[224] The CNGB complained to fellow guard leaders that Marshall was "constantly being misled and misinformed" about the NG by members of the active army or civilians at the War Department.[225] Several other top guard officers believed "the cards [were] definitely stacked [against them], and the powers that be have made up their minds that no National Guard officer will be permitted to take a division into battle."[226] A colonel from the Thirty-Eighth Division (Indiana) complained that because of McNair's replacement policies, good officers "who had given their all" were being sent home "embittered, heart-broken, and discarded."[227]

In response, Major General Milton Reckord, the influential adjutant general of Maryland and former Twenty-Ninth Infantry Division commander, mounted a letter-writing campaign starting in late 1941. His goal was to gather support from other NG leaders to resist War Department efforts to alter the character of guard units by assigning them active-duty soldiers and draftees.[228] Reckord found some support among state governors. In November 1941 the governor of Texas tried to pressure the War Department to keep guard officers in regimental command in the Thirty-Sixth Division.[229] The War Department refused, and state leaders could not stop the army from removing and reassigning personnel, as guardsmen activated for federal service no longer fell under their command. Arguments between the NG and the War Department persisted, even after the United States entered the war in December 1941 following the Japanese attack on Pearl Harbor.

Initially, the War Department aimed to have army divisions deployable by the end of 1942, but the chaos of expanding and modernizing the army made that goal unrealistic. Shifts in personnel were particularly problematic, as the army removed soldiers and officers from their units and sent them to fill vacancies elsewhere or to attend school.[230] As Major General Walker of the Thirty-Sixth Division recalled in his diaries: "It seems that everybody is either going to school, at school, returning from school, or being transferred away permanently. This keeps us in a state of confusion and uncertainty and makes it impossible to carry on unit tactical training."[231] Making matters worse, expansion of the draft in 1942 filled NG divisions with new, untrained personnel, forcing them to devote considerable time to individual training and less on collective tasks.[232]

Despite these challenges, the NG and the active army began to deploy some divisions overseas in early to mid-1942 (table 2.4), where they participated in operations in the Pacific or prepared for the invasion of North Africa. However, units continued to confront training challenges during the deployment process. Some received new draftees and equipment all the way up to the time of their arrival at the port of embarkation. Once they were overseas, units tried to find opportunities to conduct collective training in quiet sectors for a few weeks, but that did not always happen. In places like Great Britain, for example, there was insufficient space for large unit maneuvers.[233] Thus, unlike in World War I, the US Army did not have the opportunity to conduct lengthy, large-scale in-theater training.

It is difficult to determine how well the guard performed in combat, as wartime reports did not necessarily distinguish units or personnel by their affiliation with the NG. Senior guard officers suspected this was because the War Department deliberately ignored or misrepresented the success of guard divisions.[234] But in fact, NG divisions that deployed during World War II were guard in name only, as many of their original members, mobilized between 1940 and 1942, were no longer serving. In addition, many of those divisions' officers had been replaced by active-duty or recently commissioned officers.

That said, some guard divisions distinguished themselves in combat in the Pacific and European theaters. In the Pacific, the Thirty-Second, Thirty-Seventh, Fortieth, and Forty-Third Divisions served as lead elements for the liberation of the Philippines in 1945. And the Americal Division—formed from three NG regiments in 1942—fought doggedly at Guadalcanal, earning a Navy Presidential Unit Citation.[235]

However, like their active counterparts, NG divisions performed unevenly in their initial battles against veteran-led German forces in North Africa and Italy. The Germans, for instance, decimated the Thirty-Fourth Infantry Division of Wisconsin and Minnesota during battles in Tunisia

Table 2.4 National Guard World War II Deployment Timeline

Division	Theater	Date Mobilized	Date Deployed	Date Entered Battle	Time from Mobilization to Combat
26th	Europe	16 Jan 1941	27 Aug 1944	7 Sep 1944	3 years, 8 months
27th	Pacific	15 Oct 1940	10 Mar 1942	17 Jun 1944	3 years, 8 months
28th	Europe	17 Feb 1941	18 Oct 1943	22 Jul 1944	3 years, 5 months
29th	Europe	3 Feb 1941	5 Oct 1942	6 Jun 1944	3 years, 4 months
30th	Europe	16 Sep 1940	11 Feb 1944	10 Jun 1944	3 years, 9 months
31st	Pacific	25 Nov 1940	12 Mar 1944	25 Jun 1944	3 years, 7 months
32nd	Pacific	15 Oct 1940	22 Apr19 42	15 Sep 1942	1 year, 11 months
33rd	Pacific	5 Mar 1941	7 Jul 1943	11 May 1944	3 years, 2 months
34th	North Africa and Mediterranean	10 Feb 1941	12 Jan 1942	3 Jan 1943	1 year, 11 months
35th	Europe	23 Dec 1940	12 May 1944	6 Jul 1944	3 years, 7 months
36th	Mediterranean and Europe	25 Nov 1940	2 Apr 1943	13 Apr 1943	2 years, 5 months
37th	Pacific	15 Oct 1940	26 May 1942	11 Jun 1942	1 year, 8 months
38th	Pacific	17 Jan 1941	3 Jan 1944	16 Dec 1944	3 years, 11 months
40th	Pacific	3 Mar 1941	23 Aug 1942	31 Dec 1943	2 years, 9 months
41st	Pacific	16 Sep 1940	19 Mar 1942	25 Jan 1943	2 years, 4 months
42nd	Europe	14 Jul 1943	Nov 1944	Dec 1944	1 year, 5 months
43rd	Pacific	24 Feb 1941	1 Oct 1942	28 Feb 1943	2 years
44th	Europe	16 Sep 1940	5 Sep 1944	15 Sep 1944	4 years
45th	Mediterranean and Europe	16 Feb 1940	3 Jun 1943	22 Jun 1943	3 years, 4 months

Sources: Stanton and Weigley, World War II Order of Battle, 101–134; National Guard Bureau Annual Report (1946), 27; "History of the Rainbow," https://dmna.ny.gov/arng/42div/?id=history.

in 1943. Following those defeats—which were mostly due to poor planning by higher headquarters—senior British commanders recommended banishing the Thirty-Fourth to the rear for retraining. This prompted intervention by George Patton and Omar Bradley, who guaranteed they could improve the division's performance and "restore its soul." Patton also issued a veiled threat, reminding the British that embarrassing a guard unit could lead to political blowback.[236]

As promised, the Thirty-Fourth improved and, as Bradley later noted, became "one of the finest infantry outfits in World War II."[237] Over the next one to two years, other guard and active divisions also gained the experience and confidence to take on leading roles in successful ground operations.[238] For example, the Forty-Fifth Infantry Division helped lead the landings on Sicily in June 1943.[239] Three months later, the Thirty-Sixth Infantry Division was at the forefront of the invasion of Italy and, along with the Forty-Fifth, would participate in the liberation of Rome after suffering horrendous losses in a grinding battle of attrition from Salerno to Rome.[240] Its commanders would later contend that the division's losses were the result of "faulty orders" from "a West Point commander" that essentially destroyed a "fine National Guard division."[241] The Twenty-Ninth Infantry Division would suffer similarly high losses during the Normandy invasion and subsequent operations at Brest and on the road to Germany, which it would help conquer.[242]

On average, guard divisions lost 14,000 personnel each (125,630 total)—a rate similar to active-duty divisions.[243] Some divisions suffered nearly 100 percent losses, devasting the small towns from which their units were raised.[244] On the surface, these rates suggest that NG and active-duty divisions performed poorly. But as historian Peter Mansoor has shown, these losses reflect the fact that the US Army did not have enough divisions to rotate units out of combat to rest and refit. Instead, they remained on the line, receiving individual replacements from in-theater depots or from the United States. This was the case because the War Department gambled and mobilized only eighty-nine divisions to ensure that US farms and industry had the necessary personnel to remain productive.[245]

In summary, the NG proved to be a capable first-line combat reserve for the US Army during World War II. This was possible because the War Department had the time and the resources to restructure guard divisions in such a way that they were nearly indistinguishable from active units. President Roosevelt and General Marshall provided that time by starting the process of raising the standards of NG units as early as 1940, placing them on full-time orders, infusing them with veteran leadership, and intensifying training. Even after the United States entered the war, most guard units had additional months—or even years—to train before seeing combat.

The National Guard at the Dawn of the Cold War

In the decade following World War II, the NG arguably reached its highest readiness levels relative to the active army. During that period, combat veterans led many guard formations, which maintained a fairly intensive peacetime training program compared to prewar standards. At the same time, the guard enjoyed strong support from President Harry Truman, whose negative opinions about the active-duty army were based on his experience as a guard officer in World War I.[246]

Truman had big plans for the guard following World War II. In an October 1945 address to Congress, he laid out the structure of the postwar US military, which would consist of a "comparatively small" Regular US Army, US Navy, and Marine Corps and a "greatly strengthened" National Guard and Organized Reserve.[247] To strengthen the guard, the Truman administration set its peacetime strength at 425,000 enlisted soldiers.[248] Three years later, Congress provided the War Department and the president the authority to mobilize guardsmen and reservists for up to twenty-one months of active service.[249] During this period, the NG split into two organizations—the Army National Guard (ARNG) and the Air National Guard (ANG)—both of which continued to report to their respective state governors when not under federal orders.

Truman also sought drastic changes to US reserve service through a universal military training (UMT) program. Under this program, the Truman administration envisioned all eighteen-year-old men spending a year undergoing military training.[250] After that year, they would be placed in a general reserve, where they could be recalled in an emergency.[251]

The ARNG supported the UMT plan to boost its recruitment. Guard leadership calculated that many men would opt out of UMT and join the NG.[252] Such a choice was appealing because guardsmen were required to drill only about eight hours a month and two weeks in the summer. UMT, in contrast, required a year of full-time service.

Congress and the American public did not share the president's enthusiasm for UMT, despite attempts by senior cabinet officials, including Secretary of State George Marshall, to explain its importance to military readiness.[253] Conservatives in Congress balked at the financial costs.[254] Some congressmen refused to listen to debates on UMT, while others worried it was an overextension of federal power.[255] Truman continued to push for UMT until the end of his presidency, but given the lack of support, he decided to ask Congress to reauthorize selective service instead, in what would be the first peacetime draft in US history.[256] Tensions were rising between the United States and the Soviet Union, so Congress passed the Selective Service Act on 19 June 1948 to maintain "an adequate armed strength . . . to insure the security" of the United States.[257]

The Selective Service Act allowed the federal government to draft men between the ages of nineteen and twenty-six and authorized deferments for college students, those with physical and mental disabilities, and veterans.[258] The act also allowed men to avoid the draft by volunteering for one year of active duty, after which they would be discharged into the reserves and complete no more than one month of annual refresher training over five years.[259] Volunteering was appealing because draftees had to spend twenty-one consecutive months on active duty and could be recalled to active service for an additional five years.[260] Thus, many men volunteered, giving the army a huge boost in recruitment.[261]

As Congress and the president debated UMT and selective service, the ARNG faced renewed efforts to replace or marginalize it, generating a period of "cutthroat competition" between the active army and the NG.[262] Many active officers thought the NG had not lived up to expectations during World War II because of its struggles during mobilization.[263] And some, such as General Omar Bradley, worried that the NG was ill-suited for a potential fight against the Soviet Union. As he explained in his memoirs, "With our very survival seemingly at stake in the Cold War, I for one could not continue to support the fiction that the National Guard could be relied upon for anything more than local riot control."[264]

Bradley's concerns were likely shared by senior leaders in the National Military Establishment (NME)—the new name for the War Department as of 1947 (it was renamed the Department of Defense in 1949). James Forrestal, who became the first secretary of defense in September 1947, convened a special board led by assistant secretary of the army Gordon Gray to examine reserve policies for all the services.[265] Nine months later the board concluded that the NME should federalize the ARNG and merge it with the Organized Reserve, citing three reasons for this recommendation.[266] First, it wanted to improve the ARNG's responsiveness for federal missions, given that it could be mobilized for federal service only in a declared national emergency.[267] Second, transferring ARNG units from state to federal control took too long, in the board's estimation, due to rules governing the transfer of state employees and equipment to federal command.[268] And third, by placing the ARNG under federal control, the military could improve its readiness standards by allowing active-duty officers to oversee training and administration.[269]

The board's recommendations faced immediate opposition.[270] Governors from all the states, with one exception, strongly disagreed with proposals to abolish the guard.[271] Meanwhile, senior guardsmen, who had witnessed previous attempts to federalize the NG, were outraged by the recommendations.[272] The NGAUS, led by Major General Ellard Walsh of Minnesota, derided the proposal as "continuing efforts" by the "professional soldier and War Department" to discredit the guard.[273] Vowing to fight the plan "at every turn," the NGAUS appealed to Congress in 1948 and presented three main arguments.[274] First, it claimed that the guard trained more than it was given credit for. Active-duty officers estimated that guardsmen trained only about two hundred hours a year, but NGAUS representatives argued that guard leaders logged about six hundred hours a year because they had to perform various administrative and leadership tasks outside of drills or annual training. Second, it charged that the active army did not understand the guard because of "false indoctrination in the United States Military Academy," which made them ignorant of US military policy that required the guard to be a state-led force. And third, the NGAUS asserted that efforts to federalize the guard violated states' rights.[275] Ultimately, these arguments resonated with Republicans and southern Democrats.[276]

Faced with rising public criticism, Secretary of Defense Forrestal backed away from the Gray Board's findings.[277] Truman refused to comment on the matter publicly, fearing it could hurt his reelection bid.[278] Two years later, George Marshall—now the secretary of defense—revisited the issue of reserve reform. After a one-year study, Marshall proposed that the guard remain a dual state-federal force, and Truman agreed.[279] Marshall also called on guardsmen to improve their training standards.[280]

Because of time constraints, however, the guard's ability to improve training was limited. The postwar guard retained a training schedule of forty-eight two-hour drills a year plus fifteen annual training days.[281] Units spent much of that time training newly assigned soldiers, as guardsmen did not attend a basic training course prior to arriving at their units.[282] Additionally, by splitting drills into two-hour periods during the workweek, units' ability to conduct maneuvers outside of annual training was severely limited. To address this issue, the Department of Defense (DOD) considered expanding annual training from fifteen days to twenty-one or thirty, but budgetary constraints prevented it from doing so. Guard leaders also worried that such an expansion would undermine recruitment and retention and put extra pressure on the guardsmen's civilian employers.[283]

While the DOD and Congress debated its future, the ARNG rebuilt itself. Between 1947 and 1950 it expanded from a skeleton force of 97,000 to more than 324,000 soldiers organized into twenty-seven divisions, including the guard's first armored divisions (the Forty-Ninth of Texas and the Fiftieth of New Jersey).[284] Much of this growth was the result of successful efforts by the NGAUS to convince Congress to provide additional funding in 1947 for a public relations campaign to bolster ARNG recruitment. The NGAUS also successfully lobbied Congress to exempt seventeen- and eighteen-year-old men from the selective service if they enlisted in the ARNG.[285]

The reestablishment of the ARNG following World War II came in the context of major shifts in US national security strategy. One of the most important changes was passage of the National Security Act of 1947, which sought to prepare the United States for the challenges of the early Cold War.[286] In addition to replacing the War Department with the National Military Establishment, it created three coequal military departments: the Departments of the Army, Navy, and Air Force.[287] It also formally established the Joint Chiefs of Staff (JCS) and created the Central Intelligence Agency (CIA) and National Security Council (NSC).

These changes reflected the United States' emergence as a global superpower. During World War II, US gross domestic product (GDP) nearly doubled, surpassing that of its enemies and allies alike.[288] But the war also proved that the United States was vulnerable to international conflict. For more than a century, the United States had enjoyed the protection of two oceans, making attacks from adversaries in Europe or Asia unlikely. Now its new adversary—the Soviet Union—could use long-range bombers to overfly those oceans and strike the US mainland in a matter of hours.[289]

In response to the challenges and opportunities presented by the post–World War II security environment, the Truman administration adopted an activist foreign and defense policy to contain Soviet power. In a 1947 speech before Congress, amid fears of growing Soviet influence in Turkey and Greece, Truman presented his vision for a postwar US foreign policy, which would be known as the Truman Doctrine. Truman explained that the United States had to "support free peoples who are resisting attempted subjugation by armed minorities or by outside pressures."[290]

For the US military, the most important aspect of Truman's strategic reorientation was the establishment of the North Atlantic Treaty Organization (NATO) in 1949—the first US peacetime military alliance. NATO was created at the behest of France and Britain, both of which sought US military protection and support as they rebuilt their postwar economies. The French also wanted the United States to demonstrate its commitment to defending western Europe by stationing soldiers in Germany, ensuring that Americans would have to fight if the Soviet army attacked westward.[291] Supporting the NATO alliance meant that the US military had to maintain large numbers of land, air, and naval forces in Europe to contain Soviet expansion. And it had to do the same in the Pacific to rebuild Japan. In fact, by 1949, five of the ten active US divisions were deployed overseas.[292]

Although forward deployed, the US Army in the late 1940s played a relatively minor role in national security. At the time, US strategy for countering the Soviets focused on nuclear arms, leveraging the US nuclear monopoly and its advantage in bombers.[293] The US Army's mission was to defend key infrastructure abroad and to build its strength for the "eventual climactic ground attack" that would occur after nuclear bombers destroyed critical targets in the Soviet Union.[294]

As he placed his trust in the power of nuclear arms, Truman slashed defense spending.[295] Given this tightened budget, the DOD directed more than half its funding to the navy and air force, which would lead the fight against the Soviets in the event of war.[296] Rising inflation further reduced the purchasing power of the budget, which included new costs such as the $8 billion in benefits for World War II veterans.[297] The shrinking funds available to support army training, operations, and equipment created risks, but as Secretary of Defense Forrestal argued in 1947, the US nuclear monopoly allowed the United States to "assume certain risks otherwise unacceptable."[298]

These budget cuts, combined with its postwar missions, severely restricted the army's ability to prepare for war with the Soviets. For instance, it had to keep all its divisions understrength, except for the First Infantry Division stationed in Germany.[299] Demobilization and the booming economy also caused a brain drain, as many technical specialists and experienced leaders left the army for higher-paying civilian careers.[300] The ARNG, meanwhile, continued to experience shortages of active-duty instructors.[301] It also lacked adequate facilities to house its growing inventories of armored vehicles or to conduct live fire exercises with mortars and artillery.[302] Despite these challenges, the ARNG arguably reached its highest peacetime readiness levels in the late 1940s, as nearly 80 percent of its officers were combat veterans.[303] And those veteran leaders would command the guard during its first major test of the Cold War in Korea.

The Korean War

The Korean War began on 25 June 1950 when seven divisions of the North Korean People's Army (NKPA) attacked across the thirty-eighth parallel to unify the Korean peninsula under communist rule. Confident the Americans would not intervene, the North Koreans believed the war would be over in three weeks. Truman, however, quickly authorized military intervention to protect US prestige and prevent communist expansion.[304]

To lead the operation, the United States tapped General Douglas MacArthur, the former supreme Allied commander in the Pacific theater during World War II. An overconfident MacArthur assessed that a US regimental combat team (RCT) and two divisions could reverse the tide of the war. When the NKPA overran elements of the US Twenty-Fourth Infantry Division (known as Task Force Smith) at Osan on 5 July, he revised his estimate and requested six more divisions.[305] By early August, the three US divisions making up Eighth Army were on the ground in and around the southern port city of Pusan.[306]

Nearly two weeks after the Task Force Smith debacle, President Truman announced in a televised speech that he was authorizing mobilization of the ARNG.[307] The first guard units received their mobilization orders on 22 July; a year later, one-third of the ARNG would be called to active service.[308] Guardsmen mobilized that summer served for twenty-one months; those mobilized after mid-1951 served two years.[309]

At first, the Pentagon hesitated to deploy guard units outside of the United States. CSA J. Lawton Collins feared that a mass deployment of guardsmen would disrupt their home communities; plus, he understood that these men would require extensive predeployment training.[310] Nevertheless, Pentagon leaders needed the NG to provide individual replacements because divisions deployed to Korea were critically short of soldiers due to battlefield losses and the fact that most units had entered the war understrength. The DOD's rotation policy also increased the need for replacements, as soldiers in Korea were promised that they could rotate out of combat after a year.[311] Thus, the Pentagon—under the leadership of Secretary of Defense Marshall—started activating NG divisions in the fall of 1950 to provide individual replacements (table 2.5).[312] The Twenty-Eighth and Forty-Third Divisions as well as two RCTs, the 196th and

Table 2.5. Army National Guard Maneuver Units Deployed during the Korean War

Unit (State)	Deployed To	Date Activated	Date Deployed	Training Time before Combat	Casualties
28th ID (PA)	Germany	1 Sep 1950	12 Nov 1951	N/A	
40th ID (CA)	Japan, Korea	1 Sep 1950	11 Jan 1952	16 months	311 KIA, 10 MIA, 1,504 WIA
43rd ID (RI, CT, VT)	Germany	1 Sep 1950	20 Oct 1951	N/A	
45th ID (OK)	Japan, Korea	1 Sep 1950	5 Dec 1951	15 months	707 KIA, 1 MIA, 3,258 WIA
196th RCT (SD)	Alaska	1 Sep 1950	Late Jul 1951	N/A	
278th RCT (TN)	Iceland	1 Sep 1950	N/A	N/A	

Sources: Berebitsky, *Very Long Weekend*, 265–269; Doubler, *Civilian in Peace, Soldier in War*, 234; "Lineage," http://www.278acr.com/metadot/index.pl?iid =2167; "43d Division to Join 'Ike' This Month," *Washington Post*, 1 October 1951, 1; "Guardsmen Embark," *Washington Post*, 18 November 1951, M10; "National Guard Division Lands for German Duty," *Los Angeles Times*, 21 October 1951; "28th Division Set to Go to Germany," *New York Times*, 25 October 1951; Bucklin, "Those in Reserve Also Serve," 399; Rottman, *Korean War Order of Battle*, 32–33.

Abbreviations: ID, Infantry Division; KIA, killed in action; MIA, missing in action; N/A, not applicable; RCT, Regimental Combat Team; WIA, wounded in action.

278th, were the first to do so. A year later, the army activated two additional ARNG divisions—the Thirty-First and Forty-Seventh—for the same purpose.[313]

The Pentagon held off on sending full ARNG units to Korea until President Truman declared a national emergency in November 1950, following China's intervention in the war. Shortly thereafter, guard transportation companies deployed to move United Nations personnel and supplies away from the Chinese advance.[314] In the following months Lieutenant General Matthew Ridgway, commander of Eighth Army, rushed ten guard and reserve artillery battalions to Korea to stabilize the front.[315] And in the summer of 1951, four ARNG divisions and two RCTs received mobilization orders.[316]

Upon mobilization, ARNG divisions, like their active-duty counterparts, were understrength and needed additional personnel to fill their rosters.[317] The army did so with draftees, reservists, and active-duty personnel.[318] Once they were assembled at training sites in the early fall, ARNG divisions participated in a program designed to build unit proficiency in collective combat tasks, as most of them had trained only up to the company and battalion levels during the previous two years.[319] As it had during the world wars, the ARNG struggled to train because of a host of personnel issues. Recently drafted soldiers and new enlistees, for instance, arrived with no training, as the US Army did not send guardsmen to basic training courses. Many of the junior officers had not attended basic schools, meaning that they were not qualified in their respective specialties. And some branch-qualified officers were pulled away by the active army to serve as replacements for units already in Korea. Units also lost soldiers during mobilization because they were younger than eighteen years old. As one soldier from the Fortieth Infantry Division recalled, "Upon being called into active duty, about two thirds of our ranks had to be let go, seeing that they had enlisted underage."[320]

Unlike in the world wars, the active army did not purge the ARNG of its senior and midranking officers. Of course, active and reserve officers took command positions in guard units in some cases, and some had negative opinions of guardsmen. One soldier from the Fortieth Infantry recalled that his new company commander "openly expressed disdain, if not loathing for [guardsmen and] . . . talked about getting rid of [them] as soon as possible!" Meanwhile, an active-duty officer assigned to lead one of the Forty-Fifth Infantry Division's regiments let his subordinates know upon taking command that he "had no respect for National Guard officers."[321]

Despite these criticisms, many ARNG officers who mobilized in 1950 were combat veterans with the skill and experience necessary to keep their jobs and perform up to active-army standards. In fact, 65 percent of the Fortieth Infantry Division's officers were combat veterans, including its commander, Major General Daniel Hudelson, who had served as a regimental commander under Patton in World War II.[322] In the Forty-Fifth Infantry Division, 75 percent of the officers and 50 percent of the NCOs were combat veterans.[323]

For more than six months, ARNG divisions trained Stateside, focusing on basic solider skills and small-unit tactics. Training could not progress to more advanced tasks for several reasons. For instance, units could not start training immediately upon arriving at mobilization sites in September because the facilities there were not ready to receive them.[324] Units also had to release thousands of pieces of equipment to units fighting in Korea, thereby limiting the realism of their training.[325] Meanwhile, new soldiers needed to complete a six-week initial training program.[326] The Fortieth Infantry Division, for example, had to train 14,237 new recruits between October 1950 and February 1951.[327] One captain from the division later recalled, "There was a lot of lost time initially simply because you had such an influx of guys that were draftees who had been brought into the division. You virtually had to start from scratch instead of starting with unit training which is the initial objective of a mobilized Guard unit."[328]

On 18 December MacArthur asked the JCS to approve the deployment of four guard divisions to Japan, as the Soviets had started broadcasting threats to Japan over the radio.[329] But the JCS rejected MacArthur's request, suggesting that he consider reassigning forces from Korea to protect Japan.[330] Furious, MacArthur explained that he lacked sufficient forces for both missions, and in mid-January he made a second request for ARNG divisions.[331] This time, the JCS relented and offered to deploy two guard divisions to Japan, but only if MacArthur could halt the Chinese, who had recaptured Seoul in January.[332] The JCS would not allow MacArthur to expand the war by bombing bases and industry inside China.[333] Disagreements over this issue eventually led Truman to fire MacArthur in April 1951 and replace him with Ridgway.

Before MacArthur was relieved from command, however, United Nations forces stabilized the front lines. As promised, the JCS authorized the deployment of two ARNG divisions—the Fortieth and Forty-Fifth—to Japan.[334] To placate NATO and bolster US defenses elsewhere, they authorized the deployment of the Twenty-Eighth and Forty-Third Infantry Divisions to Germany and smaller deployments of guardsmen to Alaska, Iceland, and Panama.[335]

As they embarked for Japan in March 1951, the Fortieth and Forty-Fifth Divisions were unprepared for combat, having completed little to no training at the regimental and division levels.[336] As one senior NCO from the Fortieth conceded in a newspaper interview, "The division isn't quite ready yet but when we finish our training in Japan we'll be ready for whatever happens."[337] In fact, the army rated both divisions' readiness at 43 to 45 percent as they departed the United States.[338] Once they were in Japan, the two divisions resumed training, which continued to focus on basic tasks.[339] One reason for this delay was that the regiments had to reorganize into RCTs, as they had not fully completed their reorganization over the previous two years. Another reason was that because the army barred soldiers who had not completed basic training from deploying to Japan, the Forty-Fifth had to leave four thousand soldiers behind in California, although they later rejoined the unit in Japan.[340] The Fortieth had a similar experience, but it had the added burden of having to send soldiers to Korea as replacements.[341]

The individual replacement issue generated a political firestorm in 1951. That year, the NGAUS lobbied Congress to stop the practice of "stripping" ARNG units of veterans to fill units in Korea, arguing that it destroyed guard morale.[342] Pentagon leaders countered that they had no other source of replacements and augmentees.[343] The controversy intensified when Daniel Hudelson, the outspoken commander of the Fortieth Division, refused to send soldiers to Korea.[344] Normally, an officer would be removed from command for such blatant insubordination, but Hudelson was shielded by congressional supporters, who successfully pressured the army to stop pulling replacements from his division.[345]

By mid-1951, the Fortieth and Forty-Fifth Divisions were finally able to progress to more advanced training, as they neared full strength. That June, the Fortieth conducted beach landing exercises.[346] Their training was aided by officers and NCOs sent from Korea to prepare the guardsmen to counter Chinese and North Korean tactics.[347] This advanced training set the stage for the divisions' deployment to Korea to relieve units that were completing their one-year rotation.[348]

On 18 November 1951 the army ordered the Fortieth and Forty-Fifth Divisions to prepare to move to Korea.[349] The Forty-Fifth arrived first in December 1951, replacing the First Cavalry Division north of Seoul.[350] About a month later, the Fortieth arrived, relieving the Twenty-Fourth Infantry Division near Kumsong.[351] The Forty-Fifth suffered its first casualty shortly after arriving on 15 December, when First Lieutenant Jack Hancock of Poteau, Oklahoma, was killed by enemy fire.[352] The Fortieth sustained its first loss on 20 January 1952, when mortar fire killed Sergeant First Class Kenneth Kaiser Jr. of Los Angeles.[353]

By the time ARNG divisions arrived in Korea in late 1951, the character of the war had shifted from a mobile fight to a static battle of attrition.[354] To limit casualties, guard and regular divisions occupied fortified defenses on hilltops or ridges, taking advantage of the improved accuracy and responsiveness of US artillery and air support to surround themselves with protective rings of firepower.[355] The infantry's job was to keep the enemy pinned down to ensure their destruction by artillery.[356] Thus, it is difficult to assess how well ARNG divisions performed and whether they were able to execute their primary tasks—combined-arms maneuver—under the command of guard officers.

The war ended in an armistice in July 1953, as the Soviet leaders who replaced Joseph Stalin following his death in March pressured the Chinese to end the war. Millions of Koreans and Chinese died in the war, as did 33,741 US personnel.[357] Despite these losses, the United Nations achieved its original objective of preventing the Korean peninsula from falling under the control of a Soviet ally.

The US Army mobilized 138,597 guardsmen during the Korean War.[358] They made important contributions to the UN mission, providing critical logistical and artillery support in the first year of the war. Guard infantrymen served as valuable individual replacements and augmentees for active divisions. And the two ARNG divisions deployed at the end of the war relieved exhausted army units while maintaining a robust forward defense. The guard therefore fulfilled its primary role during the Korean War, as it had during the world wars. It was able to do so because it had veteran leadership and nearly a year to train and reorganize prior to deployment. But, as the next chapter shows, changing military and political circumstances prevented the army from relying on that same formula in the latter half of the twentieth century.

Chapter Three

The National Guard
as an Operational Reserve

We want the Guard and Reserve to be more responsive. It is
possible that if a conflict breaks out in the future, it'll happen in
a faster rate of speed. Thirty-nine days of training ahead of time
and counting on post-mobilization training may not be a wise
thing for us to do as we go forward.
—General Mark Milley[1]

Following the Korean War, the Department of Defense (DOD) became increasingly dependent on the Army National Guard (ARNG) to carry out its wartime and peacetime missions. To prepare it for these responsibilities, DOD improved ARNG training, personnel, and equipment standards to a level that blurred the distinction between the guard and the active army, as both components' missions and capabilities became increasingly similar. Defense policymakers took this path for two reasons. First, the army lacked sufficient active-duty personnel to compete with the Soviets, especially after the United States abolished peacetime conscription in 1973. Second, rising costs for operations, personnel, and equipment strained the army's budget, forcing it to rely on cheaper guardsmen. These costs rose because unprecedented US deficit spending enabled the DOD to transform the army into a highly skilled high-tech force in the 1980s to offset the Soviets' quantitative advantages in arms and personnel. After the Cold War, the army deepened its commitment to this way of war as the military downsized and overseas operations increased as the United States became bogged down in protracted peacekeeping and counterinsurgency operations.

Guard maneuver units, however, struggled to keep up with their growing responsibilities. Most continued to drill for only several days a month and two weeks in the summer, as they had since the early twentieth century. But that training schedule proved inadequate for building unit readiness above the battalion level in the late twentieth and early twenty-first centuries, given the increased sophistication of army equipment and tactics. And, unlike in the world wars and Korea, the guard could not assume it would have many months—if not years—to make up for training deficiencies. Instead, it would be needed to reinforce overstretched active-duty units almost immediately at the outset of a war. This chapter examines how and why this situation unfolded.

Becoming an Operational Reserve

The ARNG's primary purpose during the Cold War was to reinforce the active army in Europe in the event of war with the Soviet Union, as well as to assist civil and military authorities in the defense of the continental United States. It had to be ready to deploy to Europe because the active army was vastly outnumbered by the Soviets, who could field about twice as many soldiers (through mass conscription) and far more tanks and artillery than the United States.[2] In addition, the US government lacked the political will and ability to match the Soviets in conventional ground forces, as doing so would have caused a massive economic drain.[3]

To offset the Soviets' quantitative advantages, US presidents, starting with Truman and Eisenhower, turned to nuclear arms, as laid out in National Security Council (NSC) Document 162/2 (better known as the New Look strategy).[4] Through this strategy, the Eisenhower administration sought to maintain "a strong military posture, with [an] emphasis on the capability of inflicting massive retaliatory damage by offensive striking power."[5] And that "massive retaliatory damage" would be achieved through nuclear arms, which were far cheaper to develop and maintain than a mass conscript army.

The ARNG—and the army in general—played a relatively minor role in support of the New Look strategy. The Eisenhower administration and some senior navy and air force officers believed that, in the age of nuclear arms, airpower was decisive because land forces lacked the means to deliver such weapons via bombers and missiles.[6] Ground forces were also highly vulnerable to nuclear strikes, especially as the Soviets began to field tactical nuclear weapons.[7] Thus, in the view of chairman of the Joint Chiefs of Staff (JCS) Arthur Radford, the US Army's role in the New Look era was "the maintenance or restoration of law and order, and re-habilitation within the United States."[8]

The ARNG would play an important role in the JCS's vision, given the guard's long history of supporting civilian authorities in response to natural disasters and civil unrest. But Secretary of Defense Charles Wilson questioned the ARNG's quality and reliability. During congressional testimony in 1957, Wilson said the ARNG had become a haven for draft dodgers during the Korean War—a claim that drew condemnation from guard supporters.[9] The National Guard Association of the United States (NGAUS) countered by arguing that those who joined the ARNG were actually volunteering for service, considering that many of them deployed to Korea.[10] Shortly after making these incendiary comments, Wilson qualified his position and expressed his respect for guardsmen, but he still maintained that the ARNG system perpetuates "a low standard of training and readiness."[11]

Despite Wilson's doubts, army leadership was generally supportive of the guard during the Eisenhower administration. Army leaders likely wanted to preserve the ARNG because cutting or substantially scaling back its capabilities would have eroded the land power component of the US military. They also understood the guard's political power and therefore rejected proposals by the secretary of defense that guardsmen and their allies would certainly block.[12] That said, CSA Maxwell Taylor believed the ARNG needed to improve its training, as he explained during a 1957 interview with ABC News. If it did not, he warned, the ARNG would be unable to "perform those indispensable duties which it must perform in mobilization."[13]

Nevertheless, the ARNG's roles and responsibilities increased in the latter half of the 1950s as part of the Strategic Reserve Force (STRAF) program, under which DOD integrated one ARNG division into each active corps. During a crisis, that division had to be ready to deploy overseas in nine months or less. Those divisions not assigned to a corps would remain in the United States and serve as a strategic reserve.[14] To prepare STRAF divisions for overseas service, the ARNG devised a new training program that aimed to make select units deployable within thirty-six weeks of mobilization.[15] Before their activation, guard units would focus on building and maintaining skills in individual to company-level tasks—which were easier to train for at or near local armories.[16] Battalion- to division-level training would occur after mobilization, when a unit was fully assembled at larger and better-resourced sites managed by the active army.

Yet Secretary Wilson still had doubts about the guard's ability to meet these requirements due to its poor peacetime training standards. To raise these standards, Wilson and Taylor mandated that new guardsmen attend a six-month basic and advanced training course before reporting to their units.[17] During congressional testimony in February 1957, Secretary of the Army Wilber Brucker argued that such training was "fundamental to an adequate military posture for our Nation's defense."[18] Previously, ARNG units provided new soldiers with basic training over the course of multiple drills and during summer training, but that system did not ensure that new guardsmen received standardized training from full-time US Army instructors. Furthermore, DOD leadership in the 1950s wanted to develop more disciplined and more highly skilled soldiers, which was easier to do if the army had more oversight.[19]

NG leaders initially resisted this plan, but they were willing to compromise if the active army shortened total training time or divided it over multiple summers to reduce disruptions to guardsmen's civilian lives.[20] The fear was that six months of initial training would scare away potential recruits.[21] That said, some senior ARNG members supported the six-month basic training option. Major Generals Roy Green and John Guerard testified in February 1957 before the House Armed Services Subcommittee in support of a federally managed basic training program for guardsmen. Green recalled his service during World War II and claimed that his unit had suffered heavy attrition because he was sent men with just six or eight weeks of training. In his view, "Those men died because they were not trained."[22]

Ultimately, Wilson and Taylor compromised, authorizing a voluntary four-month basic and advanced training program for new guardsmen.[23] Two years later, it became mandatory for new enlistees who lacked prior service.[24] Thus, by 1960, 95 percent of guardsmen had attended some form of basic training, whether on active duty or as part of the new guard entrance requirements.[25] Such training almost certainly improved the quality of the ARNG by ensuring that nearly all its soldiers had six months of training overseen by professional soldiers and officers. And because units no longer had to spend their drill weekends training new soldiers, they were free to focus on more advanced tasks.[26]

Officer training also improved for guardsmen during the Eisenhower administration. In the 1950s the guard created and expanded its own state-run officer candidate schools (OCSs), which used lessons plans created by active-duty officers.[27] Enlisted soldiers could also volunteer to attend active-duty OCS or the army's Reserve Officers' Training Corps (ROTC).[28] The vast majority of prospective guard officers chose state OCS programs, which were generally less burdensome because they took place over multiple weekends throughout the year.[29] In short, by 1960, most guard officers and soldiers were completing entry programs that were the same as or similar to those undertaken by active-duty personnel.

Another significant development during this period was that the ARNG consolidated weekly two-hour drills into a single weekend drill held every month.[30] This was important because it allowed units to spend nearly an entire day together, providing more time to plan and execute advanced training. Consolidated drills also allowed units to train in the field more frequently, given that they had additional time to move to and from ranges. Two-hour drills, in contrast, were nearly over by the time soldiers showed up and leaders took attendance and issued initial guidance.[31] After about a decade of experimenting with this schedule, the National Guard Bureau (NGB) required all guard units to switch to the monthly drill model.[32]

Despite these improvements, ARNG maneuver units were still ill prepared to perform their primary mission: conduct highly mobile combined-arms operations as part of the new Pentomic division structure, which the army introduced in 1956.[33] This new scheme did away with the traditional triangular organization of infantry, armor, and airborne forces by replacing the division's three standard regiments with five mobile battle groups, which were essentially reinforced battalions composed of five infantry companies.[34] Under CSA Taylor's leadership, the US Army created this new structure to ensure that it could fight on a nuclear battlefield. Taylor believed the army needed a division that could rapidly disperse and concentrate its subordinate maneuver elements to enable their survival. These elements would also have the combat power and support capabilities to fight independently, if necessary.[35]

The ARNG adopted the Pentomic structure in 1959.[36] But, like the active-duty army, it lacked the requisite training, equipment, and highly skilled personnel to execute Pentomic division operations.[37] For instance, sixteen of twenty-seven guard divisions could field only three battle groups, instead of the standard five, due to budgetary constraints.[38] And all its divisions were short of armored personnel carriers (APCs), recoilless rifles, and radios, limiting their ability to train realistically.[39] But most important, the ARNG did not train at the battle group level due to the aforementioned changes in its peacetime training routines, which focused on company-level operations and below. And even if it could have trained at that level, the army lacked sufficient training space and the technical means to practice Pentomic operations.[40]

Despite these issues, DOD had little choice but to retain the ARNG as the army's first-line reserve. As discussed earlier, political considerations prevented it from marginalizing the guard. Moreover, the active army was facing severe personnel and officer shortages—especially in technical fields—forcing it to draw heavily on reservists to fill critical billets. And budgetary constraints and rising overhead costs limited its ability to invest in raising the guard's personnel, equipment, and training standards. High overhead costs were the result of several factors. First, the army instituted pay raises in the late 1950s as it competed with the private sector to attract and retain skilled technicians.[41] Second, the army—and DOD in general—invested more heavily in new and improved weapons and support systems.[42] The growing complexity of modern weapon systems greatly increased research and development costs, and soldiers needed longer training periods to learn how to operate and maintain this new, expensive equipment.[43] Third, DOD had to redirect more funds away from conventional ground forces to build and maintain its growing arsenal of bombers and missiles.[44]

Thus, during the Eisenhower administration, the army was unprepared for a general or limited war against the Soviet Union, as budgetary constraints significantly reduced its ability to maintain readiness.[45] For its part, the ARNG made great strides in readiness by developing a structured peacetime training program, improving entry-level training standards for officers and soldiers, and consolidating weekly training into more manageable—and potentially more productive—weekend drills. But the ARNG did not have the training, experience, and resources to execute operations above the company level, especially after the army adopted the more complex Pentomic division concept in 1956. In other words, the army's backup soldiers were not ready to replace or augment full-timers without significant and lengthy predeployment training.

The guard's situation improved somewhat during the Kennedy administration. Kennedy took office in 1961 with a vision of a better trained and more deployable ARNG. During his first State of the Union address, he presented his goal of training two guard divisions to be deployable within three weeks of notification, while others would deploy within five to eight weeks—a major change from the thirty-six-week timeline of the STRAF program.[46]

Kennedy's plan to enhance ARNG readiness supported his broader vision of an army capable of waging limited war against the Soviet Union. The president wanted these reforms because he and his advisers believed that limited wars, like Korea, were still possible—if not probable—as the Soviets' expanding nuclear arsenal made general war highly unlikely and essentially unwinnable.[47] The Berlin crisis, which began in the summer of 1961, seemingly validated these assessments. That summer, Soviet premier Nikita Khrushchev declared that the Soviet Union would no longer accept the NATO occupation of West Berlin. But the US Army—and the US military in general—was ill prepared to respond to these provocations, as it was structured, trained, and armed for nuclear war and for homeland defense, not a limited conflict.

The crisis also exposed ARNG shortcomings. During the summer of 1961, Secretary of Defense Robert McNamara requested presidential authorization to activate four ARNG divisions and supporting units to form a strategic reserve that could rapidly deploy to Europe if the crisis escalated.[48] The president, however, authorized only two divisions—the Thirty-Second Infantry (Wisconsin) and the Forty-Ninth Armored (Texas)—along with several smaller guard and reserve units, which reported for federal service on 19 September.[49] McNamara assumed that these two divisions would be deployable after four to twelve months of Stateside training and reorganization.[50] But the mobilization proceeded more slowly than anticipated, much to the disappointment of McNamara.[51] The main cause for the delay was that the mobilized guard divisions were understrength and lacked key equipment.[52] Consequently, they needed to find and absorb soldiers and acquire equipment before they could conduct full-scale exercises.

Despite their manning and equipment issues, the mobilized guard divisions reached a combat-ready rating within four months—much faster than in previous conflicts, but slower than the three- to ten-week window Kennedy had initially envisioned. Ultimately, none of the divisions deployed, and they were released from federal service in the summer of 1962.[53]

Following the Berlin crisis, the Kennedy administration crafted a new approach—called Flexible Response—for containing and, if necessary, fighting the Soviet Union. Through Flexible Response, Kennedy aimed to improve the US military's ability to fight a limited war against the Soviet Union without resorting to strategic nuclear arms.[54] In pursuit of these ends, the administration boosted defense spending by $30 billion between 1961 and 1964, which allowed the army to grow from 860,000 soldiers to more than a million.[55] Increased spending also led to modernized equipment for all sixteen active divisions and six priority guard divisions.[56] The US Army, meanwhile, revised its main doctrinal publication—Field Manual (FM) 100–5: Operations—in 1962 to include a greater emphasis on limited war.[57]

To prepare for limited war, the army abandoned the Pentomic division structure—designed for the nuclear battlefield—in favor of one better suited to a variety of operating environments. The new structure—the

Reorganized Objective Army Divisions (ROAD)—aimed to optimize the army's ability to engage in conventional combat against mechanized forces in Europe.[58] To ensure that divisions could perform a variety of missions, the ROAD flexible structure allowed division commanders to vary the numbers and types of battalions assigned to the three brigades based on the mission and the operational environment.[59] Divisions also gained additional tanks, machine guns, and antitank weapons to boost their firepower. The army began converting its Pentomic divisions to the ROAD structure in 1963 as it prepared for limited war with the Soviets.[60]

To ensure that the guard could participate in such a war, McNamara sought to accelerate ARNG deployment timelines to about eight weeks for brigades and, if possible, entire divisions.[61] Taylor and others believed such timelines were unrealistic.[62] This skepticism was backed by the historical record, given that it took guard divisions a year or more to prepare for the world wars and Korea. Nevertheless, the Pentagon continued to make plans based on the eight-week time frame in the second half of the 1960s.[63]

To improve reserve readiness for limited war, McNamara planned to downsize and merge the ARNG and US Army Reserve (USAR) into a single entity to reduce manpower shortfalls and eliminate redundancies. The Berlin crisis had revealed that many of the mobilized ARNG units were, in McNamara's view, "paper tigers"; most were around 45 percent understrength and had numerous equipment shortages.[64] Cutting the overall size of the reserve component from 700,000 to about 500,000 and merging units could reduce these problems while saving DOD an estimated $150 million per year.[65]

Congress and the NGAUS opposed McNamara's proposals. Some questioned whether the loss in personnel would undermine reserve readiness; others were concerned that the merger would leave some reservists jobless.[66] Thus, Congress rejected the merger plan in 1966.[67] However, it allowed DOD to eliminate the USAR's six maneuver divisions in 1965, freeing personnel and resources to improve manning and equipment levels in guard divisions.[68] Moving forward, the ARNG specialized primarily in maintaining maneuver units, whereas the USAR was mainly responsible for combat support, as is the case today.[69]

Although the merger plan failed, DOD was able to enact other reforms in the early and mid-1960s that almost certainly improved ARNG readiness. For instance, it increased full-time staff assigned to the ARNG by 50 percent.[70] Full-time staff members took care of a unit's administrative tasks between drills, allowing the bulk of its personnel to focus on core training tasks. The ARNG also began to reorganize according to the ROAD structure between 1962 and 1963, and guard units received their first M-60 tanks, M-113 APCs, and self-propelled artillery.[71]

More important, the ARNG improved its training standards in the mid-1960s. Training doubled from eight hours a month to sixteen starting in 1964.[72] This increase, according to the chief of the NGB, "greatly advanced the training" of ARNG units.[73] Meanwhile, the 1964 Reserve Enlistment Program (REP) allowed guardsmen to extend their initial six months of active-duty entry training if their advanced schools required it.[74] This meant that guardsmen could more easily attend technically challenging training courses that could last for a year or more. Additionally, in 1964 eight thousand guardsmen participated alongside the active-duty army in the Desert Strike exercise in the Mojave Desert, which was the US Army's largest peacetime exercise since World War II.[75] Collectively, these reforms set the ARNG down the path to becoming the operational reserve it is today.

The Vietnam War reversed much of this progress. The US Army had an advisory role in Vietnam dating back to the 1950s in support of its French allies. But by late 1963, the United States had deployed sixteen thousand troops to Vietnam in response to rising violence by insurgents. The first combat battalion arrived two years later, and US involvement rapidly transitioned to direct combat. Despite overwhelming advantages in firepower and technology, the United States failed to break the North Vietnamese will to fight. Moreover, in the words of historian Andrew Krepinevich Jr., the US Army was "neither trained nor organized to fight effectively in an insurgency conflict environment," as it was designed for conventional war against the Soviets.[76]

Initially, DOD planned to send the ARNG and USAR to reinforce active units in Vietnam.[77] However, President Lyndon Johnson refused to authorize the deployment of guardsmen, even though more than nine thousand served voluntarily as individual augmentees and nearly one hundred died in combat.[78] Johnson wanted to avoid a fight with Congress over mobilization, which had proved somewhat controversial during the Korean War and could have undercut support for his ambitious domestic programs.[79] Furthermore, General William Westmoreland—the top US commander in Vietnam—had promised President Johnson he could win the war without a major mobilization of reserve forces.[80]

Keeping the ARNG Stateside seriously degraded its readiness as well as its reputation.[81] During the war it became a haven for men seeking to avoid service in Vietnam, as the 1967 Selective Service Act exempted guardsmen from the draft.[82] In fact, between 70 and 90 percent of new guard enlistees joined to avoid conscription.[83] By 1971, when the threat of the draft had faded, many stopped attending drills and opted not to re-enlist.[84] Consequently, by the summer of 1972, the guard was under-strength by forty thousand personnel and likely had thousands of soldiers on its books who were absent without leave (AWOL).[85] The ARNG's heavy-handed tactics in response to antiwar and civil rights protests during the 1960s also tainted its public image, likely undermining its ability to recruit replacements.[86]

To support the war and maintain a credible deterrent to Soviet aggression in Europe, DOD had to cut into the guard's training and equipment budget, undermining its ability to train effectively, as the NGB complained in its 1970 annual report.[87] State governors, meanwhile, frequently called on guard units to respond to civil unrest in the late 1960s. Due to these Stateside operations and declining budgets, most guard units could train only at the platoon to company level.[88] Consequently, DOD could no longer assume that guard divisions and brigades would be able to deploy effective combat forces within two months of activation—a dubious assumption even before the Vietnam War.

The Dawn of the Total Force Era

In the wake of the Vietnam War, DOD planners searched for creative ways to rebuild the capabilities of the entire US military to deter a rapidly modernizing Soviet army. One way they did so was by turning to the ARNG as a cost-effective means to reinforce and support forward-deployed units in Europe and other theaters.

The problem was that the ARNG was not well positioned to fill that role. During the Vietnam War, most guard units conducted little to no training above the company level. And the ARNG faced a severe recruiting and retention crisis, as the end of the draft eliminated one of the main incentives for men to join the guard.[89] Those who still valued military service likely questioned whether the guard was the right fit for them.[90] As Will Tankersley, assistant secretary of defense for reserve affairs, observed, "People thought of [the guard] as a bunch of old, fat men telling war stories or as draft dodgers."[91]

With its reputation sullied, guard recruitment and retention plummeted. Officer shortages were particularly acute. For example, state OCS programs anticipated graduating 1,221 officers in 1975—far less than its goal of 2,200.[92] Resolving these personnel issues took time and attention away from training. One senior guard leader recalled that "maintaining strength had become an end in itself, while training and equipping had become peripheral issues."[93]

The Pentagon, at the urging of President Johnson, had started to investigate the feasibility of an all-volunteer force as early as 1963, due in part to rising political pressure to reform the selective service. The need for personnel to support Vietnam temporarily halted these debates, but mass protests against the draft during the Vietnam War reignited calls for reform and elevated the matter to a campaign issue during the 1968 presidential election.[94]

On the campaign trail, Republican presidential candidate Richard Nixon exploited the unpopularity of the draft and promised to transition to an all-volunteer force.[95] Upon assuming office in 1969, Nixon appointed a commission headed by Thomas S. Gates Jr., secretary of defense during Eisenhower's second term, to examine the feasibility of ending the draft. A year later, the commission recommended ending peacetime conscription, claiming that it violated individual freedom and diluted the quality of the military by filling its ranks with soldiers who did not want to serve. Nixon accepted these findings, and the all-volunteer force became law in September 1971.[96]

The army, however, depended on conscripts to fill combat arms billets, as only about 4 percent of volunteers chose the combat arms.[97] Finding volunteers to replace conscripts was particularly challenging in the 1970s—a period during which the US public held military service in low regard. A 1973 Harris poll, for instance, revealed that Americans viewed military service as an undesirable career choice.[98] Thus, by the end of 1973, the army was short about fourteen thousand soldiers.[99]

Stabilizing the army's strength while transitioning to an all-volunteer model imposed new financial burdens. The army, for example, had to invest more in pay, housing, and incentives to attract and retain volunteers, especially those with vital technical skills.[100] In fiscal year 1973 alone, the Pentagon spent $1.8 billion on these items, which would eventually consume more than 50 percent of US military spending.[101]

The army's declining strength was alarming because the Soviet military was growing and modernizing.[102] Between 1964 and 1977 the Soviet military expanded by nearly a million men, giving it a two-to-one advantage in personnel over the downsized post-Vietnam US military.[103] Soviet tank production—including newer T-62 and T-72 models—also rose from 3,100 in 1966 to 4,250 in 1970.[104] These new tanks matched or exceeded the capabilities of the US M-60.[105] In addition, Soviet deep-battle concepts provided the tactics and methods for the Warsaw Pact to coordinate its massive armies and conduct a rapid invasion of western Europe that—in theory—could occur with little warning and defeat NATO in a matter of days or weeks.[106] And the US Army could no longer plan to use nuclear arms alone to blunt and reverse such an attack.

In 1970 President Nixon provided guidance on how US military operations should unfold in the event of war with the Soviets. In a series of top-secret memos to senior US military, diplomatic, and intelligence officials, Nixon called for NATO to develop "a credible conventional defense posture to deter and, if necessary, defend against [a] conventional attack by the Warsaw Pact forces." The United States and NATO, moreover, needed to be able to sustain a conventional defense for up to ninety days without ceding significant territory.[107]

In fact, the US Army lacked the equipment, tactical concepts, and personnel to deter or defeat Soviet forces with conventional means and methods. US Army doctrine had not been revised since 1968, and it did not account for improvements in Soviet arms and tactical concepts.[108] The Vietnam War and the move to an all-volunteer force also caused a decline in the size and quality of the active army and the ARNG as morale plummeted, recruitment collapsed, and disciplinary issues skyrocketed. Nixon, in short, lacked the military means to achieve his strategic ends.

One way DOD compensated was by issuing the 1973 Total Force Policy (TFP), which would revolutionize how the military integrated reserve forces into its plans and operations. Although issued by Secretary of Defense James Schlesinger, TFP was the brainchild of his predecessor Melvin Laird, who drafted the policy in response to Nixon's decision to move to an all-volunteer military.[109] Laird believed the reserve components of the military could provide an affordable source of personnel to fill gaps in the active ranks following the end of peacetime conscription. He therefore directed his service chiefs to plan to use their respective reserve components as the "initial and primary source for augmentation of the active forces in any future emergency requiring a rapid and substantial expansion of the active forces."[110]

The TFP—combined with previous efforts to improve the military's ability to wage limited war—transformed how the army employed the ARNG. Because the army was planning to fight the Soviets conventionally and with troops forward-deployed in Europe, it could no longer plan for a lengthy reserve mobilization as it had in the world wars and Korea. Instead, reservists and guardsmen had to be ready to deploy to Europe or other theaters within weeks; otherwise, a large Soviet army could rapidly overrun NATO's forward defenses. Thus, the guard had to become an operational reserve—one that would be available at the outset of a crisis or even before a conflict began.

An early proponent of an operational guard was CSA Creighton Abrams, a decorated World War II armor officer and successor to General Westmoreland as commander of US forces in Vietnam. At the time, Abrams was seeking to expand the army from thirteen to sixteen divisions, but budgetary shortfalls stymied those plans.[111] Undeterred, Abrams looked to the ARNG's twenty-one maneuver brigades and eight divisions to "round out" new active divisions.[112] Abrams also wanted the ARNG to be more closely involved in US defense plans and operations to ensure that the American people were more invested in a future conflict than they had been in Vietnam, given that guard units were embedded in local communities throughout the United States.[113]

Abrams and his successors devised the 1973 Roundout Program to bring the army's three new divisions to full strength in wartime. These three divisions, composed of two active-duty maneuver brigades, had been created by eliminating about two-thirds of the army's combat support capabilities and placing them in the USAR.[114] The guard would then "round out" the divisions by adding another maneuver brigade. The Twenty-Ninth Brigade of the Hawaii ARNG was the first to participate in the program in 1973, along with the Twenty-Fifth Infantry Division. Over the next three years, the 256th Infantry Brigade of the Louisiana ARNG integrated with the Fifth Infantry (Mechanized) Division, and the Forty-First Infantry Brigade of the Oregon ARNG joined the Seventh Infantry Division.[115]

While it established new divisions, the army revised its doctrine and training methods. Heading this effort was the US Army Training and Doctrine Command (TRADOC), formed in 1973 by Abrams.[116] In particular, Abrams wanted TRADOC to revise the 1968 edition of FM 100–5 to improve the army's ability to meet Nixon's goal of containing a Warsaw Pact attack primarily with conventional means.[117]

To lead TRADOC, Abrams turned to Lieutenant General William DePuy, a World War II and Vietnam War veteran. DePuy came to TRADOC in 1973 with a set of assumptions about what the army's new doctrine should look like. In a 1973 briefing to newly commissioned infantry officers at Fort Benning, Georgia, DePuy laid out these assumptions and his vision for moving forward. He started with a discussion of the US Army in World War II, which, he conceded, was "not very good" and "quite awful" compared with the German army.[118] DePuy had experienced that incompetence firsthand when, as a captain, his division lost all its infantrymen in combat during the invasion of France and subsequent operations.[119]

DePuy knew that such loss rates were unacceptable in the 1970s because he believed the next war—presumably with the Soviets—would be "short, violent, and important," meaning there would be little time to recover from early defeats. He also knew that a war of attrition was unlikely. The United States did not have the infrastructure or military strength for that type of war in 1973, especially with the end of the peacetime draft. Instead, he envisioned the United States developing qualitative advantages to offset the Soviets' quantitative advantages. "One American infantry battalion," DePuy stressed to his audience of young infantry officers, "has to be worth five of theirs."[120]

The product of DePuy's vision was the 1976 revision of FM 100–5, which aimed to provide the army with the tactical concepts to "win the first battle" in a short, highly lethal war against the Soviets in Europe.[121] Historically, the US Army mobilized for war at a low state of readiness and often lost its first major battles, such as Kasserine Pass in 1943 or Task Force Smith in Korea in 1950. In the past, the Americans had the luxury of time and space to methodically build a massive army that could recover from early defeats, learn from its mistakes, and prevail in a war of attrition. The army could not rely on such a formula in the 1970s. The Soviet military vastly outnumbered NATO forces in Europe, and its mechanized and armored divisions had the ability to overrun forward-deployed US forces in a matter of weeks. What is more, over the previous decade, the Soviets had developed weapons systems, such as the T-72 tank, that, as FM 100–5 conceded, were "generally as effective as our own." Such weapons, equipped with improved fire-control computers and optics, could quickly inflict heavy losses, as the Israelis learned during a surprise attack by Soviet-armed Egyptian and Syrian forces in the 1973 Yom Kippur War. In short, FM 100–5 warned, "The first battle of [the] next war could well be [the] last."[122]

To survive and thrive on this highly lethal battlefield, the US Army would have to preserve its own formations and delay and degrade enemy forces. FM 100–5 therefore laid out a concept for an "Active Defense."[123] Divisions and brigades would forward-deploy with little tactical depth, relying on a strong screening force ahead of them to detect and degrade the advance guard and main body of a Soviet attack.[124] Once the Soviets' main body penetrated the screen, US mechanized infantry and armor would fight a mobile defense, shifting to positions protected by cover and concealment provided by natural terrain and manmade obstacles. As opportunities emerged, US mechanized and airmobile units would concentrate and strike the Soviet flanks and rear, disrupting and ultimately defeating the attack, as the Israelis did against the Egyptians and Syrians in the 1973 Yom Kippur War (see chapter 4).[125]

Active Defense required the army to revolutionize how it trained to ensure that individual soldiers and units were ready to fight on day one of a war. Prior to the 1970s, army training at the individual and collective level lacked rigor. Units did not train to a specified standard; rather, they trained on collective tasks, such as an infantry platoon attack, for a set number of hours based on how a particular instructor interpreted doctrine.[126] TRADOC therefore decided to set standards for each collective task and created the Army Training and Evaluation Program to determine a unit's ability to meet those standards. Meanwhile, at the individual soldier level, TRADOC created the Skills Qualification Test to evaluate soldiers' basic knowledge of their occupations.[127] Thus, soldiers and units—including those in the guard—started to train to standards rather than time.[128]

TRADOC, however, lacked ranges large enough for maneuver brigades to practice Active Defense.[129] To address this challenge, DePuy and the next two TRADOC commanders, Generals Paul Gorman and Don Starry, developed a National Training Center (NTC), which opened at Fort Irwin, California, in 1980.[130] For the rest of the Cold War and beyond, all US Army combat brigades and battalions cycled through the NTC, where they engaged in simulated battles against full-time role players, known as the Opposing Force, who fought according to the tactics of the Soviet armed forces. These rotations allowed the army to test new doctrine and gauge how well its units could put it into practice.

The ARNG also had to meet these higher standards, but with only a fraction of the army's resources and training time. To compensate, the DOD and NGB coordinated to improve ARNG equipment and integrate it more closely with active-duty counterparts. Throughout the 1970s the guard received newer equipment and upgrades to its existing gear to make it more interchangeable with that of the active army.[131] Integration with the active army also improved through the Roundout Program and the Affiliate Program, which paired guard and reserve battalions with an active-duty counterpart for mentorship and training support. By 1976, eighty-one ARNG battalions had such an affiliate.[132] The guard also began to participate in major exercises, such as the army's premier annual exercise, Return of Forces to Germany, which simulated a rapid reinforcement of West Germany to defend against a Soviet attack.[133] Through these programs, the army could ensure that guard units better understood their wartime roles and responsibilities.

To address personnel shortages, Congress authorized the establishment of a full-time ARNG recruitment cadre in 1978, which helped stabilize guard strength by the end of the decade.[134] These recruiters benefited from two changes to recruitment practices. First, recruits were offered $1,500 cash bonuses and $2,000 in educational aid, which appealed to young Americans during the economic downturn of the 1970s.[135] Second, they started recruiting more women and minorities.[136] In 1974, for instance, only about 33,000 minorities and 6,700 women served in the guard. By 1980, those numbers had nearly tripled to 90,083 and 16,868, respectively.[137]

Nevertheless, the ARNG still struggled to build and maintain readiness. A 1978 Congressional Budget Office (CBO) report found that 43 percent of ARNG units had a C4 (not ready) rating due to personnel and equipment issues, leading to concerns that the ARNG would be unable to deploy to Europe within ninety days of activation.[138] Senior defense officials, including the secretary of defense, shared these concerns. A year earlier, Secretary of Defense Schlesinger had complained that "even the highest priority Army reserve brigades do not become available for deployment as early as we would like."[139]

A mobilization exercise in 1976 highlighted these problems. During this exercise, the active army tested the ability of select ARNG units to deploy within thirty days of activation—a task many failed. The main reason for this failure was that the units had done a poor job screening their rosters for personnel who could not deploy due to medical reasons—a problem that would reemerge in 1991 during the lead-up to Operation Desert Storm. An after-action review also noted the disparity in annual training time between guard units (thirty-eight or thirty-nine days) and active-duty ones (about two hundred days). Administrative tasks consumed many of these guard training days, reducing actual training time to between twenty-two and twenty-eight days a year.[140]

Having so few training days seriously compromised the ARNG's ability to develop units capable of fighting according to the lofty standards of the Active Defense doctrine. Army studies from 1978, for instance, showed that soldiers needed continual practice—more than the once-a-year gunnery practice guardsmen received—to achieve the marksmanship standards of Active Defense.[141] And because guard units could not find the time to train in battalion-, brigade-, and division-level tasks, they focused on individual to company-level tasks instead.[142] This meant that, upon mobilization, guard units would have to conduct predeployment training on those higher-level tasks or deploy to combat without completing such training.

Making matters worse, equipment and personnel issues continued to plague the ARNG into the late 1970s. Although the ARNG received new equipment throughout the decade, the active army had to transfer some modern artillery and support equipment from the guard to higher-priority units in Europe in 1978.[143] Meanwhile, personnel shortages deprived the ARNG of the key technicians needed to maintain and operate its increasingly advanced equipment.[144] Many guardsmen were also overage. As one senior guard officer conceded, "We realize there are a lot of 40-year-old squad leaders who couldn't go to combat."[145]

The ARNG's struggles drew the attention of national media and internal government watchdog groups in the late 1970s.[146] In a 1977 report, the Government Accountability Office (GAO), which provides auditing, evaluation, and investigative services for Congress, assessed that the TFP was "still far from a reality, and the expectations of it may have been overstated." In the GAO's estimation, it was unrealistic to assume that many guard or reserve units could deploy to Europe within 30 to 60 days; rather, it was safer to assume they could do so within 120 to 180 days.[147] The ARNG was aware of its own deficiencies, despite optimistic assessments of its progress in the NGB's annual reports. One senior guard officer claimed in a May 1980 letter to the Carter administration, "We couldn't mobilize enough firepower to stop Snow White and the Seven Dwarfs. Our equipment is 20 to 25 years old and half of it isn't even functional."[148]

These readiness issues had enormous strategic and tactical implications. "It's not a joke," one senior DOD official for reserve affairs remarked in 1977. The "survival of our country depends on [guardsmen], and the margin for error's gone."[149] That dependence was evident by the fact that nearly 60 percent of the US Army's combat strength resided in the ARNG and USAR.[150] In addition, three US Army divisions depended on the readiness of Roundout brigades to deploy at full strength. In short, the ARNG's readiness issues were compromising the ability of the entire US Army to execute its wartime missions.

The ARNG was not alone in its struggles. The active army was also unprepared to execute the Active Defense doctrine against the Soviets. During field tests in the late 1970s, active units struggled to conduct a co-ordinated mobile defense, as prescribed by FM 100–5.[151] Active Defense, moreover, could not resolve the problem of how to defeat the Soviets in depth. In other words, even if NATO forces were successful in the initial battle, they lacked the combat power to defeat follow-on attacks by second- and third-echelon Warsaw Pact forces. And, as discussed earlier, guard and reserve forces would almost certainly fail to arrive in time to reinforce active units and enable them to absorb and defeat such attacks. Additionally, army equipment was inferior or at best equal to much of what the Soviets fielded. Thus, as one senior US Army commander admitted, "The sum total of it is that we are not ready right now to fight sustained combat in Europe."[152]

The army addressed some of these deficiencies in the 1980s as budgets increased, new equipment entered production, and concepts for defeating a Soviet attack were refined. However, the qualitative gap between the active army and the ARNG widened as guardsmen struggled to keep up with the higher standards of army doctrine and the technical sophistication of new weapons. Despite these problems, the army increased the roles and responsibilities of the ARNG.

US defense spending started to rise in the late 1970s due to concerns about the improving quality of the Soviet military.[153] Secretary of Defense Donald Rumsfeld warned, "The Soviet Union, whatever its purpose, is without question engaged in a serious, steady, and sustained effort which, in the absence of a U.S. response, could make it the dominant military power in the world."[154] The Carter and Reagan administrations heeded these warnings and took steps to mitigate the deteriorating military position of the United States relative to the Soviet Union.

President Carter ramped up defense spending, adding $15 billion to the budget between 1977 and 1981.[155] Like President Ford and Secretary Rumsfeld, Carter and his secretary of defense, Harold Brown, believed that the international system of the late 1970s presented significant threats to US interests. In a February 1981 report to Congress, Brown warned that the 1980s could become a decade "more dangerous than any we have yet known." He attributed this danger to growing Soviet military power, rising instability in the developing world, and global dependence on Mideast oil. Despite these fears, Carter and Brown conceded that defense spending could not accelerate too much, given the "severe economic difficulties" facing the country in the late 1970s.[156]

With these constraints in mind, Carter and Brown developed the so-called Offset Strategy, which aimed to improve the United States' ability to wage war not just in Europe but also in the Middle East and other strategically important areas. To do so, the United States would seek to develop qualitative advantages to "offset" the quantitative advantages of US adversaries. This idea was not new; the army had developed its Active Defense doctrine with the same goal in mind. The difference was that Carter proposed that the United States develop the military means "to defeat all potential enemies."[157] Defeat is a much more challenging task than containing and degrading a Warsaw Pact advance into West Germany, as the Nixon and Ford administrations envisioned.

President Reagan also initiated a major US military expansion and modernization effort enabled by massive growth in army funding, which increased from $34 billion in 1980 to over $75 billion by 1988.[158] Strong growth in the US economy and Reagan's unprecedented deficit spending between 1982 and 1990—about $1.4 billion more than revenue generated—enabled and sustained such expenditures.[159]

This massive spike in the US defense budget allowed the army to modernize and address many of the conceptual and technical problems that had plagued it during the 1970s. The centerpiece of the US Army's modernization effort in the 1980s was the 1982 revision of FM 100–5 known as AirLand Battle, which addressed the conceptual gaps of Active Defense. Like Active Defense, AirLand Battle envisioned the US Army defeating a Warsaw Pact invasion primarily with a high-tech, highly skilled military capable of fighting even when outnumbered.[160] But unlike Active Defense, AirLand Battle called for NATO aircraft, artillery, and cruise missiles to conduct deep attacks using new precision munitions against second- and third-echelon Soviet forces to degrade them before they reached the forward edge of the battlefield.[161] Active Defense, in contrast, focused narrowly on fighting first-echelon forces.

To practice AirLand Battle, the army expanded training activities. Between 1980 and 1989, 143 battalions cycled through the NTC. Additionally, the army established the Joint Readiness Training Center (JRTC) in 1983 at Fort Polk, Louisiana, to provide maneuver training for light infantry battalions while the NTC focused on armored and mechanized units. ARNG battalions also participated in training at these centers.[162]

In addition to revising doctrine and enhancing training, the army fielded new systems to improve its ability to execute AirLand Battle. To make that doctrine work, the army needed to ensure that its weapons systems could survive and thrive in combat against a numerically superior enemy. Toward that end, the army began planning for the so-called big-five program in the early 1970s.[163] Higher defense spending enabled the army to start fielding these systems in the early to mid-1980s, including the M1 Abrams tank and Bradley infantry fighting vehicle (IFV).

Table 3.1 Rising Costs of the All-Volunteer Force (Billions of Dollars)

Year	Personnel	Retirement Pay	Operations and Maintenance	Procurement
1980	31.1	11.9	46.6	35.3
1982	41.3	15.6	62.4	49.1
1984	48.4	16.5	80.0	86.1
1986	67.8		74.8	92.5
1988	76.6		81.6	80.1
1990	79.8		91.7	84.1

Sources: DOD Annual Report (1982), C-2; DOD Annual Report (1984), 319; DOD Annual Report (1986), 293; DOD Annual Report (1988), 325; DOD Annual Report (1990), 219.

Additionally, newly developed precision munitions enabled US aircraft and artillery to strike further and more accurately than ever before, giving the army a realistic chance of degrading second- and third-echelon forces before they reached the front.[164]

The army's big-five program and similar modernization efforts in the air force and navy drove up procurement costs from $35.3 billion in 1980 to $84.1 billion by the end of the decade (table 3.1). Operations and maintenance costs rose as well, given that the new equipment's sophisticated electronics required extensive technical support. And attracting, training, and retaining volunteers and technical specialists who could operate and maintain these systems forced the military to offer higher salaries and better benefits.

Increased defense spending helped the army modernize and become a more highly skilled force capable of deterring Soviet aggression with conventional means, but the active army was overstretched. To deter the Soviets, the army of the 1980s deployed two additional divisions to Germany and deepened its commitments to the Middle East.[165] At the same time, it maintained thousands of forces in Korea and other places across the globe. However, the army could not increase its strength—which remained at around 780,000 personnel—primarily due to budgetary constraints. DOD, in turn, looked to the guard and reserve to relieve the active force of some of these burdens.[166]

DOD increased the integration of the guard and reserve by expanding the Roundout Program from four divisions to nine, meaning that half of the army's eighteen active divisions could not deploy and fight at full strength without the guard. At the same time, the guard had ten of its own divisions that could reinforce the active army in Europe or in other secondary theaters.[167]

The Reagan administration, which was initially confident that guardsmen and reservists could live up to their heightened responsibilities, invested heavily in improving ARNG capabilities. Increased spending helped the ARNG grow its ranks from 368,254 in 1980 to 455,182 by 1988.[168] At the same time, DOD issued new Abrams tanks and Bradley IFVs to select guard units.[169] The guard, however, received this equipment at a lower rate than active units, and only two guard battalions had M1 tanks by 1989.[170]

Despite these improvements, the ARNG continued to fall short of active-army expectations. In the summer of 1987 General Bernard W. Rogers, supreme Allied commander in Europe, complained to Congress that reserve units assigned to support operations in Europe "were under-manned, underequipped and unable to perform the tasks for which they were formed."[171] Likewise, internal army reviews from 1988 determined that the ARNG suffered from substandard physical fitness, insufficient experience with modern weapons, and general inexperience in military skills relative to active forces.[172]

One reason the ARNG struggled was that its soldiers and officers were not training to the same standards as their active counterparts. A 1988 GAO report revealed that only 32 percent of guardsmen were preparing for or taking their biannual Skills Qualification Tests, compared to 74 percent of active-duty soldiers. Of the 32 percent who took the exam, only 65 percent passed, compared with a 92 percent pass rate among the active component.[173] This meant that guard personnel might need extensive predeployment training to test and validate their proficiency in basic and advanced soldiering skills, which could compromise their ability to deploy in the planned thirty- to sixty-day time frame.

Time, however, was the biggest factor preventing the guard from reaching higher readiness standards. The army designed AirLand Battle—and all the high-tech systems needed to make that doctrine work—with active-duty soldiers in mind. The active army trained throughout the year, providing numerous opportunities to learn and practice AirLand Battle in school, during field exercises, or in garrison training. The guard, in contrast, had only thirty-nine days of training each year, much of which focused on individual and small-unit tasks. A battalion conducted full maneuvers with its three companies only once a year during annual training or, in some cases, every other year. Brigade maneuvers occurred only once every four years for the select units that attended the NTC or JRTC.[174] And ARNG units had fewer opportunities to attend the NTC. In 1989, for instance, thirty-two active-duty battalions passed through the NTC, while only four guard battalions—all of which were part of the Roundout divisions—did so.[175]

Making matters worse, administrative issues often cut into training time for mission-essential tasks (METs)—those tasks the army considered critical for a unit to perform its primary functions. In the 1980s the army expected a guard or reserve unit to spend 80 percent of drill weekends on METs.[176] However, a 1989 Brookings study found that administrative tasks, such as personnel evaluations and armory maintenance, could consume nearly half a unit's drill time.[177] Making matters worse, the subordinate units of a guard division or brigade were located, on average, in a 150-mile radius and about nine miles from motor pools and training sites.[178] Units therefore lost precious hours driving to sites where they could perform individual and collective training and basic vehicle maintenance.

DOD recognized these challenges and conducted several studies to determine how to mitigate them. One such study concluded that the ARNG and reserves needed to focus on skills training for individual soldiers, rather than more advanced collective tasks.[179] Three years later, a board appointed by the secretary of defense to review the TFP concluded that during a crisis, a mobilized guard brigade or division would likely "need some post call-up training before deployment."[180] In other words, DOD was questioning whether the ARNG was capable of deploying maneuver brigades to Europe in thirty days, which was a core assumption of the TFP and the Roundout Program. Fortunately, the army never had to test that assumption against the Soviets, as the Cold War ended at the dawn of the 1990s.

The Total Force Policy Is Tested

The 1991 Persian Gulf War provided a real-world opportunity to evaluate the TFP. At first glance, the war was a resounding success for the guard and reserve and for the TFP. The ARNG deployed 297 units—37,484 personnel—to Saudi Arabia to support the war; thousands of additional guard personnel bolstered security at military installations and other facilities in Germany and Turkey and across the United States. Many of the units deployed to Saudi Arabia arrived within thirty days—far quicker than in Korea or the world wars.[181]

These success stories were largely from combat support elements. Maneuver units—infantry and armor—from the Roundout brigades were sidelined by a host of personnel and training problems that prevented them from deploying, despite two opportunities to do so. The first opportunity came in August 1990, when US Central Command (CENT-COM) dispatched two divisions—First Cavalry and Twenty-Fourth Infantry—to Saudi Arabia in response to Saddam Hussein's invasion and occupation of Kuwait. Both divisions contained a Roundout brigade from the ARNG, but the Pentagon opted to replace the guardsmen with active personnel—a decision that sparked a political firestorm in Washington.[182]

At the Pentagon, Secretary of Defense Dick Cheney and CSA Carl Vuono determined that deploying the Roundout brigades made little sense because the 1973 War Powers Act limited federal activation of reservists to ninety days, with the possibility of a ninety-day extension.[183] Vuono worried that this time frame was too restrictive, given his estimate that it would take at least sixty days to train each Roundout brigade prior to deployment.[184] In other words, by the time they completed training and arrived in theater, the Roundouts would be very close to reaching their ninety-day limit. That said, Vuono still wanted to activate the Roundouts to prove the viability of the program, which he had helped manage in the late 1980s.[185]

The CENTCOM commander, General Norman Schwarzkopf, also strongly objected to the deployment of guard maneuver units to the Persian Gulf. According to Stephen Duncan, who headed the Pentagon's Office for Reserve Affairs at the time, Schwarzkopf lacked confidence in the guard's combat readiness and found its 180-day deployment limit too restrictive.[186] Schwarzkopf also viewed Vuono's desire to deploy the Roundouts as politically motivated, telling him, "I understand your political problem, but goddammit, we're fighting a war now."[187] With support from JCS chairman General Colin Powell, Schwarzkopf succeeded in removing the Roundouts from the deployment.

The ARNG and its supporters in Congress protested this decision. Leading the opposition was Congressman Sonny Montgomery of Mississippi, a retired ARNG general and World War II veteran. Montgomery wrote a letter to Secretary Cheney in late August 1990 expressing his concern regarding DOD's decision to keep the Roundouts Stateside. Montgomery explained that he "was fully confident that [the Roundouts] can answer this challenge."[188] And in an October 1990 report, Montgomery and his allies assessed that the Roundouts were ready and could deploy within thirty days of activation.[189] He backed up his statements by supporting legislation that passed in November 1990 granting the president the authority to deploy reservists and guardsmen for up to one year.[190] These demands and the new legislation, combined with a decision by President George H. W. Bush to double the number of US forces in Saudi Arabia, convinced the Pentagon to activate the Roundouts.[191]

DOD activated the Forty-Eighth Infantry (Georgia), 155th Armored (Mississippi), and 256th Infantry (Louisiana) Brigades between 30 November and 7 December 1991.[192] Following activation, each brigade reported to an assigned readiness center for predeployment assessments, after which they were supposed to travel to the NTC to participate in progressively challenging combat simulations.[193] The Pentagon and CENTCOM hoped the brigades could complete these tasks within forty days, enabling them to deploy to Saudi Arabia in time for the looming ground offensive.[194]

In fact, a multitude of personnel issues prevented the brigades from meeting this timeline, as revealed in a series of postwar GAO investigations. The most pressing initial challenge was that brigades were critically short of trained and deployable personnel. Between 34 and 50 percent of the brigades' soldiers were nondeployable for medical reasons, requiring them to spend several weeks addressing these issues. Of those who were deployable, many were untrained or undertrained in their military occupations, as they had not yet attended key leadership or technical schools.[195]

A flawed readiness reporting system likely prevented senior active-duty and guard leaders from identifying these problems prior to activation, as revealed during congressional hearings led by Representative Les Aspin in May 1992.[196] Dishonesty was also cited as an issue. Aspin noted that when guard units were allowed to rate their own readiness, with little oversight, they sometimes inflated their readiness levels. An army inspector general's report issued after the war found that active-duty officers assigned to oversee guard units during annual training also tended to exaggerate unit performance in their assessments.[197]

Some units, such as the 256th Brigade, suffered from disciplinary problems. After a month of training at Fort Hood, Texas, sixty members of the brigade went AWOL because they felt mistreated and overworked and wanted a weekend off—an incident that attracted national media attention.[198] "A lot of guys were frustrated and tired of being lied to about getting time off," one member of the brigade explained to a newspaper reporter.[199] As a result, the 256th remained at Fort Hood until the end of the war.[200]

When the Forty-Eighth Brigade arrived at the NTC, army trainers quickly discovered that it lacked the training and experience to execute AirLand Battle tactics. One of the key problems, they told GAO investigators, was that the brigade struggled to plan and execute combined-arms tactics, which was problematic because such tactics were the central pillar of AirLand Battle. Trainers also informed the GAO that the brigade's leaders had difficulty performing basic staff work.[201] In addition, The brigade could not keep more than 30 to 40 percent of its tanks running, as it had become dependent on full-time, nondeployable civilian technicians.[202]

The officers and NCOs overseeing the Forty-Eighth's training may have harbored biases that caused them to be more critical of the guard unit than they might have been of an active unit. One member of the brigade complained in a March 1991 interview, "We were called to active duty, yet we were still treated like the National Guard. It was like being second string, sitting on the bench for the state championship football game when you expected to play." Another member told the journalist, "We got the impression a lot of people wanted us to fail." In their view, it seemed "like the Regular Army a lot of times was just giving us bad information or was just messing with us."[203] The Forty-Eighth's commander, Brigadier General William Holland, was relieved of command in January; he later claimed that the evaluators at the NTC had mistreated his unit.[204]

Because of the Forty-Eighth's poor performance at the NTC, its training had to be extended for nearly two months—twice as long as a normal rotation. Ultimately, it received a combat-ready rating on 28 February, the day the ground war ended in Iraq. Thus, the Roundout brigade concept failed its first and only real-world test, as it took about ninety days for the unit to achieve a combat-ready rating, and only after extensive predeployment training. Shortly after the war, Secretary Cheney concluded that the Roundout concept was unrealistic and that ARNG maneuver brigades should serve only in guard divisions that receive at least ninety days of training prior to deployment.[205]

The National Guard as an Operational Reserve

In the decade following Desert Storm, the entire US Army faced steep budget and personnel cuts. During this period, the army's annual budget fell by about $10 billion, and its strength plummeted from 750,600 to 482,200.[206] Pentagon leaders also looked to make deep cuts in the reserve component as they sought to free increasingly scarce resources for equipment modernization.[207]

The ARNG and its supporters in Congress and the NGAUS resisted these cuts.[208] They argued that keeping the ARNG at full strength was cost-effective given that, in their estimation, a guard unit cost 25 to 80 percent less to maintain than an active-duty one.[209] Members of Congress such as Sonny Montgomery also worried that downsizing the guard would have negative economic effects on their states and districts, as local armories might close.[210] In a letter to Secretary of Defense William Cohen, the NGAUS even warned that cuts to the guard could undermine President Clinton's 1996 reelection bid.[211]

As they fought personnel cuts, the ARNG and its supporters worked to improve the guard's power in the halls of the Pentagon. Their main effort was a campaign to elevate the chief of the NGB from a three-star to a four-star billet and to give the chief a seat on the JCS. This effort eventually succeeded in 2012, despite protests from the active army.[212] Previously, the guard had to rely on the CSA—an active-army officer—to represent it in top-level debates in the Pentagon regarding budgets and force structure.

Rising tensions between the ARNG and DOD, which spilled over into the press, led Secretary Cohen to demand a compromise.[213] DOD was pushing to downsize the reserve and guard by forty-five thousand personnel, but it agreed to drop that number to twenty thousand and enact the rest of the cuts at an undetermined date.[214] Two years later, Cohen canceled the cuts altogether due to a high demand for guardsmen and reservists for peacekeeping operations in the Balkans.[215] To cover the costs of retaining these troops, Congress raised defense spending by $112 billion between 2000 and 2005, taking advantage of the booming US economy of the late 1990s.[216] The guard also agreed to transform twelve of its forty-two maneuver brigades into support units, which were generally cheaper and met the active army's more pressing needs.[217]

Although the ARNG's importance to maneuver operations declined after the Cold War, DOD increased its use of guard and reserve units in peacekeeping, security, and counternarcotics operations.[218] In 1994 Congress passed a new law empowering the president to extend involuntary reserve mobilizations from 90 to 270 days.[219] DOD sought this extension to maximize its scarce resources following the end of the Cold War. Using the guard and reserve could also "take the heat off the regulars," as CSA Gordon Sullivan noted.[220]

Between 1994 and 2000 more than thirty thousand guardsmen and reservists deployed to peacekeeping and security assistance missions in the Balkans and the Sinai, where their responsibilities gradually increased.[221] In 2000 the Forty-Ninth Division of the Texas ARNG deployed a headquarters element to Kosovo to command active, guard, and reserve soldiers—the first time an ARNG division had done so since Korea.[222] To prepare for the deployment, the Forty-Ninth had to complete more than 108 training days in the year prior to activation, foreshadowing, according to historian Michael G. Anderson, the current guard deployment model that features an intensified training year prior to mobilization.[223] A year after the Forty-Ninth's deployment, the Pentagon gave the ARNG full responsibility for the Kosovo mission, drawing on guard divisions to manage operations in six-month rotations.[224] It did so because active-duty divisions were overworked, limiting their ability to respond to a major crisis such as a war in Korea or the Middle East.[225]

As its deployments increased, the ARNG revised its training standards. Late in the Cold War the guard attempted—and largely failed—to train effectively at the battalion and brigade levels prior to mobilization, as evidenced by the struggles of the Roundout brigades in 1991. Following Desert Storm, DOD decided to focus ARNG training on individual skills and company-level tasks as part of the Bold Shift Program.[226] The goal was to establish a foundation of basic skills that units could improve on during mobilization.[227] Meanwhile, the introduction of digital training tools in the 1990s helped build skills in tank gunnery and rifle marksmanship, as units used simulators at their own armories or nearby facilities.[228]

Although focused on company-level tasks, the ARNG conducted some training at the battalion to brigade level. Due to reductions in active-army end strength, DOD could not reduce its reliance on guard maneuver brigades. Thus, to maximize the guard's value as a combat reserve, DOD decided in 1993 to transfer all maneuver elements from the USAR to the ARNG, while giving the reserves some of the guard's excess combat support capabilities.[229] The ARNG, in turn, had to field fifteen combat brigades—seven armor, seven infantry, and one armored cavalry—that could deploy within ninety days of mobilization to ensure that the army could wage a two-theater war.[230] Every eight years, battalions from these brigades, known as the Enhanced Brigades, rotated through the NTC or JRTC.[231] Units not included in the Enhanced Brigades program (totaling around 110,000 personnel) maintained lower manpower, equipment, and training levels.[232] These units would prepare to deploy within 150 days of mobilization to reinforce an active division or corps during a crisis.[233]

As the ARNG restructured, the US military deepened its commitment to a highly skilled, high-tech way of war. However, unlike during the 1980s, the US military—and the army in particular—focused on developing lighter, more survivable forces that could rapidly deploy anywhere in the world to respond to crises ranging from major regional wars to security assistance missions.[234] In response to this shift, the army developed and fielded weapons such as the fire-and-forget Javelin antitank missile, which enhanced the ability of light—and more deployable—infantry to defend themselves against armored threats.[235] The army also fielded new unmanned aircraft and an array of other sensors to rapidly locate and destroy enemy forces.[236]

The US Army had its first opportunity to apply many of these new systems in combat following the 9/11 terrorist attacks and the ensuing global war on terrorism—a series of conflicts that brought ARNG maneuver units into combat for the first time since the Korean War.[237] Initially, however, DOD largely sidelined the guard, keeping it in a support role. The George W. Bush administration wanted to maintain a light footprint in its fight against al-Qaeda in Afghanistan, fearing that a large commitment of ground forces would make the Afghans dependent on the United States.[238]

The 2003 invasion of Iraq was far more resource intensive than the war in Afghanistan. To invade and occupy Iraq, the US Army had to activate and deploy around thirty-eight thousand guardsmen—the largest mobilization of the ARNG since the Korean War.[239] And unlike in 1991, the guard deployed maneuver units, including seven infantry battalions, that served in supporting roles, while active-army, US Marine Corps, and UK forces spearheaded the main attack.[240]

The Pentagon did not plan to deploy guard maneuver brigades until a year after the invasion, and only after they had completed more than six months of predeployment training.[241] The Pentagon and CENTCOM assumed these brigades would enter a relatively safe operating environment, but those assumptions quickly proved false, as an insurgency and civil war erupted between Iraq's Sunni and Shia communities following the fall of Saddam Hussein in 2003.[242] Escalating insurgent violence in Iraq between 2003 and 2007 forced CENTCOM to assign guard units to combat missions in Iraq or supporting roles elsewhere. To free personnel for Iraq, the army sent twenty-six hundred guardsmen to Afghanistan and tasked guard units with running peacekeeping operations in the Sinai and the Balkans.[243] In Iraq, CENTCOM eventually had to rotate thousands of guardsmen in to replace exhausted active-duty units, leading to a situation in 2005 when half the maneuver brigades deployed to Iraq were guard units.[244] This high deployment tempo would continue until 2011, when the Obama administration began to reduce US combat missions in Iraq and Afghanistan.

The prolonged deployments of guardsmen to Iraq and Afghanistan generated recruitment and retention issues as well as political backlash. The dangers of serving in Iraq and Afghanistan and the length of the deployments—around twelve months in theater plus several months of pre- and postmobilization training—led to a recruitment crisis in the mid-2000s.[245] The guard's ability to recruit members was constrained by the fact that the active army prevented some soldiers from leaving active duty in order to meet its own mission requirements.[246] Consequently, the ARNG struggled to reach recruitment quotas, falling 20 percent short in mid-2003 and around 30 percent short a year later.[247] Retention was also difficult, as some guardsmen questioned the value and purpose of their missions and the burdens placed on them and their families. For example, one Florida guardsmen deployed to Iraq in 2003 complained to a reporter that his mission was "outside the scope of what the National Guard has been used for in the past."[248]

Such views almost certainly reflected the fact that many guardsmen who deployed to Iraq between 2003 and 2005 had joined the army before 9/11. In the 1980s and 1990s guard deployments were extremely rare, and when guardsmen were deployed overseas, they went to relatively safe locations such as the Balkans and the Sinai. In addition, their missions were short—around six months—and predictable, meaning that guardsmen knew about an upcoming deployment well in advance, allowing them to prepare their employers and their families. Deployments to Iraq between 2003 and 2007, in contrast, were long, dangerous, and increasingly unpopular back home.

The unpopularity of the wars in Iraq and Afghanistan led some politicians to speak out against the extensive use of guardsmen there. Senator Bill Nelson of Florida, for instance, led a protest in September 2003 during which he argued that deploying guardsmen to Iraq was inappropriate and would discourage reenlistment.[249] Some governors worried that deployments were compromising the guard's ability to respond to state missions, as a lot of its equipment and personnel were abroad in the mid-2000s— an issue that came to light in 2005 following Hurricane Katrina.[250] This tension—and the recruitment crisis—abated by 2010, as violence in Iraq subsided and the deployment tempo decreased.[251]

Despite these concerns, the Pentagon had little choice but to deploy the guard to Iraq and other theaters simply because it lacked enough active-duty soldiers. The post–Cold War US Army had a strength of around 492,000 personnel in 2005—down from 780,800 in 1985.[252] And that downsized force was trying—unsuccessfully—to contain rising insurgent violence in Iraq and Afghanistan while also deploying and maintaining forces to support missions in Korea, the Balkans, and the Sinai. DOD's ability to expand the active army to meet these commitments was limited due to rising costs associated with the all-volunteer force and the global war on terrorism. Personnel costs, for instance, had increased from around $73.8 billion in 2000 to $111.3 billion by 2006, as the army offered larger recruiting and retention bonuses and other incentives to maintain its end strength.[253]

Although the guard was heavily involved in operations in Iraq and Afghanistan, the active army hesitated to assign it combat missions. Instead, guard units were generally given support missions such as training local forces or providing security for convoys and bases.[254] In fact, only 20 percent of guard maneuver units that deployed between 2001 and 2015 received combat assignments, such as clearing areas of insurgent groups, compared with 80 percent of their active counterparts.[255]

That said, some guard units struggled with complex combat assignments. In 2005 a shortage of active-duty troops forced commanders to assign the Second Brigade Combat Team (BCT) of the Pennsylvania ARNG to secure Ramadi—a city in western Iraq that was a major center for insurgent and terrorist groups such as al-Qaeda.[256] A US marine regiment in Ramadi cautioned that deployment of a guard brigade to such a dangerous area was a "recipe for disaster," and that warning proved accurate. Under the Second BCT's watch, al-Qaeda expanded its presence across Ramadi. A frustrated General George Casey—the overall commander of US and allied forces in Iraq—ordered the guardsmen to go on the offensive and roll back al-Qaeda's gains. But according to Casey, the brigade's initial plan was predictable and based on an incomplete intelligence picture. Casey also sensed that the guardsmen were distracted by their pending redeployment back home.[257] Thus, Casey turned to active-duty troops to clear the city instead.

The experience of the Second BCT was not an outlier. In the fall of 2005 the Forty-Eighth BCT of the Georgia guard took control over the so-called triangle of death just south of Baghdad. Like the Second, the Forty-Eighth struggled to conduct presence patrols in contested areas, allowing insurgents to expand their control. The Third Infantry Division, which oversaw the Forty-Eighth BCT, found that the brigade suffered from widespread disciplinary problems that might have contributed to its ineffectiveness. Fed up with the brigade's lackluster performance and discipline issues, senior commanders in Baghdad reassigned it to convoy security missions.[258]

After the surge of active-duty formations into Iraq in 2006, the army decided to keep guard BCTs in support roles. Over the next three years, guardsmen continued to rotate to Iraq, providing critical support to the surge while helping to hold the line in Afghanistan. In fact, by 2009, more

than 200,000 army guardsmen had served in Iraq and Afghanistan—
levels not seen since the 1950s.[259] And the new generation of guardsmen
who joined after 9/11 did so with the expectation of deploying as an operational force, not the strategic reserve of the Cold War era that rarely saw
overseas service.[260]

That said, a DOD policy decision in January 2007 restricted the ARNG's
ability to perform such missions. Driving this change was Secretary of Defense Robert Gates. In Gates's view, DOD "had pulled a bait and switch
on the National Guard and Reserve," as most of its soldiers had joined
expecting to train one weekend a month plus two weeks a year.[261] But by the
mid-2000s, many guardsmen were serving lengthy tours lasting eighteen
to twenty-one months, including four or five months of predeployment
training.[262] To reduce this burden, Gates authorized a reduction in Stateside training to just sixty or ninety days, thereby limiting the total number
of days on federal service to one year.[263] By 2015, mobilization schedules
had fallen to fifty to eighty days for brigade-sized units and thirty days
or less for company-sized units and below.[264] Gates also mandated that
guard units aim for a one-to-five mobilization-to-dwell ratio, meaning that
a one-year deployment would be followed by four nondeployment years
(the active-army ratio was one to two).[265]

By reducing Stateside training, guard units lost opportunities to
demonstrate and improve their collective skills above the company level.
The army required deploying ARNG and USAR units to restart their
training cycles at basic soldier tasks and build up to higher-level tasks
at predeployment centers staffed by active-duty personnel.[266] However,
sixty to ninety days was simply not enough time to reach proficiency in
battalion- to brigade-level tasks. Thus, once they were deployed, a theater
commander could expect guard maneuver units to perform only company-
level tasks and below.

Being forced to restart training at the individual to company level at
predeployment centers upset some guardsmen, who argued that they had
trained on many of these tasks during drill weekends and annual training.
But, as was the case in the 1970s and 1980s, administrative tasks often
consumed entire drills, as complaints by guardsmen in 2015 revealed.[267]
That same year, the National Commission on the Future of the Army
(NCFA) found that such tasks could consume up to thirty-one of a guard
unit's thirty-nine training days—far more than in the 1970s and 1980s.[268]

These administrative and training issues declined in significance
during much of the Obama administration. Guard and active unit deployments decreased as the United States withdrew from Iraq and downsized

its presence in Afghanistan in 2011—a trend that was reversed to some extent with the rise of ISIS in Iraq and Syria in 2014. That said, the United States relied on Special Operations Forces, airpower, and local allies to fight ISIS and for operations in Afghanistan. However, since destroying ISIS's territorial caliphate in 2019, CENTCOM has drawn more heavily on guard maneuver, artillery, and aviation units to prevent the group's resurgence in Iraq and Syria and to protect forces deployed in those countries from Iranian and Iranian-aligned militia attacks.[269]

As it reduced force levels in Iraq and Afghanistan, the United States cut defense spending and the size of the army. These cuts were mostly the result of the Budget Control Act of 2011 (BCA). The BCA capped defense spending at $10 trillion between fiscal years 2011 and 2021 in response to the economic downturn of the late 2000s and the Democrats' and Republicans' inability to compromise on spending and debt levels.[270] Consequently, army funding fell 14 percent between 2010 and 2015, and the size of the force declined from 563,600 active-duty soldiers in 2010 to 490,000 by 2015; meanwhile, guard strength fell from 358,200 to 350,200, and USAR strength remained unchanged at 205,000.[271]

Active-army and ARNG relations frayed during this period over two issues. First, in 2013 DOD began replacing some guard units ready for deployment with active-duty units in a policy referred to as "off-ramping." The ARNG complained that this policy disrupted the soldiers' lives and disparaged the replaced guardsmen. Active-duty officers justified off-ramping because they believed full-time units were cheaper to deploy, given that the Pentagon did not have to cover the extra cost of activating and training guardsmen.[272] Making matters worse, during a January 2014 press conference, CSA Ray Odierno claimed that guard capabilities are not interchangeable with those of the active army—a statement that contradicted what guard leaders had been claiming for decades. NGAUS leadership rejected Odierno's assertations, arguing that guard and active units "are, by design, interchangeable" and that "they train to the same standard . . . and fight under the same doctrine."[273]

The second issue that stressed relations was the active army's intention to remove all Apache attack helicopters from the ARNG by 2017, consolidating them in active formations to save an estimated $12 billion. In return, the ARNG would receive 111 transport helicopters. This decision sparked a turf war between guard and active leadership, as guardsmen feared that removal of the attack helicopters indicated their transition to a combat support force.[274] Infighting over the Apache helicopters led Congress to establish the NCFA in April 2015 to investigate the current state of the army and recommend how to optimize it for the future. Less than a year after it formed, the NCFA released its report recommending a compromise: instead of removing all Apaches from the ARNG, it recommended that the guard retain four battalions—two fewer than the guard wanted to keep. At the same time, the NCFA reaffirmed the value of the TFP and the all-volunteer force.[275]

The army had little choice but to embrace greater integration of components—a central tenet of the TFP. Since 2014, threats to US interests have multiplied, while the Pentagon's ability to grow the active-duty army to meet these threats has been constrained by budgetary shortfalls compounded by rising costs for personnel and operations.[276] The downsized US military, for instance, witnessed the birth and spread of ISIS, forcing the United States to resume a combat role in Iraq in 2014 and to expand its counterterrorism operations into neighboring Syria—while continuing the fight in Afghanistan (until the US withdrawal in 2021) and other battlegrounds. China, meanwhile, has become more assertive, militarizing the South China Sea and investing in weapons that challenge US naval and air supremacy in East Asia. Russia has also become more aggressive, seizing the Crimea in 2014 and initiating an unprovoked invasion of Ukraine eight years later.

In response to these threats, DOD has needed more support from the ARNG. As of 2019, the ARNG contained twenty-seven BCTs, forty-two multifunctional support brigades, fifty-six support brigades, two Special Forces groups, one security assistance brigade, and eight division headquarters.[277] The army drew on these forces to cover important missions such as the buildup of US military forces in eastern Europe to deter Russian aggression against NATO. In fact, in 2016 the US Army's Europe commander, Lieutenant General Ben Hodges, noted that the active-duty force was "paper thin" and he lacked "the capacity to do what I need to do without significant contributions from the guard and reserve."[278]

The main reason the army was paper thin in 2016 was a lack of funds to grow its forces. And historically, guardsmen are economical substitutes for active-duty soldiers. The average guard unit costs between 21 and 68 percent of an active unit, depending on unit type.[279] Active soldiers, who must be housed, fed, and cared for 24/7, are far more expensive than guardsmen. For example, in 2018 a junior NCO in the guard earned approximately $364 a month.[280] That soldier's active-duty counterpart made $2,733 a month in base pay plus about $1,000 in housing and living allowances, depending on locality and dependents.[281] Although its budget rose during the Trump administration, the army had to use much of that new money to invest in technology to upgrade or replace aging Cold War–era equipment.[282]

Army modernization efforts reflect a broader shift in US national security strategy from counterterrorism to Great Power conflict and changes in the character of war. The 2018 US National Defense Strategy stated: "We are facing increased global disorder, characterized by a decline in the long-standing rules-based international order—creating a security environment more complex and volatile than any we have experienced in recent memory. Inter-state strategic competition, not terrorism, is now the primary concern in U.S. national security." The strategy also acknowledged that rapid technological changes in fields such as robotics are altering the character of war.[283]

In response to these changes in the character of war and the operating environment, the army revised its operations doctrine (FM 3–0) in 2017 and again in 2022. In this new version, called Multi-Domain Battle (re-named Multi-Domain Operations in May 2018), army doctrine is based on combined-arms warfare against state adversaries after a decade-long focus on counterinsurgency.[284] To adapt to this new operational context, FM 3–0 calls for the army to develop the ability to conduct multidomain operations that can synchronize and employ weapons systems and tactics across all domains of warfare: air, land, maritime, space, and the information environment (including cyberspace).[285] This means that a maneuver commander has to be able to locate, suppress, and destroy enemy air and artillery systems (i.e., create a window of opportunity) using electronic, kinetic, and cyber capabilities that enable friendly forces to wage offensive or defensive operations. In short, success on the battlefield requires more than the integration of tanks, artillery, infantry, and airpower, as was the case during the AirLand Battle era. Now the army has to integrate all these capabilities with cyber missions, electronic attack, information operations, space-based platforms, and, in some cases, naval forces.[286] Such responsibilities were typically reserved for the highest-level commanders in the army, but now mid- and senior-level commanders on the battlefield have to be prepared to manage—or at least consider—these disparate capabilities.[287]

These changes to army training, doctrine, and technology caused senior army leaders to reexamine ARNG training and readiness standards. In 2015 ARNG director Lieutenant General Timothy Kadavy concluded that the current thirty-nine–day training period—a standard set in 1916—did not account for major changes in the art and science of warfare occurring over the last century.[288] CSA General Mark Milley echoed these concerns in an October 2015 speech to the Association of the US Army, stating, "We want the Guard and Reserve to be more responsive. It is possible that if a conflict breaks out in the future, it will happen in a faster rate of speed. Thirty-nine days of training ahead of time and counting on post-mobilization training may not be a wise thing for us to do as we go forward."[289]

After a year as director, Kadavy moved to address these training and readiness concerns through the ARNG 4.0 initiative, with the objective of improving the guard's ability "to rise to the challenges of the 21st century and meet the requirements of the Total Army."[290] Among other things, the initiative aimed to increase training for guard Armored and Stryker BCTs from thirty-nine to sixty-three days. As of 2018, those units are moving to a four-to-one deployment–to–dwell time ratio—a change from the standard five-to-one ratio set by Secretary Gates a decade earlier.[291] ARNG 4.0 is also attempting to increase deployment opportunities for guard maneuver units, including division headquarters. In 2016 the Twenty-Ninth Infantry Division (Maryland and Virginia) headquarters deployed to Kuwait to serve as headquarters for Operation Spartan Shield—a quick-reaction force for a Mideast crisis. This was the first time the Twenty-Ninth commanded units in a deployed environment since World War II.[292] Guard division headquarters have continued to rotate into this mission over the past six years, helping to command and control critical missions such as the evacuation of US forces and Afghan refugees from Afghanistan in 2021.[293]

Guard units are also receiving high-profile missions in Europe. In 2018 the 278th Armored Cavalry Regiment of the Tennessee ARNG deployed to Poland as part of NATO's enhanced forward presence mission to assure allies and partners that the alliance is willing and able to defend against Russian aggression in eastern Europe.[294] As of 2023, guard combat and support units are rotating to the Baltic states to participate in large-scale exercises in response to the Russian invasion of Ukraine.[295] In short, if NATO and Russia go to war, guardsmen will be engaged in combat at the outset of fighting—unlike during the Cold War, when guardsmen did not arrive in theater until at least thirty days later.

The ARNG is playing important roles in theaters outside Europe as well. As of 2023, guard units forward-deployed to Kuwait, Syria, and other places in the Middle East are on the front lines of a low-intensity conflict with Iran and its militant allies.[296] The ARNG is also performing important security missions in Somalia, where New Jersey guardsmen defeated an attack by al-Shabaab militants on Baledogle Airfield in 2019—the New

Jersey guard's most significant combat engagement since World War II.[297] In short, guard maneuver units are regaining combat assignments in the Middle East and Africa as active-duty units are redirected to higher-priority missions in Europe and the Pacific.

To improve its readiness for such deployments, the ARNG had been afforded additional opportunities to attend the NTC and JRTC and to integrate with active-army units for exercises. In 2016 Kadavy and Milley restarted a modified version of the Roundout Program, known as the Associated Unit Program, that integrates guard and active-duty combat and combat support units from the brigade level down in joint training exercises; eventually, these partnered units will conduct deployments together.[298] Meanwhile, the number of guard battalions rotating through the NTC and JRTC increased from two to four each year.[299]

Increased and intensified training and deployment opportunities for ARNG maneuver units will almost certainly improve their ability to reinforce and replace active units. However, the challenge for DOD will be to ensure that increased training and deployments do not eliminate the guard's cost advantage over the active army or harm recruitment and retention. This is especially concerning given the unprecedented operational tempo guardsmen have faced in recent years, which, in the words of one defense journalist, is "pushing the National Guard to the brink."[300] Indeed, as of late 2022, such pressures led to the guard's worst recruitment and retention crisis in decades, as it missed its annual recruitment quota by around seventy-five hundred personnel.[301]

How the reserve component of the Israel Defense Forces (IDF) handled similar pressures is the topic of the next case study. Unlike the US Army, the IDF practices near-universal conscription to build and maintain the active and reserve elements of its military. Nevertheless, as the next two chapters show, even reservists with extensive active experience struggle to maintain readiness in the era of high-tech, high-skilled war.

Chapter Four

The Heights of Israeli Reserve Performance

Every squad commander is a general.
—Palmach motto[1]

Since gaining independence in 1948, Israel has confronted a range of threats to its existence, from a coalition of hostile Arab armies during the Cold War to the present-day threat of a nuclear Iran. To maximize its military potential, Israel developed a highly trained reserve force composed of discharged conscripts who, in the event of war, could reinforce and augment its smaller standing army. And for the first three decades of its existence, Israel was able to swiftly mobilize and field a force that proved capable of outperforming and defeating a host of internal and external adversaries.

Israel succeeded in developing an effective reserve army for several reasons. First, it employed a cadre system—like the Germans in the world wars—that placed veteran leaders in command of reserve brigades and divisions. Second, most reservists had extensive training acquired in their two to three years of conscript duty and at least thirty days of annual training while in the reserves. That training was planned and overseen by long-service professionals, many of whom had extensive combat experience. Finally, Israeli reservists had the advantage of fighting adversaries who suffered from serious leadership, personnel, and tactical deficiencies. Combined, these factors enabled Israel to develop what one historian called history's best "citizen army" during its formative wars: the 1948 War of Independence, the 1956 Suez Crisis, the 1967 Six-Day War, and the 1973 Yom Kippur War.[2] This chapter examines how and why Israel came to field this highly effective reserve army. In doing so, it sets the stage for chapter 5's examination of how changes in these conditions after the Yom Kippur War caused a steep decline in the effectiveness of the Israeli reserve.

Laying the Foundation

Understanding how Israel developed a highly effective reserve requires an examination of the history of the militias from which the Israel Defense Forces (IDF) emerged in 1948. Early Israeli political and military leaders formed militias to protect their burgeoning communities during the British Mandate (1920–48), establishing policies and practices that the IDF later borrowed to build a highly effective reserve army. These practices included universal military service; rigorous training schedules for part-time fighters; an emphasis on aggressive, offensive-minded small-unit leadership; and the placement of veteran officers in charge of part-time soldiers. Additionally, the Jewish immigrants who came to Palestine during the Mandate had unique backgrounds that imbued them with the will and, in many cases, the skills to fight, lead, and sacrifice—traits that made them excellent soldiers.

Jewish immigrants from Europe began arriving in Ottoman Palestine in the 1880s and 1890s. Many of them fled Europe to escape the rising anti-Semitic violence and discrimination there.[3] Upon their arrival in Palestine, which had a population of around 380,000 (including 27,000 Jews), the settlers started purchasing land and establishing communities. Collectively, these communities—and the Palestinian Jewish community as a whole—were called the *Yishuv* (Hebrew for "settlement").[4]

Following World War I, the Yishuv established its first formal defense force, known as the *Haganah* (Hebrew for "defense"), in response to rising violence and civil unrest in Palestine.[5] This unrest was caused by simmering Arab anger over a 1917 declaration by Great Britain (which had conquered Palestine during the war) to support the "establishment in Palestine of a national home for the Jewish people."[6] Initially, Palestinian Arabs protested the declaration peacefully, but the protests devolved into violent riots during the 1920 *Nabi Musi* festival, leaving five Jews and four Arabs dead.[7]

Initially, the Haganah operated in secret under the leadership of the Labor Zionists—the dominant political organization in the Yishuv.[8] The Labor Zionists viewed the Haganah as a defensive force that served as an "emergency instrument that can prove useful in difficult times, but is better if not needed."[9] It was structured as a people's militia composed primarily of farmers and laborers, including women, who served voluntarily on a part-time basis.[10] About a dozen members served in full-time administrative positions.[11]

Tasked with defending the Yishuv, the Haganah faced an uncertain

Table 4.1. Demographics of Palestine during the British Mandate

Religion	1922	1931	1946
Muslim	640,798	777,403	1,175,196
Jewish	94,752	176,648	602,586
Christian	76,194	93,029	148,910
Other	8,515	10,314	15,637
Total	820,259	1,057,394	1,942,329

Source: Kramer, *History of Palestine*, 183.

and difficult security environment. Great Britain gained formal control of Palestine following the San Remo Conference in April 1920, so the Haganah had to operate under British rule.[12] In theory, Britain was supportive of the Yishuv, given its stated support for a Jewish national home. But in reality, British authorities on the ground held generally negative opinions of the Jewish immigrants and tended to favor the Arab majority.[13] What is more, they barred Jews from owning weapons, forcing the Haganah to operate clandestinely.[14] But the biggest challenge facing the Haganah was that the Jewish community was vastly outnumbered by the Arab Muslims (table 4.1), who grew increasingly hostile to the Yishuv as Jewish immigration spiked in the 1930s and 1940s.

Social and cultural conditions in the Yishuv and the structure of the Haganah offset some of these disadvantages. Namely, the Haganah could recruit immigrants who, in the words of one of the IDF's founders, were "young, passionately idealistic, and had in many cases already experienced the taste of paramilitary underground activities when defending the ghettos of Eastern Europe against anti-Semitic pogroms."[15] Among these immigrants were military veterans who had served in the British or Russian army during World War I. Some even had experience as military trainers, enabling them to develop Haganah training and leadership courses in the 1920s.[16]

For much of the 1920s the Haganah was able to train and operate in peace, but as more Jews immigrated to Palestine, tensions with Arab communities grew. Those tensions erupted into violence in August 1929 during a dispute over Jewish prayer rights at the Western Wall in Jerusalem. The Haganah was unprepared for the scale and intensity of the subsequent fighting.[17] Nevertheless, it managed to mobilize about three hundred members, dispersing them among the Jewish settlements that accepted protection.[18] These fighters—sometimes with help from British police and local civilians—were generally able to repulse the Arab attacks, taking advantage of the fact many assailants lacked firearms and operated as mobs rather than organized units.[19] Ultimately, 133 Jews and 116 Arabs died in the fighting.[20]

The leadership of the Yishuv was dissatisfied by the Haganah's performance during the 1929 riots, leading many to conclude that a greater investment in defense was needed.[21] Thus, in the 1930s they authorized expansion of the Haganah to more than fifteen thousand members and increased its cadre of full-time officers and administrators.[22] The influx of thousands of western European immigrants fleeing the rise of Nazism in Germany helped sustain this growth. This wave of immigrants was different, in that many came from more educated and affluent backgrounds; some also had experience working in mid- and senior-level positions in industry and government.[23] The Haganah tapped into this more highly skilled and wealthier pool of immigrants to improve its management, funding, and recruitment.[24]

The Haganah had an opportunity to evaluate and improve its capabilities during the Arab Revolt, which occurred in two phases between 1936 and 1939 and erupted because of anger over the continuing rise in the number of Jewish immigrants.[25] To pressure the British to halt immigration, Palestinian Arabs engaged in a labor strike that turned violent when Arab militias attacked Jewish civilians in mid-April 1936.[26] Though better organized than in 1929, the Arabs lacked the firepower to compete with the British and the Haganah.[27] The Arab militias struggled to breach the fortified defenses manned by Haganah members around Jewish settlements.[28] The violence subsided in October 1936, when the Palestinians agreed to a truce with the British. A year later, however, the attacks resumed following a British proposal—which Yishuv leaders accepted—to partition Palestine into Jewish- and Arab-controlled sectors. The British, with Haganah support, responded forcefully, crushing the revolt by 1939.[29]

During the second round of fighting, the Haganah had the opportunity to enhance its tactical competencies by partnering with the British to form the Special Night Squad (SNS). Established in 1938 under the leadership of British army captain Charles Orde Wingate, the SNS was composed of squad-sized units of select Haganah members and British soldiers who launched night raids on Arab forces inside Palestine.[30] By working with Wingate, who was an expert in irregular warfare, junior Haganah leaders learned how to think and act independently. Additionally, as Yigal Allon—who served in the SNS and became a senior IDF commander in the 1948 war—recalled, Wingate taught the Haganah how to patrol and conduct raids and ambushes, which "effectively pulled the Haganah out of its trenches" and made it "adopt a more active kind of defense."[31] Although the British abolished the SNS after the revolt, its legacy endured through Haganah leaders who formed the IDF.[32]

Following the Arab Revolt, the Haganah reorganized into three groups: Field Corps, Home Guard, and *Gadna* (a Hebrew acronym for "youth battalions"). Men between the ages of eighteen and twenty-six served in the Field Corps, which was responsible for defending settlements and conducting offensive operations.[33] Men in the Field Corps trained for six hours a month.[34] The Home Guard was composed of men and women between the ages of twenty-seven and fifty who trained six hours every three months; during crises, Home Guard members defended settlements, and some served in support of offensive operations.[35] The Gadna was a voluntary organization for boys and girls aged fifteen to eighteen. Its primary purpose was to train Jewish youth to defend the Yishuv while acting as an emergency reserve. Gadna training occurred twice a week in the evenings; members also participated in two full training days every month.[36] In short, the Haganah created a three-tier reserve structure that, unlike a traditional reserve system, lacked a sizable full-time force to augment or reinforce.

The most important structural change in the Haganah during this period was the creation of a mobile strike force known as the *Palmach* (a Hebrew acronym for "assault companies," *Plugot Machats*) in 1941.[37] The Haganah national command—in cooperation with the British—created the Palmach to defend Palestine against a feared Nazi invasion.[38] The British chose to support this effort based in part on the assessment of A. W. Lawrence (brother of T. E. Lawrence, better known as Lawrence of Arabia), a member of the British Special Operations Executive. In Lawrence's estimation, the Yishuv's military potential was high because its members were "mentally tough, highly disciplined and used to guerrilla warfare," making them ideal for waging an insurrection against the Nazis if they succeeded in occupying Palestine.[39]

The Palmach started as a small force of six hundred part-time volunteers—most of whom came from agricultural settlements (kibbutzim)—organized into six platoons.[40] Over the next seven years it became, in the words of one historian, "the heart and brain" of the Haganah.[41] Many future Israeli commanders and politicians, including nearly all IDF chiefs of the General Staff who served between 1953 and 1983, were Palmach veterans.[42]

Those interested in joining the Palmach underwent an intensive selection and training process overseen by the group's commander, Yitzhak Sadeh, a decorated World War I Russian army veteran who had immigrated to Palestine and served in several Jewish militias during the 1920s and 1930s.[43] As Palmach commander, he handpicked the best and brightest members of the Haganah to build his leadership cadre, often choosing men who had served in the SNS, including future IDF commanders Yigal Allon and Moshe Dayan.[44]

The Palmach training program aimed to develop independent and empowered tactical leaders, as evidenced by its motto: "Every squad commander is a general."[45] This mind-set was important because it would help the Haganah—and eventually the IDF—produce and sustain a military culture centered around aggressive and flexible operations. Such operations would play a critical role in the IDF's ability to offset the quantitative advantages of its larger adversaries.

During its first year of operations, the Palmach prepared for a guerrilla war against the Nazis. It started developing a more conventional force structure when the threat of invasion faded after the German defeat at El Alamein in 1942. Thus, between 1941 and 1944, the Palmach's ranks doubled to around thirteen hundred members.[46] At the same time, it began organizing its platoons into companies, battalions, and eventually brigade-level organizations.[47] These brigades were backed by a reserve of around four hundred Palmach veterans who had at least two years of active service (three to four years for reserve officers). While in the reserves, individuals trained for several weeks a year.[48] The IDF would employ similar reserve personnel and training practices during and after the 1948 War of Independence.

A Citizens' Army Goes to War

The War of Independence started as a civil war between the Yishuv and Palestinian Arabs in late 1947 when the British—financially and militarily exhausted by World War II—announced plans to withdraw from Palestine by May 1948.[49] As the withdrawal loomed, the United Nations recommended dividing Palestine into Arab-controlled and Jewish-controlled states—a plan the Yishuv accepted with reservations and the Palestinian Arabs and their allies rejected, triggering a violent confrontation.[50]

The Palestinians had reason to be confident that they could prevail militarily against the Yishuv. One reason was their potential to field a much larger military force, as their population was around twice that of the Yishuv.[51] The Palestinians also had the support of neighboring Arab states, whose armies collectively outnumbered and outgunned the

Haganah, which initially lacked tanks and artillery.[52] The Yishuv had little territorial depth to absorb an invasion, as its population was concentrated in a narrow strip of land along the Mediterranean coast. In addition, the Arabs held much of the high ground that dominated the main avenues of approach to Jewish population centers in northern and central Palestine, including Jerusalem.[53] The Yishuv, moreover, did not have any strong allies. Both the British and the Americans avoided choosing sides, as some feared an independent Jewish state would align with the Soviets, given the socialist leanings of Yishuv leaders.[54]

Qualitatively, however, the military balance favored the Yishuv. Over the past three decades it had developed a nascent army of cohesive units imbued with a strong will to fight. In addition, members of the Haganah—especially those with Palmach backgrounds—had undergone extensive training and gained some combat experience over the past two decades. In late 1947 Palmach members had completed one year of training on average, and Haganah members had an average of fifty days of training.[55] Some of the new immigrants flooding into the Yishuv after World War II also had experience serving in state armies or fighting as partisans in Europe against the Nazis.[56] The Palestinian Arabs, meanwhile, had lost many of their best fighters during the 1936 Arab Revolt.

Despite its small size, the Yishuv could maximize its resources by drawing on nearly all sectors of society. In late 1947 the Haganah had forty-five thousand members (about twenty-one hundred from the Palmach).[57] Two smaller right-wing organizations, the Irgun and Stern Gang (about three thousand fighters), operated independently and were sometimes at odds with the Haganah.[58] Individuals who were younger than eighteen, including members of the Gadna, and those who were too old to fight served in the Home Guard, filling vital support roles.[59] Yishuv members were willing to tolerate these demands because failure risked national annihilation.[60]

In terms of demographics, members of the Yishuv were much younger than their Palestinian counterparts. During the 1920s and 1930s the Yishuv's leaders sought to attract young immigrants to settle and develop the country. Many of these immigrants were well educated and physically fit, making them ideal soldiers. Palestinian society, in contrast, was older and suffered from widespread illiteracy.[61]

Still, the Yishuv had to contend with a multitude of weaknesses and shortfalls. For instance, its military lacked combat support services, such as dedicated logistics and maintenance units, forcing it improvise these capabilities for much of the war.[62] It was also woefully underequipped.

David Ben-Gurion—Israel's first prime minister—recalled in his memoirs that only about one-third of the Haganah was armed at the start of the civil war.[63] And in late 1947 not a single Haganah commander had combat experience leading a unit above the company level.[64]

Ben-Gurion recognized these weaknesses and took steps to address them.[65] In the immediate aftermath of World War II, he worked with allies and donors in Europe and the United States to raise funds and arms for the Haganah.[66] When he became head of the defense portfolio for the Jewish Agency in 1947, he and his military advisers developed contingency plans to defend against an invasion by neighboring Arab states.[67]

To prepare for such a contingency, Haganah chief of operations Yigael Yadin grouped his battalions into six new brigades: Alexandroni, Carmeli, Etzioni, Givati, Golani, and Kiryati. Meanwhile, the Palmach expanded to ten battalions and organized into three brigades: Yiftach, Harel, and Ha'Negev.[68] To staff and sustain this larger force, Ben-Gurion laid the foundation for a conscription program by requiring Israeli men and women between the ages of seventeen and twenty-five to register for national service.[69] Additionally, as civil war loomed in late 1947, Ben-Gurion mobilized the Haganah and transitioned it into a semiactive-duty force that gained extensive experience fighting and defeating Palestinian paramilitaries over the next five months.[70]

On 14 May 1948, as the British Mandate came to an end, the Yishuv declared independence and became the state of Israel. In response, the Arab League invaded with a loosely organized task force of about 23,500 soldiers from Egypt, Transjordan, Iraq, Syria, and Lebanon.[71] Abdul Rahman Azzam Pasha—secretary-general of the Arab League at the time— warned the invasion would be "a great war of destruction and slaughter that will be remembered like the massacres carried out by the Mongols and the Crusaders."[72]

The Arab League divided the invasion force into three areas of responsibility. The Syrians and Lebanese were supposed to advance into northern Palestine, while the Egyptians moved into the south. Once Israeli forces responded to these advances, the Jordanians and Iraqis were supposed to assault across Israel's narrow center to reach the sea, bisecting the defenses of the Haganah—renamed the Israel Defense Forces (IDF) on 26 May 1948—and capturing major population centers such as Tel Aviv. However, because the Arabs failed to coordinate operations, the IDF was able to defeat the northern and southern invasions in detail.[73] The Israelis did not enjoy the same level of success against the better-trained Jordanians. The Jordanian force, known as the Arab Legion, entered Palestine on

15 May and seized East Jerusalem, including the Jewish Quarter.[74] Fortunately for the Israelis, the Arab Legion failed to press deeper into central Israel as initially planned because the Jordanian king wanted to minimize his losses.[75]

During the summer of 1948 multiple UN-backed truces went into effect, buying the IDF time to reorganize and continue its transition from a people's militia to a more conventional force.[76] In June about four thousand Jews from abroad joined the IDF, enabling it to replace losses and grow. Among these foreigners were World War II veterans, some of whom were experienced pilots who helped establish the Israeli Air Force (IAF).[77] Meanwhile, to unify the Israeli military, Ben-Gurion forced independent militias to disband and integrate into the IDF.[78] The IDF also integrated the Palmach brigades into its command structure and established two new brigades, including its first armored brigade (the Eighth) using newly acquired tanks and half-tracks.[79]

By the end of the war, the IDF had grown to twelve infantry and two armored brigades that reported to one of four regional commands: Northern, Eastern, Central, and Southern (Eastern Command would later be subsumed into Central Command).[80] With these reinforcements, the IDF managed to expel the Egyptians and Syrians by early 1949, but it failed to dislodge the Arab Legion near Jerusalem, despite multiple attempts.[81]

In the end, the War of Independence was Israel's bloodiest war, costing around six thousand lives—about 1 percent of its population—plus thousands more wounded.[82] Yet the Israelis achieved their primary objective of ensuring the independence of their new state and securing most of the land allotted to them under the UN Partition Plan. And they realized that goal with an army of citizen-soldiers—the vast majority of whom started the war as part-time soldiers.

Israel was able to succeed with these part-time soldiers for several reasons. First, their adversaries were poorly led and mounted predictable, uncoordinated operations. The lone exception was Transjordan's Arab Legion; however, the legion was too small to withstand heavy attrition and therefore could not drive deeper into Israel, allowing the Israelis to concentrate on defeating the less capable Syrians, Egyptians, and Iraqis. Second, the IDF had high-quality officers and NCOs with extensive combat experience gained fighting Palestinian militants in the months leading up to the 1948 war and in the previous two decades. As Yitzhak Rabin—a Palmach veteran and future Israeli prime minister—noted in his memoir, by the end of the 1948 war, he had "been under arms for six years."[83] These experienced leaders helped preserve and improve the

IDF's fighting quality, even as new, untested soldiers entered the ranks. Third, IDF operations in 1948 were simple in comparison to the more expansive mechanized operations it would later be known for. As historian Gunther Rothenberg explains, "The War of Independence remained mainly an infantry war, fought by small units."[84] Finally, the more experienced men of the Palmach commanded most of the larger and more complex operations (about 20 percent of those killed in action were from the Palmach, even though it was only a fraction of the size of the overall Haganah/IDF).[85] The IDF would build on these experiences and lessons during the next two decades to create a highly effective citizens' army.

Building a Citizens' Army

Following the War of Independence, Israel continued to rely on conscripts and reservists for national defense. Overseeing the development of this citizens' army was David Ben-Gurion, who served as both prime minister and minister of defense, and the first three IDF chiefs of the General Staff: Yaakov Dori (1948–49), Yigael Yadin (1949–52), and Mordechai Maklef (1952–53).[86]

Ben-Gurion and his military chiefs understood that Israel faced difficult strategic circumstances that necessitated the efficient use of human capital and economic resources. Although it had secured independence, Israel was still surrounded by larger, hostile Arab states determined to destroy it.[87] If they attacked, Israel was vulnerable to being rapidly overrun due to its small size and narrow geographic configuration. It could not form a large standing army to deter or contain such an attack because of its small population and weak economy.[88] An all-volunteer force was not possible either because Israel simply lacked sufficient volunteers.[89] Making matters worse, Israel had no military allies, as its special relationship with the United States would not develop until the late 1960s.

With these challenges in mind, Ben-Gurion sought to develop an army that had the "best and most advanced training and proper military equipment, so that the superior quality of the armed forces will compensate for its inferior quantity."[90] To ensure that such a force did not cripple the tiny Israeli economy, Ben-Gurion and his advisers built the army around part-time reservists, who were cheaper to maintain than full-time professionals.[91]

The foundation of this new army was the Defense Service Law that the Knesset—the Israeli parliament—approved in September 1949. That law, which Ben-Gurion, Yadin, and Dori wrote, mandated universal military service for nearly all Israeli citizens.[92] Initially, conscripts served for twenty-four months; in 1952 the IDF extended the obligation to thirty-six months to ensure that it had sufficient personnel to meet mission requirements.[93]

The law faced resistance from some former Palmach officers, who wanted to develop a small professional army backed by a popular militia—a proposal Ben-Gurion rejected. Instead, he wanted to maximize Israel's military capacity to defend against a coordinated invasion through mass conscription and the maintenance of a large, trained reserve.[94] Ben-Gurion also believed a conscript-reserve model army could act as "an educational force for national unity" to help assimilate new immigrants into Israeli society.[95]

The law divided the IDF into three components: the standing conscript army, the reserve, and a small cadre of career officers and technicians. The conscript army was composed of all Israeli youth—including young women—drafted into the military at age eighteen. Men served mainly in the combat arms, while women served almost exclusively in support roles such as logistics, medical services, and intelligence.[96] Service exemptions were made for Arabs living in Israel, Orthodox women, married women, mothers, full-time students in *yeshivot* (traditional Jewish educational centers), and those with mental or physical disabilities. Christian and Bedouin citizens could volunteer to serve. The professional cadre oversaw training, unit administration, and technical fields.[97]

The reserve, composed of discharged conscripts, was the largest and most important element of the IDF. On its own, the standing army was too small to defeat an invasion; its role was to hold the line against an invasion for upward of seventy-two hours, buying time for the reserves to mobilize and counterattack.[98] The reserves therefore needed to be highly trained and ready to fight with little to no notice. To ensure they could perform this vital function, the IDF required all reservists to undergo intensive initial training and field exercises as conscripts.[99] Such training was "threefold tougher" than in the US Army, according to famed US Army historian S. L. A. Marshall, who observed IDF training.[100] Intense field training continued once a soldier was discharged into the reserves.

Perhaps the most important element of the early IDF's training program was that it prepared all its NCOs—whether reservists or conscripts—to think and act independently. This ensured that Israeli infantrymen were adept and agile enough to outmaneuver their larger, more cumbersome adversaries who used a less flexible Soviet-style command system. The

IDF also allowed squads to maneuver independently by dividing them into two teams composed of four to five riflemen. Controlling such a force required a trained squad leader—usually a junior NCO—who had the skills and experience to identify and exploit opportunities as they arose without waiting for direct guidance from officers at the platoon or company level. The IDF therefore conducted demanding squad leadership courses that produced highly effective infantry NCOs, giving its reserve and conscript units a distinct advantage in flexibility over the infantry of its adversaries.[101]

The IDF reserve and active-duty officer corps also benefited from this NCO training and development program, as most Israeli officers in the combat arms previously served as NCOs and likely graduated from the squad leadership course. Unlike most armies, the IDF had no officer academy or ROTC-like program, although some young men attended special high schools that provided instruction and training in a range of military topics.[102]

By drawing its officers from the enlisted ranks, the IDF could ensure that tactical-level leaders in the active and reserve forces had some experience leading soldiers. Officers leaving active duty for the reserves had at least forty-eight months of full-time experience.[103] While in the reserves, they had to meet the same training and education requirements as their active-duty counterparts.[104]

The IDF organized its reservists into eight infantry brigades commanded primarily by reserve officers.[105] Initially, some IDF commanders worried that reservists could not handle the demands of command and staff positions at the brigade level, but they had little choice, given the shortage of active-duty officers.[106] That said, the IDF worked to ensure that almost all reserve units were fully staffed and equipped in peacetime, allowing them to train more realistically and mobilize faster in a crisis.[107] And because all reservists had served on active duty, they did not have to be taught basic soldiers skills, unlike the volunteer reserve systems of the United States and Britain.

Reserve training in Israel was demanding compared to that in other armies. Until age forty-eight, every Israeli reservist trained for thirty- to forty-five days a year (fourteen to twenty-one days for older reservists in support units).[108] Each training day lasted nine to twelve hours, compared to eight hours a day or less in the reserve components of other armies.[109] And reserve officers frequently trained beyond their annual requirements to ensure the success of their respective units.[110] For example, one reserve officer claimed in an interview with an Israeli newspaper that he devoted as many as eighty days a year to the military.[111] Ultimately, chief of the General Staff (CGS) Yadin established this rigorous training approach to develop highly professional reservists who, in his words, were "regular soldiers who happened to be on leave eleven months of the year."[112]

Reserve training took place during one or two annual training sessions; the goal was for the first session to focus on advanced individual training and the second on unit-level maneuvers, although it is unclear how often this worked out in practice.[113] Concentrating reserve training in one or two sessions likely helped to build readiness—that is, a unit's ability to perform its assigned mission to the standards expected by its leadership and doctrine. As discussed in the case study of the US Army National Guard, reserve units that divided training into multiple sessions throughout the year often wasted time on routine tasks such as taking attendance, distributing equipment, and getting soldiers back into a military mindset. By concentrating training in one or two sessions, the IDF could also conduct more field maneuvers, which were difficult to complete during the ARNG's short weekend drills or the British reserves' weekday evening sessions.[114]

Reserve officers and NCOs, however, had little control over planning and assessing training, unlike in the US Army. In the IDF, these tasks were the responsibility of full-time personnel at combined-arms centers.[115] This policy, which applied to both individual and collective training events, likely improved reserve readiness in three ways.[116] First, it prevented undertrained reserve officers and NCOs from providing incomplete or unsatisfactory training to their units. Second, it ensured that units across the IDF trained at or near the same standards. Third, instructors at combined-arms centers relieved reserve officers and NCOs of the burden of preparing training events, allowing them to focus their limited time on leading units in the field or working on their own individual training and administrative requirements.

To improve the speed of mobilization, the IDF organized reserve units geographically. That is, reserve units drew personnel and supplies from nearby towns and cities, reducing the time it took soldiers to get from their homes to assembly areas.[117] To accelerate mobilization, the IDF allowed reservists to bring much of their personal equipment home with them. Therefore, when they arrived at mobilization areas, which were located outside of cities to reduce the risk of traffic inhibiting the movement of personnel and supplies, they did not have to draw that equipment from storage.[118]

Thus, by the mid-1950s, the IDF had enacted five key practices and

policies that laid the foundation for its future battlefield successes with reserve forces:

- All reservists had at least two to four years of active training and
  experience gained as conscripts.
- Reserve training was demanding, lengthy, concentrated in one or two
  periods, conducted at local armories, and managed by experienced
  full-time personnel.
- Reserve officers had the same education and training standards as
  conscripts; had served previously as enlisted soldiers, where they
  may have gained leadership experience as NCOs; and, in some cases,
  had attended the infantry squad leadership course.
- Reserve units were generally fully manned and equipped in peacetime.
- Reservists spent many years with the same unit, boosting unit
  cohesion.

These policies and practices meant that the IDF reserve had a high degree
of experience and plenty of time to train.

Sustaining this reserve army and conscript force was expensive, requiring Israel to devote a considerable percentage of its national wealth
to defense. Defense spending was around 10 percent of gross domestic
product (GDP) in 1950 and grew to nearly 15 percent by 1956; it rose even
higher in the following decades.[119] Israel was able to convince its population to accept such high levels of defense spending and the burden of
universal military service because of a legitimate fear that failing to do so
risked national annihilation. For long-time residents of the Yishuv, memories of Arab attempts to destroy their communities in 1936 and 1948
were still fresh. And new immigrants from Europe had experienced—or
narrowly escaped—the horrors of the Holocaust. Arab rhetoric calling
for the destruction of Israel borrowed from the Nazis' anti-Semitic propaganda, amplifying fears of a second Holocaust.[120]

Given these fears and the larger sense of collectivism that pervaded
Israeli society, IDF personnel were willing to serve for little pay (about
$600 a year). In fact, many troops relied on public welfare to cover living
expenses.[121] The state also taxed employers to ensure that reservists received 65 to 80 percent of their civilian pay while on duty.[122] By keeping
salaries low and using special taxes to cover reservists' pay, the IDF could
devote more of its budget to operations, training, and equipment.[123]

Although the IDF had a strong will to fight and a well-trained reserve,
it still faced numerous challenges. One challenge was the lack of a standard

army doctrine because senior and midlevel officers came from such varied backgrounds. Some had trained and fought as light infantry with the Palmach or Haganah, while others had fought with Europe's conventional armed forces during World War II.[124] To standardize the Israeli way of war, the IDF wrote new manuals and established schools and training programs between 1949 and 1954, including a battalion command course and a command and staff college that taught a mobile, combined-arms approach to warfare that fused British, Palmach, and other tactical concepts.[125] The resulting doctrine was highly flexible. For instance, it did not encourage the use of battle drills or produce detailed standard operating procedures for unit operations. Prominent IDF tacticians such as Moshe Dayan preferred soldiers and officers to improvise solutions to tactical problems, eschewing by-the-book solutions. This view was highly influenced by the organizational culture promoted by Palmach officers in the 1930s and 1940s.[126] Ultimately, what Dayan and Yadin wanted was an army that could rapidly mobilize and outfight and outmaneuver larger Arab adversaries to end wars quickly and decisively. The army needed to avoid battles of attrition, which Israel could not afford because of its small population and limited industry.[127]

Israel, however, confronted a readiness crisis in the early 1950s that constrained its ability to put its mobile warfare doctrine into practice. It lacked sufficient trucks and armored vehicles—most of which were nonoperational—to conduct and sustain mobile operations.[128] Many of the IDF's best and most experienced officers were retiring or had been promoted to senior positions, reducing the number of combat veterans in the junior and middle ranks.[129] Additionally, a spike in immigration flooded the IDF with inexperienced new conscripts between 1950 and 1955.[130] These new immigrants were subject to conscription and reserve service, forcing the IDF to devote much of its training time and resources to improving immigrant education.[131] The immigration boom also caused command and control issues, as the IDF simply lacked the leaders and facilities to train and control the expanding army. In addition, many of the new generation of Israeli military leaders demonstrated little will to fight and a lack of basic military skills in areas such as land navigation.[132] These issues were most prevalent in the reserves, which had lower-quality equipment and training than the regulars.[133]

The IDF's poor state of readiness in the early 1950s was evident in its struggles to defend against Arab paramilitary raids launched from Jordan and Egypt.[134] In fact, the IDF concluded in 1953 that only about 18 percent of its responses to these raids were effective.[135] CGS Dayan later attributed these struggles to the loss of training time caused by IDF involvement in immigration affairs and a risk-averse and overly defensive mind-set among officers.[136] Thus, during his initial years as CGS, Dayan focused much of his energy on resolving these issues.[137]

Despite confronting major budgetary constraints, Dayan implemented several organizational and training reforms that increased the army's offensive spirit and capabilities.[138] For example, he reduced IDF participation in immigration programs, freeing units to focus on training and operations.[139] He also slashed the size of support elements to free personnel for combat arms assignments.[140] To boost the IDF's offensive spirit, Dayan required infantry officers to attend paratrooper training, and he reassigned highly motivated soldiers from kibbutzim to offensive missions.[141]

Under Dayan's leadership, the IDF also made progress toward motorization and mechanization. In the year leading up to the 1956 Suez Crisis, Dayan secured a 10 percent boost in funding that enabled the IDF to more than double its tank fleet from 86 to 181 and to acquire 150 half-tracks and 60 French-made 105mm howitzers.[142] With that equipment, the IDF established its first two mechanized reserve brigades: the Twenty-Seventh and Thirty-Seventh.[143] These upgrades, in turn, prepared the IDF to compete with the Egyptian army, which was also mechanizing using new Soviet-made arms.[144]

The Suez Crisis and the Reserve Stumbles

The IDF faced its first major combat test in 1956 when Israel, alongside Great Britain and France, went to war against Egypt. Four years earlier, Gamal Abdel Nasser and fellow Egyptian army officers had overthrown the Egyptian monarchy and nationalized the Suez Canal, a vital strategic waterway for British and French shipping.[145] In retaliation, France and Britain conspired to overthrow Nasser, and they secured the support of Israel, which wanted to strike the Egyptians before they could integrate newly acquired Soviet weapons into their arsenal.[146]

After agreeing to participate in the Anglo-French operation, Ben-Gurion authorized the IDF to form a plan of attack code-named Kadesh, the biblical name of the Sinai. The operation had three primary objectives: eliminate paramilitary bases in the Sinai, destroy the Egyptian armed forces' ability to launch raids from the Sinai into Israel, and reopen the Straits of Tiran to Israeli shipping.[147] To achieve these goals, Dayan had to draw heavily on reserve forces; in fact, seven of the ten brigades that participated in the operation were from the reserves, many of which would receive demanding front-line assignments.[148] Dayan's plan was for the IDF to advance deep into the Sinai along three avenues, penetrating or bypassing the main Egyptian defenses and seizing key terrain near the Suez Canal to encircle and collapse the Egyptian army.[149]

The Seventy-Seventh Ugdah—a division-level task force—composed of three reserve brigades (First and Eleventh Infantry and Twenty-Seventh Mechanized) was responsible for the first avenue, which extended from Gaza to el-Qantara along the Mediterranean coast.[150] Meanwhile, the Ninth Brigade (reserve) was supposed to seize Sharm el-Sheikh along the southern axis and destroy Egyptian gun emplacements that harassed Israeli shipping through the Straits of Tiran.[151] The main effort, however, was along the central avenue, which passed through Abu Ageila to Ismailia on the east bank of the Suez Canal. The campaign would start here with the 202nd Parachute Battalion dropping deep into the Sinai to seize and hold the Mitla Pass, blocking a key line of communication linking Egypt's Sinai-based units with the mainland.[152] The Thirty-Eighth Ugdah (Fourth and Tenth Infantry and Thirty-Seventh Mechanized Reserve Brigades), the Seventh Armor Brigade (a conscript unit), and two additional paratrooper battalions would then attack overland on the central avenue to link up with their comrades at Mitla.[153]

Opposing the Israelis were forty-two thousand Egyptian soldiers and Palestinian paramilitaries.[154] In the northeastern Sinai, inside and around Gaza, the Egyptians stationed the Third and Eighth Infantry Divisions and several battalions of Palestinian paramilitaries supported by Egyptian national guardsmen. Farther south, the Egyptians positioned a reinforced infantry battalion near Sharm el-Sheikh.[155]

The Egyptians had the advantage of operating from prepared battle positions, but Israel had the element of surprise. The Egyptians were not expecting a significant attack into the Sinai, so they concentrated their armored forces along the Suez to counter the Anglo-French invasion force. This gave Israel an advantage in mass and firepower in the central and eastern Sinai.[156]

The war began on 29 October 1956 when Israeli paratroopers seized the Mitla Pass. Three days later, the Twenty-Seventh Infantry and First Infantry (Golani) Brigades seized el-Arish, opening the northern road into the Sinai. However, the Egyptians repelled the Tenth Infantry Brigade's attack along the central axis near Abu Ageila, where the Israelis continued to struggle until the Egyptian high command ordered a general retreat from the Sinai. When the Egyptians near Abu Ageila abandoned their defensive positions, they were cut to pieces by the more agile Israelis.[157] Farther south, the Ninth Infantry Brigade began its advance on Sharm el-Sheikh on 2 November, securing its objectives and removing the Egyptian threat to Israeli shipping three days later.[158] By 5 November, the IDF was in control of the entire Sinai, having achieved all its tactical objectives at a cost of 231 killed in action; Egyptian casualties totaled around 3,000.[159]

The lopsided casualty counts reflected the poor Egyptian leadership. In battle, Egyptian officers demonstrated a lack of courage, abandoning their men when the tide of the battle turned against them.[160] Nasser and the high command made the fatal mistake of ordering a hasty withdrawal while the Egyptians were in contact with the IDF. This forced them to engage the Israelis on the move—a type of fight the Egyptians were not prepared to wage.[161]

These mistakes mitigated some of the weaknesses of the IDF reserve system that became apparent during mobilization and in combat on the central axis. Initially, the IDF had planned to mobilize the reserves a week before launching the attack, but to preserve the element of surprise, Dayan reduced the mobilization to five days.[162] Once it began on 24 October, units struggled to muster all their forces; in some cases, only 50 percent of personnel reported for duty, which alerted units to the fact that they lacked current contact information for their soldiers.[163] They ultimately resolved this issue by broadcasting mobilization orders over the radio.[164]

Because of these delays, units had "insufficient time to study their expected tasks," as Dayan later concluded.[165] Instead, they spent time organizing equipment and personnel for movement to the front.[166] And upon their arrival in the Sinai, some units had to deploy to combat immediately, rather than gathering in tactical assembly areas where they could have developed and rehearsed plans of attack.[167]

This hasty mobilization almost certainly contributed to some of the problems reserve units faced in combat.[168] For example, the Thirty-Eighth Ugdah, which was responsible for the central axis of advance, performed poorly against the Egyptian Sixth Infantry Brigade during the battle for the Umm Qatef ridgeline.[169] Dayan wanted to seize that ridgeline to enable the Seventh Armored Brigade, as well as elements from the 202nd Parachute Brigade, to pass into the central Sinai and reinforce the paratroopers at the Mitla Pass.[170]

To execute this mission, the Thirty-Eighth Ugdah turned to the reservists of the Tenth and Fourth Infantry Brigades. The battle started well as the Fourth Brigade successfully dislodged a battalion of Egyptian national guardsmen from Kusseima, opening a southern approach to the

Umm Qatef ridgeline.[171] Meanwhile, to the north of Kusseima, the Tenth Brigade under the command of Colonel Shmuel Goder, a decorated veteran of the Soviet artillery corps in World War II, advanced west for a frontal assault on the ridgeline.[172] The Tenth, which consisted mostly of older reservists, was supposed to strike at the same time as the Fourth attacked from the south, but for unknown reasons, the Fourth never received that order and the Tenth unwittingly went to battle alone.[173] As it neared Umm Qatef, the Tenth Brigade encountered accurate antitank and artillery fire from the Egyptians entrenched along the ridgeline.[174] Rather than press the attack, as Dayan preferred, Goder halted. When Dayan forced him to resume the attack that evening, two of Goder's infantry battalions became disoriented in the dark and were unable to coordinate their assault.[175] A frustrated Dayan relieved Goder of command and replaced him with Colonel Israel Tal, a veteran of the British Jewish Brigade in World War II (and later a major figure in the IDF).[176]

The Tenth Brigade's struggles forced Dayan to send the newly formed Thirty-Seventh Mechanized Brigade (reserve) to reinforce the attack against Umm Qatef. However, having been established only a year earlier, the Thirty-Seventh was not at a high state of readiness, as it had yet to conduct any field maneuvers.[177] In addition, it had received its tanks and half-tracks only two weeks before the war, and those vehicles lacked radio communications gear.[178] Despite these issues, the Thirty-Seventh's commander, Colonel Shmuel Galinka, was highly enthusiastic about the prospect of battlefield command—perhaps because he read inaccurate intelligence reports stating that the Egyptians were collapsing at Umm Qatef.[179] Thus, he decided to concentrate his forces and conduct a frontal assault. Making matters worse, the brigade attacked at night, with vehicle headlights on, revealing their positions to the Egyptians. Unsurprisingly, the attack failed. The Thirty-Seventh suffered eighty casualties, and many of its officers were killed in action, including Galinka. Following this debacle, IDF General Headquarters canceled the Umm Qatef mission.[180]

Despite these problems, the war ended as a tactical success for the IDF in general and for the reserves in particular, having proved themselves capable of going toe-to-toe with a well-equipped albeit poorly led adversary. The reserves also overcame administrative problems to mobilize within seventy-two hours and achieved their assigned missions, with the exception of those at Umm Qatef.

That said, the Israelis were unable to secure a lasting strategic victory. A year after the war, the IDF had to withdraw from the Sinai under diplomatic pressure from the United States and the Soviet Union, which were competing for favor with the Arab states. Although Egypt eventually reoccupied the peninsula, the United Nations agreed to oversee Sharm el-Sheikh, which allowed Israeli shipping to resume unimpeded through the Straits of Tiran.[181]

Becoming an Elite Reserve

Between 1956 and 1967 the IDF implemented a series of reforms that would have important implications for the readiness of its reserves in future conflicts, as the next chapter shows. These reforms drove the IDF's evolution from a low-tech infantry army to a higher-tech force built around the armored corps and air force. Under Dayan and his predecessors, the IDF placed infantry—and the paratroopers in particular—at the center of its doctrine and operations.[182] However, as Arab armies mechanized, the next three CGSs—Chaim Laskov (1958–61), Tzvi Tzur (1961–63), and Yitzhak Rabin (1964–68)—moved tanks and the IAF into the lead.[183] Thus, throughout the 1960s, the IDF acquired hundreds of new American-made M-48 Patton tanks and British-made Centurions.[184]

Israel Tal, who ran the armored corps from 1964 to 1967, was in favor of purchasing medium tanks like the M-48 and the Centurion because they offered a balance of armored protection and mobility, making them ideal for penetrating defenses and prevailing in mobile engagements against the Soviet-made T-54/55 tanks that many Arab armies were acquiring.[185] That said, Tal's vision for armored forces—which the IDF fully embraced by 1967—lacked a combined-arms element, as he preferred armor to operate behind enemy lines without direct infantry support.[186]

To improve Israeli tanks' ability to fight unsupported, the IDF bolstered the firepower of its armor formations, mainly by fitting tanks with the British-made L7 105mm cannon.[187] This new type of tank cannon was stabilized, enabling tank crews to fire accurately on the move at targets up to fifteen hundred meters away.[188] At the same time, the IDF doubled its inventory of self-propelled artillery and mortars to provide ground commanders with mobile indirect fire systems capable of maneuvering alongside tanks and APCs.[189]

As tanks became the central arm of the Israeli army, the IDF order of battle changed (table 4.2). By 1962, the IDF fielded five armored brigades—up from one in 1956.[190] By 1967, that number would nearly double.[191] The IDF started operating its first armored division—a reserve formation—in 1961.[192]

Table 4.2 IDF Size and Order of Battle, 1948–67

Year	Active	Reserve	Maneuver Brigades
1948	80,000		3 Palmach 9 Haganah
1950	30,000	70,000–80,000	1 active armor 1 infantry brigade 1 paratrooper battalion 8 reserve infantry
1955–56	85,000–100,000 (more than half were likely reservists)		1 paratrooper 1 armor 2 mechanized 13 infantry
1962	30,000	150,000	1 paratrooper 5 armor 1 mechanized 17 infantry
1964	30,000	220,000	1 paratrooper ~ 5 armor ~ 2 mechanized ~17 infantry (including territorials*)
1966	55,000	204,000	3–4 paratrooper 5–9 armor ~ 3 mechanized ~ 17 infantry (including territorials*)
1967	55,000	225,000	3–4 paratrooper 7–9 armor 2–3 mechanized ~ 17 infantry (including territorials*) These forces were organized into 4 armored divisions or as independent brigades

Sources: Rothenberg, *Anatomy of the Israeli Army*, 58, 85, 101, 120; CIA, "The Arab-Israeli Situation," 6 April 1961, map 1; IISS, Military Balance 1964, 32; IISS, Military Balance 1966, 37; CIA, "Military Capabilities of Israel and the Arab States," 26 May 1967, 8; Dupuy, *Elusive Victory*, 338.

Note: Numbers are approximate, as the IDF kept its order of battle secret.

* Territorials were primarily infantry units focused on defensive operations along Israel's borders.

The IDF also transformed the air force, expanding its fleet of combat aircraft by 50 percent between 1956 and 1967.[193] This transformation occurred because Israeli military leaders had been underwhelmed by the IAF's performance in 1956, when they had to rely on the British and French to protect their airspace during the war. They were highly impressed by the ability of modern French and British aircraft to inflict heavy losses on the Egyptian air force.[194]

The IAF, however, was a supporting arm for the ground forces. In wartime, its primary mission was to quickly gain air superiority and then shift to providing close air support for armored forces. Despite its support function, the air force began to receive many of Israel's best and brightest conscripts, who had previously gone to the paratroopers or the armored corps.[195] Over the next thirty years, the IAF would emerge not only as the primary destination for top conscripts but also as the dominant arm in a new, high-tech Israeli way of war.

Israel's booming population and growing national wealth enabled the IDF to modernize its air and armored forces. Between 1948 and 1965, high birthrates and immigration increased Israel's population from 650,000 to 2.4 million.[196] Additionally, the Israeli economy grew by about 10 percent a year in the late 1950s and early 1960s.[197] And overhead costs remained low as the IDF continued to minimize soldiers' pay and benefits while drawing on part-time reservists for the bulk of its combat power.[198]

The Israeli public tolerated high defense spending because many believed the nation's survival was at stake. During the 1960s Egypt and other Arab powers issued statements declaring that their aim was "the destruction of Israel."[199] The Israeli public—and the government—believed that rhetoric, even though the Arabs were overmatched militarily by the Israelis, as would become evident in 1967. Israeli officials also held public lectures and wrote newspaper articles explaining why high defense spending was necessary, citing grave threats to Israeli security.[200]

The IDF's commitment to armored warfare posed challenges to reserve and conscript units, which struggled to maintain the new armored vehicles they received in the early to mid-1960s. Brigadier General Tal blamed these problems on lax maintenance standards, but he eventually came to understand that crews did not have enough time and training to learn the intricacies of the complex electrical, hydraulic, and optical systems aboard the newer Centurion and Patton tanks. Adding to this challenge was the fact that crews had to work on about ten different vehicle types. Unlike many other armies, the IDF did not have a standard line of vehicles; it had tanks and armored vehicles from Britain, France, and the United States, as well as modified versions of them. To address this challenge, Tal established a more rigorous maintenance program in 1965 that included new written standard operating procedures; maintenance workers were also assigned to specific vehicles rather than having to learn the particulars of multiple vehicle models. Within two years, the new program began to bear fruit, as reports from the field showed improvements in maintenance standards.[201]

During the 1960s the IDF also intensified reserve and conscript training, with a focus on tank and mechanized infantry units.[202] Reserve battalions, for instance, underwent rigorous summer exercises that required them to advance from individual to battalion-level maneuvers; units could also recall personnel throughout the year for remedial training or to learn how to operate newly acquired equipment.[203] Exercises for reserves units also included a joint element, integrating ground maneuvers with the air force.[204] Some commanders complained that these exercises—developed and monitored by regular officers using training materials published by the Ministry of Defense—reduced reservists' ability to tailor training to the specific needs of their units.[205] That said, the standardized training program meant that units across the IDF were training to similar standards, thereby improving the overall interoperability of Israeli ground forces.

In addition to battalion-level maneuvers, the IDF started conducting division-level exercises by the early 1960s.[206] Some of these exercises were held in the Negev desert, preparing tank crews to operate under similar conditions if called to fight the Egyptians in the Sinai. Some reservists spent their entire summer training cycle performing such maneuvers.[207]

The IDF also improved reserve personnel standards. For instance, given the poor performance of older reservists during the Sinai campaign, it reassigned those over age forty to support units.[208] IDF officers traveled to the United States to observe how the ARNG conducted armor maneuvers.[209] Others attended US Army technical schools for instruction in tank warfare and other fields. Some of those students would later become senior commanders in IDF reserve units.[210]

The continued expansion of the IDF in the late 1950s and early 1960s allowed it to place more active-duty officers in command and staff positions in reserve brigades and divisions, bolstering those units' experience levels. Active-duty officers leveraged such opportunities to gain valuable command experience, and given the slower operational tempo of reserve units, they had more time to spend with their families or to pursue professional development. As one reserve commander recalled, "There was time to learn since we didn't carry the daily burden of ongoing security and training programs." That said, service in the reserves had drawbacks. Some considered such assignments less prestigious due to the lower-quality equipment and slower tempo.[211]

Reserve units' equipment was often subpar because the IDF prioritized certain units over others. During his tenure as CGS, Rabin divided IDF ground units into two broad categories—defensive and offensive—based on the quality of each unit's personnel and equipment. Rabin assigned armor, mechanized, and parachute units—found primarily in the active component of the IDF—to offensive roles. Purely infantry units, which were more common in the reserves, were assigned to territorial defense brigades.[212] Reserve units, however, continued to figure prominently in IDF operations outside Israel in the decades that followed Rabin's tenure as CGS. But his policy foreshadowed the current era in which the IDF relies almost exclusively on conscript units for offensive operations, as discussed in the next chapter.

In summary, the IDF became a more mobile and lethal force in the decade following the Suez Crisis. And it ensured that its reserve forces could keep up with these changes by improving the training, equipment, and personnel standards of conscript and reserve units alike. The benefits of these efforts were on display in 1967 during the Six-Day War.

A Victory for the Reserves

The Six-Day War began as a conflict over Israel's National Water Carrier Project, which diverted water from the Sea of Galilee and the Jordan River to support Israeli agriculture and industry in the Negev desert. Many in the Arab world, including the Syrian government, viewed the diversion as an attempt to attract more settlers to Israel.[213] In response, the Syrian military shelled Israeli construction sites and sponsored terrorist attacks on settlements, provoking retaliatory air strikes in April 1967.[214] Because he had signed a mutual defense pact with Syria, Egyptian president Nasser deployed seven divisions and an infantry brigade to the Sinai on 14 May.[215]

To remove the Egyptian threat from its borders, Israel devised a three-phase plan using the IAF and three division-sized task forces assigned to Southern Command.[216] Northern and Central Commands would remain on the defense to deter and, if necessary, block a potential Syrian or Jordanian intervention. The IAF, meanwhile, would open the campaign with a surprise attack on air bases west of the Suez to destroy the Egyptian air force while it was still on the ground. During phase two, the army would breach the Egyptians' front-line defenses near Abu Ageila and el-Arish and drive west to seize the Giddi and Mitla Passes just east of the Suez.[217] In the final phase, the IDF would destroy the Egyptian army as it attempted to flee to mainland Egypt through the blocked passes.[218]

Among the three divisions assigned to Southern Command were multiple reserve brigades, which would play a central role in the operation. The northern division, which the IDF placed along the border with Gaza, was commanded by Brigadier General Tal. Under Tal were three maneuver elements, including the elite Seventh Armored Brigade, equipped with newer Centurion and Patton tanks.[219] The other armored brigade—the Sixtieth—was a reserve formation armed with older AMX-13s and Sherman tanks.[220] Additionally, the Israelis placed a reserve paratrooper brigade (the Fifty-Fifth) in the north to provide infantry support to help breach fortifications around Gaza.[221]

In the south, the IDF stationed a reserve division commanded by veteran Ariel Sharon, now a brigadier general. Sharon's division consisted of a mix of conscripts and reservists tasked with seizing Umm Qatef and Abu Ageila to open the central axis into the Sinai.[222] To ensure it had the necessary firepower and mobility to avoid a repeat of the failed 1956 attack at Umm Qatef, the division received several attachments, including six artillery battalions, two reserve infantry brigades, and a combat engineer battalion.[223] Sharon also received two reserve paratrooper battalions carried by helicopters and a conscript armored brigade.[224] Once Sharon breached the Umm Qatef fortifications and seized Abu Ageila, he would advance west to the Mitla and Giddi Passes to block the Egyptian retreat.[225]

Between Sharon and Tal was a second division—containing two reserve armored brigades equipped with Centurion tanks—commanded by Brigadier General Avraham Yoffe. Yoffe's main task was to advance between Tal and Sharon over severely restricted terrain to surprise the Egyptians' second line of defense and reserve in the central Sinai.[226] Once the two brigades were through these restricted areas, one would move toward Bir Lahfan to defeat an Egyptian counterattack, while the other helped Sharon envelop Egyptian defenses at Umm Qatef from the west. Later in the operation, Yoffe was supposed to advance west toward Mitla and coordinate with Tal to complete the destruction of the Egyptian army.[227]

The IDF reserves entered the war at a much higher state of readiness than in 1956 due to improvements in personnel, equipment, and training. Unlike in 1956, Israeli reservists underwent several weeks of predeployment training before entering combat, as Prime Minister Levi Eshkol approved a partial reserve mobilization on 19 May in response to the Egyptian deployment into the Sinai.[228] Having this additional training was important for two reasons. First, it allowed units to retrain individuals who had missed some or all of their annual refresher training because of school, work, or other conflicts.[229] Second, extra training helped reservists get back into a military mind-set and accustomed them to twenty-four-hour operations. Sharon's division, for instance, trained "day and night" in the Negev in the two weeks leading up to the war, with a focus on bringing reservists to the same readiness level as conscripts.[230]

However, the lengthy mobilization damaged the Israeli economy. Some businesses had to close temporarily or curtail operations as employees departed unexpectedly for military service. By late May, war seemed likely and tourism declined, costing the Israeli economy $500,000 a day.[231] These pressures convinced Eshkol and Rabin to demobilize thirty thousand reservists on 31 May in the hopes of stabilizing the economy. When the war began on 5 June, the IDF recalled demobilized personnel via radio broadcasts.[232]

As planned, the war started with an IAF attack on Egypt on the morning of 5 June 1967. Ten flights of four IAF aircraft bombed air facilities across Egypt, destroying 298 of Egypt's 420 combat aircraft. Senior Egyptian commanders concealed the results of the raid from Nasser and their subordinates, meaning that units entered battle assuming they had air support.[233]

Shortly after the raid, Israeli ground operations commenced when three IDF Ugdot (the plural of Ugdah) entered the Sinai.[234] Facing the Israelis was a large—but weak—Egyptian army of 100,000 personnel, half of whom were poorly trained reservists rushed to action because much of the standing army was deployed to Yemen.[235] The Egyptians also employed a cumbersome command and control system that passed orders and intelligence through six layers of bureaucracy between the General Staff and front-line units.[236] Such a system was ill-suited for fighting an opponent that used a highly decentralized command system that enabled it to maintain a high operational tempo.

Exploiting these advantages, the Israelis rapidly destroyed the Egyptian army in the Sinai in one of history's most lopsided campaigns. In the north, conscript units in Tal's Ugdah captured critical positions along the northern route to the Suez, defeating the Egyptian Seventh Infantry Division.[237] In the south, Israeli reservists from Sharon's Ugdah made even greater contributions in the battle to seize the Umm Qatef ridgeline from the Egyptian Second Infantry Division—the same place Egyptian forces had held off Israeli attacks during the 1956 Sinai campaign. During the battle, Sharon used a brigade of reserve paratroopers to attack and disrupt the Second Infantry Division's artillery units west of Umm Qatef, helping Israeli infantry and armor units seize the ridgeline and open the central and southern approaches to the Suez.[238]

The most significant contribution by reserve forces in the Sinai campaign came on the central axis by Yoffe's Ugdah. Yoffe, a reserve officer who had served in the British army during World War II, the Haganah, and the IDF in 1956, successfully maneuvered his Ugdah through severely restricted terrain between Sharon and Tal during the first day of the war.[239] By doing so, he caught the Egyptians by surprise, as they were not expecting tanks to advance over such rough terrain. During the ensuing engagements against elements of the Fourth Armored Division—the Egyptians' operational reserve in the Sinai—Israeli tank crews took advantage of their superior long-range gunnery skills to destroy nine Egyptian T-55s, at the cost of one Israeli tank loss, forcing the Egyptians back to Jebel Libni. The next day, Yoffe's reservists pursued and defeated the Egyptians and destroyed an additional thirty or more T-55s without suffering a single loss.[240]

When news of the Fourth Armored Division's defeat reached Cairo, the Egyptian command ordered a retreat to more defensible terrain near the Giddi and Mitla Passes.[241] However, the order caused a panic to sweep through the Egyptian ranks, leading to a rout.[242] On 9 June Nasser cut his losses and agreed to a cease-fire with the Israelis. Egypt paid dearly for its incompetence, losing more than ten thousand troops and control of the Sinai, including the eastern bank of the Suez Canal.[243]

Reservists also played a critical role in the central front against the Jordanians. Israel wanted to avoid a fight with Jordan, but King Hussein, who had signed a mutual defense pact with Egypt on 30 May, faced tremendous political pressure from his people—many of whom were Palestinian refugees—to join the battle. Thus, on 5 June the king reluctantly agreed to enter the fight.[244]

In 1948 the Jordanian army had performed well against the Israelis, but much had changed since then. It no longer had British officers in charge of its ground forces. In addition, many of its soldiers deployed to the West Bank were not professionals; they were part-time Palestinian reservists and militiamen who, unlike the Israelis, trained infrequently.[245] That said, the Jordanians still posed a threat to Israel. Several of their units were equipped with modern US-made Patton tanks, and many of its officers were professional and well trained. The seven Jordanian infantry brigades deployed inside the West Bank were arrayed in prepared battle positions supported by two armored brigades deployed near the Jordan valley, plus an Iraqi mechanized brigade in western Jordan that could serve as a counterattack force.[246]

Facing the Jordanians were seven Israeli reserve brigades and one conscript unit:

- Sixteenth Infantry Brigade (known as the Jerusalem or Etzioni Brigade), a reserve unit composed mostly of Jerusalem residents and commanded by Colonel Eliezer Amitai, a veteran of the 1948 war.[247]

- Tenth Armored Brigade (known as the Harel Brigade), commanded by Colonel Uri Ben-Ari, a veteran of the 1956 campaign and one of Israel's first tank commanders. He helped write Israeli armor doctrine in the 1960s.[248]
- Ugdah Peled, a division-sized task force commanded by Brigadier General Elad Peled, whose forces were attached to Central Command from Northern Command.[249] It had three main elements: Thirty-Seventh Armored Brigade (reserve), Forty-Fifth Armored Brigade (conscript), and Ninth Infantry Brigade (reserve).[250]
- Fourth and Fifth Infantry Brigades, both of which were reserve.[251]
- Fifty-Fifth Paratrooper Brigade, a reserve unit commanded by Colonel Mordechai "Motta" Gur, an active-duty officer and Haganah veteran whose paratroopers were mostly tough young men from the kibbutzim.[252]

Although led by veterans, the reservists in the Jerusalem sector were not as prepared as those in the Sinai. For instance, the hundreds of reservists from the Jerusalem Brigade who were demobilized in late May had to be rushed back to service—some still wearing civilian clothes—on 5 June, with little time to prepare. And units tasked with breaching obstacles, such as the paratroopers of the Fifty-Fifth, lacked sufficient quantities of Bangalore torpedoes—used to cut paths through obstacles—and grenades because those supplies had been diverted to the Sinai.[253] The reservists in the Tenth Armored Brigade and Ugdah Peled also went to battle equipped with World War II–era Sherman tanks, whose cannons could not pierce the thick frontal armor of newer Jordanian tanks.[254]

The Jordanian attack began on the morning of 5 June with the capture of the UN compound in Jerusalem and the shelling of Israeli cities.[255] Initially, the Israeli cabinet opted for a limited response, dispatching IAF fighters to strike Jordanian airfields at Mafraq and Amman.[256] But as the IAF attacked, Defense Minister Dayan decided to escalate, authorizing ground incursions into the West Bank to retake the UN compound and prevent the Jordanians from advancing into central Israel.[257] To do so, the Jerusalem Brigade would retake the UN compound and advance toward the southern wall of the Old City of Jerusalem. At the same time, the Tenth Armored Brigade (reserve) and Fourth Infantry Brigade would envelop the city from the north while seizing critical high ground along the Jerusalem–Tel Aviv road.[258] Meanwhile, reserve paratroopers from the Fifty-Fifth, who had redeployed from the Sinai to Jerusalem, would move deeper into Jerusalem on an eastwardly arch around the Old City. North of Jerusalem, Ugdah Peled was preparing to attack Jordanian army units stationed around Jenin and Nablus.[259]

Although they faced determined resistance in a difficult urban environment, the Israelis—with reservists in the lead—defeated the Jordanians in initial engagements inside Jerusalem and farther north in Jenin. Realizing his precarious position, King Hussein ordered his generals to evacuate Jerusalem on the evening of 6 June. A few hours later, he abruptly rescinded that order following a US- and USSR-led cease-fire proposal, which he and the Israelis accepted, that was supposed to go into effect at dawn on 7 June.[260] Although they had agreed to the cease-fire, the Israelis continued to attack, striking the Jordanians at Nablus in the north, while the paratroopers of Fifty-Fifth Brigade seized the Old City.[261] In total, the Jordanians lost 6,000 to 7,000 killed in action; the Israelis lost 302.[262]

The last battles of the war unfolded along the Golan Heights, where the Syrians entered the fray with air strikes in northern Israel. In retaliation, the IAF struck multiple Syrian air bases, destroying nearly half the Syrian air force.[263] Undeterred, the Syrians continued to shell Israeli communities, leading Dayan to authorize an attack by two Ugdot—both of which relied heavily on reservists—to seize the Golan Heights on the morning of 9 June.[264] After a brief but intense battle, the Israelis took the heights, as the Syrians proved incapable of mounting an effective defense and panicked once Israeli troops penetrated their lines.[265]

In total, the Arabs lost approximately 20,000 soldiers, while the Israelis suffered 776 killed in action.[266] Israel improved its strategic depth with its acquisition of the Sinai, the Golan Heights, and the West Bank—a major strategic victory for the Jewish state, which tripled the size of its territory.[267] But in doing so, the IDF had to assume new missions that would challenge its ability to maintain a ready reserve, as the next chapter shows.

IDF reserve units played important roles in all three fronts of the 1967 war, seizing Jerusalem, scaling the Golan Heights, and triggering the total collapse of the Egyptian army in the Sinai. And much of their success can be traced to the fact that many senior officers and staff were veterans of previous wars, and rank-and-file members received intensive peacetime training, unlike their adversaries' reserves. In short, the 1967 war was, in many ways, a story of contrasting reserve forces. The IDF invested in its reserves and achieved decisive results. Its adversaries neglected their reserves, which was particularly problematic for the Egyptians, whose Sinai-based force in 1967 was composed largely of reservists.

The Height of Reserve Performance

Seizing the Sinai, Golan Heights, West Bank, and Gaza Strip gave Israel more defensible borders. But those gains came with costs, as the IDF had to garrison new territory while policing a restive Palestinian population.[268] And because its conscript army was so small, the IDF had to use reservists to meet these new requirements. As an IDF spokesman reported in the summer of 1967, "We will need some of the reservists to hold the area. . . . The borders are enormous compared with what we had before. We have to guard them against attack even though we don't expect any, and we have to maintain order in the occupied areas."[269] As a result, thousands of reservists remained mobilized after the 1967 war, ushering in a new era in the history of the IDF reserve—an era that witnessed the reserve's direct involvement in an increasing number of protracted conflicts and routine security operations.

The first of these protracted engagements took place along the Suez Canal. Egypt and its allies were determined to reverse the outcome of war, declaring during the 1967 Arab Summit that there would be "no peace, no recognition, and no negotiation" with Israel.[270] Egypt and Syria worked with the Soviet Union to rebuild their military capabilities, acquiring new tanks, surface-to-air missiles (SAMs), and antitank guided missiles (AT-GMs).[271] Armed with this equipment, Egypt launched raids against IDF positions on the east bank of the canal to pressure the Israeli government to relinquish control of the Sinai.[272] But rather than back down, Israel retaliated with air and artillery strikes.[273] The resulting conflict—known as the War of Attrition—culminated in August 1970 with a US-brokered cease-fire.[274] More than four hundred Israeli soldiers were killed and hundreds more were wounded in the three-year conflict.[275]

During the War of Attrition, the IDF constructed a network of fortifications along the eastern bank of the Suez Canal known as the Bar Lev Line—named after CGS Chaim Bar Lev—to protect its soldiers from shelling and to provide early warning of Egyptian attempts to cross the canal.[276] Although conscripts initially held the line, which consisted of thirty-two strongpoints, the IDF later called on reserve units.[277] Those reservists tasked with defending the canal served on thirty-day rotations.[278] This service was demoralizing due to the unpopularity of the War of Attrition among the Israeli public and the near-constant threat of air and artillery strikes.[279] Manning the line also reduced training opportunities. In fact, for the army as whole, the period between 1967 and 1973 witnessed a 40 percent decline in training, as units had to focus on routine security operations in the Sinai, West Bank, and Golan Heights.[280] Lost training time was problematic for two reasons. First, it prevented reservists from conducting large-scale mobilization exercises.[281] This contributed to several missteps in the early days of the 1973 Yom Kippur War. Second, rotations to the canal zone and elsewhere deprived reservists of the ability to keep up with changes in IDF tactics and technologies.

IDF successes with the armored corps and air force in 1967 convinced Israeli military and political leaders that these forces and technologies would continue to be decisive in battle. The back-to-back appointments of two armored officers as CGS—Chaim Bar Lev (1968–71) and David Elazar (1971–74)—reinforced such preferences.[282] Under these two officers, the IDF crafted a new tank doctrine called Totality of the Tank. Written by Israel Tal, the doctrine assumed that tanks could fight with little to no infantry support, taking advantage of their long-range cannons to dominate the open deserts of the Sinai and the rocky expanses of the Golan Heights. Infantry would serve in supporting roles, garrisoning fortifications and consolidating the battlefield gains of armored forces.[283]

As it deepened its commitment to armored warfare, the IDF acquired hundreds of new tanks, including 150 US-made M-60 Pattons, as well as 119 combat aircraft armed with new US-made precision-guided munitions (PGMs). PGMs would become increasingly important to Israeli operations and strategy in the coming decades.[284] To improve its mobility and combined-arms capabilities, the IDF also acquired 450 M-113 APCs and 24 M-109 self-propelled howitzers.[285] In short, the IDF leveraged its warming relations with the United States to reshape itself from an infantry army into a more high-tech military centered on tanks and the air force (table 4.3).

These changes produced new budgetary and personnel stresses, especially for reservists.[286] For instance, Israel's equipment-buying spree

Table 4.3. Expansion of IDF Weapons Systems, 1967–73

Year	Combat Aircraft	Main Battle Tanks	Armored Vehicles
1967	214	1,123	Data unavailable*
1971	337	1,400	3,100
1973	354	2,119	4,367

Sources: CIA, "The 1973 Arab-Israeli War," September 1975, 28; CIA, "Military Capabilities of Israel and the Arab States," 26 May 1967, 8; US Department of State, "The Military Balance in the Mideast," 19 November 1971, 2, 19; IDA, "Assessment of Weapons and Tactics Used in the October 1973 Middle East War," 80.
*The IDF had only outdated World War II–era half-tracks until it captured Jordanian M-113s in 1967. It started receiving newer versions from the United States after the war.

following the 1967 war cost more than $100 million, according to CIA estimates.[287] To garrison and police newly occupied areas, the IDF had to double the size of its conscript force from 50,000 to 100,000, which led to growth in the reserves as conscripts completed their active-duty obligations.[288] The IDF was able to achieve this growth by recalling thousands of reservists to active duty and by increasing the maximum age for reserve service from forty-nine to fifty-five.[289]

Fortunately for Israel, changing political and economic conditions helped pay for the rising overhead costs generated by modernization and an increased operational tempo. Most important, Israel benefited from a substantial increase in military aid from the United States, which rose from $7 million in 1967 to $550 million by 1971.[290] Israel's GDP nearly doubled during the same period, softening the blow of increased defense spending.[291]

The IDF's acquisition of high-tech equipment also stressed its personnel system. Maintaining and operating new electronic fire control and target acquisition systems required soldiers and officers with advanced technical training and education. And the army was already competing for such talent with the air force, which typically received the most technically skilled conscripts.[292] That said, the pool of candidates expanded as Israeli public education standards improved and the number of Israelis with college degrees rose from just five thousand in 1950 to nearly thirty-five thousand by the early 1970s.[293]

Nevertheless, Israeli soldiers—even those who were highly educated—needed substantial time to become proficient at operating and maintaining new equipment. Thus, conscript units conducted extensive combined-arms exercises between 1967 and 1973 to learn how to operate, maintain, and integrate their new APCs, tanks, and howitzers. Time constraints limited reservists' ability to conduct similar exercises, which ultimately undermined reserve readiness.[294] For instance, a senior officer in the 679th Reserve Armor Brigade warned his commander at the outset of the 1973 Yom Kippur War that he was unready for combat because he had been given limited opportunities to train on Israel's new tanks.[295] Fortunately for the IDF, when the war started, its reserve readiness levels were high.

In September 1970 Egyptian president Nasser died unexpectedly of a heart attack—just a month after the War of Attrition ended. His successor, Anwar Sadat, concluded shortly after taking power that Egypt and its Syrian allies could conduct a limited attack to retake the Sinai and Golan.[296] He understood, however, that such an attack must unfold quickly and with little warning, taking advantage of the IDF's thinly held defensive lines along the Suez Canal and Golan Heights.[297] Telegraphing an attack would allow the Israelis to mobilize their reserves and reinforce their defenses, as they had in 1956 and 1967. Furthermore, the attack objectives would have to be limited, as Sadat knew the Israelis had recently developed as many as ten nuclear weapons they could employ if the conflict threatened Israel's survival.[298]

At 1400 on 6 October—which fell on Yom Kippur, Judaism's holiest day of the year—ten Egyptian and Syrian divisions attacked into the Golan and across the Suez Canal, having successfully disguised their military buildup as an exercise.[299] Within twenty-four hours, they overran most of the IDF's forward defenses, inflicting heavy losses on front-line Israeli conscript units.[300]

Israeli intelligence services had observed the Egyptian and Syrian buildup in the days leading up to the attack, but they and CGS Elazar had concluded that the Arabs were highly unlikely to attack because they were sure to lose against the superior Israeli military.[301] Consequently, the IDF did not mobilize its reserves, leaving the smaller conscript army and reservists from a second-tier reserve brigade (the Jerusalem Brigade) to hold the Bar Lev Line and absorb the attack by a force that outnumbered them five to one.[302] The odds were no better in the Golan, where a division-sized IDF force with around two hundred tanks faced three Syrian infantry divisions and two armored divisions with nearly a thousand tanks.[303]

There were heated internal debates among senior officials of the Israeli government whether to mobilize the reserves in the days leading up to the war. But the top Israeli military intelligence officer confidently recommended against mobilization because it could severely damage the economy, as had occurred in 1967.[304] Such damage would be compounded by the fact that Israel had to utilize thousands of civilian trucks to mobilize and transport reservists to battle, causing significant disruptions to Israeli industries and public transportation.[305] Prime Minister Golda Meir and Minister of Defense Moshe Dayan also feared that mobilization would make Israel appear to be the aggressor, possibly compromising support from the United States.[306] Senior defense planners had concluded before the war that conscripts could repel an Egyptian attack in the Sinai on their own, providing ample time for the reserves to mobilize.[307]

But the initial Israeli counterattack faced unexpectedly stiff resistance from Arab soldiers armed with new Soviet-made weapons. To improve their ability to defend against the IAF, the Egyptians and Syrians had purchased Soviet-made SAMs that inflicted heavy losses on Israeli aircraft seeking to support the embattled ground forces.[308] On the Syrian front, such systems were responsible for downing as many as thirty-five Israeli aircraft within the first twenty-four hours of fighting.[309] Meanwhile, Egyptian infantry broke through the sand berms of the Bar Lev Line using high-pressure water hoses in just two to three hours—far quicker than the Israelis anticipated.[310] Having breached the obstacles, forward elements of the Egyptian assault force seized high ground from the vastly outnumbered reservists of the Jerusalem Brigade. [311]

From these positions, Egyptian antitank teams fired thousands of newly acquired Sagger ATGMs and rocket-propelled grenades against the initial Israeli counterattack from the Sinai Division, destroying or immobilizing three hundred to four hundred IDF tanks in just thirty-six hours.[312] Such high losses were due in part to the fact that the tanks counterattacked without infantry support—a reflection of a "tank mania" that had overtaken the IDF since the Six-Day War.[313] In the Golan, the IDF suffered similar setbacks, as the Syrian onslaught nearly destroyed the elite 188th and Seventh Armored Brigades.[314]

Fortunately for the Israelis, the reserves mobilized quickly and reversed the Arab gains. In total, four Israeli reserve divisions—143rd, 146th, 162nd, and 210th—as well as reserve elements from the Thirty-Sixth Armored Division, mobilized just hours before the attack began on 6 October when Israeli intelligence services received a report from a reliable source that the Egyptians and Syrians were planning an attack that afternoon.[315] Because there was so little time, reserve officers had to hastily organize their units as they arrived at mobilization centers.[316] Deputy chief of staff Tal ordered Israeli commanders to waste no time and rush units to the front as platoons and companies, rather than wait for complete brigades and divisions to form.[317]

Several factors contributed to the speedy mobilization. As tensions with Egypt grew in the spring and summer of 1973, the IDF moved two reserve brigades closer to the Golan Heights, established a reserve base near the Suez Canal, and formed a new reserve division (210th).[318] The IDF also conducted exercises for newly formed reserve brigades and tested mobilization procedures.[319] Several days before the start of the war, some reserve units proactively staged equipment and adjusted operational plans, as fears of an invasion intensified.[320] Additionally, once mobilization began, reservists and their equipment could move almost unimpeded across Israeli roadways, taking advantage of a lack of civilian traffic during the holiday.[321]

These preparations, as Tal later recalled, allowed the IDF to enter the war "stronger than was planned."[322] In fact, within forty-eight to seventy-two hours, nearly the entire Thirty-Sixth, 210th, and 146th Reserve Armor Divisions were deployed to the Golan Heights, reinforcing the embattled conscripts.[323] On the Sinai front, the 162nd and 143rd Reserve Armor Divisions arrived even faster, reaching the front—albeit in piecemeal fashion—within twenty-four to thirty-six hours.[324] Some elements entered the fight within twelve hours of mobilization.[325]

But the first groups of reservists deployed to the Golan and the Sinai suffered heavy casualties as they encountered a more determined and capable foe than expected. The first Israeli reserve unit to reach the Golan—a tank company led by Uzi Mor—did not appreciate the gravity of the situation on the ground or realize that Syrian forces had essentially overrun the entirety of the heights. Mor's company stumbled into an ambush, losing most of its tanks. Meanwhile, in the Sinai, the Egyptians repulsed the initial counterattack by Avraham Adan's reserve division—the 162nd—near the canal zone.[326]

Despite these setbacks, Adan's and Sharon's divisions adapted. One of the most important adjustment they made was reorganizing their units into combined-arms task forces composed of tanks and infantry to suppress and destroy the Egyptian antitank teams.[327] They also benefited immensely from Egypt's decision to advance beyond the protection of its SAM umbrella on 14 October.[328] Once it did so, the character of the battle shifted into a more fluid tank-on-tank fight, which the Israelis excelled at.[329] Taking advantage of their superior gunnery, Israeli reserve tank crews destroyed 250 Egyptian tanks at a cost of just 20 of their own.[330] Buoyed by these successes, the Israelis went on the offensive, crossing the Suez on 15 October and encircling Egyptian Third Army.[331] Nine days later, the Egyptians and Syrians agreed to a cease-fire, as Israeli ground forces advanced to within artillery range of Damascus in the north and approached Cairo in the south.[332]

The success of the IDF reserve in 1973 was primarily the result of four factors. First, each of the reserve divisions had cadres of full-time personnel who were able to manage the quick mobilization and get units to the front within hours.[333] Second, each reserve division was led by veteran officers such as Sharon and Adan, who, as Dayan noted, "were the major league of the IDF."[334] In fact, Adan's division was staffed by instructors from the IDF's Armor School, who were some of the best crews in the entire army.[335] Adan had previously worked closely with his four brigade commanders, and as he recalled in his memoirs, they "instinctively understood each other."[336] Third, the IDF's intensive reserve training program ensured that tank crews excelled in gunnery; they could often fire two or more accurate shots in the time it took their adversaries to fire one.[337] Fourth, reservists were led by experienced junior officers and NCOs who were trained—and empowered—to seize the initiative amid the chaos of combat. With such training and experience, the Israeli reservists were able to outmaneuver and outshoot their adversaries, who struggled in open combat.

That said, the reserves performed unevenly in the initial days of the war due to the condensed and confused mobilization period. The full-time cadre at reserve depots were caught off guard by the sudden mobilization of 200,000 reservists between 6 and 8 October, as they had assumed at least a forty-eight-hour warning.[338] Making matters worse, much of the cadre had little practice executing such a large-scale mobilization. Since 1967, the IDF had not conducted any major mobilization exercises due to operational and budgetary pressures.[339]

Consequently, some reservists encountered chaos and confusion upon arriving at their armories. In multiple cases, tanks and other armored vehicles had been stripped of their equipment, were in storage, or had not undergone proper maintenance.[340] Because some full-time cadres had not received the mobilization orders, they refused to issue equipment to commanders when they arrived at their depots.[341] Thus, several units had to depart for the front without critical equipment. One brigade in Sharon's division, for instance, left without any half-tracks or mortars.[342] Others lacked machine guns for their tanks.[343] The two reserve divisions destined for the Sinai did not have enough heavy equipment transporters to carry tanks from mobilization centers to the fight, forcing them to drive the vehicles under their own power over long distances, leading to frequent mechanical breakdowns.[344] The IDF lacked enough trucks to move men and material, forcing it once again to requisition civilian vehicles. This brought the civilian economy to a near halt, as trucks used to load equipment from ports and to move goods across Israel became scarce.[345]

The rushed mobilization also undermined unit cohesion and readiness. The need to speed crews to the fighting forced officers to mix and match personnel as they arrived, so soldiers had to fight with men they did not know.[346] Because there was no time for refresher training before entering the fight, some officers and soldiers had to learn how to use new equipment in combat, as opposed to having several days or weeks to train beforehand.[347] And some reservists who had missed training due to other commitments had to relearn how to operate equipment on the way to the front.[348] Nevertheless, as a CIA after-action review observed in 1975, because of the reserves' superior training, "flexibility, adaptability, and high motivation," they were able to deal with the chaos of the war's opening days.[349]

In the end, the 1973 Yom Kippur War was a major tactical success for the Israeli reserves. They mobilized in less than twenty-four hours—with little to no warning—retook the initiative, and defeated well-armed and highly motivated adversaries who had the advantages of surprise and mass. In fact, no other modern reserve force has achieved such a feat. Over the past century of warfare, reservists usually had weeks, months, or even years of premobilization training before entering a major war. But the Israeli reserve proved that its veteran leaders and experienced reserve soldiers had the discipline, training, and confidence to transition within twelve to twenty-four hours from being civilians celebrating a holiday to highly effective soldiers.

A total of 2,515 Israeli soldiers died in the Yom Kippur War.[350] Among the dead were thirteen hundred Israeli officers—losses that would deprive Israel of some of its best tactical commanders.[351] Additionally, about a quarter of its tank inventory and a third of its combat aircraft were destroyed.[352] Such losses shook the IDF's confidence and revealed significant deficiencies in Israeli combined-arms capabilities.[353] Improved Arab air defense systems called into question the IAF's ability to dominate the skies, as it had in 1967.[354] The war also cost Israel about a year's worth of GDP and sullied the IDF's public standing and the reputation of its leaders—military and civilian—who were caught unprepared.[355] Such losses undermined Israel's confidence in its military might and set the stage for significant changes in the IDF's structure and capabilities over the next decade.

Israel's first generation of military and political leaders inherited a formula from the Yishuv for mitigating the reserve dilemma. They ensured that part-time soldiers had veteran leadership and underwent intensive peacetime training—a system that resembled the German reserve organization of the late nineteenth and early twentieth centuries. Israel's founders and military pioneers improved on that formula between the 1948 War of Independence and the 1967 Six-Day War by ensuring that all reservists had active-duty experience gained as conscripts and that full-time officers oversaw their training and commanded large reserve maneuver units. In doing so, they built one of history's most effective reserve forces, as evidenced by the performance of IDF reservists in the Six-Day War and the Yom Kippur War.

But to build such an effective force, Israeli leaders invested heavily in improving the IDF's joint and combined-arms capabilities following the 1956 Suez Crisis. These changes set the conditions for the IDF's transformation from a low-tech infantry army into a high-tech mechanized force that was increasingly dependent on long-service technicians. These developments improved the lethality and survivability of IDF ground units while giving them the ability to strike enemies more quickly, more accurately, and at longer ranges; at the same time, they increased the intellectual demands of soldiering for IDF conscripts and reservists and generated higher overhead costs. These rising technical demands and associated costs—when combined with major changes to Israeli society and its threat environment—would lead to a gradual erosion in the effectiveness of the IDF reserve.

Chapter Five

The Decline of the Israel
Defense Forces Army Reserve

Currently, the army's main areas are cyber warfare and precision
warfare, for which reservists are less needed.
—Brigadier General Shuki Ben-Anant[1]

Over the past forty years, the effectiveness and relevance of the IDF army reserve declined due to a combination of military, political, and socioeconomic trends that unfolded in Israel and around the world. Following the 1973 Yom Kippur War, Israel doubled down on its commitment to high-tech, high-skilled warfare to maintain a decisive qualitative edge over its adversaries and to reduce its own casualties. After the end of the Cold War, that trend accelerated as Israel confronted new adversaries and new types of threats, such as Iranian ballistic missiles and unmanned aerial vehicles (UAVs). To deter and, if necessary, confront such threats, the IDF invested more heavily in expensive stand-off precision strike capabilities, air and missile defenses, and special operations forces to carry out an "offensive-defense" strategy and strike adversaries simultaneously in depth.[2]

Conventional ground forces still played an important role in this updated war-fighting approach, but they got bogged down in protracted security operations in southern Lebanon and the Palestinian territories.[3] Such missions sapped their morale and reduced their opportunities to become proficient in the increasingly high-tech Israeli way of war. In addition, a combination of political and budgetary pressures made chiefs of the General Staff (CGSs) less inclined to train or mobilize reservists; in turn, reservists' willingness to serve declined sharply following Operation Peace for Galilee in 1982.

Combined, these factors produced a widening qualitative gap between regular and reserve ground units, leading to serious consequences. The standing IDF army—composed of conscripts and its professional cadre—was simply too small to meet Israel's national security requirements without reservists, as became apparent during the Second Intifada

(2000–2005) and the 2006 Lebanon War. During those conflicts, Israeli reservists performed poorly when thrust into battle due to insufficient training and a lack of experience in high-intensity combat missions.[4] Subsequent efforts by Israeli military leaders to improve reserve readiness largely failed because budgetary and legal constraints prevented them from increasing reservists' training time and standards. In short, changes to the IDF's way of war and Israeli society in the 1980s and 1990s compromised the effectiveness of the reserve—and, by extension, the entire army—for large-scale combat operations or protracted insurgencies. This chapter examines the decisions and events that led to this situation and their significance for Israeli national security.

Roots of the Reserve Readiness Crisis

The IDF underwent a major transformation in the decade following the Yom Kippur War, and this had profound implications for Israel's ability—and willingness—to maintain a highly trained reserve force. At the heart of this transformation was an urgent sense among IDF personnel—and Israeli society in general—that Israel had lost its qualitative military edge owing to its adversaries' acquisition of advanced Soviet-made arms. During the 1973 war, Egypt and Syria used such weaponry to render entire Israeli brigades combat-ineffective in less than two days of fighting, while temporarily neutralizing the Israeli Air Force (IAF).[5] Despite their effectiveness in 1973, the reserves sustained heavy equipment and personnel losses, especially among the officer corps.[6]

Thus, in the wake of the war, CGS Mordechai Gur (1974–78) and his successor Rafael Eitan (1978–83) aimed to expand the IDF and improve its lethality and survivability.[7] Over the next decade, the IDF doubled the number of maneuver brigades (table 5.1). It added one thousand tanks to its arsenal, and its fleet of armored personnel carriers (APCs) increased from five hundred to more than ten thousand as the IDF sought to improve the combined-arms capabilities of its ground forces.[8] To control this larger force, the IDF organized eight new divisions that could fight as part of two new corps-level headquarters that coordinated multidivision operations in wartime.[9]

To staff these organizations, the IDF convinced thousands of conscripts and reservists to volunteer for professional service, extended the age men could serve in combat units from thirty-nine to forty-four, and reduced the length of initial training for new conscripts.[10] Policy changes also

Table 5.1 IDF Army Growth, 1973–84

Year	Active	Reserve	Full-Time	Combat Brigades (Active and Reserve)*	Israeli Population
1973	83,000	180,500	11,500	36	3,180,000
1974	110,000	250,000	15,000	36	3,422,000
1976	120,000	240,000	15,000	47	3,575,000
1978	120,000	237,000	18,000	43	3,738,000
1980	120,000	240,000	15,000	56	3,922,000
1982	110,000	315,000	15,000	70	4,064,000
1984	104,000	420,000	16,000	70	4,200,000

Sources: IISS, Military Balance 1973, 33; IISS, Military Balance 1974, 34; IISS, Military Balance 1976, 34; IISS, Military Balance 1978, 38; IISS, Military Balance 1980, 43; IISS Military Balance 1982, 56; IISS, Military Balance 1984, 63; CIA, "Israel's Military Edge Continues," June 1986, 2; "Population of Israel," Jewish Virtual Library.
*Includes armor, mechanized infantry, infantry/territorial, parachute infantry, and artillery brigades.

allowed women and civilian contractors to assume greater responsibilities in support roles, freeing men to transfer to combat arms assignments.[11]

These policies, however, caused a spike in defense spending, as personnel and operations costs rose (table 5.2). Israel spent millions to purchase, repair, or upgrade armored vehicles and combat aircraft. And much of this new equipment, such as the IAF's new F-16s and F-15s, had higher per-unit costs than the platforms they replaced.[12] Such sophisticated equipment also required more technical support to maintain and operate. These costs stressed the Israeli budget and economy, especially during the first half of the 1970s.[13] During that period, defense expenditures nearly tripled, accounting for 30 percent of gross domestic product (GDP).[14] Concurrent boosts in US aid provided some relief,

Table 5.2 IDF Personnel Costs (Civilian and Military), 1972–84

Year	Total Personnel Pay (Millions NIS)	Defense Imports (Millions NIS)
1972	0.12	0.26
1974	0.29	0.72
1976	0.51	1.46
1978	1.27	3.07
1980	5.80	10.30
1982	33.00	40.30
1984	404.00	548.00

Source: Israel Central Bureau of Statistics, "Defence Expenditure in Israel," July 2017, 32, https://www.cbs.gov.il/he/publications/DocLib/2019/1758/e_print.pdf.
NIS, Israeli new shekel.

but soaring defense costs remained burdensome, especially as inflation gripped the Israeli economy.[15]

Adding to Israel's economic woes were the second-order operational costs associated with the Yom Kippur War. The death of so many Israeli soldiers had a detrimental effect on industry. As the president of the Manufacturers Association of Israel lamented in 1974, "a thousand to fifteen hundred key people are . . . missing today." The prolonged mobilization of reservists in the year after the war added to the burden because many industries had planned for reservists to be away from work for only a month or less. The mobilization of about 80 percent of the country's trucks during the war also reduced Israeli industrial production by 40 percent and construction projects by as much as 80 percent.[16] To relieve these stresses, which persisted well into the 1980s, Israeli policymakers had to make difficult choices regarding the reserves. Those choices, combined with broader changes to the Israeli threat environment and socioeconomic landscape, inadvertently undermined reserve readiness.

The reliability of the IDF reserve declined after the Yom Kippur War as it struggled to find the time and resources to keep up with changes in Israeli military doctrine and war-fighting technologies. In the immediate aftermath of the war, between 150,000 and 200,000 reservists remained on active duty for four months or more as Israel feared a resumption of hostilities.[17] Some—particularly technicians activated to repair damaged equipment—served as many as two hundred days on active duty after the war.[18] However, Israel could not afford to keep reservists on extended missions due to the impact on the economy. There was also an adverse impact on the personal and professional lives of reservists, some of whom lost their jobs because of their extended mobilization.[19] At the time, reservists had no real protection from employers who punished or sometimes fired them, even though service in the reserves was mandatory. These pressures—together with declining tensions along the Suez—convinced the IDF to release most reservists from active duty by the end of 1974.

Once they were demobilized, reservists had to contended with the new, demanding training program implemented by CGS Mordechai Gur. Gur believed that Israel's pre-1973 reserve training program—which consisted of thirty to forty-five training days a year—was insufficient "in view of the great complexity of modern warfare."[20] Thus, he doubled reserve training obligations for combat units beginning in 1975.[21] At the same time, the IDF established new combined-arms training facilities where reserve units could practice updated tactics and gain experience operating new equipment.[22] However, by the end of the decade, the program had to be scaled back to ten to forty-five days because of its negative impact on the economy and complaints from reservists.[23] Even so, some units and personnel continued to train on the higher end of that range into the 1980s due to high operational demands.[24]

In addition to updating training standards, the IDF worked to enhance the speed and efficiency of reserve mobilization. As discussed in the previous chapter, mobilization in 1973 had been hampered by the lack of vehicles to move personnel and equipment from depots to the front in a timely manner. To address this issue, the IDF acquired twenty-five hundred new trucks.[25] It also developed a digital equipment accountability and maintenance system to track vehicle readiness.[26]

The IDF reserve and active components also confronted several personnel challenges that had significant implications for readiness. For instance, there was a shortage of technicians to operate and maintain new weapons and support systems.[27] One reason for the shortfall was that Israel's improving civilian sectors of the economy—which had risen to western European standards by the late 1970s—attracted talent away from the military.[28] The IDF compensated for this by diverting some recruits with technical backgrounds from the air force to the army, although shortages persisted.[29]

The IDF struggled in the late 1970s to staff its enlarged conscript army and reserve component. One way it dealt with this challenge was to reduce conscript standards, allowing waivers for those with medical issues or criminal backgrounds.[30] It also increased the officer promotion rate, but this reduced the time officers had to learn their jobs.[31] And the aforementioned cuts in initial conscript training likely affected the quality of new soldiers.[32] All these policies had a negative downstream effect on the reserve component, as the personnel entering its ranks after completing conscript service were not as well trained and had less experience.

The reserve component confronted questions about its political reliability as well.[33] In 1977 a new right-wing political party, the Likud, won a plurality of seats in the Knesset, overturning decades of rule by the left-wing Labor Party, whose reputation had been sullied by the Yom Kippur War.[34] Once in power, the Likud charted a more aggressive settlement policy in the Palestinian territories seized in 1967—a decision that generated pushback from some reservists who, like many young Israelis, were becoming more outspoken politically.[35] Meanwhile, the establishment and expansion of settlements forced the IDF to mobilize more reservists for settlement defense.

Reservists were becoming politically active as early as 1973, when some formed a group to protest the government's mishandling of the Yom Kippur War.[36] Five years later, one hundred reservists refused to serve in the West Bank, citing their disgust over the "annexationist aims" of Prime Minister Menachem Begin's government.[37] This antisettlement activism was part of a larger movement—known as Peace Now—that attained international prominence in the late 1970s, as antiwar and antiestablishment activism came to Israel.[38]

These changes in the Israeli political and social environment affected other aspects of the IDF. Israeli youth, for instance, started questioning government policies in general and defense policies in particular. One Israeli student complained to a *New York Times* reporter in 1970 that "the war and army exhaust all our energy," and Israel is "oblivious to everything else."[39] Many Israeli youths were becoming more independent minded, turning away from the collective kibbutz ideals in favor of more individualistic and capitalistic worldviews. Television—which became widespread in Israel in the early 1970s—helped drive these developments by exposing Israeli society to the countercultural currents and consumerism of Western popular culture.[40] Consequently, large segments of Israeli society became critical of defense policies—such as high spending on military programs—and many young Israelis questioned the value of their conscript and reserve service.

By 1980, these developments in the Israeli security, social, and political environment produced five challenges related to maintaining reserve readiness and relevance:

- Reservists were becoming outspoken critics of Israeli security and settlement policies, making them a potential liability for right-wing policymakers who came to power after the 1977 national elections.
- The IDF's efforts to expand its forces by reducing entry, training, and promotion standards diluted the quality of the reserve officer and NCO corps. Additionally, more than a thousand IDF officers and NCOs perished in the 1973 war, depriving reserve units of their veteran leadership.
- The IDF's ongoing transition to a technical army posed challenges for reservists, whose training time was declining in the late 1970s.
- Budgetary constraints associated with the IDF's arms buildup—and investments in high-tech weaponry and highly skilled technicians—restricted the military's ability to increase reserve training periods.
- High operational tempos associated with policing the Palestinian territories and maintaining robust defenses to deter a renewed effort by

Egypt or Syria to recapture the Sinai or Golan deprived reserve units of training time.

All these challenges persisted, and in some cases worsened, over the next two decades.

The Start of the Decline

During the late 1970s and early 1980s, the Israeli security environment underwent a radical change. The threat of large-scale conventional war declined substantially as Egypt made peace with Israel in exchange for regaining control of the Sinai through the US-brokered Camp David Accords. Syria, meanwhile, became less of a threat to Israel without Egyptian support, especially after Syria's intervention in Lebanon in the 1980s bogged down its army.[41] Israel also gained greater protection from the United States as part of the 1981 Agreement for Strategic Cooperation, which led to intelligence sharing, combined military exercises, and weapons development projects, essentially creating Israel's first strategic military alliance.[42]

That said, Israel faced new security challenges as its armed forces became embroiled in an indecisive and unpopular war in Lebanon and as the Palestinians began to resist Israeli control more violently. In addition, Iran—a former ally—became an adversary following its 1979 revolution, eventually becoming Israel's top security threat. Under the clerical regime of Ayatollah Ruhollah Khomeini, Iran established a regional network of allies—the so-called Axis of Resistance—to expand Iranian influence across the Arab world. As part of that effort, Iran launched a campaign to attack Israel through allied and proxy groups, such as Hizballah, and to hijack the broader Arab-Israeli conflict for its own purposes. This new security environment confounded and challenged the IDF and accelerated the decline of the reserves' quality and political reliability.[43] That decline became apparent during Israel's long war in southern Lebanon (1982–2000).

The road to Israel's invasion of southern Lebanon can be traced back to the late 1960s and early 1970s. During that period, Palestinian militants from the Palestine Liberation Organization (PLO)— founded in 1964—launched dozens of attacks into northern Israel from bases inside Lebanon, where the militants relocated following their expulsion from Jordan in 1970.[44] Periodically, the Israelis retaliated with air and ground raids, such as Operation Litani in 1978.[45] The situation worsened in the mid-1970s as Lebanon descended into civil war, allowing the PLO to expand its foothold. Syria also took advantage of the chaos inside Lebanon, where it deployed military forces in 1976, opening a potential second front against Israel.

By 1982, the Israeli government—with the hawkish Ariel Sharon as defense minister—lost its patience.[46] That summer, the IDF launched a massive invasion of southern Lebanon in retaliation for a string of Palestinian terrorist attacks.[47] The invasion force consisted of nine divisions, including thousands of reservists.[48] However, conscript units spearheaded the assault, while reservists played a supporting role in most cases.[49] The goal was to destroy the PLO bases inside Lebanon, install a friendly Christian government in Beirut, and reduce Syria's influence and presence along its border with Israel.[50]

The invasion initially went well for the Israelis. Within six days of crossing into Lebanon, the IDF succeeding in pushing the PLO toward Beirut, lifting the threat of rocket and mortar attacks on Israel's northern communities.[51] The IDF also inflicted heavy losses on the Syrian army in a battle in Lebanon's Beqaa Valley.[52] During that fight, the Israelis tested their new domestically produced Merkava tank, which outperformed Syria's new Soviet-made T-72 tank.[53] In addition, the IAF downed upward of one hundred Syrian aircraft, at the cost of just one Israeli fighter, while destroying fourteen surface-to-air missile (SAM) batteries with newly developed precision-guided munitions.[54] That battle also tested one the IDF's newest reserve brigades—the 409th Paratrooper Brigade—whose special mission was to fight behind enemy lines to identify and destroy enemy armor using new antitank weaponry. The 409th used such capabilities and tactics to destroy more than a dozen Syrian tanks in the Beqaa Valley.[55]

Despite these successes, the invasion unfolded more slowly than anticipated, as the mountainous terrain and underdeveloped road networks of southern Lebanon channeled Israeli units into narrow, predictable avenues of advance. The slow advance, in turn, enabled many PLO fighters to flee northward to refugee camps in Beirut, where Israel would experience one of its most significant setbacks of the war.[56]

In September 1982 Israel's main Lebanese ally—Christian leader Bashir Gemayel—was assassinated by Syrian intelligence agents, ruining plans to install a friendly government in Beirut and fanning the flames of the civil war. Around the same time, the IDF suffered a major—and lasting—blow to its reputation during an operation in the Sabra and Shatila refugee camps in Beirut when IDF-backed Christian militants pillaged the camps, raping, wounding, and killing thousands of civilians. These incidents, combined with rising casualties, caused the Israeli public and world opinion to sour on the Lebanon operation.[57] Facing a mounting domestic and international backlash, Israel withdrew from the Beirut area a year later, taking more defensible positions in southern Lebanon.

In the south, the IDF confronted a growing Shia militant insurgency that eventually included a new Iranian-backed militant group known as Hizballah.[58] To combat these groups and defend their local Christian allies, the IDF had to keep ninety-five hundred soldiers—many of whom were reservists—inside Lebanon between 1983 and 1985.[59] By 1984, however, the rising cost in blood and treasure—and the political backlash it generated—convinced a new Israeli government led by Shimon Peres to extricate the IDF from the morass in Lebanon.[60] A year later, the Israelis completed their withdrawal, retaining a small strip of land—about ten kilometers wide—in southern Lebanon as a security buffer.[61]

Keeping thousands of reservists deployed inside Lebanon between 1982 and 1985 had multiple second-order economic, military, and political effects. Economically, the war cost Israel $2 billion to $5 billion.[62] The activation of reservists disrupted Israeli industry and transportation, though not to the same degree as in 1973. In 1982, for instance, economic production in Israel dropped 5 percent due to the prolonged reserve mobilization. The initial mobilization also disrupted public transportation, as the IDF requisitioned hundreds of buses to shuttle reservists to assembly areas near the Lebanese border.[63] Such economic hardships contributed to Israel's steep economic decline in the early 1980s, which convinced the government to curtail military spending in general and reserve funding in particular.[64]

The prolonged deployment to Lebanon also harmed reservist morale, causing a spike in disciplinary problems and reducing training opportunities. In terms of discipline, thousands of Israeli reservists protested their involvement in the war, which was unpopular due to the perception that Operation Peace for Galilee and subsequent operations in Lebanon constituted Israel's first war of choice.[65] Upward of two hundred reservists outright refused to serve in the summer of 1982, and they were often imprisoned for a month as punishment.[66] Over the next three years, thousands more signed petitions against the war and participated in antiwar protests as part of the reservist-led "There Is a Limit" movement.[67] As many as 10 percent of reservists asked to be excused from service in Lebanon, citing medical, work, or family issues. Work issues were particularly problematic for reservists, as many lost their civilian jobs after being away so long. As the head of the IDF Manpower Division noted in 1985, "Many workplaces find it difficult to abide by a reserve paratrooper who is called up for 60 days a year, so they find ways to get rid of him."[68]

Given these morale and discipline issues, some senior Israeli defense officials questioned the reliability of reserve formations, especially for controversial missions.[69] For instance, Sharon decided not to commit one reserve brigade to combat in the summer of 1982 due to fear that its men would refuse to fight.[70] Indeed, some reservists later admitted in interviews that their will to fight was very low. One reserve sergeant recalled, "The main idea [during operations in Lebanon] was to get out of that place alive." To do so, they avoided aggressive patrols in their assigned sectors.[71]

Reserve units cycled into Lebanon for one- to three-month deployments between 1982 and 1985.[72] But spending months in Lebanon deprived reservists of opportunities to train, as the IDF comptroller reported in 1984.[73] Operational experience could compensate somewhat; however, the majority of operations in the last two years of the war focused on patrols and base defense against low-tech militant groups.[74] Reservists therefore had few opportunities to learn and practice the IDF's increasingly high-tech and high-skilled conventional warfare doctrine.

Despite its heavy involvement in counterinsurgency and stability operations during the 1980s, the IDF continued to focus its training, equipment, and personnel policies on large-scale combat operations against a conventional state adversary such as Syria.[75] But budget constraints due to Israel's poor economic situation—plus distractions caused by the Lebanon conflict—undermined plans to maintain and enhance readiness to meet such contingencies.[76] These pressures forced the Ministry of Defense to slash spending by $48 million in 1983, $485 million in 1984, and $661 million in 1985.[77]

Reduced spending hit the reserves particularly hard.[78] To cut operations and maintenance costs, the IDF reduced reserve personnel strength by lowering the maximum age for drilling in a combat unit from fifty-four to fifty and by deactivating units that used older 1960s-era vehicles.[79] At the same time, it curtailed reserve training and live fire exercises. In doing so, it risked eroding the quality of the army reserve, as reports by the IDF Training Branch and comptroller warned in 1984, given that intensive peacetime training had been key to reservists' battlefield successes in 1967 and 1973.[80]

But even as Israeli defense spending fell, operations costs climbed

Table 5.3 Expansion of IDF Combat Systems, 1986–90

Year	Tanks	Combat Aircraft	Howitzers	APCs
1986	3,900	500	1,200	10,600
1988	3,850	577	1,361	10,700
1990	4,288	553	1,395	10,700

Sources: CIA, "Israel's Military Edge Continues," June 1986, 5; IISS, Military Balance 1988, 103–104; IISS, Military Balance 1990, 106–107.

due to the expansion of the IDF and its investment in new weapons. A growing population, for instance, caused the IDF reserve to expand from around 315,000 members in 1982 to 494,000 by 1988.[81] At the same time, the IDF increased its equipment inventories to arm new formations and improve the army's combined-arms capabilities (table 5.3). And much of that new equipment was expensive to buy and to operate. For example, the IAF's newly acquired F-16 and F-15 fighters cost about twice as much as the F-4s they replaced.[82]

Operating and maintaining these high-tech weapons systems required specially trained personnel, which Israel struggled to recruit and retain in the mid-1980s.[83] One reason for this difficulty was that many officers were leaving the military for more lucrative careers in Israel's booming high-tech industries.[84] Israel was experiencing a growth in these fields as young Israelis educated and trained in Silicon Valley returned home to start their own businesses.[85] To compensate, the IDF had to rely on officers and technicians with less education and training, which likely had a negative effect on the operational capabilities of the conscript and reserve force.[86]

Despite these challenges, the IDF doubled down on its commitment to a high-tech, high-skilled approach to warfare in the latter half of the 1980s under CGS Lieutenant General Dan Shomron. By the late 1980s, Shomron understood that the threat from state actors was declining. Syria was tied up in Lebanon, Iraq and Iran were at war, and Israel and Egypt had signed a peace treaty. Shomron therefore aimed to streamline the IDF while improving its technological edge in select areas to increase force lethality and survivability.[87] In a 1987 interview, Shomron argued: "We must develop weapons that allow us to come out of a war with few casualties, and in order to have this we are forced to cut the army. . . . Obviously, I am in favor of a large, top-quality, and expensive army . . . only unfortunately, these things do not go together. . . . This is why I say quality is the first thing."[88]

To improve the quality of the IDF, Shomron invested in long-range precision-guided munitions and improved intelligence capabilities—including

Israel's first photo reconnaissance satellite (launched in 1988)—to identify, track, and strike targets from afar.[89] At the same time, the IDF invested in midair refueling aircraft so that its fighters could strike further into enemy territory, as the threat from so-called far enemies such as Iraq and Iran was rising.[90] And to protect Israel from retaliatory strikes, the IDF increased its investment in missile defense technologies, developing the Arrow missile defense program with US support.[91]

Shomron oversaw improvements to the army's antitank missiles, tactical UAVs, and the Merkava tank.[92] Acquiring and upgrading this equipment, however, forced the IDF to increase annual spending by about a billion dollars in the late 1980s, further constraining its ability to invest in training for its reserves. These system upgrades also necessitated more highly skilled personnel. As Shomron explained at the time, "Operating a sophisticated weapon calls for highly professional operators, just as an advanced C2 system requires first-class human resources for its command and control."[93]

To streamline the IDF, Shomron deactivated an entire armored division and retired older personnel, while reducing the size of division and corps staff and mothballing aging aircraft and tanks.[94] Israel's increasing birthrate also allowed the IDF to be more selective in terms of which individuals it called to service, meaning that it no longer had to make the same legal and morality waivers that were common in the late 1970s. Men and women who did not want to serve were often granted waivers or discharges.[95]

Shomron's reforms were seemingly validated by the performance of the US military in the 1991 Persian Gulf War, where similar technologies and tactical concepts enabled the United States and its allies to rapidly destroy the Iraqi army while suffering few casualties. Shomron and his successors as CGS maintained their commitment to a vision of a "smaller and smarter" force.[96]

The first test for Shomron was not a high-tech war against a conventional state army; rather, it was a fight against civilians and militants armed with rocks and knives. In Gaza and the West Bank, a generation of young people who had grown up under Israeli occupation since 1967 became increasingly dissatisfied by their lack of independence and their dire economic conditions.[97] These frustrations exploded into widespread riots in Gaza in December 1987 and spread to the West Bank a month later in what became known as the First Intifada (Arabic for "shaking off").[98] Amidst the unrest, a new Palestinian militant group emerged: Hamas. By the 1990s, it would be a major and enduring threat to Israeli security.

The IDF was caught unprepared for the intifada, having spent most of its short history focused on wars against state armies.[99] Thus, the three divisions of conscripts and reservists deployed to Gaza and the West Bank in January 1988 to quell the violence had little to no training in how to deal with mass civil unrest. And IDF leaders were reluctant to train units for problems that, in their view, were largely the responsibility of the border police. Their instinctive reaction was to employ heavy-handed tactics, firing live ammunition and plastic bullets—which can be lethal at close range—into crowds of rioters and protesters.[100] Such tactics killed as many as five hundred Palestinians between 1987 and 1988, but the intifada continued unabated.[101]

The scale, intensity, and endurance of the intifada forced the IDF to deploy thousands of reservists to Gaza and the West Bank. On average, a reserve unit rotated into the territories for multiple sixty-day deployments, performing crowd control, participating in presence patrols, and manning checkpoints.[102] To get around legal restrictions that limited reserve deployments, the IDF cited national emergency procedures—known as Order 8 Call-ups—used during the War of Attrition with Egypt two decades earlier.[103]

Frequent deployments to the territories harmed reserve readiness in multiple ways. Most important, it forced reserve units to cancel training altogether or reduce it to just three days a year.[104] These cuts came after years of reduced reserve training due to the Lebanon conflict and budgetary constraints. But as IDF deputy chief of staff Ehud Barak conceded in a 1988 speech, scaling back reserve training was "the price we must pay at the moment."[105]

Reserve readiness also declined because service in the territories caused disciplinary and morale problems. Between 1988 and 1990 as many as 160 reservists—including some officers—refused to serve in the territories, citing their opposition to the IDF's heavy-handed tactics.[106] Five hundred others wrote letters to Prime Minister Yitzhak Shamir, requesting to be released from military service.[107] Reservists were also outspoken critics in the media, as they were not subject to the same censorship regulations as conscripts. For instance, one reserve soldier admitted to the *New York Times* in 1989, "I was disgusted when I got my notice [to serve in the Palestinian territories]. . . . It was against my principles to even be there."[108] Those who refused to serve faced harsh punishment, as Yitzhak Rabin—now the minister of defense—sentenced them to several months in prison.[109]

Reservists and conscripts alike were particularly upset that senior commanders provided limited guidance on the rules of engagement. Essentially, each battalion or company commander could dictate how to deal with protesters or militants, which led to "total chaos," in one soldier's estimation. Some units acted harshly, while others were more restrained. Because soldiers who acted aggressively could face criminal prosecution back home, many chose to avoid patrols or other assigned missions.[110]

Several months into the First Intifada, CGS Shomron, who later admitted he "had misjudged the events," started to take the unrest more seriously and adjusted tactics.[111] IDF commanders discarded the view that counterinsurgency and stability operations were police matters that distracted from conventional operations.[112] To prepare soldiers for such duties, they acquired more riot control gear and implemented new tactics such as establishing mobile checkpoints.[113] The Ministry of Defense also replaced reservists with conscripts and specially trained border police units, which reduced the average reserve deployment to the territories from sixty-two to forty-four days a year by the early 1990s.[114] Combined, these tactics helped quell the intifada by 1993.

From a military perspective, the First Intifada exposed deep problems within the IDF and its reserve component. Reservists demonstrated a questionable will to fight, and their tendency to speak out publicly against their missions made them a political liability.[115] Their utility for conventional operations was also on the decline because of fewer training opportunities in the 1980s. Such developments prompted some Israeli military commentators to warn that the IDF was losing its conventional war-fighting edge. As Israeli military historian Martin Van Creveld lamented at the time, "What used to be one of the world's finest fighting forces is rapidly degenerating into a fourth-class police organization."[116]

Nevertheless, Israel remained dependent on its army reserve for cultural, military, and fiscal reasons. Culturally, many Israelis valued their reserve service as a way to escape civilian life and bond with old army friends. Others argued that the reserve was a critical institution for building societal cohesion—just as Ben-Gurion had envisioned thirty years earlier.[117] Fiscally, it made sense to keep a trained reserve, as budgetary pressures prevented the IDF from developing a more expensive all-volunteer force like the US Army. Most conscripts, for instance, cost the IDF only about $90 a month, while Social Security covered much of the cost of the reserves' pay.[118]

Primarily, however, Israel remained committed to its reserve because it lacked sufficient full-time personnel. Even with an expanded conscript force, the IDF had to call thousands of reservists to action in Lebanon and in the Palestinian territories in the 1980s. In other words, the IDF could not function without the reserves, and Israeli cultural and political norms almost certainly would have prevented it from eliminating the reserves if it tried. The problem was that the qualitative gap between the reservist and the conscript was growing and would widen significantly in the 1990s and 2000s, forcing the IDF to reconsider long-held policies and norms related to reserve service.

The IDF: Distracted and Demoralized

During the mid to late 1990s, reserve readiness plummeted due to three developments. First, the Israeli security environment changed in such a way that IDF leaders thought they could meet the bulk of operational requirements with conscripts supported by few, if any, reservists. Second, operational demands and budgetary restrictions affected the IDF's ability to provide the necessary time and resources for reservist training. These constraints resulted from the IDF's ongoing evolution into a technical army, growing competition for government resources, and the increased size of the Israeli military because of rising immigration and birthrates. Third, new legislation passed in the late 1990s reduced annual reserve training requirements. Because of these developments, Israeli reservists—especially those in the combat arms—were unprepared when mobilized for war in the 2000s.

In the 1990s the IDF revised its military doctrine to focus on precision strikes conducted jointly by highly trained conscript units, the air force, and the intelligence services. This shift had begun in the 1980s under CGS Shomron but was interrupted by the First Intifada. Shomron's two successors, Ehud Barak (1991–95) and Amnon Lipkin-Shahak (1995–98), took advantage of the relative peace of the early to mid-1990s to restart and accelerate these reforms.[119] They did so based in part on lessons learned from observing the US military's stunning victory over the Iraqi army in the 1991 Persian Gulf War.[120] The United States demonstrated that modern military aircraft equipped with precision-guided munitions and informed by digital intelligence and command and control systems could destroy the ground and air forces of a formidable Arab army within weeks. Based on these lessons and its similar experience against the Syrians in 1982, the IDF adjusted its priorities and spending to focus on enhancing its precision strike capabilities.[121]

The IDF rationalized these reforms due to shifts in the threat environment. By the early to mid-1990s, Israel's main adversaries were Iran and Iraq—the so-called far threats.[122] During the Persian Gulf War, Iraq had shown its ability to threaten the Israeli homeland by launching forty ballistic missiles against Israeli cities—the first time major Israeli population centers had come under conventional military attack since 1948.[123] Iran, meanwhile, provided military and financial support for Hizballah attacks on Israeli soldiers in southern Lebanon's security zone. The Israelis also feared that Iran was developing a nuclear weapons program that could pose an existential threat to Israel.[124]

A conflict between Israel and either one of these powers would almost certainly occur primarily through long-range missiles or via militant proxies such as Hizballah. Iraq's army had largely been destroyed by the United States in the Persian Gulf War, and it lacked the ability to reconstitute its strength due to extensive sanctions imposed after that war. Iran was isolated internationally and was still recovering from the Iran-Iraq War (1980–88). Neither state—before or after their respective wars—had the ability to project and sustain substantial conventional ground forces beyond their borders. Thus, the only credible ground threat was the Syrian army, which was not well positioned for a conflict with Israel due to the country's deteriorating economy and the loss of substantial Russian military aid following the collapse of the Soviet Union.[125]

In the unlikely event of a major war, the IDF believed it could wage "offensive-defense" attacks in depth against the Syrians using new precision-guided weapons employed primarily by the air force and select—mostly conscript—ground units.[126] To combat Hizballah in the security zone, the IDF relied almost exclusively on the air force and specially trained commandos.[127]

Army reservists were rapidly become irrelevant to Israeli security. In fact, in 1993 the Ministry of Defense announced that it was reducing reliance on reservists by as much as 50 percent for everyday missions, due to the growing size of the IDF's conscript cohort.[128] The Israelis believed these reductions would save as much as $139 million a year, because the IDF would not have to pay reservists for lost civilian income.[129] And by the late 1990s, the IDF could fill operational gaps by turning to specialized conscripts battalions and border police units established for routine security operations.[130] The IDF also published an updated security doctrine—called Crossword 2000—that envisioned the ability to defend against an external attack "without being as dependent on reservists."[131]

The IDF was able to rely more heavily on the active army because its yearly intake of new conscripts increased rapidly in the late 1980s and early 1990s due to a booming population. Between 1984 and 1994 the size of the active Israeli army grew from 104,000 to 114,700, while its cadre of full-time professionals increased from 16,000 to 19,300.[132] Israel's population grew from 4.8 million in 1990 to more than 6 million by the end of the decade as hundreds of thousands of new immigrants—including thousands of youths eligible for conscription—arrived from the Soviet Union and Ethiopia.[133]

The growth of the conscript force had negative effects on reserve readiness. As conscript cohort grew, the number discharged into the reserve grew as well, leading to a massive increase in the army reserve from 315,000 in 1982 to nearly 500,000 a decade later.[134] The problem was that there were not enough missions, resources, or instructors to provide new reservists with meaningful assignments and training. Consequently, up to 40 percent of reservists were not mobilized at all or were given menial duties such as manning checkpoints.[135] This could be demoralizing for reservists, who were pulled away from their jobs and families for no clear purpose.[136]

Budgetary constraints also reduced the IDF's ability to train reservists during the 1990s. Although the Israeli economy expanded, defense spending remained near or below 10 percent of GDP—a major decline compared to the 1970s and 1980s, when it ranged between 14 and 30 percent.[137] And throughout the 1990s, actual defense expenditures and US military aid remained relatively flat at around $3 billion per year.[138]

The IDF also had to contend with rising overhead costs as it continued to maintain a large inventory of armored vehicles that consumed lots of fuel and required specialized technical support. To attract and retain the highly skilled personnel needed to operate and maintain its increasingly complicated equipment, the IDF had to invest more in pay, education, and benefits; as a result, personnel costs rose by as much as 40 percent between the late 1970s and the mid-1990s.[139] New weapons acquired in the 1990s, such as the F-15I and the Dolphin submarine, added to costs as Israel aimed to improve its long-range strike capabilities.[140] As Van Creveld argues, these equipment and personnel trends shifted "the balance from fighters in favor of technicians."[141]

Because of these two trends—flat defense spending and rising overhead costs—the IDF had to cut its conscript and reserve forces to maintain readiness. CGS Barak focused on cutting "whatever does not shoot," leading him to reduce the IDF's administrative and maintenance staff by around ten thousand billets.[142] For the reserve component, the IDF scaled back training and released men from their reserve obligations seven years ahead of schedule. And, as already noted, the IDF replaced some reserve units in the West Bank with conscripts and border police, who were generally cheaper—and less controversial—to deploy.

The reduction in reservists' service obligations was the result of a 1997 law. Until the mid-1990s, there were no restrictions on how many days reservists could train each year or how many days they could be mobilized for operational assignments. That changed in 1997 when the Knesset—with support from the Ministry of Defense—capped the yearly reserve activation period at thirty-six days, at least five of which were to be dedicated to training. However, during a state of emergency, the IDF could keep reservists activated for an unlimited period using its Order 8 mobilization authority.[143] Consequently, by the end of 1997, the average reservist was training or performing operational missions for a maximum of twenty-four days a year (most of this time was not training related), compared to the thirty to forty-five dedicated training days most reservists had in the 1960s or 1970s.[144]

The Knesset and the Ministry of Defense hoped this reduction in reserve mobilization would save $140 million a year and address the morale crisis among Israeli reservists.[145] According to a 1995 poll, as many as 72 percent of reservists considered their service demoralizing or irrelevant.[146] And according to an internal IDF poll conducted in 1996, as many as 63 percent believed Israeli society actively encouraged them to avoid reserve duty.[147] At the time, some Israeli reservists were still being reprimanded or even fired by civilian employers for participating in military training or operational assignments.[148]

Faced with such pressures, many reservists concluded that military service was not worth the personal and professional sacrifice.[149] Thus, by 1996, as many as 50 percent of reservists failed to report for duty. These high levels of absenteeism led CGS Shahak and others to warn that declining reserve morale was undermining Israel's ability to defend itself.[150] In addition, many reservists thought reserve duty was only for "suckers" and sought to be excused from mobilization and training, according to a 1997 IDF comptroller's report.[151]

These attitudes reflected substantial changes taking place in Israeli society and in Israel's strategic environment. Since the late 1970s, Israel had not faced a realistic existential threat outside of Iran's nascent nuclear program, and the recent conflict in Lebanon was unpopular among many Israeli youth.[152] Israeli society in general was suffering from a sort of military fatigue following decades of war and indecisive low-intensity conflicts. Popular attitudes toward the military were also changing, as evidenced by

Israeli films and novels that depicted military life as depressing.[153] In addition, Israel had become increasingly urban, and Israelis were focused on individualistic pursuits in the thriving private sector and tech industries rather than in the military.[154] In fact, by 2000, only 2 percent of Israelis were involved in agriculture and the kibbutzim, where many top Israeli commanders and soldiers had emerged during the 1950s and 1960s.[155]

To make reserve life more appealing for the new urban Israeli, the government reduced the burdens of military service, and the IDF improved benefits and employee protection. Pay for officers and NCOs increased, reserve facilities were renovated, and civilian employers were legally prevented from firing or disciplining reservists for attending training.[156] Universities were required to allow reservists to make up work missed due to their reserve service.[157] The IDF also created special awards and ceremonies to publicly recognize "outstanding reservists" and give them a sense of pride in their duty.[158]

Despite these efforts, reserve readiness declined significantly in the 1990s. With only six training days a year, units struggled to maintain proficiency in their military specialties. This was especially true for armored, artillery, and mechanized infantry units, which rarely had an opportunity to use their equipment because, when deployed to the West Bank, they operated mainly as dismounted infantry, manning checkpoints or escorting vehicles. Many of these same units failed to keep up with regular vehicle maintenance, meaning that those vehicles would not be ready at the start of a crisis, as had occurred in 1973.[159] Reserve officers were unable to keep up with the rising professional and educational standards of the regular army, widening the qualitative gap between conscript and reserve units.[160]

The declining experience levels of IDF trainers also undermined reserve readiness. Veteran officers and NCOs generally oversaw IDF reserve training in peacetime, in contrast to the US and other armies, where reservists generally supervised their own training. In the past, the Israelis benefited from having trainers with extensive experience in conventional military operations. But beginning in the early to mid-1980s, veteran trainers started retiring or moving into the senior ranks, and their replacements were experienced primarily in low-intensity conflict against groups such as Hizballah and Hamas.[161] These developments concerned CGS Shahak, who warned in 1997 that the reserves were losing experienced cadres and starting to perform poorly in exercises.[162]

Shahak's successor, CGS Shaul Mofaz, sought to reverse this trend. In 1999 he warned that the reserve was ill prepared to fight a major war because of inadequate training, and Israel could not fight such a war without its reserves. To improve reserve readiness, Mofaz announced plans to overhaul training.[163] First, he reduced reservists' involvement in routine security operations, allowing them to focus on field and classroom exercises.[164] The IDF attempted to rely on digital training centers and new urban combat facilities to boost the realism of exercises.[165] Additionally, the General Staff examined ways to boost the experience and professionalism of reserve units by adding more career professionals to their ranks.[166] Unfortunately for the IDF, these measures came too late to have a significant impact before the Second Intifada erupted in October 2000, forcing reservists back into high-intensity combat for the first time in more than a decade.

In summary, by the late 1990s, the IDF army reserve was no longer the elite fighting force it had been in the 1960s and 1970s. Its once rigorous peacetime training program had declined from thirty or more days to just several days a year. Meanwhile, the average reservist's motivation to serve was questionable. Reservists also had few opportunities to advance their technical skills and knowledge due to budgetary shortages, time constraints, and declining experience among Israeli trainers.

Consequences of Decline

The IDF faced back-to-back crises in the first decade of the twenty-first century—the Second Intifada (2000–2005) and the 2006 Lebanon War—both of which required it to mobilize and deploy thousands of reservists. Fortunately for Israel, the reserves' declining readiness did not have a major impact on IDF performance during the Second Intifada, as most reservists were assigned routine security missions such as manning checkpoints. Conscripts, the intelligence services, and the air force carried the burden of more complicated operations. But when reservists did have to participate in such operations, their performance was uneven at best.

The Second Intifada started on 28 September 2000 when Palestinian militants launched a wave of suicide bombings against Israeli civilians and military targets. The Palestinian Authority (PA), the interim self-governing body established in the 1990s as part of the Oslo Accords, gambled that such attacks would force Israel to make concessions in the stalled peace talks. The PA, however, miscalculated. The Israeli government's response to the uprising was robust, especially after Ariel Sharon—a well-known hawk—became prime minister in 2001.[167]

The IDF faced a much different battle space compared with the First

Intifada, which involved mostly mass protests and rioting. Instances of organized violence by groups such as Hamas were rare. During the Second Intifada, the IDF faced an urban terrorist campaign in which multiple groups—the PA, Hamas, and the Palestinian Islamic Jihad—conducted near-daily bombings and shootings against Israelis.[168]

The unprecedented scale and intensity of the violence forced the IDF to activate and deploy thousands of reservists. During the first two to three years of the intifada, as many as twenty thousand reservists were on duty at a single time, serving tours of twenty-seven to forty-three days.[169] The declaration of a national state of emergency allowed deployments to extend beyond the new service limits put in place in 1997. By generally limiting reserve units' rotations to two months, the IDF could minimize the negative impact on the civilian economy. Many reserve officers, however, worked upward of 180 days a year.[170]

The initial wave of reserve rotations to the West Bank revealed a host of equipment and training problems. Many units did not know how to operate their equipment, while others had outdated and insufficient quantities of basic supplies.[171] One reservist recalled that his unit did not have enough body armor and helmets, and each soldier had only one magazine for his rifle, rather than the standard seven magazines per rifleman.[172] And units were hastily thrown into action with little to no preparation, beyond an abbreviated three-day course on counterinsurgency tactics.[173]

The lack of training was not a major issue at first because the IDF planned to have reservists perform routine missions such as guarding the Lebanese border or operating checkpoints.[174] This freed conscripts for more difficult missions such as locating and destroying weapon-producing facilities.[175] Even so, these routine missions were often quite dangerous. Manning a checkpoint made soldiers vulnerable to sniper attacks or suicide bombers. In the words of one reservist, they were "like sitting ducks."[176]

Despite these difficult circumstances, 85 to 97 percent of reservists reported for duty when called.[177] Unlike the previous war in Lebanon, most Israelis viewed IDF operations in the Second Intifada as defensive in nature, not a war of choice.[178] Plus, Palestinian terrorists were directly targeting civilians. Thus, even though many young Israelis no longer viewed reserve service as desirable, they showed up and fought. As one reservist told a journalist, "[I] don't really like reserve duty. I like my color TV; I like my couch. But we feel like this is part of our duty."[179]

Nonetheless, there were pockets of resistance. Some reservists protested the length of mobilization or the number of Israelis who were not required to serve at all.[180] In fact, about 10 percent of the reserve force was completing the lengthier thirty-day mobilizations during the intifada. Others were still managing to obtain medical, family, or work-related deferments, and members of the ultra-Orthodox community were largely exempt from service, allowing them to pursue religious studies.[181] This created resentment among reservists who did serve.[182] In a 2001 television interview, one reservist explained that many in his unit felt like "suckers" for responding to call-ups, knowing that only about 20 percent did so.[183]

Adding to these frustrations was the ongoing employment discrimination against reservists, despite laws enacted in the 1990s to prevent such behavior.[184] During a 2000 forum with CGS Mofaz, one reservist revealed, "My boss told me that I was to blame for missing workdays, because everyone knows that anyone who really wants to get out of reserve duty has no trouble doing it, so it must be that I really wanted to be there."[185] Mofaz recalled during the same forum that he received reports of employers not hiring reservists if they participated in too many training days a year—a problem that persists today.[186]

Given such incentives to avoid service, some reservists went AWOL or refused to deploy, as many had done in the 1990s.[187] Although a few were arrested for these violations, the IDF allowed most of these incidents to go unpunished, likely hoping to avoid a repeat of the high-profile imprisonment of reservists that had captured media attention in the 1980s.[188] To make service more appealing, the IDF and the Knesset improved reserve benefits. Soldiers serving more than thirty-two days were paid an additional $27 to $42 a month, and they received life insurance coverage for the first time.[189] To oversee the improvement and management of the reserve component, the IDF created the position of chief reserve officer.[190]

The dangers of reserve service were on display in 2002 when the IDF deployed seven reserve brigades to the West Bank to participate in or support major combat operations.[191] That spring, a Palestinian suicide bomber murdered thirty civilians at a hotel in Netanya. In response, the Israelis launched Operation Defensive Shield (29 March–10 May 2002)—a massive security sweep that targeted terrorist infrastructure throughout the Palestinian territories.[192]

During the operation, Israeli reserves played a lead role in a key battle at the Jenin refugee camp between 1 and 11 April 2002. The IDF intended to sweep through the camp—which was and still is a hotbed of terrorist activity—using two brigades: the Fifth Infantry (reserve) and the more experienced First Golani Infantry (conscript).[193] However, some Israeli officers were concerned about the reserve brigade's readiness for such a difficult assignment.[194] For instance, it had no training in urban warfare, yet it was tasked to control six city blocks where thirteen thousand people resided.[195] Among those residents were hundreds of militants from the Palestinian Islamic Jihad and other groups led by veteran commander Abu Jandal, who had fought in Lebanon and served in the Iraqi army.[196] The Fifth Brigade was also short of basic equipment such as body armor and helmets, due in part to budgetary shortfalls.[197] As one reservist later surmised, "Other than the air force, this is an army that is held together by masking tape and rope and there is always a lack of equipment."[198] In addition, the Fifth Brigade was commanded by a colonel who had just been assigned to the unit, meaning that he had little to no time to assess its capabilities.[199]

The operation began on 3 April when the 340th Division (reserve) established a cordon around the refugee camp. To clear the camp, the Israelis advanced on two avenues: Fifth Brigade moved in from the northeast, and a battalion of the Golani Brigade advanced from the south.[200] The reservists moved slowly and methodically—due in part to a lack of developed intelligence on the threat environment they were entering. Once in the camp, they encountered improvised explosive devices (IEDs) and sniper fire, which killed a veteran company commander of the lead element.[201] The commander's death shocked the reservists, who were not expecting heavy resistance.[202]

The Palestinian militants were surprised that the reservists were moving into the camp on foot, rather than behind the protection of armored vehicles. A captured militant later said, "They knew that any soldier who goes into the camp on foot is going to get killed. It baffles me to see a soldier walking in front of me."[203] Faced with heavy resistance, the reservists slowed their advance to a crawl, moving only about fifty yards a day. Meanwhile, the more experienced Golani Brigade advanced steadily from the south, having placed armored bulldozers in the lead to sweep for IEDs.[204]

Upset by the slow pace of operations, senior IDF commanders ordered Fifth Brigade to increase its tempo on 6 April.[205] As the pressure mounted, a company of reservists stumbled into a booby-trapped house that killed thirteen soldiers—the IDF's largest loss of life in a single day in twenty years. At this point, Fifth Brigade adjusted its tactics. To clear the remaining portions of the camp, it placed armored bulldozers, APCs, and tanks in the lead, and any resistance was met by tank fire, snipers, and Apache attack helicopters.[206] By 11 April, the camp was under control. Thirty IDF soldiers—including twenty-three reservists—died in the operation, along with fifty Palestinians.[207]

Ultimately, the battle was an IDF success, as it cleared the camp of terrorist groups and dismantled the Palestinian Islamic Jihad's weapon-producing facilities and associated caches. But the cost was high for the reservists of Fifth Brigade, who struggled to adapt to the realities of urban combat. One company commander later said the battle "was not like what we were trained for. It was something else, because on every corner, on every house there were bombs, booby traps, people with bombs on them, [or] mines."[208] The lack of training was undoubtedly a factor in the unit's struggles. But so was the decision by senior commanders to give an underprepared reserve brigade such a challenging task.

After Defensive Shield, the IDF gradually reduced its reliance on reservists and cut the number of days they served in the territories.[209] In fact, by the mid-2000s, reservist support of routine security operations had declined 70 percent from 1980s levels.[210] Reservist training and operational time in general declined from about 10 million days in 1990 to 2.5 million by 2004.[211]

Four factors drove this trend. First, Palestinian attacks declined from a peak of 452 in 2002 to 45 in 2005 (following Defensive Shield and subsequent sweeps)—a trend that accelerated after Israel erected the first segments of the security wall to isolate Palestinian communities.[212] Second, Israel's 2005 expulsion of settlers from the Gaza Strip reduced the amount of territory the IDF had to defend.[213] Third, the IDF shifted its tactics from large security sweeps to targeted raids launched by highly trained conscripts, the air force, or the intelligence services, which ultimately pressured Hamas to agree to a cease-fire.[214] Fourth, the IDF assigned routine security missions to new conscript and border police units.[215]

As the IDF reduced reservists' involvement in security operations, it cut their training and released some reservists from their service obligations at age forty.[216] These policies were part of CGS Moshe "Bogie" Ya'alon's efforts to streamline the IDF and redirect funding toward modernization programs such as the digitalization of command, control, and intelligence systems.[217] Under Ya'alon, the air force and navy expanded their ranks, as both became more central to Israeli security doctrine. At the same time, the IDF was dealing with budget cuts. The Israeli economy was in decline due to the global recession and the negative impact of terrorism on Israeli commerce and tourism.[218] In 2003, for instance, the IDF's budget was slashed by $1.7 billion to free funding to boost the economy.[219]

Faced with declining budgets and rising operational costs associated with the Second Intifada, the IDF decided to pause nearly all reserve training in 2003.[220] As IDF ground forces commander Major General Yiftah Ron Tal explained at the time, "The [budgetary] situation has forced us to stop all training exercises for reserve units not because we don't think they need to train—they must—but because we don't have the capability to invest in resources."[221] The cuts continued over the next two years.[222]

When units had the opportunity to train, they did so in a time-constrained environment that did not realistically simulate battlefield conditions. Units at the battalion level and below typically had only one to five training days, reducing opportunities to train in the field.[223] Brigade- and division-level exercises could run longer, but most were canceled or severely curtailed between 2002 and 2006.[224] When two reserve brigades had the opportunity to train in 2006, they did so as part of a command post exercise, rather than an actual field maneuver.[225] This reduction in the quantity and quality of training almost certainly reduced Israel's reserve readiness. As one reserve NCO explained, "Once I started doing tours and doing less training, I realized my skill deteriorated. I realized I was not fit and accurate. On my last training exercise, I saw how my skills had completely gone."[226]

The Second Intifada was a costly experience for Israel. During the five-year conflict, 1,063 Israelis lost their lives, many of them civilians. For the Palestinians, the toll was even higher: 3,659 dead and 29,035 wounded.[227] The IDF and security services succeeded in suppressing the uprising, but in doing so, they had to significantly reduce their readiness for a large-scale conflict. Operational and budgetary constraints also forced the IDF to reduce reserve training standards, which had been in decline since the 1990s.

Israel had little time to recover from the Second Intifada before it confronted its next major crisis: a thirty-four-day war with Hizballah in the summer of 2006. The IDF had withdrawn from nearly all of southern Lebanon in 2000. In the decade leading up to the withdrawal, more than 150 IDF soldiers—including some reservists—died in Hizballah attacks inside the security zone. For the most part, the IDF retaliated with air strikes, artillery fire, and Special Forces raids, such as in 1993 during Operation Accountability and in 1996 during Operation Grapes of Wrath. Such operations, however, were mostly ineffective, as Hizballah continued its attacks undeterred and used civilian casualties caused by Israeli air strikes to boost its popularity among the Lebanese.[228] After the Israeli withdrawal, Hizballah attacks into northern Israel continued.

On 12 July 2006 twenty Hizballah fighters infiltrated northern Israel and ambushed a patrol of Israeli reservists from the Ninety-First Territorial Infantry Division near the village of Zar'it.[229] Three reservists died in the ambush; Hizballah kidnapped two others who later died—either in captivity or shortly after the ambush.[230] In a failed attempt to rescue the abductees, five more soldiers were killed by Hizballah mortar fire and IEDs.[231]

In the weeks prior to the ambush, the Ninety-First's commander, Brigadier General Gal Hirsch, sought to replace the reservists on the Lebanese border with better-trained regulars, given the rising tension with Hizballah. His request was denied by the CGS and Northern Command because of troop shortages. The IDF considered the Lebanon border to be a secondary theater, and its attention remained focused on the Golan Heights, the West Bank, and Gaza, which had fallen under the control of Hamas following the Israeli withdrawal in 2005.[232]

The new Israeli prime minister, Ehud Olmert, responded forcefully to the ambush, authorizing a massive aerial campaign to punish Hizballah and set the conditions for the release of the captured Israeli soldiers.[233] The air strikes were unable to stop Hizballah's short-range rocket fire. In total, nearly four thousand Hizballah rockets fell in northern Israel, killing forty-four civilians over thirty-four days.[234] To suppress the rocket fire, Olmert reluctantly authorized a ground incursion into southern Lebanon that included thousands of reservists, who, despite their limited training since 2002, had to immediately assume front-line combat roles against a determined and well-armed foe.[235]

As the IDF's attention turned to smaller-scale counterinsurgency operations, it abolished its intermediate-level corps headquarters. Therefore, during the 2006 Lebanon War, Northern Command directly controlled ground operations.[236] Its primary maneuver unit was the Ninety-First Division, which contained a mixture of regular and reserve units as well as attached special operations forces from the Egoz and Maglan units.[237] The Ninety-First controlled the entire Lebanon-Israel border until 21 July, when the 162nd Armored Division arrived from Southern Command to take over the eastern portion. The 366th Reserve Armor Division served as the theater reserve beginning on 30 July and would later enter Lebanon between 8 and 10 August.[238] Elements of the Ninety-Eighth Parachute Division and Thirty-Sixth Armored Division provided additional attachments to the Ninety-First. The Ninety-Eighth also deployed into Lebanon, conducting an air assault operation to the Litani River with reserve and regular paratroopers.[239]

The war caught the IDF at a transition point under its new CGS, Dan Halutz, who was the first air force general to rise to the IDF's seniormost rank. Shortly after taking command, Halutz developed the *Keshet* (Rainbow) Plan to enhance IDF preparedness for low-intensity conflicts such as the Second Intifada, while retaining its capability for conventional warfare.[240] To that end, the IDF invested more heavily in unmanned systems and precision strike capabilities to pinpoint and attack terrorist targets and conventional military forces.[241] Halutz believed airpower could be the decisive arm of modern warfare, meaning that Israel could, in theory, win wars with little need for ground forces.[242] However, ground forces—and reservists—would still be required to hold ground and protect Israeli territory from raids by groups such as Hizballah. In a May 2006 speech celebrating the IDF reserve, Halutz reminded reservists, "We still need you and will continue to call on you."[243]

Halutz's confidence in airpower was evident in the IDF's initial attempt to defeat Hizballah in 2006 through precision air and artillery strikes. In fact, Halutz did not mobilize army reservists at the start of the war, despite requests from front-line commanders to do so.[244] After the war, he acknowledged that this had been a mistake, but at the time, he thought a large ground operation was not politically feasible because of the casualty risks.[245] During Halutz's time as CGS, the IDF, with the exception of the Ninety-First Division, conducted minimal planning and exercises for a ground strike against Hizballah.[246] In the event such an operation was necessary, Halutz was willing to allow only a brigade- to division-sized force to enter Lebanon, as opposed to the two- to three-division force some commanders wanted.[247]

The problem with airpower is that it generally does not have the same effect on a decentralized fighting force like Hizballah as it does on a more conventional army.[248] Unlike most Arab militaries the IDF had fought in the past, Hizballah lacked a highly centralized command, control, and communications (C3) network.[249] Precision strikes against its C3 nodes, therefore, did not significantly erode the group's cohesion or its ability to fight. In addition, Hizballah fighters were difficult to identify and strike from the air, as they operated mostly as light, dismounted infantry and often wore civilian clothes and drove civilian vehicles. The IAF managed to destroy much of the group's medium- and long-range rockets systems, but the lighter, mobile short-range rockets and mortar teams were far more difficult to locate and destroy.[250] Thus, despite the IAF's best efforts, Hizballah maintained a steady barrage of close to one hundred rockets a day into northern Israel.[251]

Facing pressure to eliminate the rocket threat, CGS Halutz reluctantly authorized a ground incursion to create a buffer zone in southern Lebanon and set the conditions for the entry of a multinational peacekeeping force.[252] But casualty aversion, breakdowns in command and control, and confusion led to a haphazard deployment of ground forces into Lebanon, starting with battalion- to brigade-sized raids in late July and culminating in a four-division operation in August.[253] At no point were there more than ten thousand Israeli soldiers inside Lebanon, meaning that the actual combat power deployed against the estimated four thousand Hizballah fighters in southern Lebanon amounted to about one understrength division.[254]

Among the soldiers entering Lebanon were reservists from 551st Brigade of the Nineth-Eighth Parachute Division and a brigade from the 366th Reserve Armored Division. The Ninety-First Territorial Infantry Division had multiple assigned and attached reserve units, including one paratrooper brigade (the Fifty-Fifth), two infantry brigades (Carmeli and Alexandroni), and one armored brigade (Steel Chariots).[255] The Ninety-First also had one regional brigade—the 300th—which contained one reserve battalion.[256] The IDF's premier armored division—the Thirty-Sixth—mobilized its reserves as well, freeing its Seventh Armored Brigade (active) to enter Lebanon while the rest of the unit maintained security on the Golan Heights to deter any Syrian attempt to intervene.[257] The IDF's other active-duty armored division—the 162nd—deployed at least one reserve infantry company into Lebanon as part of the 401st Armored Brigade.[258]

The IDF in general and the reserves in particular were unprepared for a sustained ground operation against Hizballah, especially considering the prewar decision not to mobilize the reserves and the confusing and at times contradictory orders issued from Northern Command and the CGS. Making matters worse, the IDF lacked common doctrinal language for its operations and tactical tasks, leading to further confusion among regulars and reservists alike.[259] Reserve units attached to the Ninety-First Division were at a particular disadvantage because its commander, Brigadier General Hirsch, had developed esoteric operational concepts and terminology that were not shared throughout the IDF.[260]

Reserve mobilization began between 27 and 30 July, once Halutz began to seriously consider a larger-scale ground offensive into southern Lebanon.[261] Prior to mobilization, some front-line reserve units, such as the Alexandroni Brigade of the Ninety-First Division, fought defensive actions along the border, and others participated in major engagements inside Lebanon. For example, on 24 July a reserve paratrooper battalion seized the Hizballah stronghold of Maroun al-Ras.[262] In the lead-up to that battle, a reserve officer—one of the few IDF tactical leaders with previous experience in Lebanon—helped rally a special operations team from Maglan that had been paralyzed after Hizballah fire killed two of its members.[263] Despite some successes, many reserve units performed poorly in subsequent battles due to their inexperience and limited training for high-intensity combat against Hizballah, in addition to command and logistical problems.

The 366th Reserve Armor Division suffered multiple command and control breakdowns that contributed to its failed attack on Hizballah near the village of Marjayoun in early August. It had to pause or delay operations on at least one occasion due to its low readiness levels.[264] Making matters worse, the division's commander, Brigadier General Erez Zuckerman, had no training or background in managing armored operations, having spent his career in commando units.[265] Zuckerman resigned after the war, citing his failures at Marjayoun.[266]

Reservists from the Carmeli and Alexandroni Brigades experienced similar complications and delays; some of the commanders claimed these issues were caused by the unready reservists in their units.[267] The Alexandroni Brigade later recovered, helping to defeat Hizballah fighters in a series of engagements in the western sector.[268]

Reserve units also demonstrated poor discipline and lax safety standards while mobilizing in northern Israel. On 6 August a reserve paratrooper unit failed to heed warnings of rocket threats and bivouacked in an open field without wearing protective gear. An incoming rocket struck one of its vehicles, killing twelve soldiers in the war's deadliest single incident for the IDF. Press coverage of the attack provided a propaganda boost for Hizballah and undermined Israeli support for the war, given the public's sensitivity to reservists' deaths.[269]

Another problem facing reserves and regulars alike was that the IDF could not provide timely resupply to units inside Lebanon. One reason for this failure was that Northern Command barred supply convoys from entering Lebanon, given their vulnerability to IEDs and direct fire. Units therefore had to improvise aerial resupply solutions, place supplies inside heavy APCs, or use pack animals. The IDF also lacked a division-level organization to manage the flow of supplies to brigades inside Lebanon; it had abolished its division support brigades prior to the war because of their limited utility during the intifadas. The Ninety-First Division, meanwhile, had no procedures in place to track unit supply status, as postwar reports revealed. Consequently, once they were inside Lebanon, units quickly exhausted their two-day rations.[270] One Israeli soldier from the Alexandroni Brigade recalled that his unit "went as long as two-and-a-half days with daily rations of a can of tuna, a can of corn, and a couple of pieces of bread—to share between four soldiers." The same soldier reported that twenty-five soldiers in his unit collapsed from dehydration.[271]

The IDF also failed to properly maintain reserve equipment warehouses between 2003 and 2006. This forced some units to spend days addressing equipment issues because much of their gear was outdated and, in some cases, damaged. Others spent personal funds to replace or acquire basic equipment such as body armor.[272]

A second—and more serious—problem was that reservists lacked the necessary skills and experience to carry out the missions assigned to them. Hizballah's mobile ambush teams, armed with antitank missiles, posed a particular challenge to reservists who were accustomed to fighting poorly equipped Palestinian militants. In combat against the Palestinians, soldiers often took shelter inside buildings to avoid small-arms fire. But these tactics were dangerous against Hizballah fighters, who could target concentrations of soldiers with laser-guided antitank munitions. In one such incident, a Hizballah antitank missile killed nine reserve paratroopers huddled inside a house, even though intelligence reports had warned the unit to avoid sheltering in buildings.[273] Postwar studies by the IDF Northern Command concluded that this behavior reflected the fact that up to 20 percent of IDF reservists deployed to Lebanon had insufficient combat training after years of focusing on routine policing tasks in the West Bank, in Gaza, or along the Israeli-Lebanese border.[274]

To be fair, the active-duty divisions and brigade commands experienced similar difficulties in Lebanon. The 162nd Division bungled a river crossing at Wadi al-Saluki in the final days of the war, losing eleven personnel and multiple tanks as it traversed a predictable and exposed route that ran directly into Hizballah antitank defenses.[275] During the battle, none of the Israeli tank crews deployed smoke screens—standard practice in such a situation—further exposing them to enemy fire.[276] Meanwhile, the Ninety-Eighth Parachute Division had to abruptly abort a major air assault operation after failing to secure its landing zones.[277]

The war also revealed problems with reserve brigade command structures and training processes. As one IDF reserve officer explained in a journal article written two years after the war, reserve brigade commanders—who were typically full-time officers—did not lead from the front during the war, opting to work inside operations centers back in Israel.[278]

This was a problem for conscript brigades as well, but reserve battalion commanders needed closer supervision and support, given their relative inexperience. In fact, some battalion commanders had never even led their units in exercises, due to the curtailment of reserve training between 2003 and 2006.[279]

Reserve brigade commanders also did a poor job building rapport with their subordinates. This occurred because brigade-level exercises were canceled, and career officers tended to distance themselves from battalion- and company-level training.[280] Additionally, when reserve units mobilized for their three weeks of operational support, they fell under the command of a territorial brigade, not the organization and commander they would serve with in wartime. Wartime mobilization practices in 2006 further reduced cohesion, as Northern Command split some reserve brigades among multiple divisions.[281] Combined, these factors contributed to a lack of trust and understanding between reserve brigade commanders and their battalions, as evidenced by instances of reserve battalions hesitating or outright refusing to follow commands issued from brigade headquarters.[282]

Another issue was finding time to train reservists prior to combat. Some units, such as the 300th Infantry Brigade, conducted precombat training along the border.[283] Others had to be taken off the line and sent to training centers, which caused confusion and disrupted planning.[284] For instance, upon mobilization in late July, the Carmeli Brigade was ordered to report to the reserve training center at Tze'elim, but the trip to and from the center caused delays and changed the plans for a ground raid near Bint Jbeil. Brigadier General Hirsch from the Ninety-First Division eventually convinced Northern Command to send the brigade back to the front, as he believed it was already well trained.[285] Subsequent fighting revealed the unit still had considerable deficiencies.[286]

By the end of the war, nearly sixty-two thousand reservists were mobilized, although only a fraction of them entered Lebanon.[287] Those who were sent to Lebanon sustained heavy attrition, accounting for nearly half of Israel's 117 combat fatalities in the war.[288] These figures suggest a major disparity in the fighting quality of conscripts and reserves, which is not surprising, given the relative lack of training reservists had completed prior to the war. One reservist later explained to a reporter:

> In the past six years, I've only had a week's training. Soon after we arrived, we received an order to seize a nearby Shi'ite village. We knew that we were not properly trained for the mission. We told our

commanders we could control the village with firepower and there was no need to take it and be killed for nothing. Luckily, we were able to convince our commander. . . . For the last six years, we were engaged in stupid policing missions in the West Bank . . . checkpoints, hunting stone-throwing Palestinian children, that kind of stuff. The result was that we were not ready to confront real fighters like Hizballah.[289]

These struggles contributed to Israel's strategic defeat in the war. The casualties suffered by reserve units due to their poor state of readiness helped turn the Israeli public against the war. This led Prime Minister Olmert to withdraw Israeli ground forces on 14 August, having failed to achieve his primary objectives.

Israeli soldiers were disappointed by the war's outcome, as was the Israeli government, which launched an internal investigation into IDF planning and conduct. These investigations and independent media reports revealed the low level of readiness among the reserves. Many reservists themselves were upset with their performance, prompting some to blame years of neglect of the "land forces in favor of the air force [and] high-tech wizardry."[290] The IDF vowed to improve reservist training after the 2006 Lebanon War, but budgetary and legal constraints have limited its ability to do so.

Reversing the Decline

Since 2006, Israel has implemented a series of five-year plans aimed at preparing the IDF—including the army reserve—for a war against Iran and its militant allies. The 2006 Lebanon War showed that Iranian allies such as Hizballah—trained and equipped by Iran's Islamic Revolutionary Guards Corps (IRGC)—could pose a significant challenge to the IDF on the battlefield. Since 2006, Iran has greatly expanded its arsenal of missiles and UAVs, enhancing its ability to strike Israel directly.[291] And following the outbreak of the Syrian civil war in March 2011, Iran recruited and deployed armed proxies across Syria, some of which have launched rocket and UAV attacks into northern Israel.[292] Iranian-aligned militias in Iraq have also initiated UAV attacks against Israel, while the Iranian-aligned Huthi movement in Yemen presents another potential threat to Israel's south.[293] Finally, Iran has worked to supply Palestinian militants, such as Hamas and the Palestinian Islamic Jihad, with arms and support to attack Israel.[294] Combined, these threats led Israeli defense minister Yoav

Gallant to declare in April 2023 that Israel had entered "a new security era" of multifront conflicts.[295]

However, legal and budgetary constraints have complicated efforts by the last four CGSs to prepare the reserves for this multifront threat. The biggest legal obstacle was a new law approved by the Knesset in 2008 that capped reserve soldiers' service at fifty-four days over three years; NCOs were allotted seventy days, and officers eighty-four.[296] The Knesset—with support from the Ministry of Defense—drafted the law in response to complaints from reservists who felt overworked due to the high operational tempo of the Second Intifada and the 2006 Lebanon War.[297]

To improve reserve readiness while working within these constraints, the IDF mandated that reserves spend 70 percent of their time during a three-year readiness cycle focused on training, culminating in an operational deployment attached to a territorial division, such as the Ninety-First along the Lebanon border or the 877th in the West Bank. Previously, units followed a two-year cycle in which they deployed in year two, leaving little time for training.[298] Under this new program, the IDF had to submit yearly reports to the Knesset for the first time, providing updates on reserve training and readiness levels.[299] That said, fifty-four training days over three years meant that reservists trained, on average, just eighteen days a year. This was problematic because the IDF accelerated its transition into a high-tech army following the 2006 Lebanon War. In other words, reservists had more to learn in less time.

Since 2007, each CGS has attempted to work within these constraints to enhance reserve readiness as part of their five-year modernization plans. CGS Gabriel "Gabi" Ashkenazi formulated the first of these plans, known as *Tefen*, which sought to reorient the IDF away from counterterrorism and back to large-scale combat operations. To do so, the IDF reopened the courses for brigade and division commanders, started to monitor unit readiness more closely to avoid future surprises, and accelerated production of advanced versions of the Merkava tank and the Namer, a new heavy APC.[300] As part of these reforms, Ashkenazi aimed to improve reserve readiness by resuming brigade live-fire exercises, which had not occurred since the 1990s.[301] Reserve units also implemented a more rigorous inspection program to document and resolve supply shortages.[302] In 2017 the IDF announced a $500 million plan to upgrade reserve equipment to ensure that all units were fully stocked with helmets, vests, weapons, and uniforms.[303]

Ultimately, these reforms were insufficient, as IDF comptroller and press reports have revealed.[304] For example, as of late 2022, some reservists

Table 5.4 IDF Personnel Costs and Defense Imports, 1990–2015

Year	Total Employee Pay[*] (Billions NIS)	Defense Imports (Billons NIS)
1990	5.40	3.70
1995	11.51	4.70
2000	16.45	9.37
2005	18.11	11.72
2010	20.92	10.03
2015	24.82	13.78

Source: Israel Central Bureau of Statistics, "Defence Expenditure in Israel," July 2017, 29, https://www.cbs.gov.il/he/publications/DocLib/2019/1758/e_print.pdf. NIS, Israeli new shekel.
[*]Salaries of all IDF military and civilian defense personnel.

were patrolling dangerous areas in the West Bank using leased civilian cars, rather than the armored vehicles they had requested. Some of these cars were so small that soldiers could not wear their armored vests inside them.[305] Additionally, the lack of a standard supply reporting system and a faster-than-normal rotation of commanders have complicated units' ability to identify and address supply and maintenance issues.[306]

This situation worsened under CGS Benny Gantz (2011–15), who had to curtail reserve training due to severe budgetary constraints that reflected rising personnel and equipment costs (table 5.4). Personnel costs, which consumed about two-thirds of the defense budget by the mid-2010s, increased as the IDF reserve ballooned from 380,000 members in 2005 to around 500,000 a decade later due to rising immigration and high birthrates.[307] The IDF also offered reservists and conscripts better pay and benefits to improve morale—a trend that continues today, as evidenced by a 2022 Knesset bill that raised combat soldiers' pay and educational benefits.[308]

The IDF also poured money into expensive weapons programs since the Second Intifada, leading to a major uptick in defense spending (table 5.5). For instance, between 2007 and 2015, the IDF purchased advanced F-35 fighters from the United States, doubled its submarine fleet, and upgraded its tanks and APCs.[309] It also significantly expanded and modernized its air defense network to counter missile, rocket, and UAV threats.[310] At the same time, it invested hundreds of millions of shekels in laser air defense systems to enhance and diversify its air defense network.[311]

To offset rising costs, Gantz canceled all reservist deployments to the West Bank and cut brigade exercises by 50 percent in 2013.[312] A year later, he halted reserve training altogether, citing "unprecedented financial constraints."[313] Such moves prompted a warning from the state comptroller in 2014, expressing concerns about declining reserve readiness.[314]

Table 5.5 Israeli Defense Spending, 2005–18

Year	Defense Spending as Percentage of GDP	Israeli GDP (Billions of US$)	Estimated Expenditures (Billions of US$)	US Military Aid (Billons of US$)
2005	6.26	142.53	8.92	2.02
2010	5.93	234.00	13.88	2.76
2015	5.49	299.81	16.52	3.10
2018	5.35	370.59	19.76	~3.10

Sources: World Bank, "Military Expenditure (% of GDP)—Israel"; World Bank, "Israel GDP"; World Bank, "Military Expenditure (Current USD)"; "U.S. Foreign Aid to Israel," Jewish Virtual Library; Lilac Shuval, "Going Back: The Reserve System Is Not Qualified [in Hebrew]," Israel Ha-Yom, 29 December 2014.
GDP, gross domestic product.

The next CGS, Gadi Eizenkot (2015–19), took a different approach. In his estimation, the ground forces in general and the reserves particular needed a "deep change" to bolster their readiness.[315] For the reserves, this meant cutting end strength by 100,000 to free funding.[316] These cuts reduced the number of "active reservists"—those who actually participate in annual training and operations—to around 120,000.[317] With fewer reservists, the IDF could channel funding and resources to build the readiness of select units, which was a key part of Eizenkot's five-year modernization plan, known as the Gideon Plan. The IDF therefore implemented a tiered readiness system that prioritized training funds and facilities for certain units—namely, armor and paratrooper units—that would likely play a major role in a war.[318] This enabled some armored units to conduct field exercises annually, while lower-priority infantry units did so on a semiannual basis.[319]

As of early 2023, the IDF is maintaining this tiered readiness approach due to limited resources, according to a senior Israeli officer.[320] At the top of the readiness tier are reserve paratroopers and special operations units, which regularly train—on a voluntary basis—beyond the limits established by the 2008 reserve law. This practice was formalized by a 2019 policy that officially approved such intensified training. For example, the policy permits some special operations units to train between 84 and 108 days over a three-year period, and reservists in the Ninety-Eighth Paratrooper Division received an additional 16 training days.[321] However, special treatment for certain units has created resentment among reserve officers whose units were not selected for such training support.[322]

CGS Eizenkot also increased the intensity of conscript training, returning to a cycle of seventeen weeks of training followed by seventeen weeks of operational deployment—a practice abandoned in 2000 due to the demands of the Second Intifada.[323] In 2017 conscript and reserve units conducted their first corps-level exercise in nearly two decades, as the IDF aimed to boost its readiness for a war with Hizballah.[324]

Since 2013, IDF training plans have often been interrupted by conflict with Hamas and the Palestinian Islamic Jihad in the Gaza Strip, unrest in the West Bank, and other unforeseen distractions. As one midranking IDF official complained to the *Economist* in mid-2018, "It's true that the tempo of exercises have gone up," but they are often disrupted "by urgent duty when Palestinians begin rioting in Gaza or in the West Bank."[325] Additionally, in the summer of 2020 the IDF had to cancel some reserve training and mobilization due to COVID-19.[326] Rising violence in the West Bank since mid-2022 has forced the IDF to increase the scale and frequency of reserve deployments in support of routine security operations, which cuts into training time.[327] Israeli reservists' mass refusal to train as a protest against controversial judicial reforms proposed by the Benjamin Netanyahu government in 2023 caused additional distractions and disruptions in unit training.[328]

Such disruptions were particularly problematic because they coincided with reductions in conscript service.[329] In an effort to ease the economic impact of military service, the Knesset passed a bill in 2018 that reduced conscription obligations from thirty-six to thirty-two months, shrinking the standing army by seven thousand personnel.[330] Two years later, the Knesset reduced obligations by an additional two months.[331] For the reserves, this meant that soldiers discharged into its ranks had even less experience and training.

Budgetary constraints, meanwhile, continued to undermine reserve training, forcing some units to train only five days a year.[332] But, as one reservist observed, five days was "a bit of an exaggeration." His unit did not start training seriously until Sunday afternoon. The rest of the time they were "busy doing what we have to do to go home." Another reservist complained, "What level of professionalism can you reach? There's no way to learn and assimilate combat doctrine or new technology this way. Would you trust a doctor who works in his profession only five days a year?"[333]

Condensed training periods posed a particular challenge for commanders, as one IDF reserve officer detailed in a 2013 article. Limited contact with their units meant commanders struggled to build rapport and trust with their personnel. This was exacerbated by the high turnover in reserve units, as discharged conscripts enter their ranks and older reservists leave the service.[334]

Reserve units' limited training has affected the willingness and ability of CGSs to deploy reservists. This was evident in Israel's multiple wars with Palestinian militants. Over the last fifteen years, the IDF launched six major operations against Hamas and the Palestinian Islamic Jihad in the Gaza Strip: Cast Lead (2008–9), Pillar of Defense (2012), Protective Edge (2014), Guardian of the Walls (2021), Breaking Dawn (2022), and Shield and Arrow (2023). Reservists were mobilized in each operation, but the CGS largely kept them—and ground forces in general—on the sidelines.

During Operation Cast Lead, the IDF mobilized ten thousand reservists who mostly backfilled conscript units in less demanding support missions.[335] Three years later, during Operation Pillar of Defense, the IDF activated fifty-seven thousand reservists. The vast majority, however, were placed in supporting roles defending the border with Lebanon or performing routine security missions in the West Bank, freeing active-duty units to deploy closer to Gaza.[336]

Operation Protective Edge in 2014 was an outlier. During that operation, the IDF mobilized eighty-six thousand reservists, with most performing routine security assignments.[337] But the IDF also attached reserve armor companies to the Givati Brigade, which conducted a ground incursion into Gaza as part of a division-sized task force that aimed to locate and destroy Hamas tunnels used to cross into Israel. Those reserve elements performed well; in fact, one battalion commander from the Givati Brigade claimed the reservists outperformed some conscripts.[338]

During the three most recent Gaza conflicts—Guardian of the Walls, Breaking Dawn, and Shield and Arrow—the IDF did not mount ground operations against Hamas or the Palestinian Islamic Jihad, opting to rely on air and artillery strikes. Thus, the five thousand reservists mobilized for Guardian of the Walls remained in support roles.[339] A year later, during Breaking Dawn, the IDF deployed about one hundred reservists to help secure the Gaza border.[340] And in May 2023, during Shield and Arrow, the IDF mobilized only select army reservists, namely, those in intelligence and staff positions.[341]

In addition to its Gaza wars, Israel has sustained a strike campaign—known as the Campaign between the Wars—since 2013 against Iranian and Iran-associated targets in Syria to prevent the IRGC from transferring advanced arms to Hizballah and from establishing a presence on Israel's northern borders. Israel has prosecuted this campaign almost exclusively through the air or with artillery strikes.[342]

The IDF's ability to execute these missions in Gaza—as well as its strike campaign in Syria—without substantial numbers of army reservists led some to question the importance and relevance of the reserves. In 2018, for instance, Brigadier General Shuki Ben-Anat (head of IDF reservists from 2008 to 2013) claimed, "Currently the army's main areas are cyber warfare and precision warfare, for which reservists are less needed."[343]

However, the wars with Hamas since 2006 and the enduring conflict with Iran also demonstrated that Israel's conscript army was still too small to fight without the reserves, especially if those conflicts escalated into a larger regional war that forced the IDF to commit ground forces to defend its borders. As one IDF senior officer conceded in discussions with military reporters in 2001, "There was talk of creating a professional military [in the 1990s]. But we don't know how a country with a population of six million would be able to hold a permanent army of a size that meets our strategic needs . . . [we] still need thousands of tanks and artillery and infantry, and we can't keep an army like that without reserves."[344] In early 2023 retired CGS Gadi Eizenkot echoed that sentiment at a conference regarding the importance of IDF reservists today, arguing that "the reserves are critical to the operational functioning of the IDF in any war."[345]

During his time as CGS, Lieutenant General Aviv Kochavi (2019–23) was committed to bolstering reserve readiness, given concerns about a potential large-scale, multifront war with Iran. For example, between 2020 and 2022 the IDF launched a series of intense exercises involving ground forces—including surprise reserve activations—simulating a conflict with Hizballah.[346] During these exercises, reserve units had an opportunity to practice brigade- and division-level operations for the first time in nearly seven years.[347] In 2021 reserve infantry units started training as many as four times a year at a new urban warfare center.[348] Additionally, in November 2021 Israel dedicated a special $324 million fund to support ground force modernization, a twofold increase in reserve training, and a substantial boost in division-level exercises.[349] With this funding, the IDF launched its largest exercise in decades during the summer of 2022, which included the deployment of conscript and reserve paratroopers to Cyprus for a simulated conflict with Hizballah.[350]

This training was important because Kochavi also doubled down on the IDF's commitment to high-tech, high-skilled war in his five-year plan (known as *Tnufa*, Hebrew for "momentum").[351] But unlike previous plans, Kochavi's placed greater emphasis on the army.[352] Specifically, he attempted to enhance army readiness for urban warfare against groups like Hizballah and Hamas by upgrading Israeli tanks and APCs with new active protective systems such as Trophy and Iron Fist for defense against antitank guided missiles and rocket-propelled grenades. To strengthen Israel's overall precision strike capabilities, Kochavi aimed to double the number of precision-guided munitions in the Israeli arsenal by 2025.[353] Such capabilities will be incorporated into planned multidomain army units that integrate air, cyber, and ground capabilities.[354] Since assuming command of the IDF in January 2023, Kochavi's successor, CGS Herzl Halevi, has signaled his intention to maintain these efforts.[355]

However, Halevi will almost certainly face numerous political and military constraints and compulsions that will complicate any reforms aimed at improving the IDF reserves. For example, Israeli reserve forces continue to suffer from widespread readiness and morale issues. In early 2023 polling revealed that 40 percent of reservists do not show up when activated, and many question the value and purpose of their service.[356] Reserve service, in other words, has essentially become voluntary, as there is no real punishment for failing to report for duty.[357] And those who continue to show up for duty have fewer opportunities to train, given the heightened tempo of West Bank operations since mid-2022.[358]

Opportunities for reserve training, therefore, remain scarce and are declining in some cases—an issue the IDF was attempting to address as of mid-2023 by requesting additional training days beyond those allowed by the 2008 reserve law.[359] These constraints have led some in the IDF to suggest that reserve officers in key positions, such as battalion or company commanders, be replaced with more experienced regulars and career professionals.[360] Israel, however, is struggling to retain sufficient numbers of qualified career officers and technicians due to competition with the private sector, which can offer far better pay and benefits.[361] In fact, in 2014 the IDF reported that only about 12 percent of reserve battalion commanders were career professionals from the active-duty army, compared to 20 percent in 2008.[362] This challenge is compounded by the fact that, as of mid-2023, the IDF was struggling to convince high-performing reserve officers to volunteer for these demanding command positions, given the stress it puts on their civilian and family lives.[363]

In short, the entire Israeli military system—dependent on inexpensive reserve and conscript soldiers—is under tremendous strain as Israeli society becomes more individualistic and divided, the IDF's means and methods of war become increasingly technical and expensive, and operations in the West Bank and along the Gaza border chip away at available training time. There is no clear path for Israel to replace or significantly modify its military system to address these issues that have collectively eroded the readiness, reliability, and relevance of the IDF reserves. It is equally unclear whether Israel will continue to enjoy the luxury of avoiding the need to commit army reservists to combat, given the growing strength and sophistication of

Hizballah forces in Lebanon and Syria and the spread of Palestinian militancy from Gaza and into the West Bank and southern Lebanon.[364]

The IDF mitigated the challenges posed by the reserve dilemma in the 1960s and 1970s by ensuring that all reservists had served at least two to three years on active duty, were led by veteran commanders, and trained thirty days or more a year. But changing military, societal, and political conditions within Israel and across the greater Middle East deprived the IDF of the budgetary resources, political capital, and societal support to maintain that formula's viability beyond the mid-1980s.

Thus, by the early 2000s, the IDF reserve was training only a few days a year or not at all, even as the IDF embraced increasingly high-tech and highly skilled forms of warfare. Many reserve leaders were still veterans, but they lacked the same levels of combat experience as earlier generations of Israeli commanders. And although reservists still served on active duty as conscripts first, by the mid-2000s, conscripts' service obligations had fallen from thirty-six to thirty-two months and declined even further in 2020. These reductions in training and personnel standards almost certainly contributed to reservists' struggles during the Second Intifada and 2006 Lebanon War. And in the conflicts that followed, the IDF sidelined its reservists in favor of full-time soldiers and the air force—a far cry from the 1960s and 1970s, when reserve brigades and divisions spearheaded key offensives.

In short, the people's army that captured the world's attention in 1967 and 1973 was no more by the end of the twentieth century. In its place was a smaller and technologically advanced army of professionals and conscripts specializing in precision strikes against terrorists and more distant threats from Iran and its proxies. This new Israeli army excelled in such missions, destroying Iranian weapons depots in Syria and eliminating key terrorist leaders in Gaza and elsewhere.[365] But as the IDF discovered in 2006, this smaller technical army was ill suited for a protracted conflict like the Second Intifada or for a war in which the IDF suffered heavy attrition, as occurred in 1973. In such circumstances, the IDF would almost certainly have to turn to its reservists, as it did during Israel's formative wars. But the reservists of today are shadows of their former selves due to decades of neglect and decline. Consequently, as one Israeli commander acknowledged in 2019, the decline of the reserves "could gravely affect the army's readiness for the next battle."[366]

Conclusion

Knowing yourself means knowing what you can do; and since
nobody knows what he can do until he tries, the only clue to what
man can do is what man has done.
—R. G. Collingwood[1]

Over the past century, army reserve training and personnel models developed in the mid to late nineteenth century largely proved incapable of providing reservists with the skills and experiences necessary to meet the rising technical and tactical demands of warfare. The two main reserve models employed by armies since the nineteenth century—the Prussian model, built around discharged conscripts, and the Anglo-American model, built around volunteers—generally provided reservists with only one to four weeks of training each year. Standards developed for the nineteenth century's mass infantry armies simply did not give reservists—and reserve units above the company level in particular—the time they needed to develop the individual and collective skills that would allow them to thrive on the highly lethal mechanized battlefields of the twentieth and twenty-first centuries. Consequently, reservists struggled to fight as effectively as active-duty soldiers in the wars of the past century, unless they were supervised by veterans and received substantial predeployment training. In short, a long-standing qualitative gap separated reservists and active soldiers. This gap narrowed briefly due to tactical, technological, and training innovations introduced by the Prussians and others in the mid to late nineteenth century, but it widened after World War I. Armies' inability to recognize and respond to the potential shortcomings of their reserve models risked military misadventure, as the Israelis experienced in the 2006 Lebanon War, or even national collapse, as France experienced during World War II.

The widening qualitative gap between reservists and active soldiers resulted from a convergence of financial, military, and technological factors combined with broader political, socioeconomic, and cultural influences.

During World War I, industrial weapons such as the machine gun and rapid-fire artillery forced armies to devolve command and control to junior and midranking officers and NCOs who controlled increasingly dispersed and flexible formations armed with a diverse array of weapons and support systems. Such developments were necessary to ensure that soldiers could survive on the battlefield and make tactical gains. Those trends accelerated after World War I, as armies mechanized and increased their integration with air forces and, more recently, with electronic and cyberwarfare and information operations capabilities. In this context, armies became more reliant on highly skilled technicians who could devote substantial time to learning how to operate, maintain, and integrate these weapons and associated support systems. But reserve maneuver units—training for just thirty days a year or less—struggled to find the time to keep up with these developments.

Nevertheless, armies preparing for major war could not simply reduce their dependence on reservists. In some instances, political and cultural factors forced military planners to maintain their reserve models and continue to integrate reservists into combat operations, even when it was not militarily prudent to do so.[2] But the main reasons for the continued dependence on nineteenth-century reserve models were financial and military in nature. From a financial perspective, armies had to contend with rising overhead costs as they developed expensive new high-tech arms and support systems and then had to recruit, train, and retain highly skilled technicians who demanded higher pay and better benefits. These developments prevented armies from growing their active-duty ranks and thereby reducing their reliance on reservists. Mass abandonment or curtailment of conscription around the globe in the past fifty years further reduced armies' ability to fight without reservists, especially as many of the conflicts during this period, such as the US wars in Iraq and Afghanistan, were protracted and led to exhausted or overextended standing armies.

Boosting reserve training time and standards was another challenge, as higher defense spending was required to provide more time and resources. And states were generally apprehensive about spending more on their reservists, especially as they dealt with rising overhead costs for their active forces. Additional reserve training also meant recalling reservists from their civilian lives more frequently, which generated a multitude of challenges. For instance, it undermined civilian industries that depended on reservists for labor, as the French learned in the lead-up to World War II and as the Israelis learned in 1967 and 1973. Or it might inadvertently signal to adversaries that war was imminent, especially for those armies, like Israel's, that required mass reserve mobilization to execute wartime plans. Reservists themselves sometimes resented shouldering a greater military burden, given the effect it had on their civilian lives, creating disciplinary problems that could lead to political troubles for defense officials. In short, many armies remained dependent on reserve forces, despite their questionable quality, due to a host of financial, military, and political constraints and compulsions.

This situation presented defense policymakers with a dilemma as they considered how best to structure, train, and employ their army reserves. At the center of that dilemma was the question of how to balance the minimal skills reservists needed to perform their jobs adequately and the acceptable military and political costs of their inability or ability to do so. The importance of this dilemma—and its associated risks—became apparent during the world wars.

During World War I, the Great Powers' reservists proved to be poor replacements for active soldiers because they had insufficient peacetime training to prepare their bodies and minds for the shockingly violent and protracted conflict and to hone their ability to fight in loose open-order formations. For the main combatants, reservists had little to no time to complete precombat training in the late summer and fall of 1914. Thus, in the war's opening phases, many reservists broke down physically during long marches and demonstrated a limited ability to fight without close supervision from active-duty officers.

To address these readiness issues, armies generally employed one of five methods, or a combination of them (table 6.1). And in the conflicts that followed World War I, states continued to employ similar methods in response to the reserve dilemma. Each method, however, carried its own risks and benefits and might be feasible only because of unique historical circumstances.

The Germans, for instance, used a cadre system that assigned active-duty officers and NCOs to reserve units. Supervision by these veterans helped compensate for the relative inexperience of rank-and-file reservists and ensured that most German reserve units could fight at or near the same standards as units composed primarily of conscripts. German reservists also underwent more frequent peacetime training than reservists in other armies, providing additional opportunities to refresh the soldiering skills gained as conscripts.

The Americans, meanwhile, took advantage of their geographic isolation from the battlefields of World War I to completely reorganize and retrain their reservists prior to deployment. Once in Europe, they continued

Table 6.1 Historical Examples of Policy Responses to the Reserve Dilemma

Method	Exemplars	Potential Drawbacks	Potential Advantages	Key Enabling Conditions
Cadre approach—reservists led by veteran full-time personnel	German army in both world wars; Israeli army 1948–present	Resource intensive; may require large, well-trained cadre of NCOs and officers	Part-time soldiers have veteran active-duty soldiers to oversee training and operations	High levels of nationalism and/or an existential national threat that enables high defense spending and convinces many to devote considerable time and resources to military pursuits
Extend reserve training beyond the typical 1–4 weeks a year in peacetime	ARNG since 1973; IDF army reserves in 1960s and 1970s	May reduce cost savings of reservists; can stress reservists' civilian employers and family lives	Reservists have more time to learn and master the complexities of modern war-fighting tactics and technologies	High defense spending to fund additional training; reservists with the will and ability to devote additional time to military pursuits
Reorganize and retrain reserve prior to deployment	British territorials in World War I; ARNG in both world wars and Korea	Reservists unprepared to deploy rapidly; active-duty officers and NCOs must be diverted from their units to supervise reserve retraining	Reservists may more closely meet active-duty standards prior to deployment; time to purge and replace poorly performing reservists	Geographic separation from the battlefield; time and resources to devote to intensive reserve training; cadre of active officers and NCOs to oversee training programs; draft or widespread volunteerism to replace poorly performing reservists

| Fight without reserves or place reservists primarily in supporting roles/homeland defense | Russian army in World War I; Soviet army in Cold War; US Army in 1950s; IDF since 2006 | Lack of strategic depth in personnel if active army proves incapable of handling missions on its own; high defense spending to field and maintain a large standing army | No need to rely on potentially undertrained reserve soldiers for combat operations; less disruption to civilian industries by reducing the need for recalled reservists | Conscription and high defense spending to build and maintain a large standing army or (e.g., in the case of Israel) a high-tech force that can achieve many objectives through airpower and limited ground operations |
| Ignore reserve readiness issues—maintain 19th-century training models with minimal changes | Austro-Hungarian Empire in 1914; France in 1930s; Iranian military in 1980s; Israeli army in 1990s | Reserves may be woefully unprepared for combat and unable to serve as viable substitutes for active soldiers; reserve casualty rates likely to be very high | Less likely to incur high overhead costs in peacetime (i.e., no enhanced reserve training initiatives) | Political-military leadership that is distracted, unable or unwilling to invest resources and time in reserve readiness; confidence that reservists can muddle through or that their poor performance will have minimal strategic or tactical effects |

to train for weeks or months under the supervision of active-duty officers and battle-hardened allies. During this period, reserve officers who were found to be lacking in leadership, technical, or physical abilities were replaced by veterans or newly commissioned officers. In other words, the US Army essentially transformed reservists into trained conscripts or professionals. The Americans used a similar formula to build an effective reserve during World War II and the Korean War. But the US Army could do so only because it did not have to commit the bulk of its forces to combat immediately after entering the war, unlike most of its allies and adversaries in Europe.

Many states, however, did not take substantial steps to improve their reserve formations before and during the world wars, and this failure had significant costs. In the years leading up to World War I, the Austro-Hungarian Empire and Italy allowed their reserves to atrophy due to budgetary, political, and socioeconomic constraints. They did little to compensate for that decline, thrusting undertrained and physically unfit reservists into combat in 1914 and 1915, with devastating results. Similarly, France allowed its reserves to fall into disrepair in the decade leading up to World War II, even though its national defense plans depended on the readiness of reservists. When called to fight, the reserves were not up to the task, contributing to the downfall of France.

Following the world wars, armies continued to experiment with methods to address the widening qualitative gap between reservists and active-duty soldiers. Some, like the Soviet Union, decided to keep reservists in support roles, hoping to achieve wartime objectives with a huge conscript force. But doing so required mass conscription and heavy spending on military programs, which proved unsustainable in the long run. Others, like the United States in the 1950s and early 1960s, sought to prevent or, if necessary, wage wars primarily with air, missile, and naval forces, keeping reservists in supporting roles on the home front.

In the latter half of the Cold War, the United States took a different approach as it aimed to develop the capability to deter or defeat the Soviet Union primarily with conventional ground and air forces. It had to do so without peacetime conscription after 1973, forcing it to draw more heavily on the ARNG and US Army Reserve. The problem was that ARNG combat units were unprepared for these new roles, having spent the previous decade focused on homeland defense.

To enhance guard readiness, the US Army established intensive peacetime training programs for select units, requiring them to train beyond the typical thirty days a year. During a crisis, guard units continued to receive intensive predeployment training that could last several weeks or more. Yet these programs still proved inadequate, as guard combat units mobilized for the 1991 Persian Gulf War and the Second Iraq War struggled to conduct operations above the company or battalion level. Intensified peacetime training also reduced the cost savings associated with using guard units rather than active ones. The additional training burdens caused some discontent in the guard's ranks, which led to disciplinary problems in 1991 and recruitment and retention issues in the early and mid-2000s. Today, the United States continues to wrestle with the reserve dilemma as it seeks to maximize the use of guard units to ensure that the US Army can generate sufficient combat power to deter threats from Russia and China and to support contingency operations against lower-tier threats elsewhere.[3]

In the mid-twentieth century the Israelis fielded perhaps the most capable reserve force in history. Unlike other armies, the IDF used reservists to spearhead successful ground campaigns during a series of wars fought between 1948 and 1973. And Israeli reservists were able to accomplish such feats within just one to three days of being mobilized.

The key to the Israeli reserve's success was its cadre system. Like the German reserve system of the world wars, it provided reserve units with veteran active-duty leadership at the brigade level and above. Additionally, all Israeli reservists had close to three years of active service as conscripts (four or more years for officers), and once they were discharged, they trained for thirty or more days a year under the supervision of full-time officers and technicians. The Israelis also benefited from the fact that their opponents were commanded by amateur officers who failed to utilize the military potential of their Soviet-supplied arms and their motivated but poorly trained soldiers.

The conditions that enabled the Israelis' success did not last beyond the 1970s. In the 1980s and 1990s the IDF had to cut reserve training time by 50 percent or more, which led to a steep decline in reserve readiness. Operational demands forced IDF leaders to deploy reservists to the Palestinian territories and Lebanon to assist with routine security tasks the active army could not handle on its own. These remedial tasks and the unpopularity of Israel's war in Lebanon led to a decline in reservists' morale and willingness to serve, which pressured Israeli policymakers to reduce reserve training time. IDF senior leadership in the 1990s was amenable to such reductions, as they sought to build a smaller and more efficient military to confront increasingly high-tech threats from Iraq and Iran.

Nevertheless, the IDF could not allow its reserves to fall into complete disrepair. They were still needed to reinforce and augment active units in the unlikely—but not impossible—event of a large-scale conflict. Thus, since the 1990s the IDF has implemented multiple reserve reform programs, each of which has fallen short. In the late 1990s the IDF tried to bolster reserve training time and standards, but the Second Intifada and new legal restrictions on reserve training limited its ability to do so. Failure to address reserve readiness, in turn, contributed to setbacks in the 2002 Battle of Jenin and the 2006 Lebanon War, when reservists struggled in combat and undermined Israeli tactical and strategic objectives.

Since 2006, Israeli defense policymakers have attempted to improve reserve readiness by resuming brigade- and division-level exercises and increasing reservists' pay and benefits. However, budgetary shortfalls due to the prioritization of high-tech weapons programs and government infighting have forced the IDF to make deep cuts. Today, IDF leaders continue to consider ways to improve reserve readiness but, for the most part, have opted to focus on preparing select reserve units for high-intensity operations while keeping the vast majority in supporting roles carrying out important but secondary functions such as border security. In short, the IDF has been unable to find a solution to the reserve dilemma since the 1980s.

The decline of the IDF reserve and the struggles of other reservists reveal an overlooked element of modern military history: how armies' transition to volunteer technical models—a development well documented by other historians—produced a policy dilemma for defense officials with regard to reservists, whether they served first as conscripts or were volunteers with little or no active-duty experience.[4] States' ability to recognize and respond to that dilemma played a major role in shaping the dynamics of multiple conflicts in the twentieth and twenty-first centuries, including, most recently, the Russia-Ukraine war that started in 2022. In that case, Russian reservists unexpectedly thrust into combat have proved to be woefully unprepared for modern warfare. In other words, histories of modern warfare must consider the roles, capabilities, and performance of armies' reserve components. Too often, these part-time soldiers are relegated to the margins of military history and strategic studies, even though they make up the bulk of many armies.

Yet the importance of reserve maneuver units—and the importance of the reserve dilemma in general—may be short-lived. As historian John Keegan explains in *The Face of Battle*, warfare over the past century has become increasingly mechanized and thus dehumanized as machines have taken the place of people.[5] This trend has only accelerated since Keegan wrote *The Face of Battle* in the 1970s. Today, armies are fielding robotic air, ground, and maritime systems capable of operating with little to no human supervision.[6] For example, in its 2020 conflict with Armenia, Azerbaijan employed Israeli-made one-way attack UAVs—also known as loitering munitions—that can locate and strike targets with little human input.[7] Meanwhile, Russia, the United States, and others are developing new generations of semiautonomous ground vehicles that can operate without human crews.[8]

Machines can also enhance individual human performance, potentially compensating for training deficiencies. As of mid-2020, the IDF was experimenting with a new system—called Smart Shooter—that uses a rifle-mounted computer and an electro-optical sight to improve a soldier's ability to engage targets rapidly and accurately.[9] Other armies are experimenting with exoskeletons that can greatly enhance a soldier's physical strength and stamina.[10]

Such technologies portend a future in which armies will not need large numbers of soldiers. They may need only small cadres of specially trained technicians who can maintain, operate, and integrate a host of robotic air and ground systems. In such a world, the challenges and risks associated with the reserve dilemma will likely fade in importance as the need for part-time soldiers—and soldiers in general—declines. In other words, the mechanization of war, which helped make the trained reserve a viable military institution in the nineteenth century, is driving reserve maneuver units—or at least their training and personnel models—toward obsolescence or irrelevance.

However, today's armies have multiple electronic and cyberattack capabilities that can disrupt or even destroy the onboard electronic sensors of robotic systems, as demonstrated by the Russia-Ukraine war.[11] Various laws and regulations, such as those in the United States, limit the military's ability to employ machines that can kill without a human actor in the loop.[12] Robotic ground systems, moreover, face multiple technical hurdles. Unlike air systems, they must navigate extraordinarily complex and variable terrain. The Russia-Ukraine war has also underscored how today's militaries lack the industrial capacity to mass-produce high-tech weapons to replace equipment and munitions in a timely manner.[13] In short, fully robotic warfare—especially in the land domain—is not imminent.

Thus, despite their questionable readiness levels relative to active-duty soldiers, reservists will likely play prominent roles in the wars of the near future. Indeed, as we have seen since early 2022, both Russia and Ukraine have had to draw extensively on reserve and militia forces to reinforce their overextended armies and to compensate for heavy battlefield losses.[14] As General Valerii Zaluzhnyi, Ukraine's top military commander, noted in a May 2023 interview, "The war is started by career soldiers and finished by teachers, engineers, accountants."[15] How such citizen-soldiers— be they wartime volunteers, draftees, or recalled reservists—will be employed in wars of the future and how states will structure, train, and equip them in peacetime are less certain. What is clear is that each state and society will formulate and enact reserve policies in ways that reflect its unique political, military, cultural, and socioeconomic contexts. And as they do so, each state—or at least the ones preparing for major war—will almost certainly have to contend with the enduring challenge of building and maintaining reserve readiness in an era of increasingly high-tech and high-skilled warfare. As recent history suggests, overcoming or mitigating this challenge will likely require significant modifications to the structure, capabilities, and roles of the trained reserve—a type of military organization formed in response to the circumstances of the mid-nineteenth century that has proved ill suited to the realities of mechanized warfare.

Notes

Series Editor's Foreword

1. On Palmer, see I. B. Holley Jr., *General John M. Palmer, Citizen Soldiers, and the Army of a Democracy* (Westport, CT: Greenwood, 1982).

2. John McAuley Palmer, "Memorandum for the Committee on Civilian Components, Office of the Consultant in Military History, Subject: Inter-relations between Professional and Non-professional Personnel in the Armed Forces of a Democratic State," 9 January 1948, 12, box 78, folder 33, George C. Marshall Papers, George C. Marshall Library, Lexington, VA.

Preface

1. Mordechai Gur, chief of staff of the Israel Defense Forces, quoted in "Gur Outlines Challenge of Training Our Soldier," *Jerusalem Post*, 26 January 1978, 2.

2. Matthew Cox, "Army National Guard Mechanized Infantry Forces Arrive in Syria to Protect Oil Fields," Military.com, 31 October 2019.

3. Thomas Gibbons-Neff, "How a 4-Hour Battle between Russian Mercenaries and U.S. Commandos Unfolded in Syria," *New York Times*, 24 May 2018.

4. Loren Schulman, Twitter post, 31 October 2019, https://twitter.com/LorenRaeDeJ/status/1189893621937573888.

5. Charlie Anderson, "How a Few Good 'Bastards' from the Army National Guard Helped Secure the Kabul Airport," *Task and Purpose*, 22 September 2021.

6. See Reid Forgrave, "Minnesota National Guard Commander Details Mission to Evacuate Afghan Refugees," *Stars and Stripes*, 17 October 2021, https://www.stripes.com/branches/army/2021-10-17/minnesota-national-guard-commander-details-mission-evacuate-afghan-refugees-3273421.html.

7. Eugenia Kiesling, *Arming against Hitler: France and the Limits of Military Planning* (Lawrence: University Press of Kansas, 1996).

8. David French, *Raising Churchill's Army: The British Army and the War against Germany 1919–1945*, new ed. (New York: Oxford University Press, 2001).

9. Michael Doubler, *Civilian in Peace, Soldier in War: The Army National Guard, 1636–2000* (Lawrence: University Press of Kansas, 2003).

10. Ute Frevert, *A Nation in Barracks: Modern Germany, Military Conscription, and Civil Society* (New York: Berg, 2004).

11. Michael Howard, *War in European History*, updated ed. (New York: Oxford University Press, 2001), 120; John Keegan, *The Face of Battle: A Study of*

Agincourt, Waterloo, and the Somme (New York: Penguin Books, 1978), 319–320; Antulio J. Echevarria II, *After Clausewitz: German Military Thinkers before the Great War* (Lawrence: University Press of Kansas, 2000), 36–38.

12. See Michael O'Hanlon's comments at the October 2015 Association of the United States Army conference, made available by the US Army Training and Doctrine Command at https://www.youtube.com/watch?v=T1qcObRb1tU (accessed 20 September 2016).

13. Despite its long history, the historiography of the Army National Guard (ARNG) is underdeveloped compared to that of the active-duty US Army. The most comprehensive histories of the guard are Doubler's *Civilian in Peace, Soldier in War* and Jim Hill's *The Minute Man in Peace and War: A History of the National Guard* (Mechanicsburg, PA: Stackpole, 1964). However, both works downplay or overlook many of the guard's shortcomings and failures. The other main historical work on the ARNG is Martha Derthick's *The National Guard in Politics* (Cambridge, MA: Harvard University Press, 1965), which concentrates on how the guard's political influence in Congress and state legislatures shaped its history. However, Derthick's work predates the important changes in the guard's roles and capabilities following the Vietnam War (e.g., the ARNG's evolution into an operational reserve once the United States ended peacetime conscription). There are also several works on particular guard regiments and divisions during the world wars: Jonathan Bratten, *To the Last Man: A National Guard Regiment in the Great War, 1917–1919* (Fort Leavenworth, KS: Army University Press, 2020); Michael Weaver, *Guard Wars: The 28th Infantry Division in World War II* (Bloomington: Indiana University Press, 2010); Joseph Balkoski, *Beyond the Beachhead: The 29th Infantry Division in Normandy* (New York: Dell Books, 1989). These books provide valuable insights into the evolution and performance of these units, including how long periods of training and reorganization before deployment allowed them to perform their missions effectively. This book expands on and complements these works by including them in the conversation in chapters 2 and 3 and by showing how the ARNG's evolving capabilities and performance were related to broader developments in military history.

14. The historiography of the IDF army reserve is also undeveloped. Most works, such as Martin Van Creveld's *The Sword and the Olive: A Critical History of the Israeli Defense Force* (New York: Public Affairs, 2008) and Stuart A. Cohen's *Israel and Its Army: From Cohesion to Confusion* (New York: Routledge, 2008), combine the story of the army reserve with the history of the army in general. This is understandable because the IDF is so heavily dependent on reservists and because active units have reservists in their ranks. In other words, the story of the IDF ground forces is the story of the IDF reserves. This book expands on that body of work by exploring how Israeli reservists' capabilities and performance relate to broader trends in military history and by accounting for recent developments in the history of the IDF reserves, such as ongoing efforts to improve reserve readiness as part of the *Tnufa* plan (2019 to present) and the intensifying shadow war with Iran and its militant proxies.

15. Most of these personal papers can be found at the National Guard Association of the United States library in Washington, DC. They provide insights into readiness challenges over the past century that historians often overlook when assessing the National Guard and its performance in major US wars.

16. *Maarachot* articles are available in Hebrew at https://www.maarachot .idf.il/.

17. The views expressed in this book are my own and do not reflect those of the Defense Intelligence Agency, Department of Defense, US Army, National Guard, or Maryland Army National Guard.

Chapter 1. The Reserve Dilemma

1. Howard, *War in European History*, 120.

2. R. R. Palmer, "Frederick the Great, Guibert, Bulow: From Dynastic to National War," in *The Makers of Modern Strategy from Machiavelli to the Nuclear Age*, ed. Peter Paret (Princeton, NJ: Princeton University Press, 1986), 111; Frevert, *Nation in Barracks*, 15.

3. Frevert, *Nation in Barracks*, 15; Paul M. Kennedy, *The Rise and Fall of Great Powers: Economic Change and Military Conflict from 1500 to 2000* (New York: Vintage Books, 1989), 51–55, 58–59.

4. Terence Wise, *Medieval European Armies* (Oxford: Osprey, 2012), 6; Helen Nicholson, *Medieval Warfare: Theory and Practice of War in Europe, 300–1500* (New York: Palgrave, 2003), 57.

5. Steven Ross, *From Flintlock to Rifle: Infantry Tactics, 1740–1866* (London: Frank Cass, 1996), 19–21, 22, 24.

6. Richard W. Stewart, ed., *American Military History*, vol. 1, *The United States Army in a Global Era, 1917–2008* (Washington, DC: US Army Center of Military History, 2009), 30–31, 47; Doubler, *Civilian in Peace, Soldier in War*, 7.

7. Allan R. Millett, Peter Maslowski, and William B. Feis, *For the Common Defense: A Military History of the United States from 1607 to 2012* (New York: Free Press, 2012), 48; Russell F. Weigley, *The American Way of War: A History of United States Military Strategy and Policy* (Bloomington: Indiana University Press, 1977), 4, 11; Antulio J. Echevarria II, *Reconsidering the American Way of War: US Military Practice from the Revolution to Afghanistan* (Washington, DC: Georgetown University Press, 2014), 65.

8. Stewart, *American Military History*, vol. 1, 114.

9. Gunther E. Rothenberg, *The Art of Warfare in the Age of Napoleon* (Bloomington: Indiana University Press, 1981), 11.

10. Ibid., 32, 97; John Keegan, *A History of Warfare* (New York: Vintage Books, 2012), 349.

11. Rothenberg, *Art of Warfare in the Age of Napoleon*, 133.

12. John Lynn, "States in Conflict: 1661–1773," in *The Cambridge Illustrated History of Warfare*, ed. Geoffrey Parker (New York: Cambridge University Press, 1995), 193, 198.

13. Philip Mansel, *Paris between Empires: Monarchy and Revolution 1814–1852* (New York: St. Martin's Press, 2003), 6, 8.

14. Frevert, *Nation in Barracks*, 10–11, 15.

15. Ross, *From Flintlock to Rifle*, 45.

16. Wilbur Gray, *Prussia and the Evolution of the Reserve Army: A Forgotten Lesson of History* (Carlisle, PA: Strategic Studies Institute, 1992), 3.

17. Lynn, "States in Conflict: 1661–1773," 206.

18. Ross, *From Flintlock to Rifle*, 146.

19. Gray, *Prussia and the Evolution of the Reserve Army*, 5–6.

20. Ibid., 6; Dennis Showalter, "The Prussian Landwehr and Its Critics, 1813–1819," *Central European History* 4, 1 (1971): 15.

21. Howard, *War in European History*, 94–96.

22. Michael Howard, *The Franco-Prussian War: The German Invasion of France 1870–1871*, 2nd ed. (New York: Routledge, 2001), 9–10.

23. Ross, *From Flintlock to Rifle*, 158.

24. Dennis Showalter, *The Wars of German Unification*, 2nd ed. (New York: Bloomsbury Academic, 2015), 39; Keegan, *Face of Battle*, 134–135.

25. Geoffrey Wawro, *The Franco-Prussian War: The German Conquest of France in 1870–1871* (New York: Cambridge University Press, 2003), 2; Kennedy, *Rise and Fall of Great Powers*, 160.

26. Showalter, *Wars of German Unification*, 24, 79.

27. Ibid., 24, 86; Frevert, *Nation in Barracks*, 48.

28. Frevert, *Nation in Barracks*, 57.

29. Ibid., 50.

30. Showalter, *Wars of German Unification*, 24; Showalter, "Prussian Landwehr and Its Critics," 3; Howard, *Franco-Prussian War*, 12.

31. Frevert, *Nation in Barracks*, 86; Showalter, *Wars of German Unification*, 38–39.

32. Showalter, *Wars of German Unification*, 26.

33. Echevarria, *After Clausewitz*, 13.

34. Ibid.; Millett, Maslowski, and Feis, *For the Common Defense*, 114–115.

35. Wawro, *Franco-Prussian War*, 58.

36. Geoffrey Wawro, *Warfare and Society in Europe, 1792–1914* (New York: Routledge, 2003), 59, 68, 72.

37. William H. Russell, *The British Expedition to the Crimea* [1858], rev. ed. (New York: Routledge & Sons, 1877), 2.

38. Wawro, *Warfare and Society in Europe*, 32.

39. Kennedy, *Rise and Fall of Great Powers*, 184.

40. John Gooch, *Armies in Europe* (New York: Routledge, 1980), 87.

41. William H. McNeill, *The Pursuit of Power: Technology, Armed Force, and Society since A.D. 1000* (Chicago: University of Chicago Press, 1984), 235.

42. Howard, *Franco-Prussian War*, 5.

43. Showalter, *Wars of German Unification*, 61.

44. McNeill, *Pursuit of Power*, 235.

45. Ibid., 246–247; Michael Solka and Darko Pavlovic, *German Armies 1870–71*, vol. 1 (London: Opsrey, 2004), 37.

46. Philip Bobbit, *The Shield of Achilles: War, Peace, and the Course of History* (New York: Anchor Books, 2002), 188.

47. Showalter, *Wars of German Unification*, 28.

48. Ibid., 46; Gooch, *Armies in Europe*, 68.

49. Wawro, *Franco-Prussian War*, 47.

50. This is how Helmuth von Moltke (the younger) described an unplanned mobilization on the eve of World War I, as detailed by Holger H. Herwig in *The Marne, 1914: The Opening of World War I and the Battle that Changed the World* (New York: Random House, 2011), 14.

51. John Keegan, *The First World War* (New York: Vintage Books, 2000), 28.

52. Showalter, *Wars of German Unification*, 25.

53. Martin Van Creveld, *Command in War* (Cambridge, MA: Harvard University Press, 1985), 104–105, 107.

54. Showalter, *Wars of German Unification*, 88–89.

55. Ibid., 62, 91.

56. Wawro, *Franco-Prussian War*, 43.

57. Ibid., 43.

58. Ibid., 54; Echevarria, *After Clausewitz*, 38–39.

59. Wawro, *Warfare and Society in Europe*, 77.

60. Solka and Pavlovic, *German Armies 1870–71*, 43; Frevert, *Nation in Barracks*, 159.

61. Wawro, *Franco-Prussian War*, 43.

62. Ibid., 42–43.

63. Showalter, *Wars of German Unification*, 79, 58.

64. Bobbit, *Shield of Achilles*, 179.

65. See John Brewer, *The Sinews of Power: War, Money and the English State, 1688–1783*, reprint ed. (Cambridge, MA: Harvard University Press, 1990).

66. Wawro, *Franco-Prussian War*, 42.

67. Ibid., 41.

68. Wawro, *Warfare and Society in Europe*, 85.

69. David G. Chandler and Hazel R. Watson, *Atlas of Military Strategy: The Art, Theory and Practice of War, 1618–1878* (New York: Arms & Armor, 1997), 190; Williamson Murray, "The Industrialization of War," in Parker, *Cambridge Illustrated History of Warfare*, 235; Wawro, *Warfare and Society in Europe*, 90.

70. Kennedy, *Rise and Fall of Great Powers*, 185, 186.

71. McNeill, *Pursuit of Power*, 245; Ross, *From Flintlock to Rifle*, 177.

72. Wawro, *Warfare and Society in Europe*, 86, 89.

73. Murray, "Industrialization of War," 236.

74. Kennedy, *Rise and Fall of Great Powers*, 186; Eugen Weber, *Peasants into Frenchmen* (Stanford, CA: Stanford University Press, 1976), 293.

75. Howard, *Franco-Prussian War*, 29, 35.

76. Ibid., 29–31.

77. Ibid., 32; Frederick Martin, *The Statesman's Yearbook 1868* (London: Palgrave Macmillan, 1868), 77.

78. Howard, *Franco-Prussian War*, 29, 39.

79. Ibid., 34.

80. Ibid., 67; Showalter, *German Wars of Unification*, 237–238.

81. Wawro, *Warfare and Society in Europe*, 109; Howard, *Franco-Prussian War*, 70–71, 80.

82. Wawro, *Warfare and Society in Europe*, 111; Murray, "Industrialization of War," 237.

83. Solka and Pavlovic, *German Armies: 1870–71*, 43; Helmuth Moltke, *The Franco-German War of 1870–71* [1893] (Auckland, NZ: Pickle Partners, 2013), 35, 56, 73.

84. Wawro, *Warfare and Society in Europe*, 115–117.

85. Ibid., 111–113; Howard, *Franco-Prussian War*, 105; Michael Clodfelter, *Warfare and Armed Conflicts: A Statistical Reference to Casualty and Other Figures, 1500–2000*, 2nd ed. (Jefferson, NC: McFarland, 2002), 211.

86. Wawro, *Warfare and Society in Europe*, 113–114; Howard, *Franco-Prussian War*, 94, 96.

87. Murray, "Industrialization of War," 240.

88. Wawro, *Warfare and Society in Europe*, 118.

89. Ibid., 225; John Gooch, *The Italian Army and the First World War* (New York: Cambridge University Press, 2014), 37.

90. David R. Stone, *The Russian Army in the Great War: The Eastern Front 1914–1917* (Lawrence: University Press of Kansas, 2015), 34–35.

91. Weber, *Peasants into Frenchmen*, 294.

92. Moltke, *Franco-German War of 1870–71*, 5.

93. Edward M. Coffman, *The Regulars: The American Army, 1898–1941* (Cambridge, MA: Harvard University Press, 2004), 4–5; Derthick, *National Guard and Politics*, 45; Millett, Maslowski, and Feis, *For the Common Defense*, 343–344.

94. Doubler, *Civilian in Peace, Soldier in War*, 141; Hill, *Minute Man in Peace and War*, 172–173.

95. LTC James Parker, *The Militia Act of 1903*, 3–4, https://www.jstor.org/stable/25119439?seq=1#page_scan_tab_contents; Derthick, *National Guard in Politics*, 27.

96. David French, *The British Way in Warfare, 1688–2000* (London: Unwin Hyman, 1990), 101, 107; Brewer, *Sinews of Power*, 30, 33, 61.

97. Byron Farwell, *Mr. Kipling's Army: All the Queen's Men*, reprint ed. (New York: W. W. Norton, 1987), 153, 156, 158, 163.

98. Bruce I. Gudmundsson, *The British Expeditionary Force 1914–15* (New York: Osprey, 2005), 11.

99. The main exception would be Japan, which rapidly industrialized in the latter half of the nineteenth century and produced a modern army, complete with a reserve system. See Edward Drea, *Japan's Imperial Army: Its Rise and Fall,*

1853–1945 (Lawrence: University Press of Kansas, 2009), 56, 66, 75. In the medieval era, China developed the bureaucracy to pay for a professional army, but it made limited use of civilian militias until Mao created village militias in the 1970s. See David A. Graf and Robin Higham, eds., *A Military History of China*, 2nd ed. (Lexington: University Press of Kentucky, 2012).

100. McNeill, *Pursuit of Power,* 256.

101. John A. English and Bruce I. Gudmundsson. *On Infantry*, rev. ed. (Westport, CT: Praeger, 1994), 4–5.

102. Dennis Showalter, *Tannenberg Clash of Empires, 1914* (Washington, DC: Brassey's, 2004), 120–121.

103. English and Gudmundsson, *On Infantry,* 5.

104. Robert Citino, *Path to Blitzkrieg: Doctrine and Training in the German Army, 1920–39* (Mechanicsburg, PA: Stackpole Books, 1999), 14; Peter Hart, *Fire and Movement: The British Expeditionary Force and the Campaign of 1914* (New York: Oxford University Press, 2014), 20.

105. Howard, *War in European History,* 103.

106. Wawro, *Warfare and Society in Europe,* 136–138.

107. English and Gudmundsson, *On Infantry,* 5.

108. Wawro, *Warfare and Society in Europe,* 137.

109. Williamson Murray, "Towards World War," in Parker, *Cambridge Illustrated History of Warfare*, 243; Tenney L. Davis, *The Chemistry of Powder and Explosives*, reprint ed. (New York: Angriff Press, 2012), 331–368.

110. McNeill, *Pursuit of Power,* 242.

111. Howard, *War in European History,* 103–104; Bruce I. Gudmundsson, *On Artillery* (Westport, CT: Praeger, 1993), 6.

112. Gudmundsson, *On Artillery,* 21, 6–7.

113. Keegan, *First World War,* 6–7.

114. Holger H. Herwig, *The First World War: Germany and Austria-Hungry, 1914–1918*, 2nd ed. (London: Bloomsbury, 2014), 49.

115. Echevarria, *After Clausewitz,* 13–15, 31–32, 38–39.

116. Gooch, *Italian Army and the First World War,* 14–15; Kennedy, *Rise and Fall of Great Powers,* 212; Geoffrey Wawro, *A Mad Catastrophe: The Outbreak of World War I and the Collapse of the Habsburg Empire* (New York: Basic Books, 2014), 6–7.

117. See examples in the case studies in subsequent chapters and in Wawro, *Mad Catastrophe,* 9, 80.

118. Gooch, *Italian Army and the First World War,* 20, 58.

119. Fiorello Ventresco, "Loyalty and Dissent: Italian Reservists in America during World War I," *Italian American* 4, 1 (Fall/Winter 1978): 93, 95.

120. Wawro, *Mad Catastrophe,* 146, 159, 148 (quote), 151.

121. For a full account of the numerous deficiencies of the Austro-Hungarian military, see Wawro, *Mad Catastrophe*.

122. Jonathan M. House, *Combined Arms Warfare in the Twentieth Century* (Lawrence: University Press of Kansas, 2001), 26; Showalter, *Tannenberg,* 123.

The French also sent older reservists overseas to help defend colonies and free regulars to return to France. See Max Boot, *Invisible Armies: An Epic History of Guerilla Warfare from the Ancient Times to the Present* (New York: W. W. Norton, 2013), 182.

123. Gudmundsson, *British Expeditionary Force*, 19.

124. Some units conducted training on basic tasks such as rifle marksmanship. See J. G. W. Hyndson, *From Mons to the First Battle of Ypres* [1933] (Auckland, NZ: Pickle Partners, 2015), loc. 84, 220, Kindle.

125. Hart, *Fire and Movement*, 94–96, 108; Herwig, *First World War*, 70.

126. Hart, *Fire and Movement*, 47–48; "Reservists of Crediton," *Western Times*, 17 November 1914; Hyndson, *From Mons to the First Battle of Ypres*, loc. 78.

127. Hart, *Fire and Movement*, 47–48; "Physique of the Army Reservists," *Aberdeen Journal*, 14 August 1914, 6.

128. Bruce I. Gudmundsson, *Stormtroop Tactics: Innovation in the German Army, 1914–1918* (Westport, CT: Praeger, 1995), 11–13, 195; Hart, *Fire and Movement*, 86–87. On the eve of the war, as many of 65 percent of reservists in some counties in England were former regulars. See J. G. Hicks, "The National Reserve," *Royal United Services Institution* 57 (1913): 666; "Our Troops in France," *Times*, 20 August 1914.

129. Herwig, *Marne*, 68.

130. Dennis Showalter, "Maneuver Warfare," in *The Oxford Illustrated History of the First World War*, 2nd ed., ed. Hew Strachan (New York: Oxford University Press, 2014), 46; Keegan, *History of Warfare*, 358–359; Heinz Guderian, *Achtung-Panzer! The Development of Tank Warfare* [1937], trans. Christopher Duffy (London: Cassell, 2012), 41.

131. Murray, "Towards World War," 273; Showalter, "Maneuver Warfare," 46; Peter Young, *The British Army: 1642–1970* (London: William Kimber, 1967), 220.

132. Murray, "Towards World War," 273. See the discussion of territorial unit histories in Ray Westlake and Mike Chappell, *British Territorial Units 1914–18* (Oxford: Osprey, 2013). The long period of training also reflected the fact that Britain lacked the infrastructure to rapidly mobilize, equip, and train personnel at the start of the war, as described by Denis Winter in *Death's Men: Soldiers of the Great War* (New York: Penguin, 2014), 37–49. There were also political concerns that volunteer armies sent to Europe might be slaughtered due to insufficient training and equipment, as discussed by Nicholas Lambert in *Planning Armageddon* (Cambridge, MA: Harvard University Press, 2012), 307. For more details on particular territorial units and experiences, see John Hartley, *6th Battalion the Cheshire Regiment in the Great War: A Territorial Battalion on the Western Front, 1914–1918* (South Yorkshire, UK: Pen & Sword, 2017).

133. German General Staff, Memo: War against France, 1905, translated into English at http://ghdi.ghi-dc.org/sub_document.cfm?document_id=796.

134. Showalter, *Tannenberg*, 33–34, 61, 123. Of particular concern was that,

given their larger populations and industrial strength, Russia and the United States could reinforce France and Britain. According to Holger Afflerbach, "The Strategy of the Central Powers, 1914–1917," in Strachen, *Oxford Illustrated History of the First World War*, 29, Germany and its allies had a total mobilized strength of around 5.5 million soldiers; its French and Russian adversaries could mobilize around 7 million soldiers, plus 350,000 British soldiers, in 1914. Keegan, *First World War*, 38.

135. Showalter, *Tannenberg*, 124.

136. Drea, *Japan's Imperial Army*, 66, 75; Frevert, *Nation in Barracks*, 159–160, 163.

137. Gudmundsson, *Stormtroop Tactics*, 23.

138. *The Statesman's Yearbook 1914* (London: Macmillan, 1914), 901; Walter Bloem, *The Advance from Mons 1914: The Experiences of a German Infantry Officer* [1916], trans. G. C. Wynne (West Midlands, UK: Helion, 2011), loc. 153, Kindle.

139. *Statesman's Yearbook 1914*, 902.

140. Bloem, *Advance from Mons*, loc. 153.

141. Erwin Rommel, *Infantry Attacks* [1935] (Barnsley, UK: Greenhill Books, 1990), 2.

142. Gudmundsson, *Stormtroop Tactics*, 3–5.

143. Erich Ludendorff, *My War Memories: 1914–1918* (London: Hutchinson, 1919), 55–56, 66.

144. Herwig, *Marne*, 28.

145. Bloem, *Advance from Mons*, loc. 378.

146. Ludendorff, *My War Memories*, 96; Showalter, *Tannenberg*, 188–190.

147. Erich von Falkenhayn, *The German General Staff and Its Critical Decisions, 1914–1916* [1919] (Auckland, NZ: Pickle Partners, 2013), loc. 297, Kindle. For more on battles on the eastern front and the demands on reservists, see Herwig, *First World War*, 144–148.

148. The exception was the US Army. See chapter 2.

149. A similar dynamic occurred in World War II, as discussed by Paul Fussell in *The Boys' Crusade: The American Infantry in Northwestern Europe, 1944–1945* (New York: Modern Library, 2003), loc. 387, Kindle. Fussell's comments are about American divisions in World War II, but similar trends unfolded in other armies in both world wars as a unit's original veteran and reserve members died, were wounded or captured, or moved to other positions.

150. Citino, *Path to Blitzkrieg*, 15–16.

151. For a discussion of the dangers of close-order tactics, see Rommel, *Infantry Attacks*, 29–30; Keegan, *First World War*, 6–7. Rommel was a junior infantry officer in World War I.

152. Robert Citino, *Blitzkrieg to Desert Storm: The Evolution of Operational Warfare* (Lawrence: University Press of Kansas, 2017), 19.

153. Ibid.; Ricardo Herrera, "History, Mission Command, and the Auftragstaktik Infatuation," *Military Review*, July–August 2022, 55.

154. Gudmundsson, *Stormtroop Tactics*, 18.

155. English and Gudmundsson, *On Infantry*, 63.

156. Rommel, *Infantry Attacks*, 3–4, 10.

157. Gudmundsson, *Stormtroop Tactics*, 24.

158. Citino, *Path to Blitzkrieg*, 16.

159. English and Gudmundsson, *On Infantry*, 18–19, 20; Citino, *Path to Blitzkrieg*, 16.

160. Gudmundsson, *Stormtroop Tactics*, 171.

161. "Infantry Tactics, 1914–1918," *Royal United Services Institute* 64 (1919): 461.

162. Citino, *Path to Blitzkrieg*, 16; "Infantry Tactics, 1914–1918," 461.

163. "Infantry Tactics, 1914–1918," 468–469.

164. Heinz Guderian, *Panzer Leader* [1952], trans. Constantine Fitzgibbon, 2nd ed. (Cambridge, MA: Da Capo Press, 2002), 20.

165. Basil Henry Liddell Hart, "Man-in-the-Dark Theory," *Royal Engineers Journal* 33 (1921): 6–7.

166. Citino, *Blitzkrieg to Desert Storm*, 3, 21–22.

167. Jonathan Baily, "The First World War and the Birth of Modern Warfare," in *The Dynamics of Military Revolution, 1300–2050*, ed. Williamson Murray and MacGregor Knox (New York: Cambridge University Press, 2001), 142, 135.

168. Keegan, *Face of Battle*, 319–320.

169. Quoted in Williamson Murray, "May 1940: Contingency and Fragility of the German RMA," in Murray and Knox, *Dynamics of the Military Revolution*, 159.

170. Liddell Hart, "Man-in-the-Dark Theory," 13–15.

171. For example, German soldiers in the early 1930s had to take multiweek training courses in vehicle maintenance and operations. Hans Von Luck, *Panzer Commander: The Memoirs of Colonel Hans Von Luck* (New York: Dell Books, 1989), 14.

172. See Kiesling, *Arming against Hitler*, 7, 84.

173. Howard, *War in European History*, 120.

174. For a discussion of the changing character of battle, see Keegan, *Face of Battle*, 308–320.

175. Herwig, *First World War*, 25.

176. See Kiesling, *Arming against Hitler*, chap. 4.

177. Robert A. Doughty, *The Seeds of Disaster: The Development of French Army Doctrine, 1919–39* (Mechanicsburg, PA: Stackpole Books, 2014), 187–188; Robert Doughty, "The French Armed Forces, 1918–1940," in *Military Effectiveness*, vol. 2, *The Interwar Period*, new ed., ed. Williamson Murray and Allan R. Millett (New York: Cambridge University Press, 2010), 62.

178. Doughty, *Seeds of Disaster*, 187; Alistair Horne, *To Lose a Battle: France 1940*, reprint ed. (New York: Penguin Books, 2007), 74–75.

179. Kiesling, *Arming against Hitler*, 169–170.

180. Ibid., 168–169.

181. Doughty, *Seeds of Disaster*, 17.

182. Ibid., 20–21.

183. Kiesling, *Arming against Hitler*, 13.

184. Ibid., 86.

185. Ibid.

186. Doughty, *Seeds of Disaster*, 31.

187. Kiesling, *Arming against Hitler*, 99; Horne, *To Lose a Battle*, 73.

188. Doughty, *Seeds of Disaster*, 31–32.

189. Kiesling, *Arming against Hitler*, 175, 181, 183.

190. Doughty, *Seeds of Disaster*, 29; Kiesling, *Arming against Hitler*, 86; Horne, *To Lose a Battle*, 61–63.

191. Kiesling, *Arming against Hitler*, 182, 175, 181, 183.

192. Horne, *To Lose a Battle*, 139; Kiesling, *Arming against Hitler*, 39.

193. Horne, *To Lose a Battle*, 139–140.

194. Ibid., 150, 147–149, 144.

195. Kiesling, *Arming against Hitler*, 85; Doughty, "French Armed Forces," 43.

196. John Keegan, *The Second World War* (New York: Penguin Books, 2005), 73, 83; Kiesling, *Arming against Hitler*, 174. The Germans also had the advantage of recent combat experience in Poland, which they used to inform their training and plans in the lead-up to the May 1940 invasion of France. See Gerhard L. Weinberg, *A World at Arms: A Global History of World War II* (New York: Cambridge University Press, 1994), 122.

197. Kiesling, *Arming against Hitler*, 85.

198. French, *Raising Churchill's Army*, 64, 14–16, 62–64, 158–159.

199. Ibid., 14–15, 171–172; David A. Jones, "Pinchbeck Regulars? The Role and Organisation of the Territorial Army, 1919–1940" (Ph.D. diss., Oxford University, 2016), 133.

200. French, *Raising Churchill's Army*, 53, 172, 53–54, 62–63.

201. For an extensive examination of this issue, see Jones, "Pinchbeck Regulars?" 224.

202. French, *Raising Churchill's Army*, 53–54; Jones, "Pinchbeck Regulars?" 144–145.

203. Jones, "Pinchbeck Regulars," 138.

204. Young, *British Army*, 232.

205. UK National Archive, "Casualties Suffered by the British Expeditionary Force May–June 1940," https://www.nationalarchives.gov.uk/education /worldwar2 /theatres-of-war/western-europe /investigation/invasion/sources /docs/1/enlarge.htm.

206. David M. Glantz and Jonathan M. House, *When Titans Clashed: How the Red Army Stopped Hitler* (Lawrence: University Press of Kansas, 2015), 30.

207. David M. Glantz, *The Military Strategy of the Soviet Union* (New York: Routledge, 2001), 94.

208. Williamson Murray, "The World at War: 1941–45," in Parker, *Cambridge Illustrated History of Warfare*, 317.

209. Glantz, *Military Strategy of the Soviet Union*, 95.

210. Drea, *Japan's Imperial Army*, 68, 197–199.

211. John Gooch, *Mussolini's War: Fascist Italy from Triumph to Collapse, 1934–1943* (New York: Pegasus Books, 2020), 431, 509.

212. Williamson Murray, "The World in Conflict," in Parker, *Cambridge Illustrated History of Warfare*, 299; Stephen Bull, *Second World War Infantry Tactics: The European Theatre* (Barnsley, UK: Pen & Sword, 2012), 3.

213. Bull, *Second World War Infantry Tactics*, 3.

214. Horne, *To Lose a Battle*, 88.

215. In his memoirs, Colonel Hans Von Luck recalled that when he applied for a position in the army in the 1920s, there were 1,000 or more applicants for just 140 positions. Von Luck, *Panzer Commander*, 12.

216. Ibid., 13–14; Guderian, *Panzer Leader*, 23.

217. Von Luck, *Panzer Commander*, 20; Manfred Messerschmidt, "German Military Effectiveness between 1919 and 1939," in Murray and Millett, *Military Effectiveness*, 2:245.

218. Guderian, *Achtung-Panzer*, 232, 236.

219. Kennedy, *Rise and Fall of Great Powers*, 307–310.

220. Jürgen Förster, "From Blitzkrieg to Total War: Germany's War in Europe," in *A World at Total War: Global Conflict and the Politics of Destruction, 1937–1945*, ed. Roger Chickering, Stig Forster, and Bernd Greiner (New York: Cambridge University Press, 2005), 97–98.

221. *Officership* is a term used by militaries to describe the professional standards of an officer. For example, see the RAND Corporation's definition of *officership* at https://www.rand.org/content/dam/rand/pubs/monograph_reports/MR470/mr470.appb.pdf.

222. The best example of this is the Israel Defense Forces in the 1973 Yom Kippur War, as explored in chapter 4. The US Army also worried about this issue, as discussed in chapter 3.

223. This issue is explored in full in chapters 4 and 5.

224. For a discussion of tanks' improved targeting capabilities, see Bruce I. Gudmundsson, *On Armor* (Westport, CT: Praeger, 2004), 158, 166–167. Also see US Army, *Worldwide Equipment Guide*, 4-15, https://odin.tradoc.army.mil/WEG.

225. T-90 MBT capabilities are listed in US Army, *Worldwide Equipment Guide*, 4-32. For the integration of range finders and tanks' increased stability between the 1960s and the 1980s, see ibid., 4-10–4-32.

226. Randolph Saunders, "A Short History of GPS," US Air Force, https://www.schriever.af.mil/News/Article-Display/Article/734934/a-short-history-of-gps-development/. For an example of the high degree of accuracy of modern missiles, see the Center for Strategic and International Studies (CSIS) Missile Defense Project profile of the Iskander missile at https://missilethreat.csis.org/missile/ss-26-2/.

227. Saunders, "Short History of GPS."

228. See Lester W. Grau and Charles K. Bartles, *The Russian Reconnaissance Complex Comes of Age* (Fort Leavenworth, KS: Foreign Military Studies Office, 2018).

229. Office of the Secretary of Defense (OSD), "Fire Support," http://www.gulflink.osd.mil/irfna/irfna_refs/n28en023/firespt.htm; Thomas Bryant, Gerald Morse, Leslie Novak, and John Henry, "Tactical Radars for Ground Surveillance," *Lincoln Laboratory Journal* 12, 2 (2000): 341–352.

230. See National Reconnaissance Office (NRO) histories of the Corona, Gambit, and Hexagon programs at http://www.nro.gov/history/csnr/corona/index.html and http://www.nro.gov/history/csnr/gambhex/index.html.

231. Central Intelligence Agency (CIA), "The Cutting Edge: Soviet Mechanized Infantry in Combined Arms Operations," August 1987, 2, https://www.cia.gov/readingroom/docs/CIA-RDP89T00296R000400390004-0.pdf.

232. Ingo Trauschweizer, *The Cold War U.S. Army: Building Deterrence for Limited War* (Lawrence: University Press of Kansas, 2008), 8–9.

233. CIA, "Cutting Edge," 2.

234. US Department of the Army, *Soviet Army Operations* (Washington, DC: US Government Printing Office, 1978), 2–1; CIA, "Flexibility in Soviet Offensive Concepts," July 1975, https://www.cia.gov/readingroom/docs/CIA-RDP86T00608R000700190003-3.pdf.

235. CIA, "Readiness of Soviet Forces in Central Europe," September 1987, v, https://www.cia.gov/readingroom/docs/1987-09-01.pdf.

236. US Marine Corps Intelligence Activity (MCIA), *Soviet/Russian Army and Artillery Design and Practices, 1945–1995* (Quantico, VA: US Government Printing Office, 1995), 101.

237. Digitized command and control systems that emerged in the late twentieth century made these vehicles even more expensive. For instance, the US Army's Force XXI Battle Command Brigade and Below System, which was added to army vehicles in the late 1990s, cost an additional $20,000 per vehicle. See Chad Samuels, "Connecting the Battlespace," *Armor and Mobility*, May 2010, 4, http://www.tacticaldefensemedia.com/pdf/am/2010_may.pdf. For more on tank armor advancements, see MCIA, *Soviet/Russian Army and Artillery Design and Practices*, 101. CIA, "Readiness of Soviet Forces in Central Europe," 1–2.

238. Ibid.

239. Beatrice Heuser, *The Evolution of Strategy* (New York: Cambridge University Press, 2011), 503.

240. BBC, "The Last Man to Do National Service," *BBC News*, 1 June 2015, http://www.bbc.com/news/magazine-32929829.

241. US Defense Intelligence Agency (DIA), *Russia Military Power* (Washington, DC: US Government Printing Office, 2017), 11, 54.

242. International Institute for Strategic Studies (IISS), "Military Balance 2017," 186.

243. US Defense Finance and Accounting Service (DFAS), "Pay Charts

1949–2016," https://www.dfas.mil/militarymembers/payentitlements/Pay-Ta bles/PayTableArchives.html.

244. Lester W. Grau and Charles K. Bartles, *The Russian Way of War* (Fort Leavenworth, KS: Foreign Military Studies Office, 2016), 4, 8.

245. CIA, "Soviet Strategy and Capabilities for Multi-Theater War," June 1985, 17, https://www.cia.gov/readingroom/document/cia-rdp87t00495r0007007600 02-9. For a detailed analysis of the German reserves in the late Cold War, see Jeannine V. De Soet, "Defence Reviews in Times of Economic Turmoil: British and German Reserve Forces in Transformation (2010–2015/1970–1979)" (Ph.D. diss., Kings College, 2019).

246. Carl Karlsson, "The Swedish Military Can't Retain Enough Troops. Here's Why," *Task and Purpose*, 4 April 2018, https://taskandpurpose.com /sweden-military-retention.

247. "Polish Army to Train 36 Thousand Reserve Troops," *Defense 24*, 12 February 2016, https://www.defence24.com/polish-army-to-train-36-thousand -reserve-troops; "Compulsory Military Service Will Not Be Reintroduced in Poland," *Defense 24*, 27 February 2015, https://www.defence24.com/compulso ry-military-service -will-not-be-reintroduced-in-poland.

248. "South Korea to Reduce Length of Mandatory Military Service," *Channel News Asia*, 28 July 2018, www.channelnewsasia.com/news/asia/south-ko rea-military-service-reduce-length-army-10569914; "S. Korea's Army to Create Reserve Forces Command," *Korean Herald*, 6 April 2018, http://www.korea herald.com/view.php?ud=20180406000215. Taiwan may be considering similar reforms, as outlined in Ian Easton, Mark Stokes, Cortez Cooper, and Arthur Chan, *Transformation of Taiwan's Reserve Forces* (Santa Monica, CA: RAND Corporation, 2017).

249. Brendan Balestrieri and Won-Geun Koo, "South Korea Needs a Wake-up Call on Its Reservist Crisis," *War on the Rocks*, 26 July 2022.

250. "Syrian Army Ends Calls for Reserve Military Personnel: Newspaper," *Xinhua*, 29 October 2018, http://www.xinhuanet.com/english/2018-10/29/c _137566893.htm.

251. Mary Ilyushina, "Russian Army Ramps up Recruitment as Steep Casualties Thin the Ranks," *Washington Post*, 16 June 2022.

252. "Strained Syrian Army Calls up Reserves; Some Flee," Reuters, 4 September 2012, https://www.reuters.com/article/us-syria-crisis-army-deserters /strained-syrian-army-calls-up-reserves-some-flee-idUSBRE8830CH20120 904.

Chapter 2. The United States Confronts the Reserve Dilemma

1. Theodore Roosevelt, *An Autobiography by Theodore Roosevelt* [1923] (New York: Astounding Stories, 2017), 164.

2. Richard W. Stewart, ed., *American Military History*, vol. 1, *The United*

States Army and the Forging of a Nation, 1775–1917 (Washington, DC: US Army Center of Military History, 2009), 115.

3. Brian McAllister Linn, *The Echo of Battle: The Army's Way of War* (Cambridge, MA: Harvard University Press, 2009), 13–16, 20–21.

4. Derthick, *National Guard in Politics*, 24; Hill, *Minute Man in Peace and War*, 172–173.

5. Coffman, *Regulars*, 4–5; Derthick, *National Guard in Politics*, 2; Doubler, *Civilian in Peace, Soldier in War*, 141.

6. Millett, Maslowski, and Feis, *For the Common Defense*, 292–294; Charles Dick, "Our Second Line of Defense," *Washington Post*, 6 July 1902, 22.

7. Derthick, *National Guard in Politics*, 25–26.

8. Ibid., 27.

9. "New Law for Militia," *Washington Post*, 22 March 1902, 11; "Militia Bill Signed," *Washington Post*, 22 January 1903, 4.

10. "Militia Bill Signed," 4.

11. Derthick, *National Guard in Politics*, 27.

12. Doubler, *Civilian in Peace, Soldier in War*, 144.

13. Derthick, *National Guard in Politics*, 27.

14. James Parker, "The Militia Act of 1903," *North American Review* 177, 561 (August 1903): 279.

15. Dick, "Our Second Line of Defense," 22.

16. Doubler, *Civilian in Peace, Soldier in War*, 151.

17. Millett, Maslowski, and Feis, *For the Common Defense*, 296.

18. "Militia Bill Signed," 4.

19. Derthick, *National Guard in Politics*, 42; Doubler, *Civilian in Peace, Soldier in War*, 144; "Regulars and Militia to Form One Great Army," *New York Times*, 28 June 1908, SM1.

20. Derthick, *National Guard in Politics*, 28.

21. Doubler, *Civilian in Peace, Soldier in War*, 154; US Army War College, *Statement of a Proper Military Policy for the United States* (Washington, DC: US Government Printing Office, 1916), 24–25.

22. Joseph M. Balkoski, *The Maryland National Guard: A History of Maryland's Military Force* (Glen Burnie, MD: Toomey Press, 1997), 40.

23. US Army War College, *Statement of a Proper Military Policy*, 21, 25.

24. Doubler, *Civilian in Peace, Soldier in War*, 156; US Army War College, *Statement of a Proper Military Policy*, 25.

25. US Army War College, *Statement of a Proper Military Policy*, 24.

26. Derthick, *National Guard in Politics*, 33–34.

27. Doubler, *Civilian in Peace, Soldier in War*, 157.

28. "Outline Army Policy," *Washington Post*, 7 January 1916, 2.

29. Derthick, *National Guard in Politics*, 36–38; "Assistant Secretary Breckinridge Also Quits; Both Resignations Are Promptly Accepted," *Washington Post*, 18 February 1916, 11.

30. Doubler, *Civilian in Peace, Soldier in War*, 157–158; "Assistant Secretary Breckinridge Also Quits," 1.

31. Geoffrey Wawro, *Sons of Freedom: The Forgotten American Soldiers Who Defeated Germany in World War I* (New York: Basic Books, 2018), 69.

32. Millett, Maslowski, and Feis, *For the Common Defense*, 307.

33. Ibid.; Derthick, *National Guard in Politics*, 33.

34. Millett, Maslowski, and Feis, *For the Common Defense*, 307.

35. War Department Annual Report (1917), 893, National Guard Memorial Library, Washington, DC; Wawro, *Sons of Freedom*, 39.

36. War Department Annual Report (1917), 893.

37. Weaver, *Guard Wars*, 4.

38. Eric B. Setzekorn, *The U.S. Army Campaigns of World War I: Joining the Great War, April 1917–April 1918* (Washington, DC: US Department of the Army, 2017), 5.

39. Wawro, *Sons of Freedom*, 54–55.

40. Coffman, *Regulars*, 203.

41. Millett, Maslowski, and Feis, *For the Common Defense*, 313–314.

42. Wawro, *Sons of Freedom*, 16; Christopher Capozzola, *Uncle Sam Wants You: World War I and the Making of the Modern American Citizen* (New York: Oxford University Press, 2008), 18.

43. Richard W. Stewart, ed., *American Military History*, vol. 2, *The United States Army in the Global Era, 1917–2008* (Washington, DC: US Army Center of Military History, 2010), 21.

44. Militia Bureau Annual Report (1918), 10; Militia Bureau Annual Report (1917), 51, National Guard Memorial Library, Washington, DC.

45. Donald Smythe, *Pershing: General of the Armies* (Bloomington: University of Indiana Press, 2007), 8–9; National Guard Association, *Proceedings of the National Guard Association of the United States: 1913*, 17–18, National Guard Memorial Library, Washington, DC.

46. Doubler, *Civilian in Peace, Soldier in War*, 149.

47. Wawro, *Sons of Freedom*, 69.

48. Jerry Cooper, *The Rise of the National Guard: The Evolution of the American Militia, 1865–1920* (Lincoln: University of Nebraska Press, 1997), 167.

49. "DC Guard to Drop All Married Men," *Washington Post*, 12 April 1917, 5.

50. Cooper, *Rise of the National Guard*, 167; War Department Annual Report (1918), 1103, 1111; Militia Bureau Annual Report (1917), 31; John F. O'Ryan, *The Story of the 27th Division* [1921] (London: Franklin Classics, 2018), 583.

51. Mark Calhoun, *General Lesley J. McNair: Unsung Architect of the U.S. Army* (Lawrence: University Press of Kansas, 2015), 50; War Department Annual Report (1918), 1, 1106.

52. "Recruiting Shows 1,750,000 Volunteer," *New York Times*, 5 August 1917, 12; O'Ryan, *Story of the 27th Division*, 605; John Kennedy Ohl, *Minuteman: The Military Career of General Robert S. Beightler* (Boulder, CO: Lynne Rienner, 2001), 23.

53. War Department, *Order of Battle of the United States Land Forces in the World War* [1931] (Washington, DC: US Government Printing Office, 1988), 179.

54. Wawro, *Sons of Freedom*, 74; Militia Bureau Annual Report (1918), 18.

55. "State Soldiers to Be . . . to New Armies," *Chicago Daily Tribune*, 7 June 1917, 2.

56. "Only Those Fit for War Service Will Lead Men," *Chicago Daily Tribune*, 12 December 1917, 2.

57. War Department Annual Report (1918), 1109, 1111.

58. Ibid.; "Generals Being Examined for Service in France," *St. Louis Post*, 12 December 1917, 3.

59. Setzekorn, *U.S. Army Campaigns of World War I*, 37–38; Militia Bureau Annual Report (1918), 126.

60. Coffman, *Regulars*, 204–205; William O. Odom, *After the Trenches: The Transformation of the U.S. Army, 1918–1939* (College Station: Texas A&M Press, 1999), 19.

61. War Department Annual Report (1918), 1104–1105; "National Guard Units Being Consolidated," *Atlanta Constitution*, 25 September 1917, 7.

62. "National Guard Units Being Consolidated," 7; War Department Annual Report (1918), 1105.

63. War Department Annual Report (1918), 1102; Henry J. Reilly, *Americans All; the Rainbow at War: Official History of the 42nd Rainbow Division in the World War* (New York: FJ Heer, 1936), 26.

64. William Manchester, *American Caesar: Douglas MacArthur 1880–1964* (Boston: Little, Brown, 1978), 84.

65. Smythe, *Pershing*, 7–8.

66. "Intensive Drill in the U.S. 2 Months, Then to Europe," *Chicago Daily Tribune*, 17 July 1917, 2.

67. "16 Weeks' Training of War Forces Here," *New York Times*, 6 October 1917, 7.

68. Setzekorn, *U.S. Army Campaigns of World War I*, 27; Wisconsin War History Commission, *The 32nd Division in the World War 1917–1919* (Madison: Wisconsin Printing Company, 1920), 30.

69. Setzekorn, *U.S. Army Campaigns of World War I*, 30.

70. Joint War Commission of Michigan and Wisconsin, *The 32nd Division in the World War 1917–1919* (Madison: Wisconsin Printing Company, 1920), 30; Bratten, *To the Last Man*, 22.

71. Setzekorn, *U.S. Army Campaigns of World War I*, 44.

72. "Army Trains Now under One Head," *New York Times*, 14 January 1918, 6.

73. Ohl, *Minuteman*, 31.

74. Henry Benwell, *History of the Yankee Division* (Boston: Cornhill, 1919), 25; War Department Annual Report (1918), 8; Wawro, *Sons of Freedom*, 84; John J. Pershing, *My Experiences in the World War* (New York: Frederick A. Stokes, 1931), 17–18.

75. Data from War Department, *Order of Battle of the United States Land Forces in the World War*, 113–288.

76. Strachan, *Oxford Illustrated History of the First World War*, 246; Reilly, *Americans All*, 100.

77. H. G. Proctor, *The Iron Division: National Guard of Pennsylvania in the World War* (Philadelphia: John C. Winston, 1919), 23.

78. Wawro, *Sons of Freedom*, 137–138.

79. Ibid., 136–138.

80. Critique of the Second Phase of GHQ-Directed Maneuvers, November 1941, 1, Lesley McNair Papers, box 2, unnumbered folder: Speeches and Writings (1941–42), Library of Congress, Washington, DC.

81. Pershing, *My Experiences in the World War*, 112; Wawro, *Sons of Freedom*, 137–138.

82. John J. Pershing diary, entries for 29 May and 2 July 1918, 82, 98, John J. Pershing Papers, Diaries, Notebooks, and Address Books, 1882–1925, Library of Congress, https://www.loc.gov/resource/mss35949.00103/?st=gallery.

83. Pershing diary, entry for 2 July 1918, 98.

84. Pershing diary, entry for 6 March 1918, 55.

85. Ohl, *Minuteman*, 31.

86. Richard S. Faulkner, "'Gone Blooey': Pershing's System for Addressing Officer Incompetence and Inefficiency," *Army History* 95 (Spring 2015): 14.

87. Calhoun, *General Lesley J. McNair*, 53.

88. "Brig. Gen. Martin Tells of Injustice to Officers during Argonne Offensive," *Washington Post*, 21 February 1919, 5.

89. Doubler, *Civilian in Peace, Soldier in War*, 181.

90. Faulkner, "'Gone Blooey,'" 11.

91. Ibid.

92. Doubler, *Civilian in Peace, Soldier in War*, 187.

93. McNair personally witnessed several guard units losing cohesion and performing poorly in combat during World War I, as described in Wawro, *Sons of Freedom*, 318–321.

94. Benwell, *History of the Yankee Division*, 3.

95. Manchester, *American Caesar*, 92.

96. Doubler, *Civilian in Peace, Soldier in War*, 183.

97. Wawro, *Sons of Freedom*, 216–220, 318–320, 370–372.

98. Millett, Maslowski, and Feis, *For the Common Defense*, 328.

99. Wawro, *Sons of Freedom*, xxiv, xxvi.

100. Calhoun, *General Lesley J. McNair*, 50; War Department Annual Report (1918), 1, 1106. For an example of how guard personnel helped train and mentor new soldiers, see Bratten, *To the Last Man*, 24.

101. Some blamed the struggles of the Twenty-Sixth, Twenty-Eighth, and Thirty-Fifth Divisions on guard leaders. See Wawro, *Sons of Freedom*, 216–220, 318–320, 370–372.

102. Benwell, *History of the Yankee Division*, xii.

103. Coffman, *Regulars*, 205.

104. Cooper, *Rise of the National Guard*, 171; Doubler, *Civilian in Peace, Soldier in War*, 186.

105. National Guard Bureau (NGB), Annual Report (1921), 6; NGB Annual Report (1923), 9–10, National Guard Memorial Library, Washington, DC.

106. Doubler, *Civilian in Peace, Soldier in War*, 186.

107. "Brig. Gen. Martin Tells of Injustice," 5; Doubler, *Civilian in Peace, Soldier in War*, 188.

108. "Brig. Gen. Martin Tells of Injustice," 5.

109. Millett, Maslowski, and Feis, *For the Common Defense*, 343–344; Derthick, *National Guard in Politics*, 45.

110. Stewart, *American Military History*, vol. 2, 59–60; Hill, *Minute Man in Peace and War*, 310.

111. "New Army Policy Fixed by Harding," *New York Times*, 25 July 1921, 4.

112. Doubler, *Civilian in Peace, Soldier in War*, 188; Millett, Maslowski, and Feis, *For the Common Defense*, 344; John A. Boyd, "America's Army of Democracy: The National Army, 1917–1919," *Army History* 109 (Fall 2018): 7–8.

113. War Department Annual Report (1928), 8.

114. Doubler, *Civilian in Peace, Soldier in War*, 188.

115. Hill, *Minute Man in Peace and War*, 297; Doubler, *Civilian in Peace, Soldier in War*, 188; Derthick, *National Guard in Politics*, 56.

116. Doubler, *Civilian in Peace, Soldier in War*, 188.

117. Ibid., 189.

118. Odom, *After the Trenches*, 19–22.

119. Ibid., 23; Coffman, *Regulars*, 263.

120. Coffman, *Regulars*, 263.

121. Ibid.; War Department, *Field Service Regulation 1923* (Washington, DC: US Government Printing Office, 1923), 11.

122. Ibid., 11–12; Odom, *After the Trenches*, 42, 51.

123. War Department, *Field Service Regulation 1923*, 12–13.

124. Coffman, *Regulars*, 233.

125. War Department Annual Report (1929–30), 136.

126. NGB Annual Report (1922), 6.

127. NGB Annual Report (1924), 39.

128. Hill, *Minute Man in Peace and War*, 348.

129. Doubler, *Civilian in Peace, Soldier in War*, 190.

130. NGB Annual Report (1924), 18.

131. NGB Annual Report (1926), 27.

132. Based on personal experience, it typically takes one day to get units to exercise sites and one day to return.

133. NGB Annual Report (1924), 18.

134. NGB Annual Report (1921), 15.

135. NGB Annual Report (1924), 25; NGB Annual Report (1928), 2; NGB Annual Report (1929), 30.

136. NGB Annual Report (1922), 10–12.

137. See the case of Omar Bradley and his assignment to the Hawaii National Guard in 1927, as discussed in Omar N. Bradley and Clay Blair, *A General's Life* (New York: Simon & Schuster, 1984), 59, 70.

138. Singleton to Marshall, 1 March 1934, George C. Marshall Papers, box 1, 1/20: March 1934, George C. Marshall Research Library, Lexingtion, VA.

139. NGB Annual Report (1922), 50.

140. NGB Annual Report (1924), 5.

141. Doubler, *Civilian in Peace, Soldier in War*, 191; NGB Annual Report (1928), 2–3.

142. Doubler, *Civilian in Peace, Soldier in War*, 191.

143. Derthick, *National Guard in Politics*, 46–48, 51–52.

144. Doubler, *Civilian in Peace, Soldier in War*, 191.

145. NGB Annual Report (1941), 8.

146. Doubler, *Civilian in Peace, Soldier in War*, 191.

147. NGB Annual Report (1931), 14; NGB Annual Report (1934), 11.

148. NGB Annual Report (1932), 13.

149. Doubler, *Civilian in Peace, Soldier in War*, 193, 194.

150. Morris Shepard, bill number 73 H.R. 5645, 6 June 1933, 2, http://congressional.proquest.com:80/congressional/docview/t47.d48.9769_s.rp.135?accountid=14696.

151. Doubler, *Civilian in Peace, Soldier in War*, 194.

152. Millett, Maslowski, and Feis, *For the Common Defense*, 356.

153. Stewart, *American Military History*, vol. 2, 68.

154. NGB Annual Report (1946), 30.

155. Coffman, *Regulars*, 270.

156. Calhoun, *General Lesley J. McNair*, 153–154.

157. NGB Annual Report (1936), 1.

158. NGB Annual Report (1934), 23; CNGB, Annual Report (1940), 36.

159. NGB Annual Report (1941), 8, 67.

160. NGB Annual Report (1936), 1.

161. NGB Annual Report (1941), 11.

162. Calhoun, *General Lesley J. McNair*, 55.

163. Stewart, *American Military History*, vol. 2, 69–70.

164. Odom, *After the Trenches*, 129.

165. War Department, *FM 100–5: Tentative Field Service Regulations: Operations* (Washington, DC: US Government Printing Office, 1939), 7.

166. Ibid., 7; Odom, *After the Trenches*, 134.

167. NGB Annual Report (1939), 12–13, 24.

168. NGB Annual Report (1936), 13; CNGB, Annual Report (1938), 18.

169. NGB Annual Report (1936), 10.

170. Ibid., 11; NGB Annual Report (1937), 9–11; NGB Annual Report (1938), 17; NGB Annual Report (1939), 24.

171. COL Clifford Early to COL George Marshall, 22 January 1936, Marshall Papers, box 2, 2/26: January 1936.

172. Marshall to McNair, 16 August 1939, Marshall Papers, box 76, 76/28: McNair Correspondence; *The Papers of George Catlett Marshall*, ed. Larry I. Bland, Sharon Ritenour Stevens, and Clarence E. Wunderlin Jr. (Lexington, VA: George C. Marshall Foundation, 1981–); electronic version based on *The Papers of George Catlett Marshall*, vol. 2, *"We Cannot Delay," July 1, 1939–December 6, 1941* (Baltimore: Johns Hopkins University Press, 1986), 181–183.

173. COL Marshall to BG Frank Bolles, 2 January 1934, Marshall Papers, box 1, 1/16, January 1934.

174. Singleton to COL Marshall, 1 March 1934, Marshall Papers, box 1, 1/20: March 1934; COL Marshall to CG 6th Corps, 27 September 1934, Marshall Papers, box 1, 1/28: September 1934.

175. MAJ A. D. Goudreau to COL Marshall, 25 August 1934, Marshall Papers, box 1, 1/27: August 1934.

176. Stewart, *American Military History*, vol. 2, 61.

177. War Department Annual Report (1941), 6.

178. Kennedy, *Rise and Fall of Great Powers*, 332.

179. Coffman, *Regulars*, 289.

180. Ibid., 374.

181. Doubler, *Civilian in Peace, Soldier in War*, 197.

182. Stewart, *American Military History*, vol. 2, 72.

183. NGB Annual Report (1941), 14.

184. NGB Annual Report (1940), 7; Weaver, *Guard Wars*, 41; Balkoski, *Beyond the Beachhead*, 20.

185. NGB Annual Report (1941), 8, 67.

186. NGB Annual Report (1940), 15.

187. NGB Annual Report (1941), 20; Weaver, *Guard Wars*, 22, 34.

188. NGB Annual Report (1946), 26.

189. NGB Annual Report (1941), 26.

190. Despite popular myths, many American men resisted and resented service during World War II. See Amy Rutenberg, *Rough Draft: Cold War Military Manpower Policy and the Origins of the Vietnam-Era Draft Resistance* (Ithaca, NY: Cornell University Press, 2019).

191. Weaver, *Guard Wars*, 17, 26.

192. Critique of the Second Phase of GHQ-Directed Maneuvers, November 1941, 2; NGB Annual Report (1941), 29.

193. Critique of the Second Phase of GHQ-Directed Maneuvers, November 1941, 3; Bradley and Blair, *General's Life*, 91, 96.

194. Peter J. Mansoor, *The GI Offensive in Europe: The Triumph of American Infantry Divisions* (Lawrence: University Press of Kansas, 1999), 19.

195. Christopher R. Gabel, *The U.S. Army GHQ Maneuvers of 1941* (Washington, DC: US Army Center of Military History, 1991), 197–202.

196. CNGB John F. Williams to MG Ellard Walsh, 1 April 1941, Ellard Walsh Papers, box 3, unnumbered folder: John F. Williams (Apr 41–Jan 43), National Guard Memorial Library, Washington, DC.

197. Anthony Leviero, "Fort Dix Soldiers Get Modern Arms," *New York Times*, 9 October 1940, 14.

198. NGB Annual Report (1946), 26; NGB Annual Report (1941), 25.

199. Doubler, *Civilian in Peace, Soldier in War*, 203.

200. Ibid., 197; Rutenberg, *Rough Draft*, 45–47.

201. NGB Annual Report (1941), 16–17.

202. Balkoski, *Beyond the Beachhead*, 24.

203. John Norris, "Army to Fuse Guard, Regular Officer Corps," *Washington Post*, 19 September 1941, 8.

204. Mansoor, *GI Offensive in Europe*, 16–17.

205. General Forces of the United States Army, undated 1941–42, 1–2, McNair Papers, box 2, unnumbered folder: Speeches and Writings (1941–42).

206. Quoted in Weaver, *Guard Wars*, 6.

207. Balkoski, *Beyond the Beachhead*, 27.

208. Conference in the Office of the Chief of Staff, 8 February 1941, Marshall Papers, box 61, 61/13: Civilians (Training of), 1941.

209. Calhoun, *General Lesley J. McNair*, 82–83.

210. Quoted in Balkoski, *Beyond the Beachhead*, 27.

211. McNair to Marshall, 7 October 1941, Marshall Papers, box 76, 76/31: McNair Correspondence.

212. Dennis Showalter, "Global Yet Not Total: The U.S. War Effort and Its Consequences," in Chickering et al., *World at War*, 113; Ohl, *Minuteman*, 32.

213. Ohl, *Minuteman*, 91.

214. Ibid., 76, 78–80, 82–83.

215. Weaver, *Guard Wars*, 11, 13.

216. Bradley and Blair, *General's Life*, 109; Conference in the Office of the Chief of Staff, 8 February 1941.

217. Weaver, *Guard Wars*, 14.

218. George Marshall to Ellard Walsh, 30 July 1941, Walsh Papers, box 24, folder 2: Correspondence Files of MG Ellard Walsh, 1940–1958.

219. Ohl, *Minuteman*, 91; Mansoor, *GI Offensive in Europe*, 59.

220. Ohl, *Minuteman*, 91–92.

221. Mansoor, *GI Offensive in Europe*, 57.

222. Fred Walker, *From Texas to Rome with General Fred L. Walker: Fighting World War II and the Italian Campaign with the 36th Infantry Division, as Seen through the Eyes of Its Commanding General* [1969] (El Dorado Hills, CA: Savas, 2014), loc. 409, 677, Kindle

223. Presentation to the Army War College by MG EA Walsh, 5 February 1953, Walsh Papers, box 7, folder 4: Department of the Army (General Correspondence).

224. Ohl, *Minuteman*, 91.

225. CNGB John F. Williams to MG George E. Leach, 24 January 1942, Walsh Papers, box 24, folder 2: Correspondence Files of MG Ellard Walsh, 1940–1958.

226. Milton Reckord to Ellard Walsh, 26 August 1943, Walsh Papers, box 3, unnumbered folder: Select Correspondence of MG Ellard Walsh (42–75).

227. Williams to Leach, 24 January 1942.

228. Weaver, *Guard Wars*, 10–11.

229. Walker, *From Texas to Rome*, loc. 988.

230. Mansoor, *GI Offensive in Europe*, 21, 26.

231. Walker, *From Texas to Rome*, loc. 1207.

232. Millett, Maslowski, and Feis, *For the Common Defense*, 381.

233. Mansoor, *GI Offensive in Europe*, 29, 50.

234. CNGB John F. Williams to MG Ellard Walsh, 24 November 1943, Walsh Papers, box 3, unnumbered folder: John F. Williams (Apr 41–Jan 43).

235. Doubler, *Civilian in Peace, Soldier in War*, 210, 204.

236. Rick Atkinson, *An Army at Dawn: The War in North Africa, 1942–1943* (New York: Henry Holt, 2002), 667, 684.

237. Bradley and Blair, *General's Life*, 157.

238. As discussed in Mansoor, *GI Offensive in Europe*, 5–9, 13, 14.

239. Doubler, *Civilian in Peace, Soldier in War*, 205.

240. Ibid.; Rick Atkinson, *The Day of Battle: The War in Sicily and Italy* (New York: Henry Holt, 2007), 347.

241. Atkinson, *Day of Battle*, 349.

242. Doubler, *Civilian in Peace, Soldier in War*, 205–206.

243. Ibid., 205–207.

244. NGB Annual Report (1946), 31; Atkinson, *Army at Dawn*, 512.

245. Mansoor, *GI Offensive in Europe*, 10–11.

246. George Q. Flynn, *The Draft: 1940–1973* (Lawrence: University Press of Kansas, 1993), 101.

247. Steven L. Rearden, *History of the Office of the Secretary of Defense: The Formative Years, 1947–1950* (Washington, DC: US Government Printing Office, 1984), 14; Harry S. Truman, Address before a Joint Session of the Congress on Universal Military Training, 23 October 1945, https://www.trumanlibrary.org/publicpapers/index.php?pid=183.

248. Doubler, *Civilian in Peace, Soldier in War*, 224.

249. Doris M. Condit, *History of the Office of the Secretary of Defense*, vol. 2, *The Test of War, 1950–1953* (Washington, DC: US Government Printing Office, 1988), 31.

250. Stewart, *American Military History*, vol. 2, 214; Bradley and Blair, *General's Life*, 482; Universal Military Training, Digest of H.R. 4278 (a Bill to Enact the National Security Training Act of 1947), as Reported to the House of Representatives, 1, https://congressional-proquest-com.proxy-um.researchport.umd.edu/congressional/docview/t21.d22.cmp-1948-sas-0004?accountid=14696.

251. Rearden, *History of the Office of the Secretary of Defense*, 14; Universal Military Training, Digest of H.R. 4278, 1.

252. NGB Annual Report (1947), 113.

253. George Marshall, testimony of 17 March 1948, 4–5, George Marshall Foundation, http://marshallfoundation.org/library/digital-archive/universal-military-training/.

254. Doubler, *Civilian in Peace, Soldier in War*, 228; Universal Military Training, Digest of H.R. 4278, 1.

255. Bradley and Blair, *General's Life*, 482; Derthick, *National Guard in Politics*, 101.

256. Bradley and Blair, *General's Life*, 482–483.

257. Doubler, *Civilian in Peace, Soldier in War*, 228; Selective Service Act of 1948, https://www.loc.gov/rr/frd/Military_Law/pdf/act-1948.pdf.

258. Doubler, *Civilian in Peace, Soldier in War*, 228; Selective Service Act of 1948, 6.

259. Hill, *Minute Man in Peace and War*, 502.

260. Ibid.; Selective Service Act of 1948, 3.

261. Hill, *Minute Man in Peace and War*, 502.

262. Eisenhower to JL Devers, 28 April 1947, Walsh Papers, box 24, folder 2: Correspondence Files of MG Ellard Walsh, 1940–1958; Additional Questions for MG Milton A. Reckord and MG Walsh, undated 1948, 18, Walsh Papers, box 24, folder 2: Correspondence Files of MG Ellard Walsh, 1940–1958.

263. Bradley and Blair, *General's Life*, 483; Eisenhower to Devers, 28 April 1947.

264. Bradley and Blair, *General's Life*, 483.

265. Doubler, *Civilian in Peace, Soldier in War*, 229; John Norris, "Blow Dealt Federalized Guard Plan," *Washington Post*, 10 December 1948, 1.

266. Rearden, *History of the Office of the Secretary of Defense*, 106.

267. "Transfer of Guard to Army Advocated," *Washington Post*, 11 August 1948, 9.

268. Ibid.

269. Bradley and Blair, *General's Life*, 483; Doubler, *Civilian in Peace, Soldier in War*, 229.

270. Bradley and Blair, *General's Life*, 483; Gordon Gray, oral history interview, 18 June 1973, 25, Harry S. Truman Library, Independence, MO.

271. Gray oral history interview, 26.

272. Derthick, *National Guard in Politics*, 77–78; "Ex-General of Guard Hits Army Talk," *Washington Post*, 2 January 1949.

273. "Truman Aide Accused of Arrogance," *Washington Post*, 4 January 1948, M5.

274. Derthick, *National Guard in Politics*, 81; "Guard Rebels at Plan for Absorption into Army," *Washington Post*, 12 August 1948, 1.

275. Additional Questions for Reckord and Walsh, undated 1948, 18, 15, 21.

276. Derthick, *National Guard in Politics*, 81; "Guard Rebels at Plan for Absorption into Army."

277. Gray oral history interview, 24–26.

278. Rearden, *History of the Office of the Secretary of Defense*, 106–107.

279. Condit, *History of the Office of the Secretary of Defense*, 492.

280. "Guard Change Held Essential by Marshall," *Washington Post*, 25 October 1950, 1.

281. NGB Annual Report (1949), 14.

282. US Congress, Senate Committee on Armed Services, Hearings on Universal Military Training, March–April 1948, 80th Cong., 2nd sess., 871.

283. Presentation to the Army War College by MG EA Walsh, 5 February 1953, Walsh Papers, box 7, folder 1: Department of Defense General Correspondence.

284. NGB Annual Report (1950), 7, 11; Hill, *Minute Man in Peace and War*, 498.

285. Derthick, *National Guard in Politics*, 72, 97.

286. US Congress, National Security Act of 1947, https://www.cia.gov/library/readingroom/docs/1947-07-26.pdf.

287. Doubler, *Civilian in Peace, Soldier in War*, 227; Millett, Maslowski, and Feis, *For the Common Defense*, 451.

288. John Lewis Gaddis, *The Cold War: A New History*, reprint ed. (New York: Penguin Books, 2006), 8–9; Melvyn P. Leffler, *For the Soul of Mankind: The United States, the Soviet Union, and the Cold War* (New York: Hill & Wang, 2008), 41.

289. Office of the Secretary of Defense Annual Report (1949), 4, National Guard Memorial Library, Washington, DC.

290. Campbell Craig and Fredrik Logevall, *America's Cold War: The Politics of Insecurity*, reprint ed. (Cambridge, MA: Belknap, 2012), 77–79.

291. Ibid., 97, 98.

292. Citino, *Blitzkrieg to Desert Storm*, 117.

293. Linn, *Echo of Battle*, 155.

294. Ibid., 155–159; Millett, Maslowski, and Feis, *For the Common Defense*, 446.

295. Linn, *Echo of Battle*, 152; Stewart, *American Military History*, vol. 2, 214; Bradley and Blair, *General's Life*, 474.

296. Stewart, *American Military History*, vol. 2, 214.

297. Bradley and Blair, *General's Life*, 474, 487; Office of the Secretary of Defense, National Defense Budget Estimates for FY 2015, April 2014, 76, https://comptroller.defense.gov/Portals/45/Documents/defbudget/fy2015/FY15_Green_Book.pdf.

298. Gaddis, *Cold War*, 35.

299. Citino, *Blitzkrieg to Desert Storm*, 117; Combat Studies Institute, *Sixty Years of Reorganizing for Combat: A Historical Trends Analysis* (Fort Leavenworth, KS: Combat Studies Institute Press, 1999), 16.

300. Stewart, *American Military History*, vol. 2, 205; Millett, Maslowski, and Feis, *For the Common Defense*, 451.

301. NGB Annual Report (1949), 19.

302. Statement of Colonel CM Boyer, Executive Director, Reserve Officers Association, to the House Armed Services Committee Investigating the Reserve Training Program, June 1953, Walsh Papers, box 24, folder 3: Reserve Policy Board; William Berebitsky, *A Very Long Weekend: The National Guard in Korea, 1950–1953* (Shippensburg, PA: White Mane, 1996), 179.

303. Doubler, *Civilian in Peace, Soldier in War*, 226; NGB Annual Report (1949), 5.

304. Bruce Cumings, *The Korean War: A History*, reprint ed. (New York: Modern Library, 2011), 11–12.

305. Ibid., 14–15.

306. T. R. Fehrenbach, *This Kind of War: The Classic Korean War History*, 50th anniversary ed. (Dulles, VA: Brassey's, 2000), 108–109.

307. Doubler, *Civilian in Peace, Soldier in War*, 231–232.

308. NGB Annual Report (1951), 1.

309. Berebitsky, *Very Long Weekend*, 5.

310. DOD press release, 11 September 1941, Walsh Papers, box 7, unnumbered folder: Department of Defense General Correspondence; Berebitsky, *Very Long Weekend*, 6; Clay Blair, *The Forgotten War: America in Korea, 1950–1953* (New York: Times Books, 1987), 121.

311. Millett, Maslowski, and Feis, *For the Common Defense*, 457, 463.

312. Berebitsky, *Very Long Weekend*, xi; John Norris, "Fresh Troops Build up Units Now in Korea," *Washington Post*, 13 February 1951, 1.

313. Berebitsky, *Very Long Weekend*, 250.

314. Ibid., 29.

315. David Halberstam, *The Coldest Winter: America and the Korean War* (New York: Hyperion, 2008), 495–496.

316. "National Guard Divisions Get Call to Duty," *Los Angeles Times*, 1 August 1950, 1.

317. Berebitsky, *Very Long Weekend*, 178.

318. Millett, Maslowski, and Feis, *For the Common Defense*, 462–463; Kevin Starr, *Embattled Dreams: California in War and Peace, 1940–1950* (New York: Oxford University Press, 2003), 309–310.

319. "Gen. Clark Warns National Guard to Train Quickly," *Washington Post*, 15 August 1950, B11; Berebitsky, *Very Long Weekend*, 179; "Guard Not Ready for Early Combat," *New York Times*, 11 February 1951, 10.

320. Berebitsky, *Very Long Weekend*, 118, 17.

321. Ibid., 18.

322. Kenny A. Franks, *Citizen Soldiers: Oklahoma's National Guard* (Norman: University of Oklahoma Press, 1984), 143; "Gen D. H. Hudelson, Dissident on Korea," *New York Times*, 3 February 1970, 43; Starr, *Embattled Dreams*, 308–309.

323. Franks, *Citizen Soldiers*, 143.

324. Ibid.

325. Doubler, *Civilian in Peace, Soldier in War*, 232.

326. Berebitsky, *Very Long Weekend*, 189.

327. Doubler, *Civilian in Peace, Soldier in War*, 235.

328. Berebitsky, *Very Long Weekend*, 187.

329. Blair, *Forgotten War*, 550.

330. Condit, *History of the Office of the Secretary of Defense*, 91; Franks, *Citizen Soldiers*, 144.

331. Blair, *Forgotten War*, 639.

332. Franks, *Citizen Soldiers*, 144; Blair, *Forgotten War*, 639.

333. Manchester, *American Caesar*, 621–622.

334. Franks, *Citizen Soldiers*, 144.

335. Berebitsky, *Very Long Weekend*, xi, 5.

336. "Guard Not Ready for Early Combat," 10.

337. "40th Division Gets Japan Duty Orders," *Los Angeles Times*, 25 February 1951, 16.

338. Berebitsky, *Very Long Weekend*, 125, 194, 196.

339. "California Guard Unit Now Training in Japan," *Los Angeles Times*, 1 May 1951, 9.

340. Franks, *Citizen Soldiers*, 144–145.

341. Berebitsky, *Very Long Weekend*, 129.

342. "Raids by Services on Guard Assailed," *New York Times*, 23 October 1951, 17.

343. Harold Hinton, "Use of Guardsmen Clarified by Army," *New York Times*, 12 September 1951, 17.

344. Berebitsky, *Very Long Weekend*, 202; Starr, *Embattled Dreams*, 308.

345. Berebitsky, *Very Long Weekend*, 202; Starr, *Embattled Dreams*, 308.

346. "40th Completes Landing Exercises," *Los Angeles Times*, 30 June 1951, 4.

347. "U.S. 45th Division Battles in Korea," *New York Times*, 31 December 1951, 2.

348. Memorandum of telephone conversation with Secretary of Defense General George C. Marshall, 19 February 1951, Acheson Papers—Secretary of State File, 1, https://www.trumanlibrary.gov/library/personal-papers/mem oranda-conversations-file-1949-1953/february-1951-0?documentid=32&page number=1.

349. Berebitsky, *Very Long Weekend*, 128, 135.

350. John Miller Jr., Owen J. Curroll, and Margret E. Tackley, *Korea: 1951–1953*, reprint ed. (Washington, DC: Center of Military History, 1997), 206.

351. Ibid., 208; "New Division in Action," *New York Times*, 10 March 1952, 2.

352. "45th Division Revealed to Be Fighting in Korea," *Washington Post*, 29 December 1951, 6.

353. "40th Suffers First Fatality in Korea," *Los Angeles Times*, 29 January 1952, 1.

354. Doubler, *Civilian in Peace, Soldier in War*, 236–237.

355. House, *Combined Arms Warfare*, 201.

356. English and Gudmundsson, *On Infantry*, 157.

357. Millett, Maslowski, and Feis, *For the Common Defense*, 473, 474.

358. Flynn, *Draft*, 123.

Chapter 3. The National Guard as an Operational Reserve

1. Michelle Tan, "Top Army General Outlines Plans for New Brigades, New Technologies," *Army Times*, 21 January 2016.

2. Main Trends in Soviet Capabilities and Policies: 1957–1962, US National Intelligence Estimate (NIE) 11-4-57, 12 November 1957, 24, Digital National Security Archives.

3. Trauschweizer, *Cold War U.S. Army*, 28–29.

4. A. J. Bacevich, *The Pentomic Era: The U.S. Army between Korea and Vietnam* (Washington, DC: NDU Press, 1986), 12–13; National Security Council, NSC-162/12, 5, https://fas.org/irp/offdocs/nsc-hst/nsc-162-2.pdf.

5. National Security Council, NSC-162/12, 5.

6. Trauschweizer, *Cold War U.S. Army*, 18–19; Bacevich, *Pentomic Era*, 15, 47.

7. House, *Combined Arms Warfare*, 189–190.

8. Bacevich, *Pentomic Era*, 47.

9. J. W. Davis, "General Cries 'Lie' as Wilson Says Draft Evaders Used Guard," *Washington Post*, 2 February 1957, A1.

10. Ibid.

11. "Wilson Says System, Not Guardsmen, His Target," *Washington Post*, 2 February 1957, A1.

12. Derthick, *National Guard in Politics*, 139.

13. Kenneth Weiss, "Taylor Says Guard Fails in Training," *Washington Post*, 4 February 1957, A1.

14. Doubler, *Civilian in Peace, Soldier in War*, 245; National Guard Bureau (NGB) Annual Report (1960), 12.

15. NGB Annual Report (1960), 35.

16. NGB Annual Report (1954), 15–16; NGB Annual Report (1956), 22; Office of the Secretary of Defense (OSD) Annual Report (1958), 99.

17. Derthick, *National Guard in Politics*, 118–119; Weiss, "Taylor Says Guard Fails in Training," A1.

18. US Congress, "[No. 22] Review of the Reserve Program; Hearings before Subcommittee No. 1 of the Committee of Armed Services House of Representatives, Eighty-Fifth Congress, First Session, 4–21 February 1957," 687, https://congressional.proquest.com/congressional/docview/t29.d30.hrg-1957-ash-0020?accountid=14696.

19. The army's need for highly skilled soldiers is a central topic in Brian McAllister Linn, *Elvis's Army: Cold War GIs and the Atomic Battlefield* (Cambridge, MA: Harvard University Press, 2016), 78–81, 99, 101, 133, 188.

20. Derthick, *National Guard in Politics*, 118–119; "National Guard Hits New Plan," *Washington Post*, 10 January 1957.

21. Weiss, "Taylor Says Guard Fails in Training," A1.

22. John Norris, "Two Guard Generals Favor Long Training," *Washington Post*, 20 February 1957, A1, A13.

23. Derthick, *National Guard in Politics*, 119; Weiss, "Taylor Says Guard Fails in Training," A1.

24. NGB Annual Report (1958), 30.

25. NGB Annual Report (1960), 7.

26. US Congress, "[No. 22] Review of the Reserve Program," 724.

27. NGB Annual Report (1958), 30; NGB Annual Report (1961), 28.

28. NGB Annual Report (1960), 37.

29. NGB Annual Report (1961), 34.

30. NGB Annual Report (1958), 38; Doubler, *Civilian in Peace, Soldier in War*, 239.

31. NGB Annual Report (1963), 12.

32. Doubler, *Civilian in Peace, Soldier in War*, 239.

33. John B. Wilson, *Maneuver and Firepower: The Evolution of Divisions and Separate Brigades* (Washington, DC: US Army Center of Military History, 1998), 274.

34. Doubler, *Civilian in Peace, Soldier in War*, 244.

35. Bacevich, *Pentomic Era*, 49–51, 105–106.

36. NGB Annual Report (1960), 33.

37. For more on the active-duty army's struggles with Pentomic operations, see Linn, *Elvis's Army*, 228–229.

38. Jerry Landauer, "New Plan to Cut Guard Detailed," *Washington Post*, 9 July 1958, A10.

39. OSD Annual Report (1960), 40–42.

40. Linn, *Elvis's Army*, 218, 228–229.

41. Ibid., 160–161, 170.

42. OSD Annual Report (1958), 13.

43. Office of the Special Assistant for National Security Affairs, "Summary Evaluation of Our Actual and Potential Capabilities to Fulfill Current Military Commitments and Basic Objectives as Outlined in NSC 5906/1," 1 December 1960, 2 Special Assistant Series, Presidential Subseries, box 5, Meetings with President Volume 2 (2), Dwight D. Eisenhower Presidential Library and Museum, Abilene, KS.

44. Bacevich, *Pentomic Era*, 100–101; Office of the Special Assistant for National Security Affairs, "Summary Evaluation of Our Actual and Potential Capabilities," 3–4.

45. Office of the Special Assistant for National Security Affairs, "Summary Evaluation of Our Actual and Potential Capabilities," 3.

46. NGB Annual Report (1961), 30.

47. Trauschweizer, *Cold War U.S. Army*, 121.

230 Notes to Pages 83–84

48. DOD, Memorandum to the President: Military Build-up and Possible Action in Europe, 1, John F. Kennedy Presidential Library and Museum, Boston, MA, https://www.jfklibrary.org/Asset-Viewer/Archives/JFKPOF-077-007.aspx (accessed 23 February 2018).

49. CIA, Berlin Crisis Chronology, 1961, 74, Central Intelligence Agency (CIA) Reading Room, https://www.cia.gov/library/readingroom/docs/1961-05 -01.pdf (accessed 23 February 2018).

50. DOD, Memorandum to the President: Military Build-up and Possible Action in Europe, 1, 8.

51. John Norris, "McNamara Faces Fight over Guard-Cut Plan," *Washington Post*, 28 May 1962, A2.

52. US Congress, Subcommittee on Preparedness Investigation, Committee on Armed Services, Senate, Proposal to Reline the Army National Guard and the Army Reserve Forces, Part 1, March 1965, 19–20, https://congressional .proquest.com/congressional/docview/t29.d30.hrg-1965-sas-0011?accountid =14696; Linn, *Elvis's Army*, 330–331.

53. Doubler, *Civilian in Peace, Soldier in War*, 251, 252.

54. Stewart, *American Military History*, vol. 2, 267.

55. Trauschweizer, *Cold War U.S. Army*, 123; Stewart, *American Military History*, vol. 2, 277.

56. Trauschweizer, *Cold War U.S. Army*, 123.

57. US Department of the Army, *FM 100–5: Operations* (Washington, DC: US Government Printing Office, 1962), 6–7, 12–13.

58. Wilson, *Maneuver and Firepower*, 293; Combat Studies Institute, *Sixty Years of Reorganizing for Combat*, 23.

59. Wilson, *Maneuver and Firepower*, 297.

60. Trauschweizer, *Cold War U.S. Army*, 116, 117, 120.

61. Robert McNamara, Memorandum for the President: Reorganization of the Army National Guard and Reserves, 7 December 1961, 2, JFK Library, https://www.jfklibrary.org/Asset-Viewer/Archives/JFKPOF-077-007.aspx; US Congress, Subcommittee on Preparedness Investigation, Committee on Armed Services, Senate, Proposal to Reline the Army National Guard and the Army Reserve Forces, Part 2, March–April 1965, 376, https://congressional .proquest.com/congressional/result/congressional/congdocumentview?accoun tid=14696&groupid=95583&parmId=1784FCC5420&rsId=1784FCC4B05.

62. Maxwell D. Taylor, *Swords and Plowshares: A Distinguished Soldier, Statesman, and Presidential Advisor Tells His Story* (New York: W. W. Norton, 1972), 208–209.

63. US Congress, Subcommittee on Preparedness Investigation, Part 2, 376.

64. US Congress, Subcommittee on Preparedness Investigation, Part 1, 12; John Norris, "McNamara Urges Guard-Cut Plan but Governors Stiffen Opposition," *Washington Post*, 3 July 1962, A1; McNamara, Memorandum for the President: Reorganization of the Army National Guard and Reserves, 1–2.

65. McNamara, Memorandum for the President: Reorganization of the Army

National Guard and Reserves, 1–2; US Congress, Subcommittee on Preparedness Investigation, Part 1, 2.

66. "McNamara Merger of Army Reserve Fails to Get Policy Board's Backing," *Washington Post*, 24 December 1964, A9; "Merger of Guard, Reserve Seen Killed for This Year," *Washington Post*, 12 August 1965, A2; US Congress, Subcommittee on Preparedness Investigation, Part 1, 3.

67. Doubler, *Civilian in Peace, Soldier in War*, 255.

68. Stewart, *American Military History*, vol. 2, 283.

69. Trauschweizer, *Cold War U.S. Army*, 133.

70. John Norris, "New Look Pays off for Reserves, Guard," *Washington Post*, 2 December 1963, A1.

71. NGB Annual Report (1963), 9; NGB Annual Report (1964), 42.

72. US Congress, Subcommittee on Preparedness Investigation, Part 1, 409.

73. Ibid., 410.

74. NGB Annual Report (1964), 29.

75. Ibid., 36.

76. Andrew Krepinevich Jr., *The Army and Vietnam* (Washington, DC: Johns Hopkins University Press, 2009), 3, 4.

77. Millett, Maslowski, and Feis, *For the Common Defense*, 525.

78. National Guard Bureau, "Remembering the Vietnam War: 50th Commemoration," https://www.nationalguard.mil/Features/2016/Vietnam/.

79. Flynn, *Draft*, 170.

80. Millett, Maslowski, and Feis, *For the Common Defense*, 525.

81. Around twenty-seven hundred guardsmen eventually served in Vietnam following the Tet offensive, which prompted President Johnson to authorize a partial mobilization of the guard. See Michael G. Anderson, *Mustering for War* (Fort Leavenworth, KS: US Army University Press, 2021), 3.

82. Millett, Maslowski, and Feis, *For the Common Defense*, 526.

83. Richard Lock-Pullan, "An Inward-Looking Time: The United States Army, 1973–1976," *Journal of Military History* 67, 2 (April 2003): 492; Flynn, *Draft*, 229.

84. John B. Conaway and Jeff Nelligan, *Call out the Guard! The Story of Lieutenant General John B. Conaway and the Modern Day National Guard* (Paducah, KY: Turner, 1997), 52–53.

85. "Pentagon Acts on Recruiting for Reserves," *Washington Post*, 9 June 1972, A23.

86. Bob Horton, "Army Acts to Upgrade Guard and Reserve," *Washington Post*, 4 February 1969, A6.

87. Doubler, *Civilian in Peace, Soldier in War*, 258; NGB Annual Report (1970), 7.

88. NGB Annual Report (1970), 7, 32.

89. NGB Annual Report (1976), 27.

90. Lewis Sorley, *Thunderbolt: From the Battle of the Bulge to Vietnam and*

Beyond; General Creighton Abrams and the Army of His Times (New York: Simon & Schuster, 1992), 184–185.

91. Martha Hamilton, "Recruiting: New Work for Guard, Reserves," *Washington Post*, 27 January 1977, DC1.

92. NGB Annual Report (1975), 26.

93. Conaway and Nelligan, *Call out the Guard!* 68.

94. Bernard D. Rostker, *I Want You! The Evolution of the All-Volunteer Force* (Washington, DC: RAND Corporation, 2006), 3, 29, 4.

95. "HHH Calls Nixon Irresponsible on Draft," *Washington Post*, 18 August 1968, A15.

96. Gates Commission, *The Report of the President's Commission on the All-Volunteer Force* (Washington, DC: US Government Printing Office, 1970), vii, 5–6; Rostker, *I Want You!* 4.

97. Stewart, *American Military History*, vol. 2, 375.

98. For 1973 Harris poll results, see Robert H. Scales Jr., *Certain Victory* (London: Brassey's, 1994), 6–7.

99. Stewart, *American Military History*, vol. 2, 376.

100. OSD Annual Report (1978), 102, 117.

101. Office of the US Secretary of Defense, *National Security Strategy of Realistic Deterrence: Secretary of Defense Melvin R. Laird's Annual Defense Department Report FY 1973* (Washington, DC: US Government Printing Office, 1972), 60.

102. Gaddis, *Cold War*, 212.

103. OSD Annual Report (1978), 9.

104. Leffler, *For the Soul of Mankind*, 238.

105. This is according to General William DePuy, as described by Saul Bronfield, "Fighting Outnumbered: The Impact of the Yom Kippur War on the U.S. Army," *Journal of Military History* 71, 2 (2007): 476.

106. According to the US Army's main publication on Soviet doctrine, Soviet forces planned to win the war within fifteen to twenty-one days. US Department of the Army, *Soviet Army Operations*, 3–5; US Department of the Army, *FM 100–5: Operations* (Washington, DC: US Government Printing Office, 1976), 2–32.

107. President Richard Nixon to Secretary of State, Secretary of Defense, Director of OEP, Director of CIA, and Director of Arms Control and Disarmament Agency, 25 November 1970, 1, 2, National Security Decision Memorandum 95: US Strategy and Forces for NATO, Nixon Library and Museum, http://www.nixonlibrary.gov/virtuallibrary/documents/nsdm/nsdm_095.pdf.

108. FM 100–5 (Operations) had last been revised in 1968; it was not updated until 1976.

109. That decision came as a result of the Gates Commission's 1970 report, which recommended ending conscription. See Gates Commission, *Report of the President's Commission on an All-Volunteer Force*.

110. Office of the US Secretary of Defense, Memorandum: Support for

Guard and Reserve Forces, 21 August 1970; Conaway and Nelligan, *Call out the Guard!* 346–347.

111. Stephen M. Duncan, *Citizen Warriors: America's National Guard and Reserve Forces and the Politics of National Security* (New York: Presidio, 1997), 144–145.

112. US Department of the Army, *Department of the Army Historical Series: Fiscal Year 1974* (Washington, DC: Center of Military History, 1978), 3.

113. Stewart, *American Military History*, vol. 2, 380. But as other historians have shown, the main purpose of the TFP was to maximize manpower because the United States could no longer rely on conscription and to compensate for smaller budgets in the 1970s. For an example of this argument, see James Carafano, "Total Force Policy and the Abrams Doctrine: Unfulfilled Promise, Uncertain Future," Heritage Foundation, 18 April 2005.

114. Duncan, *Citizen Warriors*, 144–145; Stewart, *American Military History*, vol. 2, 380. For the changing count of US divisions, see Trauschweizer, *Cold War U.S. Army*, 244.

115. James T. Brady, "Ready to Serve? The 48th, 155th, and 256th Brigades and the Roundout Concept during Operations Desert Shield and Desert Storm" (M.A. thesis, US Army Command and General Staff College, 2007), 5–6.

116. Bronfield, "Fighting Outnumbered," 470.

117. See the discussion in Lock-Pullan, "Inward-Looking Time," 488.

118. Briefing by LTG DePuy at Fort Polk, LA, 7 June 1973, reprinted in Robert M. Swain, ed., *Select Papers of General William E. DePuy* (Fort Leavenworth, KS: US Army Command and General Staff College, 1995), 59.

119. Thomas Ricks, *The Generals* (New York: Penguin Books, 2012), 2.

120. Briefing by LTG DePuy, in Swain, *Select Papers*, 59.

121. US Department of the Army, *FM 100–5* (1976), 1–1.

122. Ibid., 1–1, 2–2.

123. Lock-Pullan, "Inward-Looking Time," 506.

124. Stewart, *American Military History*, vol. 2, 382.

125. US Department of the Army, *FM 100–5* (1976), 3–4, 3–5.

126. Anne Chapman, *The Army's Training Revolution, 1973–1990* (Fort Monroe, VA: TRADOC, 1994), 3.

127. Ibid., 7.

128. For an example and a discussion, see the transcript of the 13 April 1976 briefing by MG P. F. Gorman, BG M. G. Thurman, and BC C. J Wright on "Training Support for Reserve Components," Paul F. Gorman Papers, US Army Combat Studies Institute Press digital archive, https://cgsc.contentdm.oclc.org/digital/collection/p16040coll10.

129. US Department of the Army, *Department of the Army Historical Series: Fiscal Year 1978* (Washington, DC: Center of Military History, 1980), 27–28.

130. Chapman, *Army's Training Revolution*, 9.

131. Doubler, *Civilian in Peace, Soldier in War*, 281.

132. NGB Annual Report (1976), 1.

133. NGB Annual Report (1978), 29; NGB Annual Report (1980), 34.

134. NGB Annual Report (1978), 21.

135. "Army to Offer Bonuses for Joining the Reserves," *New York Times*, 8 December 1978, A12.

136. NGB Annual Report (1975), 23.

137. NGB Annual Report (1976), 31; NGB Annual Report (1978), 17; NGB Annual Report (1975), 30; NGB Annual Report (1980), 31.

138. Congressional Budget Office (CBO), *Improving the Readiness of the Army Reserve and National Guard: A Framework for Debate* (Washington, DC: US Government Printing Office, 1978), 16–17, 11.

139. Duncan, *Citizen Warriors*, 144.

140. CBO, *Improving the Readiness of the Army Reserve and National Guard*, 18, 20.

141. See General Gorman's "Posture Statement of the Chief of Staff of the Army, 1977," 2–3, Gorman Papers, US Army Combat Studies Institute Press digital archive.

142. NGB Annual Report (1975), 33; NGB Annual Report (1978), 28.

143. Bernard Weinraub, "Ill-Prepared National Guard Short of Men and Weapons," *New York Times*, 15 July 1979, E3; "Guard and Reserve Losing Equipment to Units in Europe," *New York Times*, 17 January 1978, 36.

144. Weinraub, "Ill-Prepared National Guard Short of Men and Weapons," E3.

145. Robert Kaylor, "Where Are the Weekend Warriors," *Los Angeles Times*, 18 October 1978, C8.

146. Weinraub, "Ill-Prepared National Guard Short of Men and Weapons," E3; Harold Logan, "Guard, Reserve at a Curious Crossroads," *Washington Post*, 27 June 1977, A2.

147. Comptroller General of the United States, *What Defense Says about Issues in Defense Manpower Commission Report—A Summary* (Washington, DC: US Government Printing Office, 1977), 9.

148. Ronald Yates, "53 National Guard Adjutants Criticize Carter Plans in Unprecedented Move," *Washington Post*, 7 May 1980, A4.

149. Logan, "Guard, Reserve at a Curious Crossroads," A2.

150. Ibid.; Yates, "53 National Guard Adjutants Criticize Carter Plans," A4.

151. Linn, *Echo of Battle*, 209.

152. Ibid.

153. Executive Office of the President of the United States, *Historical Tables: Budget of the United States Government: Fiscal Year 2005* (Washington, DC: US Government Printing Office, 2004), 162.

154. Office of the US Secretary of Defense, *Annual Defense Department Report: FY 1978, Secretary of Defense, Donald H. Rumsfeld* (Washington, DC: US Government Printing Office, 1977), 3.

155. Executive Office of the President, *Historical Tables*, 162.

156. Office of the US Secretary of Defense, *Annual Defense Report: Fiscal*

Year 1982, Secretary of Defense, Harold Brown (Washington, DC: US Government Printing Office, 1981), x, iii.

157. Ibid., 131, x, 69, 135.

158. DOD Annual Report (1986), 294; DOD Annual Report (1988), 326; DOD Annual Report (1990), 220.

159. These expenditures were also aided by cuts in government spending elsewhere. For more on spending cuts, see Leffler, *For the Soul of Mankind*, 346; Katherine Blakeley, "Defense Spending in Historical Context: A New Reagan-esque Buildup?" *CSBA*, 8 November 2017, https://csbaonline.org/reports /defense-spending-in-historical-context; Benjamin M. Friedman, "Learning from the Reagan Deficits," *American Economic Review* 82, 2 (1992): 299.

160. US Department of the Army, *FM 100–5: Operations* (Washington, DC: US Government Printing Office, 1982), 33. The 1986 and 1982 versions of FM 100–5 are nearly identical.

161. For a full discussion, see Trauschweizer, *Cold War U.S. Army*, 224–225.

162. US Department of the Army, *Historical Summary: FY 1989*, 254–255, https://history.army.mil/html/bookshelves/collect/dahsum.html.

163. Stewart, *American Military History*, vol. 2, 383–384.

164. Bronfield, "Fighting Outnumbered," 493.

165. Trauschweizer, *Cold War U.S. Army*, 244. For more on the expanding commitment of US forces to the Middle East and the conflict with Iran, see David Crist, *The Twilight War: The Secret History of America's Thirty-Year Conflict with Iran* (New York: Penguin Books, 2012).

166. DOD Annual Report (1989), 226, 129.

167. Ibid., 128–129.

168. NGB Annual Report (1980), 28, 74; NGB Annual Report (1988), 31, 110.

169. DOD Annual Report (1986), 41; US Department of the Army, *Historical Summary: FY 1983*, 104.

170. US Department of the Army, *Department of the Army Historical Series: Fiscal Year 1989* (Washington, DC: Center of Military History, 1998), 151.

171. Duncan, *Citizen Warriors*, 41.

172. William Robbins, "As Reliance on the National Guard Grows, so Do Questions about Readiness," *New York Times*, 10 September 1989, 30.

173. General Accountability Office (GAO), *Readiness of Army Guard and Reserve Support Forces* (Washington, DC: US Government Printing Office, 1988), 4.

174. Brady, "Ready to Serve?" 39–42.

175. US Department of the Army, *Historical Summary: FY 1989*, 154–155.

176. Ibid., 152–153.

177. Martin Binkin and William W. Kaufman, *U.S. Army Guard and Reserve: Realities and Risks* (Washington, DC: Brookings, 1989), 23.

178. GAO, *Management Initiatives Needed to Enhance Reservists' Training* (Washington, DC: US Government Printing Office, 1989), 3, 34.

179. US Department of the Army, *Historical Summary: FY 1989*, 152–153.

180. Final Report of the Total Force Policy Study Group, 4 January 1991, 5, Hollinger box 30: Force Structure Misc. (1990), folder: Total Force Policy Study, National Guard Education Foundation Library, Washington, DC.

181. NGB Annual Report (1991), 25, 82.

182. GAO, *Army Training: Replacement Brigades Were More Proficient than Guard Roundout Brigades* (Washington, DC: US Government Printing Office,1992), 1; Richard M. Swain, *"Lucky War": Third Army in Desert Storm* (Fort Leavenworth, KS: Combat Studies Institute, 2011), 8, 40.

183. Dick Cheney, response to Les Aspin, 18 September 1990, Hollinger box 31, folder: Guard Call-up, National Guard Education Foundation Library.

184. Duncan, *Citizen Warriors*, 37.

185. Norman Schwarzkopf, *It Doesn't Take a Hero: The Autobiography of General Norman Schwarzkopf* (New York: Bantam Books, 1992), 323.

186. Duncan, *Citizen Warriors*, 36–37, 40.

187. Schwarzkopf, *It Doesn't Take a Hero*, 323.

188. Letter from Congressman Montgomery to Hon. Richard Cheney, August 1990, 1, Hollinger box 31, folder: Guard Call-up, National Guard Education Foundation Library.

189. "Iraq, Saudi Arabia, and the Reserve Components: Missing Lessons for the Future Force Structure," 15 October 1990, 6–7, Hollinger box 31, folder: Guard Call-up, National Guard Education Foundation Library.

190. Conaway and Nelligan, *Call out the Guard!* 176.

191. Doubler, *Civilian in Peace, Soldier in War*, 313.

192. Major General Ensslin Jr., National Guard Association, "How Roundout Works—Updated Paper," n.d., 2, Hollinger box 31, folder: Guard Call-up, National Guard Education Foundation Library.

193. Conaway and Nelligan, *Call out the Guard!* 176–177.

194. GAO, *National Guard: Peacetime Training Did Not Adequately Prepare Combat Brigades for Gulf War* (Washington, DC: US Government Printing Office, 1991), 4.

195. GAO, *Army Training*, 4, 22, 3, 24–25.

196. Les Aspin to members of the Committee on Armed Services, Topic: Combat Power from the Reserve Component, 7 May 1992, 7, Hollinger box 30: Force Structure, folder: Total Force Policy Study, National Guard Education Foundation Library.

197. Report cited in Brady, "Ready to Serve?" 32–33.

198. Elizabeth Hudson, "40 in Guard Ruled AWOL at Fort Hood," *Washington Post*, 8 February 1991, A33.

199. Louis Sahagun and John Broder, "40 AWOL Guardsmen Come Back," *Los Angeles Times*, 8 February 1991, A11.

200. Brady, "Ready to Serve?" 95.

201. GAO, *National Guard*, 3, 14, 18.

202. Cheney Says Guard Units May Need Reorganizing," *Washington Post*, 15 March 1991, A34.

203. Peter Applebome, "Guardsmen Return from War They Didn't Fight," *New York Times*, 27 March 1991, A14.

204. Associated Press, "Unit Was Mobilized and Treated Badly," *New York Times*, 5 March 1991, A18; James Kittfield, *Prodigal Soldiers: How the Generation of Officers Born of Vietnam Revolutionized the American Style of War*, paperback ed. (Dulles, VA: Potomac Books, 1997), 352.

205. "Cheney Says Guard Units May Need Reorganizing," A34.

206. OSD Annual Report (1999), B-2; John S. Brown, *Kevlar Legions: The Transformation of the United States Army 1989–2005* (Washington, DC: US Army Center of Military History, 2012), 124–125.

207. Graham Bradley, "Army Postpones Some Guard Cuts to Ease Dispute," *Washington Post*, 7 June 1997, A6.

208. Colin L. Powell, *My American Journey* (New York: Ballentine Books, 2010), 550.

209. Graham Bradley, "National Guard, Regular Army in Tug of War," *Washington Post*, 20 October 1997, A12.

210. John Lancaster, "Cheney Says Hill Hampers Troop Cuts," *Washington Post*, 26 October 1991, A1.

211. "Rethink the Army National Guard," *New York Times*, 27 December 1995, A14.

212. Bradley, "National Guard, Regular Army in Tug of War," A12.

213. Bradley, "Army Postpones Some Guard Cuts," A6.

214. Brown, *Kevlar Legions*, 166; Bradley, "Army Postpones Some Guard Cuts," A6; Bradley, "National Guard, Regular Army in Tug of War," A12.

215. Associated Press, "Cohen Shelves Cut in Reserve Ranks," *Washington Post*, 21 December 1999, A5.

216. Brown, *Kevlar Legions*, 168.

217. Bradley, "National Guard, Regular Army in Tug of War," A12.

218. Eric Schmitt, "Military Planning an Expanded Role for the Reserves," *New York Times*, 25 November 1994, A22. For an excellent account of the NG's activities in the 1990s, see Miranda Summers Lowe, "The Gradual Shift to an Operational Reserve: Reserve Component Mobilizations in the 1990s," *Military Review*, May 2019.

219. US Department of the Army, *Department of the Army Historical Series: Fiscal Year 1995* (Washington, DC: Center of Military History, 2004), 54.

220. Schmitt, "Military Planning Expanded Role for Reserves," A22.

221. Doubler, *Civilian in Peace, Soldier in War*, 352–357; Steven Lee Myers, "Army to Shorten Tours of Reserves Serving Overseas," *New York Times*, 5 March 2000, 1.

222. Steven Lee Myers, "National Guard Unit Adds Dimension to a Peacekeeper Role," *New York Times*, 18 June 2000, 4.

223. Anderson, *Mustering for War*, 23.

224. Steven Lee Myers, "Army Will Give National Guard the Entire U.S. Role in Bosnia," *New York Times*, 5 December 2000, A8.

225. Steven Lee Myers, "Army Weighs an Expanded Role for National Guard Combat Units," *New York Times*, 4 August 2000, A1.

226. Doubler, *Civilian in Peace, Soldier in War*, 338.

227. RAND Corporation, "The Army Makes a Bold Shift: Improving Reserve Training," 2001, https://www.rand.org/pubs/research_briefs/RB3019/index1.html.

228. NGB Annual Report (1995), 32.

229. US Department of the Army, *Department of the Army Historical Series: Fiscal Year 1997* (Washington, DC: Center of Military History, 2005), 8; DOD Annual Report (1995), 245.

230. US Department of the Army, *Historical Summary: FY 1995*, 54–55; DOD Annual Report (1995), 245.

231. Brown, *Kevlar Legions*, 181.

232. US Department of the Army, *Historical Summary: FY 1995*, 54–55; Bradley, "National Guard, Regular Army in Tug of War," A12.

233. DOD Annual Report (1995), 36; Brown, *Kevlar Legions*, 181.

234. Brown, *Kevlar Legions*, 98, 140.

235. Unlike the army's existing antitank missile, the TOW, the Javelin was a top attack missile—that is, it struck tanks at the top, where the armor was thinnest and most vulnerable. Brown, *Kevlar Legions*, 98.

236. Ibid., 145–146, 148–149.

237. For the definitive history of the ARNG's mobilization to support operations in Iraq and Afghanistan, see Anderson, *Mustering for War*.

238. Steven Coll, *Directorate S: The C.I.A. and America's Secret Wars in Afghanistan and Pakistan* (New York: Penguin Books, 2018), 134.

239. NGB Annual Report (2003), 32; Kevin Sullivan, "Weekend Warriors No More," *Washington Post*, 19 July 2003, A1.

240. Terry L. Sellers, Gregory Fontenot, E. J. Degen, and David Tohn, "On Point: The United States Army in Operation Iraqi Freedom," *Naval War College Review* 59, 2 (2006): article 14.

241. Thom Shanker, "U.S. to Use Mix of Regular, National Guard, and Reserve Troops in Iraq," *New York Times*, 24 July 2003, A10.

242. US Army War College, *The U.S. Army in the Iraq War*, vol. 1, *Invasion, Insurgency, and Civil War (2003–2006)* (Carlisle, PA: US Army War College Press, 2019), 36, 64–66.

243. NGB Annual Report (2003), 32.

244. "About the Army National Guard," http://www.nationalguard.mil/AbouttheGuard/ArmyNationalGuard.aspx.

245. Vernon Loeb, "Protests Grow over Year-Long Army Tours," *Washington Post*, 20 September 2003, A13.

246. US Department of the Army, *Historical Summary: FY 2004*, 46.

247. Loeb, "Protests Grow over Year-Long Army Tours," A13; Eric Schmitt, "Guard Reports Serious Drop in Enlistment," *New York Times*, 17 December 2004, A32.

248. Sullivan, "Weekend Warriors No More," A1.

249. Loeb, "Protests Grow over Year-Long Army Tours," A13.

250. Robert Pear, "Bush Policies Are Weakening National Guard," *New York Times*, 27 February 2006, A10; Anderson, *Mustering for War*, 39–40.

251. US Department of the Army, *Department of the Army Historical Series: Fiscal Year 2010* (Washington, DC: Center of Military History, 2015), 31.

252. Brown, *Kevlar Legions*, 75.

253. OSD Annual Report (2005), A-1.

254. US Army War College, *U.S. Army in the Iraq War*, vol. 1, 376; National Commission on the Future of the Army (NCFA), "Recent Experience in Reserve and Guard Readiness, Mobilization, and Operational Deployment," 10 April 2015, 2; US Department of the Army, *Historical Summary: FY 2004*, 42.

255. NCFA, "Recent Experience in Reserve and Guard Readiness," 2.

256. For an account of the experiences of the Second Brigade Combat Team (Pennsylvania ARNG) in Iraq by the unit's commander, see John L. Gronski, "2/28 BCT Goes to War," 1 July 2007, http://www.milvet.state.pa.us/PAO/pr/2006_07_01.htm.

257. US Army War College, *U.S. Army in the Iraq War*, vol. 1, 377, 604–606.

258. Ibid., 506, 507.

259. National Guard Bureau, *Posture Statement 2010* (Washington, DC: NGB, 2010), 6.

260. Steve Beynon, "Cheated and Guilty: The Struggle for Troops Who Missed out on Combat," Military.com, 24 August 2021, https://www.military.com/daily-news/2021/08/24/cheated-and-guilty-struggle-troops-who-missed-out-combat.html.

261. Robert Gates, *Duty: Memoirs of a Secretary at War* (New York: Knopf, 2014), 7.

262. Jim Garamone, "DOD Clarifies Reserve-Component Mobilization Policy," 16 April 2007, http://www.army.mil/article/2681/dod-clarifies-reserve-component-mobilization-policy/; NCFA, "Recent Experience in Reserve and Guard Readiness," 2.

263. Garamone, "DOD Clarifies Reserve-Component Mobilization Policy."

264. National Guard Bureau, *Posture Statement 2015* (Washington, DC: NGB, 2015), 24.

265. NCFA, *National Commission on the Future of the Army: Report to the President and Congress of the United States* (Washington, DC: US Government Printing Office, 2016), 64.

266. NCFA, "Minutes from NGAUS Conference, Nashville, TN," 12 September 2015, 4; Anderson, *Mustering for War*, 50.

267. NCFA, "Audio Recording of Part 1 of the Public Meeting, June 18, 2015."

268. NCFA, "Mandatory Training Requirements and Mobilization Force Generation Installations Information Paper," 9 September 2015, 1–2.

269. "1st Battalion, 125th Infantry Regiment 'Task Force Viking' Lights up the Sky," USCENTCOM, n.d., https://www.centcom.mil/MEDIA/IMAGERY

/igphoto/2003140008/; Matthew Cox, "Army National Guard Mechanized Infantry Forces Arrive in Syria to Protect Oil Fields," Military.com, 31 October 2019, https://www.military.com/daily-news/2019/10/31/army-national-guard -mechanized-infantry-forces-arrive-in-syria-to-protect-oil-fields.html.

270. Todd Harrison, "What Has the Budget Control Act of 2011 Meant for Defense?" *CSIS*, 1 August 2016, https://www.csis.org/analysis/what-has-budget -control-act-2011-meant-defense.

271. NCFA, *National Commission on the Future of the Army*, 39, 122.

272. Ibid., 3.

273. "National Guard Chafes at Comments of Army Top Officer," *Army Times*, 14 January 2014, https://www.usatoday.com/story/news/nation/2014/01/14 /army-national-guard-readiness/4472077/.

274. NCFA, *National Commission on the Future of the Army*, 1; Ben Watson, "Army, National Guard Fight over Apache Helicopters," Defense One, 8 April 2014, https://www.defenseone.com/politics/2014/04/army-national-guard-fight -over-apache-helicopters/82150/.

275. NCFA, *National Commission on the Future of the Army*, foreword, 3, 91, 2–3.

276. CBO, "Growth in DOD's Budget from 2000 to 2014," 20 November 2014, https://www.cbo.gov/publication/49764.

277. ARNG, "By the Numbers" 2019, https://www.army.nationalguard.mil /About-Us/By-the-Numbers/.

278. SGT Dennis Glass, "Lt. Gen. Hodges: U.S. Army Europe Needs Reserve Components to Be Successful," 9 June 2016, https://www.usar.army.mil /News/News-Display/Article/795255/lt-gen-hodges-us-army-europe-needs -reserve-components-to-be-successful//.

279. OSD, "Report to Congress: Unit Cost and Readiness for the Active and Reserve Components of the United States," 20 December 2013, 4.

280. This figure was generated using the ARNG's drill paycheck calculator, https://www.nationalguard.com/pay/calculator.

281. US Army base pay figures for 2018 are available at Defense Finance and Accounting Service (DFAS), "Military Pay Charts—1949 to 2018," https:// www.dfas.mil/militarymembers/payentitlements/military-pay-charts.html. A housing allowance calculator is available at Defense Travel Management Office, "BAH Calculator," http://www.defensetravel.dod.mil/site/bahCalc.cfm.

282. Jed Judson, "The Army Is Creating a Modernization Command to Keep Projects on Track," *Defense News*, 9 October 2017, https://www.defensenews. com/digital-show-dailies/ausa/2017/10/09/the-army-is-creating-a-new-mod ernization -command-to-keep-projects-on-track/.

283. US Department of Defense, *Summary of the 2018 National Defense Strategy of the United States* (Washington, DC: US Government Printing Office, 2018), 1.

284. US Department of the Army, *FM 3–0: Operations* (Washington, DC: US

Government Printing Office, 2017), foreword; TRADOC, "General Townsend Announces MDO at LANPAC," YouTube, 23 May 2018.

285. US Department of the Army, *FM 3–0: Operations*, 1–6, 1–7.

286. Ibid.

287. "Multi-Domain Task Forces: A Glimpse at the Army of 2035," Association of the US Army, 2 March 2022, https://www.ausa.org/publications/multi-domain-task-forces-glimpse-army-2035.

288. C. Todd Lopez, "Army National Guard Director: Two Weeks Annually, Weekend per Month Enough?" https://www.army.mil/article/158810/army_national_guard_director_two_weeks_annually_weekend_per_month_enough.

289. Tan, "Top Army General Outlines Plans."

290. US Army National Guard, "ARNG 4.0: Focused Readiness," 2017, http://www.nationalguard.mil/Resources/ARNG-Readiness/.

291. Matthew Cox, "Army Guard Plans for Short-Notice Deployments, More Training Days," Military.com, 2 May 2018, https://www.military.com/daily-news/2018/05/02/army-guard-plans-short-notice-deployments-more-training-days.html.

292. US Army Center for Army Lessons Learned, *Observation Report: USARCENT Intermediate Division Headquarters (IDHQ) Operation Spartan Shield, 29th Infantry Division* (Fort Leavenworth, KS: CALL, 2018), 2.

293. SSG Marc Heaton, "29th ID Returns to USA after Spartan Shield Rotation," Virginia Army National Guard, 25 March 2022, https://va.ng.mil/News/Article/2977468/29th-id-returns-to-usa-after-spartan-shield-rotation/.

294. National Guard Bureau, *Posture Statement 2019* (Washington, DC: NGB, 2019), 17. For more on the Enhanced Forward Presence initiative, see NATO, "NATO's Enhanced Forward Presence Factsheet," May 2017, https://www.nato.int/nato_static_fl2014/assets/pdf/pdf_2017_05/1705-factsheet-efp.pdf.

295. SSG Zane Craig, "Pennsylvania Army National Guard Supports Defender Europe 22," National Guard Bureau, 3 June 2022, https://www.nationalguard.mil/News/Article/3051557/pennsylvania-army-national-guard-supports-defender-europe-22/.

296. "Task Force Spartan," US Army Central, n.d., https://www.usarcent.army.mil/About/Units/Task-Force-Spartan/.

297. Drew Lawrence, "How New Jersey Guardsmen Thwarted One of the Largest Somali Terror Attacks in Decades," Military.com, 28 December 2022, https://www.military.com/daily-news/2022/12/28/how-new-jersey-guardsmen-thwarted-one-of-largest-somali-terror-attacks-decades.html; John Vandiver, "Soldiers Reveal in Depth How 2019 Attack on Somali Airfield Was Repelled," *Stars and Stripes*, 28 December 2022, https://www.stripes.com/branches/army/2022-12-28/new-jersey-national-guard-somalia-8565947.html.

298. Michelle Tan, "Army Units Change Patches as Part of Active, Guard, and Reserve Pilot Program," *Army Times*, 19 August 2016, https://www.armytimes

.com/pay-benefits/military-benefits/2016/08/19/army-units-change-patches
-as-part-of-active-guard-and-reserve-pilot-program/.

299. National Guard Bureau, *Posture Statement 2019*, 11; Erich B. Smith, "Readiness Enhanced with Army National Guard," National Guard Bureau, 26 February 2018, http://www.nationalguard.mil/News/Article/1450485/readiness-enhanced-with-army-national-guard-40/.

300. Jeff Schogol, "Constant Mobilizations May Be Pushing the National Guard to the Brink," *Task and Purpose*, 17 March 2021.

301. Lolita Baldor, "National Guard Struggles as Troops Leave at Faster Pace," AP News, 8 October 2022, https://apnews.com/article/health-middle-east-covid-government-and-politics-987f5dbc245858f372eaeeb3edc018bd.

Chapter 4. The Heights of Israeli Reserve Performance

1. "Organizational Structure and Combat Forces," http://www.irgon-haagana.co.il/show_item.asp?levelid=61005&itemid=49699&itemtype=3&prm=t=4.

2. See Zeev Schiff, *A History of the Israeli Army, 1874 to the Present: Israel's Foremost Military Expert Tells the Story of the World's Best Citizen Army* (New York: Macmillan, 1985).

3. Gunther E. Rothenberg, *The Anatomy of the Israeli Army* (London: B. T. Batsford, 1979), 14; Anita Shapira, *Israel: A History* (Waltham, MA: Brandis University Press, 2012), 7, 12.

4. Shapira, *Israel*, 28–30.

5. Mordechai Naor, *Ha'Hagana* (Tel Aviv: IDF, 1985), 54.

6. Bruce Hoffman, *Anonymous Soldiers: The Struggle for Israel, 1917–1947* (New York: Vintage Books, 2015), 6.

7. Gudrun Kramer, *A History of Palestine: From the Ottoman Conquest to the Founding of the State of Israel* (Princeton, NJ: Princeton University Press, 2011), 207, 208; Anita Shapira, *Land and Power: The Zionist Resort to Force, 1881–1948* (Stanford, CA: Stanford University Press, 1999), 110; Hoffman, *Anonymous Soldiers*, 11.

8. Reuven Gal, *A Portrait of the Israeli Soldier* (New York: Praeger, 1986), 3.

9. Shapira, *Land and Power*, 125.

10. Rothenberg, *Anatomy of the Israeli Army*, 23; Hoffman, *Anonymous Soldiers*, 9; Van Creveld, *Sword and the Olive*, 26.

11. Rothenberg, *Anatomy of the Israeli Army*, 23; Van Creveld, *Sword and the Olive*, 26.

12. Shapira, *Israel*, 75.

13. Hoffman, *Anonymous Soldiers*, 7.

14. "The Foundations of the Hagana," http://www.irgon-haagana.co.il/show_item.asp?levelid=61005&itemid=49697&itemtype=3&prm=t=4.

15. Yigal Allon, *The Making of Israel's Army* (London: Sphere Books, 1971), 18.

16. Van Creveld, *Sword and the Olive*, 24–25.

17. Rothenberg, *Anatomy of the Israeli Army*, 24–25.

18. Benny Morris, *Righteous Victims: A History of the Zionist-Arab Conflict, 1881–1998*, reprint ed. (New York: Vintage Books, 2011), 119.

19. Hillel Cohen, *Year Zero of the Arab-Israeli Conflict 1929* (Waltham, MA: Brandeis University Press, 2015), 106; "Activity during the Early Years," http://www.irgon-haagana.co.il/show_item.asp?levelid=61005&itemid=49698&itemtype=3&prm=t=4; Rothenberg, *Anatomy of the Israeli Army*, 24; Morris, *Righteous Victims*, 114–116.

20. Morris, *Righteous Victims*, 116.

21. Rothenberg, *Anatomy of the Israeli Army*, 23–24.

22. Van Creveld, *Sword and the Olive*, 43.

23. Kramer, *History of Palestine*, 240.

24. Van Creveld, *Sword and the Olive*, 38; Hoffman, *Anonymous Soldiers*, 38–39.

25. Rothenberg, *Anatomy of the Israeli Army*, 18.

26. Benny Morris, *1948: A History of the First Arab-Israeli War* (New Haven, CT: Yale University Press, 2008), 16; Yigal Eyal, "The Arab Revolt, 1936–1939: A Turning Point in the Struggle for Palestine," in *A Never-ending Conflict: A Guide to Israeli Military History*, ed. Mordechai Bar-On (New York: Praeger, 2004), 22.

27. Laila Parsons, *The Commander: Fawzi al-Qawuqji and the Fight for Arab Independence 1914–1948* (New York: Hill & Wang, 2016), 127–129.

28. Eyal, "Arab Revolt, 1936–1939," 24.

29. Morris, *1948*, 18, 19–20.

30. Tom Segev, *One Palestine, Complete: Jews and Arabs under the British Mandate* (New York: Owl Books, 2001), 430; Schiff, *History of the Israeli Army*, 13.

31. Allon, *Making of Israel's Army*, 21.

32. Segev, *One Palestine, Complete*, 430.

33. "Organizational Structure and Combat Forces," http://www.irgon-haagana.co.il/show_item.asp?levelid=61005&itemid=49699&itemtype=3&prm=t=4.

34. "Command and Training," http://www.irgon-haagana.co.il/show_item.asp?levelid=61005&itemid=49701&itemtype=3&prm=t=4.

35. "Organizational Structure and Combat Forces"; "Command and Training."

36. "Organizational Structure and Combat Forces."

37. "Activity during the Early Years," http://www.irgon-haagana.co.il/show_item.asp?levelid=61005&itemid=49698&itemtype=3&prm=t=4.

38. Colin Shindler, *A History of Modern Israel* (New York: Cambridge University Press, 2008), 36–37.

39. Hoffman, *Anonymous Soldiers*, 116.

40. "Organizational Structure and Combat Forces"; Schiff, *History of the Israeli Army*, 18.

41. Gal, *Portrait of the Israeli Soldier*, 7.

42. Yitzhak Rabin, *The Rabin Memoirs*, expanded ed. (Berkley: University of California Press, 1997), 13; Van Creveld, *Sword and the Olive*, 51.

43. Schiff, *History of the Israeli Army*, 17.

44. Ibid.; Martin Van Creveld, *Moshe Dayan* (London: Weidenfeld & Nicolson, 2004), 47, 52.

45. Gal, *Portrait of the Israeli Soldier*, 7; "Organizational Structure and Combat Forces."

46. Schiff, *History of the Israeli Army*, 19.

47. Allon, *Making of Israel's Army*, 30; Rabin, *Rabin Memoirs*, 14.

48. Allon, *Making of Israel's Army*, 32; Schiff, *History of the Israeli Army*, 19.

49. Ahron Bregman, *Israel's Wars: A History since 1947*, 3rd ed. (New York: Routledge, 2010), 11–12, 14.

50. Ibid.,12.

51. Gal, *Portrait of the Israeli Soldier*, 9.

52. Kenneth M. Pollack, *Arabs at War: Military Effectiveness, 1948–1991* (Lincoln, NE: Bison Books, 2004), 15, 169.

53. Rabin, *Rabin Memoirs*, 23.

54. Rothenberg, *Anatomy of the Israeli Army*, 42–43.

55. Ibid., 51.

56. "Staff H.Q. Haganah," *Palestine Post*, 1 January 1948, 4.

57. Bregman, *Israel's Wars*, 15.

58. Ibid.

59. Allon, *Making of Israel's Army*, 43.

60. Shapira, *Israel*, 158.

61. Morris, *1948*, 81, 82.

62. Allon, *Making of Israel's Army*, 43.

63. David Ben-Gurion, *Memoirs* (Cleveland, OH: World Publishing, 1970), 86.

64. Rothenberg, *Anatomy of the Israeli Army*, 46.

65. Neil Silberman, *A Prophet from Amongst You: The Life of Yigael Yadin* (Boston: Addison-Wesley, 1993), 87.

66. Van Creveld, *Sword and the Olive*, 63.

67. Rabin, *Rabin Memoirs*, 19.

68. Rothenberg, *Anatomy of the Israeli Army*, 45.

69. Bregman, *Israel's Wars*, 15.

70. Ariel Sharon, *Warrior: An Autobiography*, 2nd ed. (New York: Simon & Schuster, 2002), 40, 44.

71. Allon, *Making of Israel's Army*, 15; Bregman, *Israel's Wars*, 24.

72. Ronen Bergman, *Rise and Kill First: The Secret History of Israel's Targeted Assassinations* (New York: Random House, 2018), 25.

73. Howard M. Sachar, *A History of Israel: From the Rise of Zionism to Our Time* (New York: Knopf, 2007), 316.

74. Morris, *1948*, 210; Rabin, *Rabin Memoirs*, 32.

75. Morris, *1948*, 188–189; Pollack, *Arabs at War*, 272.

76. Allon, *Making of Israel's Army*, 46.

77. Morris, *1948*, 85.

78. Ben-Gurion, *Memoirs*, 90–91.

79. Rothenberg, *Anatomy of the Israeli Army*, 54; Schiff, *History of the Israeli Army*, 30.

80. Schiff, *History of the Israeli Army*, 30; Allon, *Making of Israel's Army*, 49–50.

81. Pollack, *Arabs at War*, 280–282.

82. Van Creveld, *Moshe Dayan*, 69.

83. Rabin, *Rabin Memoirs*, 44.

84. Rothenberg, *Anatomy of the Israeli Army*, 65.

85. Van Creveld, *Moshe Dayan*, 69.

86. Gal, *Portrait of the Israeli Soldier*, 11.

87. Allon, *Making of Israel's Army*, 59.

88. Gal, *Portrait of the Israeli Soldier*, 12.

89. Arie Niger, "A New Model for the Reserve Army [in Hebrew]," *Maarachot*, 20 May 2002, 34.

90. Allon, *Making of Israel's Army*, 56, 60; Yitzhak Greenburg, "The Swiss Armed Forces as a Model for the IDF Reserve System—Indeed?" *Israel Studies* 18, 3 (Fall 2013): 100–101.

91. Allon, *Making of Israel's Army*, 56, 60; Meir Finkel, *Studies in Generalship* (Stanford, CA: Hoover Institution Press, 2021), 224.

92. Rothenberg, *Anatomy of the Israeli Army*, 71.

93. Finkel, *Studies in Generalship*, 225.

94. Rothenberg, *Anatomy of the Israeli Army*, 71–73.

95. Bregman, *Israel's Wars*, 42.

96. Allon, *Making of Israel's Army*, 56–57.

97. Bregman, *Israel's Wars*, 45; Rothenberg, *Anatomy of the Israeli Army*, 72.

98. Emanuel Sakal, *Soldier in the Sinai: A General's Account of the Yom Kippur War*, trans. Moshe Tlami (Lexington: University Press of Kentucky, 2014), 68.

99. Israeli Ministry of Aliyah and Immigrant Absorption, *Military Service*, 7th ed. (Jerusalem: Publications Department, 2016), 44, http://archive.moia.gov.il/Publications/idf_en.pdf; International Institute for Strategic Studies (IISS), Military Balance 2018, 340.

100. English and Gudmundsson, *On Infantry*, 169.

101. Ibid., 167–168.

102. For an example, see the experience of Gal Hirsch in *Defensive Shield: An Israeli Special Forces Commander on the Front Lines of Counterterrorism*, trans. Reuven Ben-Shalom (New York: Gefen Books, 2016), 13.

103. Israeli Ministry of Aliyah, *Military Service*, 44; IISS, Military Balance 2018, 340.

104. "Career Planning for Reserve Officers," *Jerusalem Post*, 29 July 1953, 2.

105. Two armored brigades were added by 1956. Rothenberg, *Anatomy of the Israeli Army*, 82, 85.

106. Ibid., 82.

107. Gal, *Portrait of the Israeli Soldier*, 12.

108. Louis Williams, *Israel Defense Forces: A People's Army* (Tel Aviv: Israeli Ministry of Defense, 1989), 12; Kenneth Love, "Israel's Forces Outweigh Arabs," *New York Times*, 30 August 1955, 14.

109. "Men 20 to 49 Being Called," *Jerusalem Post*, 30 June 1950, 3; "Annual Reserve Service [in Hebrew]," *Davar*, 6 August 1954, 19–20.

110. "High Praise for Reserves in North," *Jerusalem Post*, 17 September 1952, 3; "Annual Reserve Service," 19–20.

111. Sraya Shapiro, "Part-Time Civilians," *Jerusalem Post*, 15 March 1954, 4.

112. Allon, *Making of Israel's Army*, 56–57.

113. "Reserve Duty Year to Start April 1," *Jerusalem Post*, 5 July 1951, 3.

114. See the experience of ARNG as described in chapters 2 and 3. For British army practices, see "Your Time: How Much Will It Take?" https://apply.army .mod.uk/what-we-offer/reserve-soldier/reserve-soldier-time.

115. Ash Sherwood, "The Training Aspect of Reserve Battalion Combat Readiness" (M.A. thesis, US Army Command and General Staff College, 1983), 33.

116. Ibid.; CIA, "National Intelligence Estimate: Israel," 29 June 1972, 6, https://www.cia.gov/library/readingroom/docs/DOC_0001518685.pdf.

117. Greenburg, "Swiss Armed Forces as a Model for the IDF Reserve System," 104–106.

118. Yigal Yadin, "Establishment of the IDF Reserve Force [in Hebrew]," *Maarachot*, 20 July 1984, 18, 19.

119. Central Bureau of Statistics, "Defence Expenditure in Israel, 1950–2014," August 2016, 12, https://www.cbs.gov.il/he/publications/DocLib/2016/1651/e _print.pdf.

120. Moshe Brilliant, "Tel Aviv Is Tense," *New York Times*, 29 October 1956, 3.

121. Rothenberg, *Anatomy of the Israeli Army*, 76, 80, 81.

122. Love, "Israel's Forces Outweigh Arabs," 14.

123. Unfortunately, there is no publicly available data regarding the breakdown of IDF spending in the 1950s. I assume, however, that the IDF devoted a large percentage of its resources to operations, training, and equipment, given that all the CGSs of the period focused on those aspects of the military.

124. Rothenberg, *Anatomy of the Israeli Army*, 80.

125. Rabin, *Rabin Memoirs*, 48; Rothenberg, *Anatomy of the Israeli Army*, 80; Dov Glazer, "They Did It Their Way," in *Mission Command in the Israel Defense Forces*, ed. Gideon Avidor (Dahlonega: University of North Georgia Press, 2021), 107–109.

126. Glazer, "They Did It Their Way," 126–127.

127. Van Creveld, *Sword and the Olive*, 106–107.

128. Rothenberg, *Anatomy of the Israeli Army*, 87; Meir Finkel, *Military*

Agility: Ensuring Rapid and Effective Transition from Peace to War (Lexington: University Press of Kentucky, 2020), 12–13.

129. Gal, *Portrait of the Israeli Soldier*, 13.

130. Bregman, *Israel's Wars*, 39; Rothenberg, *Anatomy of the Israeli Army*, 84.

131. Allon, *Making of Israel's Army*, 57.

132. Rothenberg, *Anatomy of the Israeli Army*, 79; Glazer, "They Did It Their Way," 118–119.

133. Itzik Ronen, "Is the Reserve Army Sinking [in Hebrew]," *Maarachot*, 6 June 2013, 31.

134. Schiff, *History of the Israeli Army*, 71.

135. Rothenberg, *Anatomy of the Israeli Army*, 89.

136. Ibid., 88; Finkel, *Studies in Generalship*, 175.

137. Moshe Dayan, *Moshe Dayan: Story of My Life; an Autobiography* (New York: William Morrow, 1976), 172–173; Rothenberg, *Anatomy of the Israeli Army*, 91.

138. Dayan, *Story of My Life*, 172–173.

139. Rothenberg, *Anatomy of the Israeli Army*, 91.

140. Dayan, *Story of My Life*, 172–173.

141. Ibid., 93; Finkel, *Studies in Generalship*, 183–184, 189.

142. Finkel, *Military Agility*, 13; Gudmundsson, *On Artillery*, 155; Rothenberg, *Anatomy of the Israeli Army*, 100–101.

143. Rothenberg, *Anatomy of the Israeli Army*, 100.

144. Bregman, *Israel's Wars*, 55.

145. Pollack, *Arabs at War*, 29; Schiff, *History of the Israeli Army*, 88.

146. Schiff, *History of the Israeli Army*, 88, 90.

147. Rothenberg, *Anatomy of the Israeli Army*, 105; Meir Amit, "Sinai System—the IDF's First Test as a Regular Army [in Hebrew]," *Maarachot*, 20 January 1987, 4.

148. Edward Luttwak and Daniel Horowitz, *The Israeli Army* (New York: HarperCollins, 1975), 157; Pollack, *Arabs at War*, 31.

149. Moshe Dayan, *Diary of the Sinai Campaign* (New York: Harper & Row, 1966), 61.

150. Pollack, *Arabs at War*, 32–33.

151. Luttwak and Horowitz, *Israeli Army*, 156–157; Schiff, *History of the Israeli Army*, 95.

152. Dayan, *Diary of the Sinai Campaign*, 36.

153. George W. Gawrych, *Key to the Sinai: The Battles for Abu Ageila in the 1956 and 1967 Arab-Israeli Wars* (Fort Leavenworth, KS: Combat Studies Institute, 1990), 22, 24.

154. CIA, "Middle East Situation," 7 March 1956, 2, https://www.cia.gov/readingroom/docs/CIA-RDP79R00890A000700030020-5.pdf.

155. Trevor M. Dupuy, *Elusive Victory: The Arab-Israeli Wars, 1947–1974* (New York: Harper & Row, 1978), 144, 146.

156. Pollack, *Arabs at War*, 31–33.

157. Schiff, *History of the Israeli Army*, 93.

158. Dayan, *Story of My Life*, 255–256; Van Creveld, *Sword and the Olive*, 147.

159. Schiff, *History of the Israeli Army*, 93, 96–97; Israel Ministry of Foreign Affairs, "The Sinai Campaign," n.d., https://mfa.gov.il/mfa/aboutisrael/history/pages/the%20sinai%20campaign%20-%201956.aspx.

160. Pollack, *Arabs at War*, 41.

161. Schiff, *History of the Israeli Army*, 93.

162. Dayan, *Diary of the Sinai Campaign*, 38; Van Creveld, *Sword and the Olive*, 142.

163. Dayan, *Diary of the Sinai Campaign*, 69–70, 86.

164. Ibid., 69; "Tel Aviv Is Tense," 1.

165. Dayan, *Diary of the Sinai Campaign*, 85–86; Ronen, "Is the Reserve Army Sinking," 31.

166. Luttwak and Horowitz, *Israeli Army*, 146.

167. Amit, "Sinai System," 4.

168. Dayan, *Diary of the Sinai Campaign*, 85–86.

169. Gawrych, *Key to the Sinai*, 14, 24.

170. Dayan, *Diary of the Sinai Campaign*, 115.

171. Gawrych, *Key to the Sinai*, 25, 37–40.

172. Ibid., 24, 50.

173. Dupuy, *Elusive Victory*, 165; Yigal Henkin, *The 1956 Suez War and the New World Order in the Middle East: Exodus in Reverse* (Lanham, MD: Lexington Books, 2015), 148.

174. Dupuy, *Elusive Victory*, 165.

175. Dayan, *Diary of the Sinai Campaign*, 118.

176. Dupuy, *Elusive Victory*, 167.

177. Henkin, *1956 Suez War*, 152.

178. Finkel, *Military Agility*, 16–17.

179. Henkin, *1956 Suez War*, 152.

180. Dupuy, *Elusive Victory*, 167, 168.

181. Dayan, *Story of My Life*, 259.

182. Finkel, *Studies in Generalship*, 106.

183. Gawrych, *Key to the Sinai*, 106; Allon, *Making of Israel's Army*, 69–72; Paul Kohn, "Israel Army Completes Manoeuvres," *Jerusalem Post*, 22 July 1960, 4; Glazer, "They Did It Their Way," 126.

184. Israel had about a thousand tanks by 1967, whereas in 1957 its tank arsenal was only two hundred to three hundred. See CIA, "Military Capabilities of Israel and the Arab States," 26 May 1967, 4, https://www.cia.gov/library/readingroom/docs/CIA-RDP79T00826A002000010049-0.pdf.

185. Gawrych, *Key to the Sinai*, 69.

186. English and Gudmundsson, *On Infantry*, 170.

187. Rothenberg, *Anatomy of the Israeli Army*, 122.

188. Gudmundsson, *On Armor*, 166–167.

189. Gudmundsson, *On Artillery*, 155.

190. CIA, "The Arab-Israeli Situation," 6 April 1961, map 1, https://www.cia.gov/readingroom/docs/CIA-RDP79S00427A000400060001-9.pdf.

191. Dupuy, *Elusive Victory*, 338; IISS, Military Balance 1966, 37.

192. Sharon, *Warrior*, 180; Van Creveld, *Sword and the Olive*, 159.

193. David Rodman, *Combined Arms Warfare in Israeli Military History: From the War of Independence to Operation Protective Edge* (Brighton, UK: Sussex Academic Press, 2019), 21.

194. Schiff, *History of the Israeli Army*, 99; Gawrych, *Key to the Sinai*, 67–69.

195. Gawrych, *Key to the Sinai*, 67–69.

196. Van Creveld, *Sword and the Olive*, 156.

197. World Bank, "Military Expenditure (% of GDP)—Israel," https://data.worldbank.org/indicator/MS.MIL.XPND.GD.ZS?end=2018&locations=IL&start =1960&view=chart; World Bank, "Israel GDP," https://data.worldbank.org/country/israel?view=chart; "U.S. Foreign Aid to Israel," Jewish Virtual Library, https://www.jewishvirtuallibrary.org/total-u-s-foreign-aid-to-israel-1949-present.

198. Irving Heymont, "Israeli Defense Forces," *Military Review*, 8 February 1967, 41

199. Bregman, *Israel's Wars*, 61.

200. Shimon Peres, "Strategy, Security, and Deterrents," *Jerusalem Post*, 19 April 1961; Van Creveld, *Sword and the Olive*, 155.

201. Rothenberg, *Anatomy of the Israeli Army*, 123–124.

202. Meir Pilewski, "Talks on the Training of Troops—Training of Troops in the Reserve [in Hebrew]," *Maarachot*, 21 January 1962, 28.

203. "Summer Training in Reserve Battalions [in Hebrew]," *Maarachot*, 21 November 1965, 23–25; Gal, *Portrait of the Israeli Soldier*, 42–43.

204. "A Reserve Armor Unit 'Attacked' Three Targets with Air Support [in Hebrew]," *Harut*, 2 November 1961, 4.

205. "Summer Training in Reserve Battalions," 23–25; Gilad Pasternak, "The Field and Terrain Capabilities of the Infantry Fighter on the Modern Battlefield [in Hebrew]," *Maarachot*, 8 August 2022, 32–33.

206. Gawrych, *Key to the Sinai*, 71; Van Creveld, *Sword and the Olive*, 159.

207. Gawrych, *Key to the Sinai*, 71–72; Kohn, "Israel Army Completes Manoeuvres," 4.

208. Gawrych, *Key to the Sinai*, 72.

209. Jac Weller, "Israeli Armor: Lessons from the Six-Day War," *Military Review*, November 1971, 46.

210. Ori Orr, *These Are My Brothers: A Dramatic Story of Heroism during the Yom Kippur War* (Tel Aviv: Contento Publishing, 2003), 14, 21.

211. Ibid., 14, 21, 23–24, 30, 33, 12, 28.

212. Rabin, *Rabin Memoirs*, 66.

213. Moshe Gat, "Nasser and the Six Day War, 5 June 1967: A Premeditated Strategy or an Inexorable Drift to War?" *Israel Affairs* 11, 4 (October 2005): 614.

214. David Lesch, *The Arab-Israeli Conflict: A History*, 1st ed. (New York: Oxford University Press, 2007), 205.

215. Bregman, *Israel's Wars*, 73; Morris, *Righteous Victims*, 302; Abraham Rabinovich, *The Battle for Jerusalem: An Unintended Conquest*, 50th anniversary ed. (Middleton, DE: Jewish Publication Society, 2017), 34.

216. Michael B. Oren, *Six Days of War: June 1967 and the Making of the Modern Middle East* (New York: Presidio, 2003), 178; Rabin, *Rabin Memoirs*, 98.

217. Gawrych, *Key to the Sinai*, 88.

218. Chaim Herzog, *The Arab-Israeli Wars: War and Peace in the Middle East* (New York: Vintage, 2015), 157.

219. Oren, *Six Days of War*, 178, 179.

220. Ibid.; Pollack, *Arabs at War*, 64.

221. Bregman, *Israel's Wars*, 75; Oren, *Six Days of War*, 179.

222. Sharon, *Warrior*, 187.

223. Bregman, *Israel's Wars*, 75.

224. Ibid.; Steven Pressfield, *The Lion's Gate: On the Front Lines of the Six Day War* (New York: Sentinel, 2014), 209; Rothenberg, *Anatomy of the Israeli Army*, 142.

225. Gawrych, *Key to the Sinai*, 88.

226. Bregman, *Israel's Wars*, 75; Sharon, *Warrior*, 183, 187.

227. Gawrych, *Key to the Sinai*, 88.

228. Bregman, *Israel's Wars*, 74–75; Ronen, "Is the Reserve Army Sinking," 31.

229. Charles Mohr, "Rapid Mobilization of Reservists a Key Factor in Israeli Victory," *New York Times*, 13 June 1967, 18.

230. Sharon, *Warrior*, 181.

231. Terrence Smith, "Reserve Call-up Costly to Israel," *New York Times*, 29 May 1967, 4.

232. Rabin, *Rabin Memoirs*, 93, 95; Rabinovich, *Battle for Jerusalem*, 66.

233. Kenneth M. Pollack, *Armies of Sand: The Past, Present, and Future of Arab Military Effectiveness* (New York: Oxford University Press, 2018), 2–3.

234. Morris, *Righteous Victims*, 319.

235. Guy Laron, *The Six Day War: The Breaking of the Middle East* (New Haven, CT: Yale University Press, 2017), 59.

236. Oren, *Six Days of War*, 160.

237. Pollack, *Arabs at War*, 64.

238. Gawrych, *Key to the Sinai*, 96, 108–109.

239. Simon Dunstan, *The Six Day War 1967: Sinai* (Oxford: Osprey, 2012), loc. 386, Kindle.

240. Pollack, *Arabs at War*, 71.

241. Ibid.; Morris, *Righteous Victims*, 319.

242. Pollack, *Arabs at War*, 72.

243. Morris, *Righteous Victims*, 327.

244. Bregman, *Israel's Wars*, 86–87; Rabinovich, *Battle for Jerusalem*, 65.

245. Rabinovich, *Battle for Jerusalem*, 82.

246. Bregman, *Israel's Wars*, 74.

247. Oren, *Six Days of War*, 186.

248. Rabinovich, *Battle for Jerusalem*, 54.

249. Oren, *Six Days of War*, 193.

250. Simon Dunstan, *The Six Day War 1967: Jordan and Syria* (Oxford: Osprey, 2013), loc. 513, Kindle; Rothenberg, *Anatomy of the Israeli Army*, 144.

251. Dunstan, *Six Day War 1967: Jordan and Syria*, loc. 513.

252. Rabinovich, *Battle for Jerusalem*, 29, 52.

253. Ibid., 107, 200.

254. Oren, *Six Days of War*, 194.

255. Ibid., 185–186; Pollack, *Arabs at War*, 298, 300.

256. Bregman, *Israel's Wars*, 87; Pollack, *Arabs at War*, 297.

257. Oren, *Six Days of War*, 190–191.

258. Ibid.; Pollack, *Arabs at War*, 300–301.

259. Oren, *Six Days of War*, 206, 191.

260. Pollack, *Arabs at War*, 314; Oren, *Six Days of War*, 238, 239–240.

261. Oren, *Six Days of War*, 242–243.

262. Pollack, *Arabs at War*, 315.

263. Pollack, *Armies of Sand*, 3.

264. Schiff, *History of the Israeli Army*, 140; Bregman, *Israel's Wars*, 90; Rothenberg, *Anatomy of the Israeli Army*, 144; Dunstan, *Six Day War 1967: Jordan and Syria*, loc. 585.

265. Pollack, *Armies of Sand*, 17.

266. Ibid., 18.

267. CIA, "Israel: Problems behind the Battle Lines," 10 May 1972, 2, https://www.cia.gov/readingroom/docs/CIA-RDP85T00875R001100130058-9.pdf.

268. Instability was at a low level in the Palestinian territories in the late 1960s and early 1970s compared to the unrest that would occur in the 1980s and 1990s. However, Palestinian militants and their supporters sometimes resorted to terrorism, such as the attack by the Palestinian terrorist group Black September on Israeli athletes during the 1972 Munich Olympics.

269. Terrence Smith, "Israel Demobilizing Slowly and without Fanfare," *New York Times*, 24 June 1967, 5.

270. Gal, *Portrait of the Israeli Soldier*, 18.

271. Bregman, *Israel's Wars*, 93–95.

272. CIA, "The 1973 Arab-Israeli War," September 1975, 10, https://www.cia.gov/readingroom/docs/1975-09-01A.pdf.

273. CIA, "The Suez Canal Front," 3 August 1970, 2, https://www.cia.gov/readingroom/docs/CIA-RDP79R00967A000200030012-7.pdf.

274. CIA, "1973 Arab-Israeli War," 10.

275. Bregman, *Israel's Wars*, 100–101; Shapira, *Israel*, 319.

276. Bregman, *Israel's Wars*, 97.

277. Rothenberg, *Anatomy of the Israeli Army*, 171.

278. Abraham Rabinovich, *The Yom Kippur War: The Epic Encounter that Transformed the Middle East*, rev. and updated ed. (New York: Schocken, 2007), 128.

279. Bregman, *Israel's Wars*, 101; Ammon Rubinstein, "6 Days Plus 3 Years: Israel Asks, 'Ma, Ihieh Hassof? Whit Will Be the End?'" *New York Times*, 31 May 1970, 157.

280. Finkel, *Military Agility*, 40.

281. Sakal, *Soldier in the Sinai*, 97.

282. Rothenberg, *Anatomy of the Israeli Army*, 157–158.

283. Rabinovich, *Yom Kippur War*, 56.

284. US Department of State, "The Military Balance in the Mideast," 19 November 1971, 2, 19, https://www.cia.gov/readingroom/docs/LOC-HAK-18-3-39-6.pdf; Institute for Defense Analysis (IDA), "Assessment of Weapons and Tactics Used in the October 1973 Middle East War," 80, https://www.cia.gov/library/readingroom/docs/LOC-HAK-480-3-1-4.pdf.

285. US Department of State, "Military Balance in the Mideast," table IV.

286. "Tougher Front Line by Increasing Reserve Duty," *Jerusalem Post*, 7 April 1970, 8.

287. CIA, "The Suez Canal Front," 3 August 1970, https://www.cia.gov/library/readingroom/docs/CIA-RDP79R00967A000200030012-7.pdf; CIA, "Israeli Development of the Occupied Territories," November 1969, 10, https://www.cia.gov/library/readingroom/docs/CIA-RDP84-00825R000100610001-8.pdf.

288. Defense Intelligence Agency (DIA), "The Arab-Israeli Conflict," October 1973, 1; https://www.cia.gov/library/readingroom/docs/LOC-HAK-480-2-3-3.pdf; CIA, "Military Capabilities of Israel and the Arab States," 8.

289. Gal, *Portrait of the Israeli Soldier*, 19; James Feron, "Israel Lifts Top Age for Reserve Duty from 49 to 55," *New York Times*, 1 November 1969, 3.

290. CIA, "National Intelligence Estimate: Israel," 29 June 1972, 16, https://www.cia.gov/readingroom/docs/DOC_0001518685.pdf; "U.S. Foreign Aid to Israel," n.d., Jewish Virtual Library, https://www.jewishvirtuallibrary.org/total-u-s-foreign-aid-to-israel-1949-present.

291. World Bank, "Israel GDP."

292. Rothenberg, *Anatomy of the Israeli Army*, 161.

293. Rubinstein, "6 Days Plus 3 Years"; Israeli Ministry of Foreign Affairs, "Higher Education in Israel," 1 December 2011, https://mfa.gov.il/MFA/AboutIsrael/Education/Pages/Higher_education_Israel-Selected_data_2010-11.aspx.

294. Rothenberg, *Anatomy of the Israeli Army*, 160.

295. Orr, *These Are My Brothers*, 57.

296. Bregman, *Israel's Wars*, 109.

297. CIA, "1973 Arab-Israeli War," introduction.

298. Van Creveld, *Sword and the Olive*, 221.

299. Rabinovich, *Yom Kippur War*, 16.

300. CIA, "1973 Arab-Israeli War," 11.

301. Avraham Adan, *On the Banks of the Suez: An Israeli General's Personal Account of the Yom Kippur War*, reprint ed. (New York: Presidio Press, 1991), 3–4.

302. Ibid., 107; Rabinovich, *Yom Kippur War*, 18.

303. DIA, "Arab-Israeli Conflict," 2.

304. Rabinovich, *Yom Kippur War*, 41.

305. Yuval Elizur, "Flaw Seen in Israel Mobilization," *Washington Post*, 23 November 1973.

306. CIA, "1973 Arab-Israeli War," 101.

307. Rabinovich, *Yom Kippur War*, 33.

308. CIA, "1973 Arab-Israeli War," introduction.

309. DIA, "Arab-Israeli Conflict," 9.

310. CIA, "1973 Arab-Israeli War," 77.

311. Sharon, *Warrior*, 294.

312. CIA, "1973 Arab-Israeli War," 16.

313. Sharon, *Warrior*, 304; CIA, "1973 Arab-Israeli War," 16.

314. Van Creveld, *Sword and the Olive*, 229–231.

315. IDA, "Assessment of Weapons and Tactics Used in the October 1973 Middle East War," 30; Orr, *These Are My Brothers*, 47–48; Van Creveld, *Sword and the Olive*, 224.

316. Adan, *On the Banks of the Suez*, 6–7, 13–15.

317. Rothenberg, *Anatomy of the Israeli Army*, 183.

318. Finkel, *Studies in Generalship*, 19–21.

319. Ibid., 21; Finkel, *Military Agility*, 33.

320. Orr, *These Are My Brothers*, 37–39, 42–44.

321. Rabinovich, *Yom Kippur War*, 68.

322. Finkel, *Studies in Generalship*, 22.

323. CIA, "1973 Arab-Israeli War," 62–63. The Thirty-Sixth Armor Division would become a regular, conscript unit after the war.

324. Ibid., 110.

325. Ibid.; Adan, *On the Banks of the Suez*, 13.

326. Rabinovich, *Yom Kippur War*, 212, 304–305.

327. CIA, "1973 Arab-Israeli War," 18.

328. Shapira, *Israel*, 475.

329. IDA, "Assessment of Weapons and Tactics Used in the October 1973 Middle East War," 7; CIA, "1973 Arab-Israeli War," 101; Sakal, *Soldier in the Sinai*, 12–15.

330. Shapira, *Israel*, 475.

331. For an in-depth account of the Israeli crossing, see Amiram Ezov, "The Crossing Challenge: The Suez Canal Crossing by the Israel Defense Forces during the Yom Kippur War of 1973," *Journal of Military History* 82, 2 (April 2018): 461–490.

332. CIA, "1973 Arab-Israeli War," 101.

333. Orr, *These Are My Brothers*, 37–39, 42–44.

334. Ibid., 58; CIA, "1973 Arab-Israeli War," 83; "Record Number of Reserve Generals Mobilized," *Jerusalem Post*, 16 October 1973, 2; Rabinovich, *Yom Kippur War*, 290.

335. CIA, "1973 Arab-Israeli War," 83.

336. Adan, *On the Banks of the Suez*, 8.

337. IDA, "Assessment of Weapons and Tactics Used in the October 1973 Middle East War," 7.

338. Rabinovich, *Yom Kippur War*, 168.

339. Sakal, *Soldier in the Sinai*, 97.

340. Rabinovich, *Yom Kippur War*, 168; CIA, "1973 Arab-Israeli War," 110; Adan, *On the Banks of the Suez*, 8.

341. Rabinovich, *Yom Kippur War*, 448.

342. Van Creveld, *Sword and the Olive*, 241.

343. Rabinovich, *Yom Kippur War*, 168.

344. Adan, *On the Banks of the Suez*, 10–11; Sharon, *Warrior*, 291.

345. Elizur, "Flaw Seen in Israel Mobilization."

346. CIA, "1973 Arab-Israeli War," 110–111.

347. Orr, *These Are My Brothers*, 57.

348. Rabinovich, *Yom Kippur War*, 219.

349. CIA, "1973 Arab-Israeli War," 111.

350. Drew Middleton, "Israel's Forces Show New Vigor: Bolstered after 73 Battles," *New York Times*, 27 July 1975, 12.

351. Gal, *Portrait of the Israeli Soldier*, 24; Middleton, "Israel's Forces Show New Vigor."

352. CIA, "1973 Arab-Israeli War," 49; IDA, "Assessment of Weapons and Tactics Used in the October 1973 Middle East War," 6.

353. CIA, "1973 Arab-Israeli War," 107–108.

354. IDA, "Assessment of Weapons and Tactics Used in the October 1973 Middle East War," 83.

355. Van Creveld, *Sword and the Olive*, 251–252; Adan, *On the Banks of the Suez*, vii.

Chapter 5. The Decline of the Israel Defense Forces Army Reserve

1. Hagai Amit, "The Israeli Army's Big Windfall—Massive Cuts in Reserve Duty," *Haaretz*, 29 October 2018, https://www.haaretz.com/israel-news/business/.premium-the-army-s-big-windfall-massive-cuts-in-reserve-duty-1.6601182.

2. Finkel, *Studies in Generalship*, 202.

3. Ibid., 200–202.

4. Other scholars have discussed this trend, including Van Creveld, *Sword and the Olive*, 322; Yagil Levy, "The Decline of the Reservist Army," *Military and Strategic Affairs* 3, 3 (December 2011): 70; and Arie Perlinger, "The Changing Nature of the Israeli Reserve Forces," *Armed Forces and Society* 37,

2 (December 2009): 232. This chapter expands on those arguments by showing how these changes in the IDF reserve were rooted in decisions and events that occurred in the 1970s and early 1980s and how they have unfolded over the past decade. Additionally, this book contextualizes the decline of the IDF reserves by linking that development to the broader trends in military history explored in chapter 1.

5. Finkel, *Studies in Generalship*, 147.

6. See the experience of reserve units in the 210th Division in Orr, *These Are My Brothers*, 127, 160.

7. Finkel, *Studies in Generalship*, 148–149.

8. Institute for Defense Analysis (IDA), "Assessment of Weapons and Tactics Used in the October 1973 Middle East War," 10, 80; Central Intelligence Agency (CIA), "The 1973 Arab-Israeli War," 28; International Institute for Strategic Studies (IISS), Military Balance 1975, 34; IISS, Military Balance 1985, 43; CIA, "Israel's Military Edge Continues," 1–2; Yoel Marcus, "Israel's Self-Inflicted Wounds," *New York Times*, 24 April 1977, SM7.

9. CIA, "Comments on Military Situation in the Mid East," October 1975, 1–2, https://www.cia.gov/readingroom/docs/CIA-RDP86T00608R000700100005 -0.pdf; Van Creveld, *Sword and the Olive*, 254; Finkel, *Studies in Generalship*, 149.

10. Joshua Brilliant, "Army to Reduce Reserve Duty," *Jerusalem Post*, 1 March 1976, 2; Finkel, *Studies in Generalship*, 151.

11. Van Creveld, *Sword and the Olive*, 263; "No Cuts in Reserve Duty as IDF Strength Grows," *Jerusalem Post*, 27 April 1977, 1.

12. "Israel Air Force Said Seeking to Buy More F-15 Planes," *Jerusalem Post*, 4 December 1977.

13. Finkel, *Studies in Generalship*, 150.

14. CIA, "Israel's Case for US Assistance," 2–3.

15. Van Creveld, *Sword and the Olive*, 252.

16. Henry Kamm, "Israel, Used to Surviving Must Now Face Long-Term Challenges," *New York Times*, 2 February 1974, 3.

17. Moshe Brilliant, "Israel's Economy Burdened by War," *New York Times*, 27 January 1974, 158.

18. "Employers Must Rehire Reservist," *Jerusalem Post*, 4 August 1974, 3.

19. Ibid.; Brilliant, "Israel's Economy Burdened by War," 158; Kamm, "Israel, Used to Surviving."

20. "Gur Outlines Challenge of Training Our Soldier," *Jerusalem Post*, 26 January 1978, 2.

21. CIA, "Comments on Military Situation in the Mid East," 1–2; "Army Speeds up Armament, Training Projects," *Jerusalem Post*, 1 April 1974, 1; "Army to Pay Grants to Reservists," *Jerusalem Post*, 5 September 1974, 3.

22. "New Training Facility for Infantrymen, Paratroops," *Jerusalem Post*, 29 July 1976, 2.

23. CIA, "Comments on Military Situation in the Mid East," 1–2; "Army

Speeds up Armament, Training Projects," 1; "Army to Pay Grants to Reservists," 3.

24. Roni Daniel, "30 to 40 Days [in Hebrew]," *Kadashot*, 18 July 1984, 3.

25. Yuval Elizur, "Flaw Seen in Israel Mobilization," *Washington Post*, 23 November 1973.

26. Van Creveld, *Sword and the Olive*, 258.

27. "No Cuts in Reserve Duty."

28. CIA, "The Arab-Israeli Military Balance: Impact of the Egyptian-Israeli Peace Treaty," 16 October 1979, 2, https://www.cia.gov/readingroom/docs/CIA -RDP83R00184R002600290006-7.pdf.

29. "No Cuts in Reserve Duty."

30. Brilliant, "Army to Reduce Reserve Duty."

31. Van Creveld, *Sword and the Olive*, 262.

32. Finkel, *Studies in Generalship*, 151.

33. Yagil Levy, "The Army Reserve Stinks [in Hebrew]," *Army and Strategy* 3, 3 (December 2011): 54.

34. Finkel, *Studies in Generalship*, 259; Shapira, *Israel*, 357.

35. Van Creveld, *Sword and the Olive*, 259–260.

36. Hirsch Goodman, "Reservists Protest State of the Nation," *Jerusalem Post*, 21 March 1974, 8.

37. "Reservists Unable to Guard Settlements in Territories," *Jerusalem Post*, 23 August 1978, 2.

38. Shapira, *Israel*, 369, 385.

39. "Peace and War Has Become Part of Israeli Daily Life 'What Will Be the End?'" *New York Times*, 31 May 1970.

40. CIA, "Israel: Problems behind the Battle Lines," 4; Ammon Rubinstein, "6 Days Plus 3 Years: Israel Asks, 'Ma, Ihieh Hassof? What Will Be the End?'" *New York Times*, 31 May 1970, 157; Shapira, *Israel*, 341.

41. CIA, "Arab-Israeli Military Balance," 1–2.

42. Van Creveld, *Sword and the Olive*, 307.

43. This is a core theme of Cohen, *Israel and Its Army*.

44. Ibid., 285; Stuart A. Cohen and Aharon Klieman, eds., *Routledge Handbook on Israeli Security* (New York: Routledge, 2018), 51.

45. Van Creveld, *Sword and the Olive*, 285.

46. Ibid., 289.

47. CIA, "Military Lessons Learned by Israel and Syria from the War in Lebanon," May 1984, 5, https://www.cia.gov/readingroom/document/cia-rdp 87t00217 r000700080010-3.

48. Thomas M. Davis, *40km into Lebanon: Israel's 1982 Invasion* (Washington, DC: NDU Press, 1987), 77–79; Van Creveld, *Sword and the Olive*, 291; Henry Kamm, "Israel Preoccupied with Men at War," *New York Times*, 22 June 1982, A10.

49. IDF, "The First Lebanon War," https://www.idf.il/en/minisites/wars -and -operations/first-lebanon-war-1982/. For an account of an Israeli reservist

in a support role, see Dov Yermiya, *My War Diary: Lebanon, June 5–July 1, 1982*, trans. Hillel Schenker (Jerusalem: Mifras, 1983).

50. CIA, "Military Lessons Learned by Israel and Syria," 5.

51. Van Creveld, *Sword and the Olive*, 297.

52. CIA, "Escalation of the Israeli-Syrian Confrontation and the Soviet Reaction," 9 June 1982, 2, https://www.cia.gov/readingroom/docs/CIA-RDP83 B01027 R000100040014-8.pdf.

53. Van Creveld, *Sword and the Olive*, 296.

54. Ibid., 295; Finkel, *Studies in Generalship*, 81, 203.

55. Gal Perel, "The IDF, the IDF, They Are Coming—End of the War, End of the Reserves [in Hebrew]," Dado Center, 15 April 2023, 1–2.

56. Van Creveld, *Sword and the Olive*, 292.

57. Ibid., 297, 298.

58. Ibid., 302–305.

59. CIA, "Israel Preparing Withdrawal Options," 17 October 1984, 2, https://www.cia.gov/readingroom/document/cia-rdp85t00287r001302230001-2.

60. Israeli Ministry of Foreign Affairs, "The Lebanon War," 2013, https://mfa.gov.il/mfa/aboutisrael/history/pages/operation%20peace%20for%20galilee%20-%201982.aspx.

61. Van Creveld, *Sword and the Olive*, 303.

62. Ibid., 302.

63. Eric Pace, "Israel Is Raising Taxes to Cover Costs of War," *New York Times*, 14 June 1982, A12; Kamm, "Israel Preoccupied with Men at War," A10.

64. Joshua Brilliant, "Training Hours Down in IDF Due to Budget Cut," *Jerusalem Post*, 15 April 1984, 2.

65. Drew Middleton, "Israel's Defense as Good as Ever?" *New York Times*, 19 May 1985, A60.

66. CIA, "Military Lessons Learned by Israel and Syria," 3; "Reservist Jailed for Not Serving in Lebanon," *Jerusalem Post*, 22 October 1982, 2.

67. CIA, "The Israel Defense Forces after the War in Lebanon," April 1986, 1, https://www.cia.gov/readingroom/docs/CIA-RDP88T00096R000200180002-0.pdf; David Shipler, "Israel's Longest Year," *New York Times*, 7 June 1983, A2.

68. Joshua Brilliant, "Yaron Wants Law to Protect Reservists' Job Security," *Jerusalem Post*, 10 January 1985, 2.

69. Sagi Turan, "Not Givat Halfon—the Challenges of Command in the Reserve Units [in Hebrew]," *Maarachot*, 21 February 2013, 46–47.

70. CIA, "Israel Defense Forces after the War in Lebanon," 1.

71. William Claiborne, "Israel Studies Lessons of Lebanon War," *Washington Post*, 31 March 1986, A18.

72. Gal, *Portrait of the Israeli Soldier*, 44; Hirsch Goodman, "Insight into Reorganization: Israel Defense Forces," *Jerusalem Post*, 31 May 1983, 7.

73. Hirsch Goodman, "Unlearned Lessons: Israel Defence Forces," *Jerusalem Post*, 14 May 1984, 7.

74. Claiborne, "Israel Studies Lessons of Lebanon War," A16.

75. CIA, "Israel Defense Forces after the War in Lebanon," iv.

76. Ibid., 3; CIA, "Israel: Economic Problems Facing the Shamir Government," December 1983, 1, https://www.cia.gov/library/readingroom/docs/CIA -RDP84 S00927R000200070002-4.pdf.

77. CIA, "Israel Defense Forces after the War in Lebanon," 3.

78. Middleton, "Israel's Defense as Good as Ever?" A60.

79. "Reservists' Quitting Age to Be Lowered to 50," *Jerusalem Post*, 17 October 1985, 2; Kenneth Brower, *The Israel Defense Forces* (Ramat Gan, Israel: Begin-Sadat Center, 2018), 15.

80. Brilliant, "Training Hours Down in IDF"; Goodman, "Unlearned Lessons," 7.

81. IISS, Military Balance 1984, 63; CIA, "Israel's Military Edge Continues," 1–2, 5; IISS, Military Balance 1988, 103.

82. US Air Force, "F-15 Eagle," http://www.af.mil/AboutUs/FactSheets /Display/tabid/224/Article/104501/f-15-eagle.aspx. Data on prices of the F-4 are difficult to find. One estimate places the price at around $16.4 million in 2008 dollars, bringing it close to $18 million in 2015 dollars. See "McDonnell Douglas F-4 Phantom II," Aircraft Compare, http://www.aircraftcompare.com /helicopter-airplane/McDonnell-Douglas-F-4-Phantom-II/437.

83. Goodman, "Unlearned Lessons," 7.

84. CIA, "Israel Defense Forces after the War in Lebanon," 1.

85. Israeli Ministry of Foreign Affairs, "Sectors of the Israeli Economy," https://mfa.gov.il/mfa/aboutisrael/economy/pages/economy-%20sectors%20 of%20the%20economy.aspx.

86. CIA, "Israel Defense Forces after the War in Lebanon," 1–2.

87. CIA, "Israel: Political-Military Situation," 4 December 1987, 2, https://www .cia.gov/library/readingroom/docs/CIA-RDP90T00114R000700770001-7.pdf.

88. Quoted in Raphael D. Marcus, *Israel's Long War with Hizballah: Military Innovation and Adaptation under Fire* (Washington, DC: Georgetown University Press, 2018), 131–132.

89. Ibid., 131; E. L. Zorn, "Israel's Quest for Satellite Intelligence," *Studies in Intelligence* 10 (Winter–Spring 2001): 33–38; Finkel, *Studies in Generalship*, 194.

90. CIA, "Israeli Military Capabilities for Striking PLO Bases," 20 December 1985, 2, https://www.cia.gov/library/readingroom/docs/CIA-RDP90T01298 R000300330001-5.pdf.

91. Middleton, "Israel's Defense as Good as Ever?" A60; "Arrow (Israel)," Missile Defense Advocacy Alliance, n.d., https://missiledefenseadvocacy.org /defense-systems/arrow-israel/.

92. CIA, "The Israeli-Syrian Arms Race," 1 May 1988, iv, https://www.cia .gov/library/readingroom/docs/CIA-RDP89S01450R000300250001-7.pdf; Finkel, *Studies in Generalship*, 193–194.

93. Anthony Cordesman, *Military Balance in the Middle East VI: Arab-Israeli Balance* (Washington, DC: CSIS, 1998), 3, 197.

94. CIA, "Israel: Political-Military Situation," 2, 4.

95. Van Creveld, *Sword and the Olive*, 310.

96. Marcus, *Israel's Long War with Hizballah*, 132, 133; Efrain Karsh, *From Rabin to Netanyahu: Israel's Troubled Agenda* (New York: Routledge, 2013), 81–82.

97. CIA, "Near East and South Asia Review," 14 February 1986, 3, https://www.cia.gov/library/readingroom/docs/CIA-RDP05S02029R000300760003-8.pdf; Sergio Catignani, *Israeli Counterinsurgency and the Intifadas: Dilemmas of a Conventional Army* (New York: Routledge, 2008), 77.

98. Defense Intelligence Agency (DIA), "The Israel Defense Forces and the Palestinian Uprising," 1 April 1988, 2, https://www.cia.gov/library/readingroom/docs/CIA-RDP92T00277R000600170002-1.pdf.

99. For a more detailed account, see Finkel, *Studies in Generalship*, 24.

100. Catignani, *Israeli Counterinsurgency and the Intifadas*, 82.

101. Stuart A. Cohen, "How Did the Intifada Affect the IDF?" *Conflict Quarterly* 14 (Summer 1994): 9–10.

102. Abraham Rabinovich, "A Burden of Sixty Days," *Jerusalem Post*, 9 December 1988, B8.

103. DIA, "Israel Defense Forces and the Palestinian Uprising," 4, 6–7.

104. Ibid., iii, 3; "All Combatants Will Serve 60 Reserve Days a Year [in Hebrew]," *Maariv*, 13 May 1988, 1.

105. "Increase in Reserve Duty Expected," *Jerusalem Post*, 25 February 1988, 2.

106. DIA, "Israel Defense Forces and the Palestinian Uprising," 8; Joel Brinkley, "Israel Mired in the West Bank," *New York Times*, 7 May 1989, A60.

107. Benny Morris, "Serving Their Term," *Jerusalem Post*, 3 June 1988, A4.

108. Brinkley, "Israel Mired in the West Bank," A30.

109. Van Creveld, *Sword and the Olive*, 350.

110. Catignani, *Israeli Counterinsurgency and the Intifadas*, 85, 86.

111. Finkel, *Studies in Generalship*, 29–31.

112. Cohen, "How Did the Intifada Affect the IDF?" 9.

113. Ibid., 10; Finkel, *Studies in Generalship*, 33.

114. "Israel's Border Police Replace Gaza Troops," *New York Times*, 12 March 1989, A18.

115. Levy, "Army Reserve Stinks," 54.

116. Karsh, *From Rabin to Netanyahu*, 81–83.

117. "Reserve Duty for Israelis: A Way of War," *New York Times*, 25 May 1986, A4.

118. Van Creveld, *Sword and the Olive*, 311.

119. Finkel, *Studies in Generalship*, 198–200.

120. Cohen, *Israel and Its Army*, 42.

121. Cordesman, *Military Balance in the Middle East VI*, 27; Arieh O'Sullivan, "IDF Plans Calls for Greater Readiness," *Jerusalem Post*, 3 February 1999, 5.

122. Cohen, *Israel and Its Army*, 40.

123. Cohen and Klieman, *Routledge Handbook on Israeli Security*, 56; Shapira, *Israel*, 424.

124. Cohen, *Israel and Its Army*, 40.

125. Cohen and Klieman, *Routledge Handbook on Israeli Security*, 54.

126. Van Creveld, *Sword and the Olive*, 351; Finkel, *Studies in Generalship*, 202.

127. Finkel, *Studies in Generalship*, 35, 37.

128. Evelyn Gordon, "IDF to Use 50% Fewer Reservists by 1996," *Jerusalem Post*, 29 September 1993, 1.

129. Ibid; Michael Rotom, "IDF Shifting Reserve Burden," *Jerusalem Post*, 2 July 1993, 5; Turan, "Not Givat Halfon," 46.

130. Arieh O'Sullivan, "Conscripts Replace Reservists in West Bank," *Jerusalem Post*, 3 December 1998, 4.

131. Arieh O'Sullivan, "Reservists to Train More," *Jerusalem Post*, 13 June 1999, 3.

132. IISS, Military Balance 1984, 63.

133. "Population of Israel," Jewish Virtual Library; Cohen, "How Did the Intifada Affect the IDF?" 13.

134. Anthony Cordesman, *The Arab-Israeli Military Balance in 2010* (Washington, DC: CSIS, 2010), 8.

135. Van Creveld, *Sword and the Olive*, 311–312.

136. Yael Ben Horin, "Leadership Test: Being a Regular Reserve Brigade Commander [in Hebrew]," *Maarachot*, 20 September 2008, 72.

137. Cohen, *Israel and Its Army*, 59; World Bank, "Military Expenditure (% of GDP)—Israel."

138. "U.S. Foreign Aid to Israel," Jewish Virtual Library.

139. Van Creveld, *Sword and the Olive*, 319.

140. Cordesman, *Military Balance in the Middle East VI*, 10; Van Creveld, *Sword and the Olive*, 320–321.

141. Van Creveld, *Sword and the Olive*, 322.

142. Cohen, *Israel and Its Army*, 93, 95.

143. Ibid.; Liat Collins and Arieh O'Sullivan, "Reserve Duty Bill Goes to 1st Reading," *Jerusalem Post*, 27 November 1997, 4.

144. Arieh O'Sullivan, "IDF Tries to Make Reservists Feel at Home," *Jerusalem Post*, 31 December 1997, 4; Williams, *Israel Defense Forces*, 12; Kenneth Love, "Israel's Forces Outweigh Arabs," *New York Times*, 30 August 1955, 14.

145. Liat Collins, "New Law Eases Reservists' Burden," *Jerusalem Post*, 23 December 1997, 1.

146. Van Creveld, *Sword and the Olive*, 351.

147. Arieh O'Sullivan, "50% of Reservists Would Opt out if They Could," *Jerusalem Post*, 11 September 1996, 1.

148. Arieh O'Sullivan, "Lower Motivation Is Weakening IDF," *Jerusalem Post*, 14 August 1996, 1.

149. Arieh O'Sullivan, "Reserve Commanders Declare War on Service Evaders," *Jerusalem Post*, 11 September 1996, 1.

150. Van Creveld, *Sword and the Olive*, 351; O'Sullivan, "Lower Motivation Is Weakening IDF," 1; "Reservists Form Lobby to Cut Duty," *Jerusalem Post*, 25 September 1994; Perlinger, "Changing Nature of the Israeli Reserve Forces," 232.

151. O'Sullivan, "Lower Motivation Is Weakening IDF," 1; Ehud Eilam, "Military, Economic and Social Challenges of the IDF Reserve System [in Hebrew]," *Maarachot*, 20 May 2002, 31.

152. O'Sullivan, "Lower Motivation Is Weakening IDF," 1.

153. Cohen, *Israel and Its Army*, 58, 57.

154. Itzik Ronen, "Is the Reserve Army Sinking [in Hebrew]," *Maarachot*, 20 June 2013.

155. Shapira, *Israel*, 393.

156. Levy, "Decline of the Reservist Army," 70; Arieh O'Sullivan, "Knesset to Pass Reserve Bill Today," *Jerusalem Post*, 22 December 1997, 3; "Giving Reservists Their Due," *Jerusalem Post*, 17 July 1997, 6; O'Sullivan, "IDF Tries to Make Reservists Feel at Home," 4.

157. Collins, "New Law Eases Reservists' Burden," 1.

158. O'Sullivan, "Reserve Commanders Declare War on Service Evaders," 1.

159. Arieh O'Sullivan, "Reserve Training Lax," *Jerusalem Post*, 8 May 1997, 9.

160. Aryeh Niger, "A New Model for the Reserve Army [in Hebrew]," *Maarachot*, 20 May 2002, 37–38.

161. Cordesman, *Military Balance in the Middle East VI*, 16; Cohen, *Israel and Its Army*, 49; O'Sullivan, "Reserve Training Lax," 9.

162. Cordesman, *Military Balance in the Middle East VI*, 16.

163. O'Sullivan, "Reservists to Train More," 3.

164. O'Sullivan, "Conscripts Replace Reservists in West Bank," 4.

165. O'Sullivan, "Reservists to Train More," 3; Finkel, *Studies in Generalship*, 45.

166. Yaron Buskila, "Reserve Battalion as a Profession," *Maarachot*, 20 August 2020, 66.

167. Catignani, *Israeli Counterinsurgency and the Intifadas*, 102, 103.

168. Ibid., 105.

169. Arieh O'Sullivan, "20,000 Reservist Enough for Now," *Jerusalem Post*, 1 April 2002, 3; Catignani, *Israeli Counterinsurgency and the Intifadas*, 146; Eric Schichter, "Reservist Groups Express Outrage over Latest Service Extension Bill," *Jerusalem Post*, 14 March 2003, A3.

170. Catignani, *Israeli Counterinsurgency and the Intifadas*, 146, 148.

171. Boaz Zalmanovich, "Reservists in the Face of Fire [in Hebrew]," *Maarachot*, 20 February 2007, 62.

172. Arieh O'Sullivan, "Reservists Ill-Equipped for West Bank," *Jerusalem Post*, 11 December 2000, 4.

173. Arieh O'Sullivan, "All Combat Reservists to Be Drafted within a Year," *Jerusalem Post*, 2 November 2000, 1.

174. Matthew Gutman, "Reserves of Strength," *Jerusalem Post*, 12 April 2002, B7.

175. Yosef Goell, "Reservist Get the Message," *Jerusalem Post*, 10 April 2001, 6.

176. Ibid.; O'Sullivan, "Reservists Ill-Equipped for West Bank," 4.

177. O'Sullivan, "20,000 Reservist Enough for Now," 3.

178. Catignani, *Israeli Counterinsurgency and the Intifadas*, 107.

179. Gutman, "Reserves of Strength," B7.

180. Schichter, "Reservist Groups Express Outrage," A3.

181. Catignani, *Israeli Counterinsurgency and the Intifadas*, 146.

182. Schichter, "Reservist Groups Express Outrage," A3.

183. Goell, "Reservist Get the Message," 6.

184. Schichter, "Reservist Groups Express Outrage," A3.

185. Calev Ben David, "Employers' Attitude to IDF Reservists Is Troubling," *Jerusalem Post*, 1 December 2000, A4; "Employers Fire and Do Not Hire People Who Serve in the Reserve, [in Hebrew]," *Walla News*, 22 June 2022.

186. Ben David, "Employers' Attitude to IDF Reservists Is Troubling."

187. Amos Harel, "13 Elite Reservists Refuse to Serve in Territories," *Haaretz*, 22 December 2003; Cordesman, *Military Balance in the Middle East VI*, 152.

188. Catignani, *Israeli Counterinsurgency and the Intifadas*, 139.

189. Arieh Sullivan, "Reservists Welcome Government's Compensation Deal," *Jerusalem Post*, 25 April 2001, 3.

190. Catignani, *Israeli Counterinsurgency and the Intifadas*, 148.

191. Meir Finkel, "Their Training Will Be Straight [in Hebrew]," *Bayin Maarachot*, 2 June 2022, https://www.maarachot.idf.il/2022.

192. Catignani, *Israeli Counterinsurgency and the Intifadas*, 111; Finkel, "Their Training Will Be Straight."

193. Lou DiMarco, *Concrete Hell: Urban Warfare from Stalingrad to Iraq* (Oxford: Osprey, 2012), 200.

194. Catignani, *Israeli Counterinsurgency and the Intifadas*, 145–146.

195. Tracy Wilkinson, "The Battle that Defines the Israeli Offensive," *Los Angeles Times*, 21 April 2002; Gutman, "Reserves of Strength," B1.

196. DiMarco, *Concrete Hell*, 177.

197. Catignani, *Israeli Counterinsurgency and the Intifadas*, 145; Gutman, "Reserves of Strength," B1, B7; Zalmanovich, "Reservists in the Face of Fire," 62.

198. Catignani, *Israeli Counterinsurgency and the Intifadas*, 146.

199. DiMarco, *Concrete Hell*, 201.

200. Ibid., 207.

201. Ibid., 177–178; Wilkinson, "Battle that Defines the Israeli Offensive."

202. "Jenin Combat Began with Gunfire, Ended by Bulldzoers," CNN, 4 May 2002, https://www.cnn.com/2002/WORLD/meast/05/04/jenin.combat/index.html.

203. Ibid.

204. DiMarco, *Concrete Hell*, 200–205.

205. Ibid.

206. Gutman, "Reserves of Strength," B1; DiMarco, *Concrete Hell*, 205; Catignani, *Israeli Counterinsurgency and the Intifadas*, 114.

207. Gutman, "Reserves of Strength," B1.

208. Catignani, *Israeli Counterinsurgency and the Intifadas*, 145.

209. Richard Weitz, *The Reserve Policies of Nations: A Comparative Analysis* (Carlisle, PA: Strategic Studies Institute, 2014), 106.

210. Ronen, "Is the Reserve Army Sinking," 33.

211. Eyal Krolitzky, "Reserve System—Directions and Trends [in Hebrew]," *Maarachot*, 20 May 2004, 41.

212. IISS, Military Balance 2006, 167.

213. Ibid.

214. Catignani, *Israeli Counterinsurgency and the Intifadas*, 108; Bergman, *Rise and Kill First*, 563–564; Krolitzky, "Reserve System—Directions and Trends," 41.

215. Arieh O'Sullivan, "Reservists Try to Revive Plan to Lessen Duties," *Jerusalem Post*, 13 February 2004, 4; IISS, Military Balance 2010, 257; IISS, Military Balance 1998, 131.

216. Yoaz Hendel, "The Reserves Comeback," *Strategic Assessment* 10, 4 (February 2008): 38.

217. Marcus, *Israel's Long War with Hizballah*, 136.

218. Catignani, *Israeli Counterinsurgency and the Intifadas*, 42.

219. Margot Dudekevitch, "Budget Cuts Force IDF to Halt Training for Reservists," *Jerusalem Post*, 6 February 2003, 2; Catignani, *Israeli Counterinsurgency and the Intifadas*, 143.

220. O'Sullivan, "Reservists Try to Revive Plan to Lessen Duties," 4; Ofer Segal, "Reservist Ground Training—Past and Present [in Hebrew]," *Maarachot*, 20 May 2004, 50.

221. Dudekevitch, "Budget Cuts Force IDF to Halt Training for Reservists," 2.

222. Hendel, "Reserves Comeback," 37.

223. Segal, "Reservist Ground Training—Past and Present," 51.

224. Marcus, *Israel's Long War with Hizballah*, 136; Horin, "Leadership Test," 74.

225. Finkel, *Studies in Generalship*, 91.

226. Catignani, *Israeli Counterinsurgency and the Intifadas*, 144.

227. Ibid., 105.

228. Ibid., 240, 68–96, 69–70.

229. Amos Harel and Avi Issacharoff, *34 Days: Israel, Hezbollah, and the War in Lebanon* (New York: St. Martin's Press, 2008), 11.

230. Matt M. Matthews, *We Were Caught Unprepared: The 2006 Hezbollah-Israeli War* (Fort Leavenworth, KS: Combat Studies Institute Press, 2008), 34.

231. Hirsch, *Defensive Shield*, 221.

232. Ibid., 213–215, 209; Harel and Issacharoff, *34 Days*, 8–9.

233. IDF, "The Second Lebanon War," n.d., https://www.idf.il/en/minisites/wars-and-operations/second-lebanon-war/.

234. Ibid.; Harel and Issacharoff, *34 Days*, vii.

235. For example, some of these reservists fought in the Battle of Maroun al-Ras, as described in Hirsch, *Defensive Shield*, 257.

236. Ibid., 314.

237. Ibid., 245, 250; Winograd Commission Report, January 2007, 317, http://go.ynet.co.il/pic/news/vinograd/vinograd.pdf.

238. Winograd Commission Report, 317.

239. Ibid., 320; Hirsch, *Defensive Shield*, 360–361.

240. Anthony Cordesman and Ionut C. Popescu, "Israel and Syria: The Military Balance and Prospects for War," Center for Strategic and International Studies (CSIS), 15 August 2007, 80–81, https://csis-website-prod.s3.amazonaws.com/s3fs-public/legacy_files/files/media/csis/pubs/070815_cordesman_israel_syria.pdf.

241. Ibid.; Avi Kober, "Israel's Security Model," in Cohen and Klieman, *Routledge Handbook on Israeli Security*, 310.

242. Avi Kober, "The Israeli Defense Forces in the Second Lebanon War: Why the Poor Performance?" *Journal of Strategic Studies* 31, 1 (February 2008): 22.

243. Fay Cashman Greer, "We Still Need You," *Jerusalem Post*, 17 May 2006, 6.

244. Eitan Shamir, *Transforming Command: The Pursuit of Mission Command in the U.S., British, and Israeli Armies* (Stanford, CA: Stanford University Press, 2011), 151; Hirsch, *Defensive Shield*, 250–251.

245. Harel and Issacharoff, *34 Days*, 121; Hirsch, *Defensive Shield*, 237; Finkel, *Studies in Generalship*, 51, 95.

246. Finkel, *Studies in Generalship*, 51.

247. Hirsch, *Defensive Shield*, 237; Finkel, *Studies in Generalship*, 93.

248. Hirsch, *Defensive Shield*, 288.

249. Harel and Issacharoff, *34 Days*, 131.

250. Bregman, *Israel's Wars*, 273–274, 276–278.

251. Matthews, *We Were Caught Unprepared*, 39.

252. Winograd Commission Report, 125.

253. Ibid., 317; Finkel, *Studies in Generalship*, 133–135; Hirsch, *Defensive Shield*, 195, 251, 277; Winograd Commission Report, 317.

254. Amos Harel, "Halutz, Olmert and Adam Are Going to Sweat [in Hebrew]," *Haaretz*, 25 January 2017, https://www.haaretz.co.il/misc/2007–01–25/ty-article/0000017f-e6f2-da9b-a1ff-eeff8f570000; David Eshel, "Lebanon 2006: Did Merkava Challenge Its Match?" *Armor Magazine*, January–February 2007, 13.

255. Amos Harel, "Battle-tested Reservists Take Charge after Second

Lebanon War Crises," *Haartez,* 14 May 2010, https://www.haaretz.com/2010
-05-14/ty-article/battle-tested-reservists-take-charge-after-second-lebanon
-war-crises/0000017f-e3c7-d568-ad7f-f3ef19d30000; Hirsch, *Defensive Shield,*
296, 300.

256. Hirsch, *Defensive Shield,* 310.

257. Winograd Commission Report, 130, 371; Hirsch, *Defensive Shield,* 271,
295.

258. Harel and Issacharoff, *34 Days,* 220.

259. Hirsch, *Defensive Shield,* 284–288, 297, 302–303.

260. Winograd Commission Report, 318.

261. Harel and Issacharoff, *34 Days,* 154; Hirsch, *Defensive Shield,* 289.

262. Hirsch, *Defensive Shield,* 293, 257–258, 272.

263. Harel and Issacharoff, *34 Days,* 132–133; Yoni Chetboun, *Under Fire:
Diary of an Israeli Commander on the Battlefield,* trans. Jessica Setbon (New
York: Gefen, 2017).

264. Harel, "Battle-tested Reservists Take Charge"; Winograd Commission
Report, 320.

265. Matthews, *We Were Caught Unprepared,* 50.

266. Yossi Yehoshua, "Lebanon War Commander Resigns," *Ynet,* 1 June
2007, https://www.ynetnews.com/articles/0,7340,L-3407286,00.html.

267. Harel, "Battle-tested Reservists Take Charge"; Hirsch, *Defensive Shield,*
305–307, 325–326, 329.

268. Hirsch, *Defensive Shield,* 327.

269. Harel and Issacharoff, *34 Days,* 188, 153, 188.

270. Harel and Issacharoff, *34 Days,* 178–180, 11.

271. Larry Derfner, "Lambs to the Slaughter?" *Jerusalem Post,* 24 August
2006, https://www.jpost.com/magazine/features/lambs-to-the-slaughter.

272. Winograd Commission Report, 339–341; Yaakov Katz and Amir Bohbot,
The Weapon Wizards: How Israel Became a High-Tech Military Superpower (New
York: St. Martin's Press, 2017), 14.

273. Raphael D. Marcus, "Military Innovation and Tactical Adaptation in the
Israel-Hizbullah Conflict: The Institutionalization of Lesson-Learning in the
IDF," *Journal of Strategic Studies* 38, 4 (2015): 520.

274. "Report: A Fifth of IDF Reservists Have Poor Combat Readiness,"
Haaretz, 4 April 2007, https://www.haaretz.com/1.4814454.

275. Harel and Issacharoff, *34 Days,* 222–224.

276. Daniel Helmer, "Not Quite Counterinsurgency: A Cautionary Tale for
U.S. Forces Based on Israel's Operation Change of Direction," *Armor Magazine,*
January–February 2007, 10.

277. Harel and Issacharoff, *34 Days,* 233.

278. Horin, "Leadership Test," 71, 77.

279. Hirsch, *Defensive Shield,* 257.

280. Horin, "Leadership Test," 74.

281. Hirsch, *Defensive Shield,* 212–213, 296.

282. Horin, "Leadership Test," 74–77.

283. Hirsch, *Defensive Shield*, 310.

284. Winograd Commission Report, 132.

285. Hirsch, *Defensive Shield*, 296–297.

286. Harel, "Battle-tested Reservists Take Charge."

287. Harel and Issacharoff, *34 Days*, 153.

288. Weitz, *Reserve Policies of Nations*, 107.

289. Matthews, *We Were Caught Unprepared*, 49.

290. Yehuda Avner, "A Battalion Commander's Anger," *Jerusalem Post*, on-line ed., 22 August 2006, http://www.jpost.com/Opinion/Op-Ed-Contributors/A-battalion-commanders-anger.

291. "Iran's Ballistic Missiles," Center for Strategic and International Studies (CSIS), 14 June 2018, https://missilethreat.csis.org/country/iran/; Tzvi Joffre, "IRGC Commander: If Israel Starts a War, It Will End with Its Destruction," *Jerusalem Post*, 11 November 2021.

292. "IDF Says Armed Drone Captured by Syria Near Golan Was Iranian, Not Israeli," *Times of Israel*, 21 September 2019, https://www.timesofisrael.com/idf-says-armed-drone-captured-by-syria-near-golan-was-iranian-not-israeli/.

293. Anna Ahronheim, "Two Iranian Drones Shot Down over Iraq Were Heading to Israel," *Jerusalem Post*, 21 March 2021; Seth Frantzman, "The Vast Iran-Hezbollah Drone Threat Is Escalating—Analysis," *Jerusalem Post*, 2 July 2022, https://www.jpost.com/middle-east/article-711029.

294. Dion Nissenbaum, "Israel Says Iran Tried to Fly Arms to Hamas Using Drones," *Wall Street Journal*, 7 March 2022.

295. Emanuel Fabian, "Gallant Warns Multi-Front War Far More Likely for Israel than Limited Conflicts," *Times of Israel*, 20 April 2023, https://www.timesofisrael.com/gallant-warns-multi-front-war-far-more-likely-for-israel-than-limited-conflicts/.

296. "Israel: Regulation of Military Reserve Service," 2 March 2008, Library of Congress, https://www.loc.gov/law/foreign-news/article/israel-regulation-of-mil itary-reserve-service/.

297. Amit, "Israeli Army's Big Windfall."

298. Ibid.; Krolitzky, "Reserve System—Directions and Trends," 41.

299. Rebecca Anna Stoil, "Long-awaited Reserve Law to Finally Pass," *Jerusalem Post*, 31 March 2008.

300. Finkel, *Studies in Generalship*, 162–163.

301. Tal Inbar, "IDF Ground Forces' Operational Capability to Increase to 79 Percent," *Israel Defense*, 20 June 2011.

302. Hendel, "Reserves Comeback," 39.

303. Yaakov Katz, "IDF Plans to Invest NIS 2 Billion to Overall Reservists' Equipment," *Jerusalem Post*, 21 March 2007, 4.

304. Yaron Druckman, "IDF Reservists in Shabby Shape, Comptroller Says in Damning Report," *Ynet*, 29 December 2014.

305. Korin Elbaz, "The Reserves on the Fence Demand Armored Vehicles

[in Hebrew]," *Ynet*, 4 November 2022, https://www.ynet.co.il/news/article/sk4ntdgri#!/replace.

306. Horin, "Leadership Test," 73; Druckman, "IDF Reservists in Shabby Shape."

307. As of 2015, Israel had the highest birthrate among Organization for Economic Cooperation and Development (OECD) countries: 3.1 children per woman, compared with an average of 1.5 to 2.0 in other countries. See "Why Are There so Many Children in Israel," Taub Center, February 2019, http://taubcenter.org.il/why-are-there-so-many-children-in-israel/; Motti Bassok, "Secrets of the Defense Budget Revealed," *Haaretz*, 21 October 2010.

308. Andrea Samuels, "Tuitions Scholarship Should Be Available to All IDF Soldiers," *Jerusalem Post*, 4 June 2022; O'Sullivan, "Reservists Try to Revive Plan to Lessen Duties," 4.

309. Shimon Shiffer, "Israel Buys Dolphin Submarine," *Ynet*, 5 May 2011; "IDF's New Submarine Model to Be Named after Lost INS Dakar," *Jerusalem Post*, 11 October 2018; "F-35 for Israel," Lockheed Martin, n.d., https://www.lockheedmartin.com/en-us/products/f-35/f-35-global-partnership/f-35-israel.html; Finkel, *Studies in Generalship*, 159.

310. Jeremey J. Sharp, "U.S. Foreign Aid to Israel," Congressional Research Office, 10 June 2015, 12–15, https://www.fas.org/sgp/crs/mideast/RL33222.pdf.

311. Emanuel Fabian, "Biden Views Defense Tech at Airport, Including Iron Dome, New Laser-Based Iron Beam," *Times of Israel*, 13 July 2022, https://www.timesofisrael.com/biden-views-defense-tech-at-airport-including-iron-dome-new-laser-based-iron-beam/.

312. Yaakov Lappin and Lahav Harkov, "IDF Cancels All Operational Duty for Reserves," *Jerusalem Post*, 3 June 2013.

313. "All Israeli Army Reserve Training Cancelled for 2014," *Times of Israel*, 20 May 2014.

314. Yaakov Lappin, "IDF Has Improved Ability to Call up Reserves under Fire," *Jerusalem Post*, 27 November 2014.

315. Amos Harel, "If Israel Had to Enter Gaza Today, the Israeli Army Would Have a Big Problem," *Haaretz*, 2 September 2018.

316. Amos Harel, "The Israeli Army's New Target: Itself," *Haaretz*, 6 June 2015.

317. "Employers Fire and Do Not Hire People Who Serve in the Reserve."

318. Harel, "Israeli Army's New Target: Itself."

319. Yaakov Lappin, "IDF Ground Forces Reserve Training in Multiple Potential Scenarios," *Jerusalem Post*, 22 March 2013.

320. Yonah Jeremy Bob, "Top Defense Officials Debate if IDF Reserves Are Ready or in Chaos," *Jerusalem Post*, 19 January 2023.

321. Assaf Golan, "How Many Reserve Days Does a Fighter in Flotilla 13 Perform? [in Hebrew]," *Israel Ha-Yom*, 20 February 2019.

322. Hanan Greenwood, "The New Fighting Pattern of Combat Reservists [in Hebrew]," *Israel Ha-Yom*, 9 February 2021.

323. Amos Harel, "Retired General's Solution to Israeli Army's Flaws: Fewer Tanks, More Training," *Haaretz*, 3 February 2018.

324. Amos Harel, "Israeli Army Can Defeat Hizballah in Massive Drill, but Reality Is More Complicated," *Haaretz*, 6 September 2017.

325. "Stand Uneasy," *Economist*, 22–28 September 2018, 44–45.

326. "The Recruitment of Reserve Battalions Was Cancelled until the End of the Summer [in Hebrew]," *Israel Ha-Yom*, 4 June 2020.

327. Yossi Yehoshua, "Due to the Wave of Terrorism, the IDF Will Ask the Knesset for Exceptional Permission to Recruit Reserves [in Hebrew]," *Ynet*, 4 December 2022.

328. Yaniv Kubovich, "Israeli Army Officials Report 'Disturbing' Decline in Combat Reservists Showing up for Duty," *Haaretz*, 22 March 2023.

329. Greenwood, "New Fighting Pattern of Combat Reservists."

330. Israeli Ministry, *Military Service*, 7th ed., 44, http://archive.moia.gov.il/Publications/idf_en.pdf; IISS, Military Balance 2018, 40; Sasson Hadad and Shmuel Even, "Do Limited Resources Threaten the IDF's New Multi-Year Plan," INSS Insight 1195, 17 July 2019, https://www.inss.org.il/publication/do-limited -resources-threaten-the-idfs-new-multiyear-plan/.

331. Yoav Limor, "The Dangers of Shortening Compulsory Service," *Israel Ha-Yom*, 3 July 2020.

332. Amos Harel, "Today, the Israeli Army Plans with Bravado but Executes with Fear," *Haaretz*, 29 December 2018; Amit, "Israeli Army's Big Windfall."

333. Harel, "Today, the Israeli Army Plans with Bravado."

334. Turan, "Not Givat Halfon," 46–50.

335. Harel, "Today, the Israeli Army Plans with Bravado."

336. RAND Corporation, *From Cast Lead to Protective Edge: Lessons from Israel's Wars in Gaza* (Washington, DC: RAND, 2017), 48, 49.

337. Yaakov Lappin, "IDF Mobilizing 10,000 Reservists after Israel Targets Senior Hamas Commanders," *Jerusalem Post*, 21 August 2014.

338. RAND Corporation, *From Cast Lead to Protective Edge*, 89–90, 116.

339. Anna Ahronheim, "Tel Aviv Battered in Unprecedented Gaza Barrage," *Jerusalem Post*, 12 May 2021; Judah Gross, "Gantz: Gaza Operation Aims to 'Strike Hamas Hard,' Make It 'Regret' Rockets," *Times of Israel*, 11 May 2021.

340. Anna Ahronheim, "Gantz Approves Draft of over 25,000 Reservists after IDF Strikes in Gaza," *Jerusalem Post*, 6 August 2022.

341. Alon Hachmon, "Despite the Escalation, the IDF Is in No Rush to Carry out Extensive Reserve Recruitment [in Hebrew]," *Maariv*, 10 May 2023.

342. Anna Ahronheim, "MABAM: Israel's Strategy to Chase Iran, Proxies out of Syria," *Jerusalem Post*, 8 October 2022.

343. Amit, "Israeli Army's Big Windfall."

344. Arieh O'Sullivan, "Reservists' Burden to Be Eased," *Jerusalem Post*, 23 August 2001, 2.

345. Bob, "Top Defense Officials Debate if IDF Reserves Are Ready."

346. Judah Gross, "IDF Launches Surprise Reservist Drill amid Month-long Exercise Series in North," *Times of Israel*, 1 November 2021; Anna Ahronheim, "Israel to Simulate War with Hezbollah in Cyprus," *Jerusalem Post*, 29 May 2022; Lilac Shoval, "IDF Begins Multi-Theater Exercise Lethal Arrow [in Hebrew]," *Israel Ha-Yom*, 25 October 2020.

347. Judah Gross, "Eyeing Northern Threats, IDF Puts over a Billion Shekels into Training for 2022," *Times of Israel*, 18 November 2021.

348. Greenwood, "New Fighting Pattern of Combat Reservists."

349. Gross, "Eyeing Northern Threats"; Amir Bohbot, "IDF to Invest NIS 1 Billion as It Prepares for War in Lebanon, Syria," *Jerusalem Post*, 18 November 2021.

350. Emanuel Fabian, "IDF Special Forces Head to Cyprus to Train for Fight against Hezbollah," *Times of Israel*, 29 May 2022.

351. Anna Ahronheim, "New Year, New Multi-Dimensional Combat Unit in the IDF," *Jerusalem Post*, 1 January 2020.

352. Eran Otel, "Turn on the Light, Extinguish the Fire: Israel's New Way of War," *War on the Rocks*, 19 January 2022.

353. "Israel's New 'Iron Fist' Active Protection System Completes Interception Tests," *Israel Defense*, 13 December 2022, https://www.israeldefense.co.il /en/node/56600; Anna Ahronheim, "IDF Appoints General to Lead New Iran Command as Threat Escalates," *Jerusalem Post*, 13 February 2020.

354. Ahronheim, "New Year, New Multi-Dimensional Combat Unit"; Judah Gross, "In 1st Drill, IDF's Ghost Unit Tests out New Tactics with Jets, Tanks and Robots," *Times of Israel*, 23 July 2020.

355. Emanuel Fabian, "Netanyahu, Treasury and Defense Officials Agree on Multi-Year Defense Budget," *Times of Israel*, 23 February 2023.

356. Bob, "Top Defense Officials Debate if IDF Reserves Are Ready or in Chaos"; Lilac Shuvel, "Empty under the Stretcher: A Significant Decrease in the Rate of People Enlisting in the Reserves [in Hebrew]," *Israel Ha-Yom*, 13 February 2023.

357. Aharon Kalman, "The Government Needs to Understand: Every Reserve Day Is Voluntary [in Hebrew]," Channel 7 News, 29 March 2023.

358. Shuvel, "Empty under the Stretcher."

359. Ibid.

360. Yaron Buskila, "Reserve Battalion as a Profession [in Hebrew]," *Maarachot*, 20 August 2020, 64–66; Perel, "The IDF, the IDF, They Are Coming," 11.

361. Yaakov Lapin, "IDF Fights Daily Battle to Hold on to Career Soldiers," *Jerusalem Post*, 11 August 2016.

362. Amos Harel, "12 Percent of Reserve Battalion Commanders in the IDF—Permanent Personnel," *Haaretz*, 19 February 2014.

363. Perel, "The IDF, the IDF, They Are Coming," 11.

364. Isabel Debre, "With West Bank in Turmoil, New Palestinian Militants Emerge," Associated Press, 3 March 2023.

365. Eyal Cohen and Kevin Huggard, "What Can We Learn from the Escalating Israeli Raids in Syria?" Brookings Institution, 6 December 2019.

366. Anna Aronheim, "IDF Cancels Drills for Reservists over Budget Problems," *Jerusalem Post*, 14 August 2019.

Conclusion

1. R. G. Collingwood, *The Idea of History* (New York: Oxford University Press, 1994), 10.

2. For example, see chapter 3's discussion of how guard supporters in Congress forced the military to use guard divisions for combat missions during the Korean War and unsuccessful efforts to deploy guard maneuver brigades to Iraq in 1991.

3. See the mission statement of First Army, which is responsible for overseeing the mobilization of ARNG and USAR units in wartime, at https://www.first.army.mil/content.aspx?ContentID=199.

4. Howard, *War in European History*, 120.

5. Keegan, *Face of Battle*, 331–340.

6. For more, see Paul Scharre, *Army of None: Autonomous Weapons and the Future of War* (New York: W. W. Norton, 2018).

7. Stephen Bryen, "Armed Drones Revolutionizing the Future of War," *Asia Times*, 9 December 2020, https://asiatimes.com/2020/12/armed-drones-revolutionizing-the-future-of-war/.

8. "Russia's Uran-9 Robot Tank," *National Interest*, 6 January 2019; Kyle Mizokami, "What Will the Army's M1 Abrams Tank Replacement Look Like?" *Popular Mechanics*, 6 November 2020, https://www.popularmechanics.com/military/weapons/a34588107/army-m1a2-abrams-tank-replacement-clues/.

9. Eyal Boguslavsky, "Indian Navy Procuring Smart Shooter 'SMASH 2000' Rifle Sights," *Israel Defense*, 12 July 2020, https://www.israeldefense.co.il/en/node/46950.

10. Paula Froelich, "France, China Developing Biologically Engineered Super Soldiers," *New York Post*, 19 December 2020, https://nypost.com/2020/12/19/france-china-developing-biologically-engineered-super-soldiers/.

11. See, for example, Kyle Mizokami, "This Is the ATV-Mounted Jammer that Took Down an Iranian Drone," *Popular Mechanics*, 22 July 2019, https://www.popularmechanics.com/military/weapons/a28471436/lmadis-iranian-drone/. For more on the Russia-Ukraine war and the role of electronic warfare, see Jack Watling and Nick Reynolds, "Ukraine at War: Paving the Road from Survival to Victory," *RUSI*, 4 July 2022, 10–11.

12. See Scharre, *Army of None*.

13. Sam Skove, "A Lack of Machine Tools Is Holding Back Ammo Production, Army Says," *Defense One*, 3 March 2023, https://www.defenseone.com/threats/2023/03/us-artillery-production-ukraine-limited-lack-machine-tools-army-official-says/383615/.

14. "Russia Sending Large Number of Reserve Troops to Sievierodonetsk, Ukrainian Governor Says," Reuters, 18 June 2022, https://www.reuters.com /world/europe/russia-sending-large-number-reserve-troops-sievierodonetsk -ukrainian-governor-2022-06-18/; David Stern, "Ukrainian Reservists Shift from Civilian Life to War Zone Battlefields," *Washington Post*, 23 April 2022, https://www.washingtonpost.com/world/2022/04/23/ukraine-civilian-reser vists-fight-russians/.

15. Orianna Lyla, Twitter post, 13 May 2023, https://twitter.com/Lyla_lilas /status/1657234883847106560.

Bibliography

Archival Sources

Central Intelligence Agency (CIA) Reading Room (https://www.cia.gov/library /readingroom/home):
  CIA—Arab-Israeli Military Balance
  CIA—Berlin Crisis Chronology
  CIA—Korean War Weekly Highlights
  CIA—Middle East Situation Reports
  CIA—National Intelligence Estimates
  CIA—Presidential Daily Briefings
  CIA—Yom Kippur War Reporting and Analysis
  Defense Intelligence Agency (DIA) Reports
  Institute for Defense Analysis (IDA) Reports on Yom Kippur War
  US State Department Reports
Digital National Security Archive (https://nsarchive.gwu.edu/digital-national -security -archive):
  US National Intelligence Estimates
Dwight D. Eisenhower Presidential Library and Museum, Abilene, KS (https:// www.eisenhowerlibrary.gov/):
  Declassified Documents—Defense Matters
  Office of the Special Assistant for National Security Affairs, Special Assistant Series, Presidential Subseries
Federation of American Scientists Online Archive (https://fas.org/irp/offdocs /nsc-hst/nsc-162-2.pdf):
  US National Security Strategy Documents (1953 to Present)
George C. Marshall Foundation, Washington, DC:
  Public Testimony of George C. Marshall
George C. Marshall Research Library, Lexington, VA:
  George C. Marshall Papers
Haganah Digital Document Repository, Israel (http://www.irgon-haagana.co.il /show_item.asp?itemId=182&levelId=61014&itemType=0&template=31)
Harry S. Truman Library, Independence, MO (https://www.trumanlibrary.org /publicpapers/index.php?pid=183):
  Dean Acheson Papers
  Harry S. Truman Papers
  Oral History Interviews with Gordon Gray

Ike Skelton Combined Arms Research Library, Fort Leavenworth, KS (http://
    cgsc.cdmhost.com/cdm/landingpage/collection/p4013coll9):
    Obsolete Military Manuals
John F. Kennedy Presidential Library and Museum, Boston, MA (https://www
    .jfklibrary.org/Asset-Viewer/Archives/JFKPOF-077-007.aspx):
    DOD Presidential Memos
Library of Congress, Washington, DC:
    John J. Pershing Papers
    Lesley McNair Papers
National Commission on the Future of the Army Digital Reading Room (http://
    www.ncfa.ncr.gov/)
National Guard Memorial Library, Washington, DC:
    Ellard Walsh Papers
    John F. Williams Papers
    Militia Bureau Annual Reports
    Milton Reckord Papers
    National Guard Association Conference Records
    National Guard Association Meeting Minutes and Reports
    National Guard Bureau Annual Reports
    1991 Persian Gulf War Correspondences and Documents
    Office of the Secretary of Defense (OSD) Annual Reports
    State Adjutants General Annual Reports
    Total Force Policy Study Group
    War Department Annual Reports
UK National Archive Online:
    World War II Documents (https://www.nationalarchives.gov.uk/education
        /worldwar2/)
US Army Command and General Staff College Library, Fort Leavenworth, KS:
    Papers of Paul F. Gorman
    Select Papers of General William E. DePuy
US Army War College, Iraq War Study Archive:
    Declassified Documents (https://ahec.armywarcollege.edu/CENTCOMIRAQ
        -papers/index.cfm)

Governmental and Military Sources

British Army. *Transforming the British Army: An Update*. London: UK Ministry
    of Defense, 2013.
Central Bureau of Statistics. *Defense Expenditure in Israel, 1950–2014*. Jerusa-
    lem: Central Bureau of Statistics, 2016.
Comptroller General of the United States. *What Defense Says about Issues in
    Defense Manpower Commission Report—A Summary*. Washington, DC: US
    Government Printing Office, 1977.
Congressional Budget Office. *Improving the Readiness of the Army Reserve and*

National Guard: A Framework for Debate. Washington, DC: US Government Printing Office, 1978.

Congressional Research Service. *U.S. Foreign Aid to Israel.* Washington, DC: Congressional Research Service, 2018.

Defense Intelligence Agency. *Iran Military Power.* Washington, DC: US Government Printing Office, 2009.

Executive Office of the President of the United States. *Historical Tables: Budget of the United States Government: Fiscal Year 2005.* Washington, DC: US Government Printing Office, 2004.

Gates Commission. *The Report of the President's Commission on the All-Volunteer Force.* Washington, DC: US Government Printing Office, 1970.

General Staff (War Office). *Germany Infantry in Action (Minor Tactics).* Calcutta: Government of India Press, 1941.

Government Accountability Office. *Army and Marine Corps M198 Howitzer: Maintenance Problems Are Not Severe Enough to Accelerate Replacement System.* Washington, DC: US Government Printing Office, 1995.

———. *Army Training: Replacement Brigades Were More Proficient than Guard Roundout Brigades.* Washington, DC: US Government Printing Office, 1992.

———. *Management Initiatives Needed to Enhance Reservists' Training.* Washington, DC: US Government Printing Office, 1989.

———. *National Guard: Peacetime Training Did Not Adequately Prepare Combat Brigades for Gulf War.* Washington, DC: US Government Printing Office, 1991.

———. *Readiness of Army Guard and Reserve Support Forces.* Washington, DC: US Government Printing Office, 1988.

IDF. *Deterring Terror: How Israel Confronts the Next Generation of Threats.* English translation of the official strategy of the Israel Defense Forces. Cambridge, MA: Harvard Kennedy Center, 2016.

Israeli Ministry of Aliyah and Immigrant Absorption. *Military Service.* 7th ed. Jerusalem: Publications Department, 2016.

Joint History Office. *Selected Works of General John W. Vessey, Jr., USA: Tenth Chairman of the Joint Chiefs of Staff: 22 June 1982–30 September 1985.* Washington, DC: Joint History Office, 2008.

Joint War Commission of Michigan and Wisconsin. *The 32nd Division in the World War 1917–1919.* Madison: Wisconsin Printing Company, 1920.

National Commission on the Future of the Army. *National Commission on the Future of the Army: Report to the President and Congress of the United States.* Washington, DC: US Government Printing Office, 2016.

National Guard Bureau. *The Army National Guard: A Great Value for America.* Washington, DC: NGB, 2012.

———. *Posture Statement: 2010.* Washington, DC: NGB, 2010.

———. *Posture Statement: 2011.* Washington, DC: NGB, 2011.

———. *Posture Statement: 2012.* Washington, DC: NGB, 2012.

———. *Posture Statement: 2013.* Washington, DC: NGB, 2013.

————. *Posture Statement: 2014.* Washington, DC: NGB, 2014.

————. *Posture Statement: 2015.* Washington, DC: NGB, 2015.

————. *Posture Statement: 2016.* Washington, DC: NGB, 2016.

————. *Posture Statement: 2017.* Washington, DC: NGB, 2017.

————. *Posture Statement: 2018.* Washington, DC: NGB, 2018.

————. *Posture Statement: 2019.* Washington, DC: NGB, 2019.

Office of the US Secretary of Defense. *Annual Defense Department Report: FY 1978, Secretary of Defense, Donald H. Rumsfeld.* Washington, DC: US Government Printing Office, 1977.

————. *Annual Defense Report: Fiscal Year 1982, Secretary of Defense, Harold Brown.* Washington, DC: US Government Printing Office, 1981.

————. Memorandum: Support for Guard and Reserve Forces. 21 August 1970.

————. *National Defense Budget Estimates for FY 2001.* Washington, DC: US Government Printing Office, 2000.

————. *National Defense Budget Estimates for FY 2015.* Washington, DC: US Government Printing Office, 2014.

————. *National Security Strategy of Realistic Deterrence: Secretary of Defense Melvin R. Laird's Annual Defense Department Report FY 1973.* Washington, DC: US Government Printing Office, 1972.

UK Ministry of Defense. *Reserves in the Future Force 2020: Valuable and Valued.* London: TSO, 2013.

US Army. *Worldwide Equipment Guide.* https://odin.tradoc.army.mil/WEG.

US Army Center for Army Lessons Learned. *Observation Report: USARCENT Intermediate Division Headquarters (IDHQ) Operation Spartan Shield, 29th Infantry Division.* Fort Leavenworth, KS: CALL, 2018.

US Army National Guard. *The Army National Guard: A Great Value for America.* White paper. Washington, DC: ARNG, 2012.

————. "ARNG 4.0: Focused Readiness." 2017. https://www.nationalguard .mil/Resources/ARNG-Readiness/.

————. *National Guard by the Numbers.* Washington, DC: ARNG, 2015.

US Army Training and Doctrine Command. *The Operational Environment and the Changing Character of War.* Washington, DC: US Government Printing Office, 2019.

US Army War College. *Statement of a Proper Military Policy for the United States.* Washington, DC: US Government Printing Office, 1916.

————. *The U.S. Army in the Iraq War,* vol. 1, *Invasion, Insurgency, and Civil War (2003–2006).* Carlisle, PA: US Army War College Press, 2019.

US Congress. *Acts of the Second Congress of the United States* [1791]. Washington, DC: Library of Congress, 2019.

————. The National Security Act of 1947. https://www.cia.gov/library/read ingroom/docs/1947-07-26.pdf.

————. Selective Service Act of 1948. https://www.loc.gov/rr/frd/Military _Law/pdf/act-1948.pdf.

US Defense Intelligence Agency. *Russian Military Power.* Washington, DC: US Government Printing Office, 2017.

US Department of the Army. *The Army Vision (2018).* https://www.army.mil /e2/downloads/rv7/vision/the_army_vision.pdf.

———. *Department of the Army Historical Series: Fiscal Year 1974.* Washington, DC: Center of Military History, 1978.

———. *Department of the Army Historical Series: Fiscal Year 1978.* Washington, DC: Center of Military History, 1980.

———. *Department of the Army Historical Series: Fiscal Year 1983.* Washington, DC: Center of Military History, 1990.

———. *Department of the Army Historical Series: Fiscal Year 1989.* Washington, DC: Center of Military History, 1998.

———. *Department of the Army Historical Series: Fiscal Year 1995.* Washington, DC: Center of Military History, 2004.

———. *Department of the Army Historical Series: Fiscal Year 1997.* Washington, DC: Center of Military History, 2005.

———. *Department of the Army Historical Series: Fiscal Year 2000.* Washington, DC: Center of Military History, 2011.

———. *Department of the Army Historical Series: Fiscal Year 2004.* Washington, DC: Center of Military History, 2015.

———. *Department of the Army Historical Series: Fiscal Year 2010.* Washington, DC: Center of Military History, 2015.

———. *FM 3–0: Operations.* Washington, DC: US Government Printing Office, 2017.

———. *FM 6–0: Command and Staff Organizations and Operations.* Washington, DC: US Government Printing Office, 2014.

———. *FM 7–8: Infantry Rifle Platoon and Squad.* Washington, DC: US Government Printing Office, 1992.

———. *FM 7–10: The Infantry Rifle Company.* Washington, DC: US Government Printing Office, 1990.

———. *FM 23–5: U.S. Rifle—Caliber .30 M1.* Washington, DC: US Government Printing Office, 1965.

———. *FM 100–2-2: The Soviet Army: Specialized Warfare and Rear Area Support.* Washington, DC: US Government Printing Office, 1984.

———. *FM 100–2-3: The Soviet Army: Troops, Organization, and Equipment.* Washington, DC: US Government Printing Office, 1991.

———. *FM 100–5: Operations.* Washington, DC: US Government Printing Office, 1949, 1962, 1976, 1982, 1986.

———. *Historical Summary* (1969 to present). https://history.army.mil/html /bookshelves/collect/dahsum.html.

———. *Operating Manual 9–1005–319–10: M-16 and M-4 Rifle.* Washington, DC: US Government Printing Office, 2010.

———. *Soviet Army Operations.* Washington, DC: US Government Printing Office, 1978.

————. *TC 3–21.20: Infantry Battalion Collective Task Publication.* Washington, DC: US Government Printing Office, 2012.

US Department of Defense. Pay and Benefits Charts (1949 to present). https://www.dfas.mil/militarymembers/payentitlements/Pay-Tables/PayTableArchives.html.

————. *Selected Manpower Statistics, Fiscal Year 1982.* Washington, DC: US Government Printing Office, 1982.

————. *Summary of the 2018 National Defense Strategy of the United States.* Washington, DC: US Government Printing Office, 2018.

US Government. *Budget FY 2015—Table 5.1—Budget Authority by Function and Subfunction: 1976–2019.* Washington, DC: US Government Printing Office, 2014.

US Marine Corps Intelligence Activity. *Soviet/Russian Army and Artillery Design and Practices: 1945–1995.* Quantico, VA: US Government Printing Office, 1995.

US National Reconnaissance Office (NRO). "The Gambit and Hexagon Programs." Center for the Study of National Reconnaissance, 2012. https://www.nro.gov/History-and-Studies/Center-for-the-Study-of-National-Reconnaissance/The-GAMBIT-and-HEXAGON-Programs/.

US National Security Council. *NSC 162/2: Basic National Security Strategy.* 30 October 1953.

War Department. *Field Service Regulation 1923.* Washington, DC: US Government Printing Office, 1923.

————. *FM 7–10: Infantry Field Manual: Rifle Company, Rifle Regiment.* Washington, DC: US Government Printing Office, 1942.

————. *FM 7–20: Infantry Field Manual: Rifle Battalion.* Washington, DC: US Government Printing Office, 1942.

————. *FM 7–40: Infantry Field Manual: Rifle Regiment.* Washington, DC: US Government Printing Office, 1942.

————. *FM 23–10: Basic Field Manual: U.S. Rifle, Caliber .30, M1903.* Washington, DC: US Government Printing Office, 1940.

————. *FM 100–5: Tentative Field Service Regulations: Operations.* Washington, DC: US Government Printing Office, 1939.

————. *Order of Battle of the United States Land Forces in the World War* [1931]. Washington, DC: US Government Printing Office, 1988.

————. *Statement of a Proper Military Policy for the United States.* Washington, DC: US Government Printing Office, 1915.

Winograd Commission Report. January 2007. http://go.ynet.co.il/pic/news/vinograd/vinograd.pdf.

Books and Articles

Adan, Avraham. *On the Banks of the Suez: An Israeli General's Personal Account of the Yom Kippur War.* Reprint ed. New York: Presidio Press, 1991.

Allon, Yigal. *The Making of Israel's Army*. London: Sphere Books, 1971.

Ambrose, Stephen E. *Upton and the Army*. Baton Rouge: LSU Press, 1992.

Anderson, Michael G. *Mustering for War*. Fort Leavenworth, KS: US Army University Press, 2021.

Atkinson, Rick. *An Army at Dawn: The War in North Africa, 1942–1943*. New York: Henry Holt, 2002.

———. *The British Are Coming: The War for America, Lexington to Princeton, 1775–1777*. New York: Henry Holt, 2019.

———. *The Day of Battle: The War in Sicily and Italy, 1943–1944*. New York: Henry Holt, 2007.

———. *The Guns at Last Light: The War in Western Europe, 1944–1945*. New York: Henry Holt, 2013.

Avidor, Gideon, ed. *Mission Command in the Israel Defense Forces*. Dahlonega: University of North Georgia Press, 2021.

Bacevich, A. J. *The Pentomic Era: The U.S. Army between Korea and Vietnam*. Washington, DC: NDU Press, 1986.

Baker, Chris. "British Army Reserves and Reservists." http://www.longlongtrail .co.uk/soldiers/a-soldiers-life-1914-1918/enlisting-into-the-army/brit- ish-army -reserves-and-reservists/.

Balkoski, Joseph. *Beyond the Beachhead: The 29th Infantry Division in Nor- mandy*. New York: Dell Books, 1989.

———. *The Maryland National Guard: A History of Maryland's Military Force*. Glen Burnie, MD: Toomey Press, 1997.

Barlone, D. *A French Officer's Diary: 23 August 1939–01 October 1940* [1942], trans. L. V. Cass. 1st paperback ed. New York: Cambridge University Press, 2011.

Bar-On, Mordechai, ed. *A Never-ending Conflict: A Guide to Israeli Military History*. New York: Praeger, 2004.

Barthas, Louis. *Poilu: The World War I Notebooks of Corporal Louis Barthas, Barrelmaker, 1914–1918* [1978], trans. Edward M. Strauss. New Haven, CT: Yale University Press, 2014.

Beckett, Ian, Timothy Bowman, and Mark Connelly. *The British Army and the First World War*. New York: Cambridge University Press, 2017.

Ben-Gurion, David. *Memoirs*. Cleveland, OH: World Publishing, 1970.

Benwell, Henry. *History of the Yankee Division*. Boston: Cornhill, 1919.

Berebitsky, William. *A Very Long Weekend: The National Guard in Korea, 1950–1953*. Shippensburg, PA: White Mane, 1996.

Bergman, Ronen. *Rise and Kill First: The Secret History of Israel's Targeted As- sassinations*. New York: Random House, 2018.

Binkin, Martin, and William W. Kaufman. *U.S. Army Guard and Reserve: Re- alities and Risks*. Washington, DC: Brookings, 1989.

Black, Jeremy. *The Age of Total War: 1860–1945*. Lanham, MD: Rowman & Littlefield, 2010.

———. *Rethinking Military History*. New York: Routledge, 2004.

————, ed. *War in the Modern World: Since 1815*. New York: Routledge, 2003.

Blair, Clay. *The Forgotten War: America in Korea, 1950–1953*. New York: Times Books, 1987.

Blakeley, Katherine. "Defense Spending in Historical Context: A New Reaganesque Buildup?" *CSBA*, 8 November 2020. https://csbaonline.org/reports /defense-spending-in-historical-context.

Blasko, Dennis J. *The Chinese Army Today: Tradition and Transformation for the 21st Century*. 2nd ed. New York: Routledge, 2012.

Bloem, Walter. *The Advance from Mons 1914: The Experiences of a German Infantry Officer* [1916], trans. G. C. Wynne. West Midlands, UK: Helion, 2011.

Bobbit, Philip. *The Shield of Achilles: War, Peace, and the Course of History*. New York: Anchor Books, 2002.

Boot, Max. *Invisible Armies: An Epic History of Guerilla Warfare from the Ancient Times to the Present*. New York: W. W. Norton, 2013.

Boyd, John A. "America's Army of Democracy: The National Army, 1917–1919." *Army History* 109 (Fall 2018): 6–27.

Bradley, Omar N., and Clay Blair. *A General's Life*. New York: Simon & Schuster, 1984.

Bratten, Jonathan. *To the Last Man: A National Guard Regiment in the Great War, 1917–1919*. Fort Leavenworth, KS: Army University Press, 2020.

Bregman, Ahron. *Israel's Wars: A History since 1947*. 3rd ed. New York: Routledge, 2010.

Brewer, John. *The Sinews of Power: War, Money and the English State, 1688–1783*. Reprint ed. Cambridge, MA: Harvard University Press, 1990.

Bronfield, Saul. "Fighting Outnumbered: The Impact of the Yom Kippur War on the U.S. Army." *Journal of Military History* 71, 2 (2007): 465–498.

Brower, Kenneth. *The Israel Defense Forces*. Ramat Gan, Israel: Begin-Sadat Center, 2018.

Brown, John S. *Kevlar Legions: The Transformation of the United States Army 1989–2005*. Washington, DC: US Army Center of Military History, 2012.

Bryant, Thomas, Gerald Morse, Leslie Novak, and John Henry. "Tactical Radars for Ground Surveillance." *Lincoln Laboratory Journal* 12, 2 (2000): 341–352.

Bucklin, Steven. "Those in Reserve Also Serve: The South Dakota National Guard during the Korean War." *South Dakota History* 30, 4 (Winter 2000): 391–411.

Bull, Stephen. *Second World War Infantry Tactics: The European Theatre*. Barnsley, UK: Pen & Sword, 2012.

————. *World War II Infantry Tactics: Squad and Platoon*. Oxford: Osprey, 2004.

Bury, Patrick, and Sergio Catignani. "Future Reserves 2020, the British Army and the Politics of Military Innovation during the Cameron Era." *International Affairs* 95, 3 (May 2019): 681–701.

Calhoun, Mark. *General Lesley J. McNair: Unsung Architect of the U.S. Army*. Lawrence: University Press of Kansas, 2015.

Capozzola, Christopher. *Uncle Sam Wants You: World War I and the Making of the Modern American Citizen.* New York: Oxford University Press, 2008.

Carafano, James. "Total Force Policy and the Abrams Doctrine: Unfulfilled Promise, Uncertain Future." Heritage Foundation, 18 April 2005.

Catignani, Sergio. *Israeli Counterinsurgency and the Intifadas: Dilemmas of a Conventional Army.* New York: Routledge, 2008.

Chandler, David G., and Hazel R. Watson. *Atlas of Military Strategy: The Art, Theory and Practice of War, 1618–1878.* New York: Arms & Armor, 1997.

Chapman, Anne W. *The Army's Training Revolution, 1973–1990.* Fort Monroe, VA: TRADOC, 1994.

Cheney, Dick. *In My Time: A Personal and Political Memoir.* New York: Threshold Editions, 2010.

Chetboun, Yoni. *Under Fire: Diary of an Israeli Commander on the Battlefield*, trans. Jessica Setbon. New York: Gefen, 2017.

Chickering, Roger, Stig Forster, and Bernd Greiner, eds. *A World at Total War: Global Conflict and the Politics of Destruction, 1937–1945.* New York: Cambridge University Press, 2005.

Chivers, C. J. *The Gun.* New York: Simon & Schuster, 2011.

Citino, Robert. *Blitzkrieg to Desert Storm: The Evolution of Operational Warfare.* Lawrence: University Press of Kansas, 2017.

———. *Path to Blitzkrieg: Doctrine and Training in the German Army, 1920–39.* Mechanicsburg, PA: Stackpole Books, 1999.

Clodfelter, Michael. *Warfare and Armed Conflicts: A Statistical Reference to Casualty and Other Figures, 1500–2000.* 2nd ed. Jefferson, NC: McFarland, 2002.

Coffman, Edward M. *The Old Army: A Portrait of the American Army in Peacetime, 1784–1898.* New York: Oxford University Press, 1988.

———. *The Regulars: The American Army, 1898–1941.* Cambridge, MA: Harvard University Press, 2004.

Cohen, Eliot A., Michael J. Eisenstadt, and Andrew J. Bacevich. *Knives, Tanks, and Missiles: Israel's Security Revolution.* Washington, DC: Washington Institute for Near East Policy, 1998.

Cohen, Hillel. *Year Zero of the Arab-Israeli Conflict 1929.* Waltham, MA: Brandeis University Press, 2015.

Cohen, Stuart A. "How Did the Intifada Affect the IDF?" *Conflict Quarterly* 14 (Summer 1994): 7–22.

———. *Israel and Its Army: From Cohesion to Confusion.* New York: Routledge, 2008.

Cohen, Stuart A., and Aharon Klieman, eds. *Routledge Handbook on Israeli Security.* New York: Routledge, 2018.

Coll, Steven. *Directorate S: The C.I.A. and America's Secret Wars in Afghanistan and Pakistan.* New York: Penguin Books, 2018.

Collingwood, R. G. *The Idea of History.* New York: Oxford University Press, 1994.

Collins, J. Lawton. *Lightning Joe: An Autobiography*. New York: Presidio Press, 1994.

Combat Studies Institute. *Sixty Years of Reorganizing for Combat: A Historical Trends Analysis*. Fort Leavenworth, KS: Combat Studies Institute Press, 1999.

Conaway, John B., and Jeff Nelligan. *Call out the Guard! The Story of Lieutenant General John B. Conaway and the Modern Day National Guard*. Paducah, KY: Turner, 1997.

Condit, Doris M. *History of the Office of the Secretary of Defense*, vol. 2, *The Test of War, 1950–1953*. Washington, DC: US Government Printing Office, 1988.

Cooper, Jerry. *The Rise of the National Guard: The Evolution of the American Militia, 1865–1920*. Lincoln: University of Nebraska Press, 1997.

Cordesman, Anthony. *The Arab-Israeli Military Balance in 2010*. Washington, DC: CSIS, 2010.

———. *Iran's Military Forces and Warfighting Capabilities*. Westport, CT: Praeger, 2007.

———. *The Israeli and Syrian Conventional Military Balance*. Washington, DC: CSIS, 2008.

———. *Military Balance in the Middle East VI: Arab-Israeli Balance*. Washington, DC: CSIS, 1998.

Cordesman, Anthony, and Ionut C. Popescu. "Israel and Syria: The Military Balance and Prospects for War." Center for Strategic and International Studies (CSIS), 15 August 2017.

Craig, Campbell, and Fredrik Logevall. *America's Cold War: The Politics of Insecurity*. Reprint ed. Cambridge, MA: Belknap, 2012.

Crist, David. *The Twilight War: The Secret History of America's Thirty-Year Conflict with Iran*. New York: Penguin Books, 2012.

Cumings, Bruce. *The Korean War: A History*. Reprint ed. New York: Modern Library, 2011.

Dandeker, Christopher, Neil Greenberg, and Geoffrey Orme. "The UK's Reserve Forces: Retrospect and Prospect." *Armed Forces and Society* 37, 2 (2011): 341–360.

Dastrup, Boyd L. *The King of Battle: A Branch History of the U.S. Army's Field Artillery*. Fort Monroe, VA: US Army Training and Doctrine Command, 1992.

Davenport, Christian. *As You Were: To War and Back with the Black Hawk Battalion of the Virginia National Guard*. Hoboken, NJ: John Wiley & Sons, 2009.

Davis, Tenney L. *The Chemistry of Powder and Explosives*. Reprint ed. New York: Angriff Press, 2012.

Davis, Thomas M. *40km into Lebanon: Israel's 1982 Invasion*. Washington, DC: NDU Press, 1987.

Dayan, Moshe. *Diary of the Sinai Campaign*. New York: Harper & Row, 1966.

———. *Moshe Dayan: Story of My Life; an Autobiography*. New York: William Morrow, 1976.

Derthick, Martha. *The National Guard in Politics.* Cambridge, MA: Harvard University Press, 1965.

DiMarco, Lou. *Concrete Hell: Urban Warfare from Stalingrad to Iraq.* Oxford: Osprey, 2012.

Doubler, Michael D. *Civilian in Peace, Soldier in War: The Army National Guard, 1636–2000.* Lawrence: University Press of Kansas, 2003.

Doughty, Robert A. *The Seeds of Disaster: The Development of French Army Doctrine, 1919–39.* Mechanicsburg, PA: Stackpole Books, 2014.

Douglas-Home, Charles. *Britain's Reserve Forces.* London: Royal United Service Institute, 1969.

Drea, Edward J. *Japan's Imperial Army: Its Rise and Fall, 1853–1945.* Lawrence: University Press of Kansas, 2009.

Drylie, Kenneth. *The National Training Center and Fort Irwin.* Charleston, SC: Arcadia, 2018.

Duncan, Stephen M. *Citizen Warriors: America's National Guard and Reserve Forces and the Politics of National Security.* New York: Presidio, 1997.

Dunstan, Simon. *Centurion vs T-55: Yom Kippur War 1973.* Oxford: Osprey, 2009.

———. *The Six Day War 1967: Jordan and Syria.* Oxford: Osprey, 2013.

———. *The Six Day War 1967: Sinai.* Oxford: Osprey, 2012.

Dupuy, Trevor M. *Elusive Victory: The Arab-Israeli Wars, 1947–1974.* New York: Harper & Row, 1978.

Easton, Ian, Mark Stokes, Cortez Cooper, and Arthur Chan. *Transformation of Taiwan's Reserve Forces.* Santa Monica, CA: RAND Corporation, 2017.

Echevarria, Antulio J., II. *After Clausewitz: German Military Thinkers before the Great War.* Lawrence: University Press of Kansas, 2000.

———. *Reconsidering the American Way of War: US Military Practice from the Revolution to Afghanistan.* Washington, DC: Georgetown University Press, 2014.

Eilam, Ehud. *Israel's Way of War: A Strategic and Operational Analysis, 1948–2014.* Jefferson, NC: McFarland, 2016.

El-Shazly, Saad. *The Crossing of the Suez* [1980]. San Francisco: American Mideast Research, 2002.

English, John A., and Bruce I. Gudmundsson. *On Infantry.* Rev. ed. Westport, CT: Praeger, 1994.

Ezov, Amiram. "The Crossing Challenge: The Suez Canal Crossing by the Israel Defense Forces during the Yom Kippur War of 1973." *Journal of Military History* 82, 2 (April 2018): 461–490.

Falkenhayn, Erich von. *The German General Staff and Its Critical Decisions, 1914–1916* [1919]. Auckland, NZ: Pickle Partners, 2013.

Farwell, Byron. *Mr. Kipling's Army: All the Queen's Men.* Reprint ed. New York: W. W. Norton, 1987.

Faulkner, Richard S. "'Gone Blooey': Pershing's System for Addressing Officer Incompetence and Inefficiency." *Army History* 95 (Spring 2015): 6–25.

Fehrenbach, T. R. *This Kind of War: The Classic Korean War History*. 50th anniversary ed. Dulles, VA: Brassey's, 2000.

Finkel, Meir. *Military Agility: Ensuring Rapid and Effective Transition from Peace to War*. Lexington: University Press of Kentucky, 2020.

———. *Studies in Generalship*. Stanford, CA: Hoover Institution Press, 2021.

Flynn, George Q. *The Draft: 1940–1973*. Lawrence: University Press of Kansas, 1993.

Franks, Kenny A. *Citizen Soldiers: Oklahoma's National Guard*. Norman: University of Oklahoma Press, 1984.

French, David. *The British Way in Warfare, 1688–2000*. London: Unwin Hyman, 1990.

———. *Raising Churchill's Army: The British Army and the War against Germany 1919–1945*. New ed. New York: Oxford University Press, 2001.

French, John. *1914*. London: Constable, 1919.

Frevert, Ute. *A Nation in Barracks: Modern Germany, Military Conscription, and Civil Society*. New York: Berg, 2004.

Friedman, Benjamin M. "Learning from the Reagan Deficits." *American Economic Review* 82, 2 (1992): 299–304.

Fussell, Paul. *The Boys' Crusade: The American Infantry in Northwestern Europe, 1944–1945*. New York: Modern Library, 2003.

———. *The Great War and Modern Memory*. 25th anniversary ed. New York: Oxford University Press, 2000.

Gabel, Christopher R. *The U.S. Army GHQ Maneuvers of 1941*. Washington, DC: US Army Center of Military History, 1991.

Gaddis, John Lewis. *The Cold War: A New History*. Reprint ed. New York: Penguin Books, 2006.

Gal, Reuven. *A Portrait of the Israeli Soldier*. New York: Praeger, 1986.

Gat, Moshe. "Nasser and the Six Day War, 5 June 1967: A Premeditated Strategy or an Inexorable Drift to War?" *Israel Affairs* 11, 4 (October 2005): 608–635.

Gates, Robert. *Duty: Memoirs of a Secretary at War*. New York: Knopf, 2014.

Gawrych, George W. *Key to the Sinai: The Battles for Abu Ageila in the 1956 and 1967 Arab-Israeli Wars*. Fort Leavenworth, KS: Combat Studies Institute, 1990.

Glantz, David M. *The Military Strategy of the Soviet Union: A History*. New York: Routledge, 2001.

Glantz, David M., and Jonathan M. House. *When Titans Clashed: How the Red Army Stopped Hitler*. Lawrence: University Press of Kansas, 2015.

Gooch, John. *Armies in Europe*. New York: Routledge, 1980.

———. *The Italian Army and the First World War*. New York: Cambridge University Press, 2014.

———. *Mussolini's War: Fascist Italy from Triumph to Collapse, 1934–1943*. New York: Pegasus Books, 2020.

Graf, David A., and Robin Higham, eds. *A Military History of China*. 2nd ed. Lexington: University Press of Kentucky, 2012.

Grau, Lester W., and Charles K. Bartles. *The Russian Reconnaissance Complex Comes of Age*. Fort Leavenworth, KS: Foreign Military Studies Office, 2018.

———. *The Russian Way of War*. Fort Leavenworth, KS: Foreign Military Studies Office, 2016.

Graves, Robert. *Good-bye to All That* [1929]. New York: Anchor Books, 1998.

Gray, Wilbur. *Prussia and the Evolution of the Reserve Army: A Forgotten Lesson of History*. Carlisle, PA: Strategic Studies Institute, 1992.

Greenberg, Yitzhak. "The Swiss Armed Forces as a Model for the IDF Reserve System—Indeed?" *Israel Studies* 18, 3 (Fall 2013): 95–111.

Greentree, David, and Adam Hook. *German Infantryman vs British Infantryman: France 1940*. Oxford: Osprey, 2015.

Grenier, John. *The First Way of War: American War Making on the Frontiers*. New York: Cambridge University Press, 2005.

Griffith, James. "After 9/11, What Kind of Reserve Soldier?" *Armed Forces and Society* 35, 2 (2009): 214–240.

———. "Reserve Forces after the Cold War: An International Perspective." *Armed Forces and Society* 37, 2 (2011): 209–215.

Griffith, Paddy. *Battle Tactics of the Western Front: The British Army's Art of Attack, 1916–1918*. New Haven, CT: Yale University Press, 1994.

———. *Forward into Battle: Fighting Tactics from Waterloo to the Near Future*. Novato, CA: Presidio, 1990.

Gronski, John L., Kurt Nielsen, and Alfred Smith. "2/28 BCT Goes to War." 1 July 2006. http://www.milvet.state.pa.us/PAO/pr/2006_07_01.htm.

Guderian, Heinz. *Achtung-Panzer! The Development of Tank Warfare* [1937], trans. Christopher Duffy. London: Cassell, 2012.

———. *Panzer Leader* [1952], trans. Constantine Fitzgibbon. 2nd ed. Cambridge, MA: Da Capo Press, 2002.

Gudmundsson, Bruce I. *The British Expeditionary Force 1914–15*. New York: Osprey, 2005.

———. *On Armor*. Westport, CT: Praeger, 2004.

———. *On Artillery*. Westport, CT: Praeger, 1993.

———. *Stormtroop Tactics: Innovation in the German Army, 1914–1918*. Westport, CT: Praeger, 1995.

Halberstam, David. *The Coldest Winter: America and the Korean War*. New York: Hyperion, 2008.

Halleck, H. W. *Elements of Military Art and Science*. 3rd ed. New York: D. Appleton, 1862.

Harel, Amos, and Avi Issacharoff. *34 Days: Israel, Hezbollah, and the War in Lebanon*. New York: St. Martin's Press, 2008.

Harish, Katoch. *Territorial Army: Future Challenges*. Delhi: Vij Books India, 2013.

Hart, Peter. *Fire and Movement: The British Expeditionary Force and the Campaign of 1914*. New York: Oxford University Press, 2014.

Hartley, John. *6th Battalion the Cheshire Regiment in the Great War: A Territorial*

Battalion on the Western Front, 1914–1918. South Yorkshire, UK: Pen & Sword, 2017.

Hendel, Yoaz, "The Reserves Comeback." *Strategic Assessment* 10, 4 (February 2008): 33–41.

Henkin, Yigal. *The 1956 Suez War and the New World Order in the Middle East: Exodus in Reverse.* Lanham, MD: Lexington Books, 2015.

Henry, Mark, and Mike Chappell. *The US Army in World War II: Northwest Europe.* Oxford: Osprey, 2012.

Herrera, Ricardo. "History, Mission Command, and the Auftragstaktik Infatuation." *Military Review,* July–August 2022.

Herwig, Holger H. *The First World War: Germany and Austria-Hungry, 1914–1918.* 2nd ed. London: Bloomsbury, 2014.

———. *The Marne, 1914: The Opening of World War I and the Battle that Changed the World.* New York: Random House, 2011.

Herzog, Chaim. *The Arab-Israeli Wars: War and Peace in the Middle East.* New York: Vintage, 2015.

Heuser, Beatrice. *The Evolution of Strategy.* New York: Cambridge University Press, 2011.

Heymont, Irving. "Israeli Defense Forces." *Military Review,* 8 February 1967.

Hicks, J. G. "The National Reserve." *Royal United Services Institution* 57 (1913): 661–666.

Hill, Jim. *The Minute Man in Peace and War: A History of the National Guard.* Mechanicsburg, PA: Stackpole, 1964.

Hirsch, Gal. *Defensive Shield: An Israeli Special Forces Commander on the Front Lines of Counterterrorism,* trans. Reuven Ben-Shalom. New York: Gefen Books, 2016.

Hobsbawm, E. J. *Nations and Nationalism since 1780: Programme, Myth, Reality.* 2nd ed. New York: Cambridge University Press, 2012.

Hodgson, Godfrey. *The Colonel: The Life and Times of Henry Stimson, 1867–1950.* New York: Knopf, 1990.

Hoffman, Bruce. *Anonymous Soldiers: The Struggle for Israel, 1917–1947.* New York: Vintage Books, 2015.

Holley, I. B., Jr. *General John M. Palmer, Citizen Soldiers, and the Army of a Democracy.* Westport, CT: Greenwood, 1982.

Horne, Alistair. *To Lose a Battle: France 1940.* Reprint ed. New York: Penguin Books, 2007.

House, Jonathan M. *Combined Arms Warfare in the Twentieth Century.* Lawrence: University Press of Kansas, 2001.

Howard, Michael. *The Franco-Prussian War: The German Invasion of France 1870–1871.* 2nd ed. New York: Routledge, 2001.

———. *The Lessons of History.* Reprint ed. New Haven, CT: Yale University Press, 1992.

———. *War in European History.* Updated ed. New York: Oxford University Press, 2001.

Hughes, Daniel J., ed. *Moltke on the Art of War: Selected Writings.* New York: Ballantine Books, 1993.

Hyndson, J. G. W. *From Mons to the First Battle of Ypres* [1933]. Auckland, NZ: Pickle Partners, 2015.

"Infantry Tactics, 1914–1918." *Royal United Services Institute* 64 (1919): 460–466.

Jacobs, Jeffery A. *The Future of the Citizen-Soldier Force: Issues and Answers.* Lexington: University Press of Kentucky, 1994.

Junger, Ernst. *The Storm of Steel* [1920]. London: Chatto & Windus, 1929.

Kahalani, Avigdor. *The Heights of Courage: A Tank Leader's War on the Golan* [1984]. New York: Praeger, 1992.

Karsh, Efrain. *From Rabin to Netanyahu: Israel's Troubled Agenda.* New York: Routledge, 2013.

Katz, Sam. *Merkava Main Battle Tank MKs I, II & III.* Oxford: Osprey, 1997.

Katz, Yaakov, and Amir Bohbot. *The Weapon Wizards: How Israel Became a High-Tech Military Superpower.* New York: St. Martin's Press, 2017.

Keegan, John. *The Face of Battle: A Study of Agincourt, Waterloo, and the Somme.* New York: Penguin Books, 1978.

———. *The First World War.* New York: Vintage Books, 2000.

———. *A History of Warfare.* New York: Vintage Books, 2012.

———. *The Second World War.* New York: Penguin Books, 2005.

Keene, Shima D. *The Effective Use of Reserve Personnel in the U.S. Military: Lessons from the United Kingdom Reserve Model.* Carlisle, PA: Strategic Studies Institute, 2015.

Kennedy, Paul M. *The Rise and Fall of Great Powers: Economic Change and Military Conflict from 1500 to 2000.* New York: Vintage Books, 1989.

Kiesling, Eugenia. *Arming against Hitler: France and the Limits of Military Planning.* Lawrence: University Press of Kansas, 1996.

Kittfield, James. *Prodigal Soldiers: How the Generation of Officers Born of Vietnam Revolutionized the American Style of War.* Paperback ed. Dulles, VA: Potomac Books, 1997.

Knight, Roger. *Britain against Napoleon: The Organization of Victory, 1793–1815.* New York: Penguin Books, 2013.

Kober, Avi. "The Israeli Defense Forces in the Second Lebanon War: Why the Poor Performance?" *Journal of Strategic Studies* 31, 1 (February 2008): 3–40.

Kramer, Gudrun. *A History of Palestine: From the Ottoman Conquest to the Founding of the State of Israel.* Princeton, NJ: Princeton University Press, 2011.

Krepinevich, Andrew, Jr. *The Army and Vietnam.* Baltimore: Johns Hopkins University Press, 2009.

Lambert, Nicholas A. *Planning Armageddon.* Cambridge, MA: Harvard University Press, 2012.

Laron, Guy. *The Six Day War: The Breaking of the Middle East.* New Haven, CT: Yale University Press, 2017.

Leffler, Melvyn P. *For the Soul of Mankind: The United States, the Soviet Union, and the Cold War.* New York: Hill & Wang, 2008.

Lesch, David W. *The Arab-Israeli Conflict: A History.* 1st ed. New York: Oxford University Press, 2007.

Levy, Yagil. "The Army Reserve Stinks." *Army and Strategy* 3, 3 (December 2011): 53–62.

———. "The Decline of the Reservist Army." *Military and Strategic Affairs* 3, 3 (December 2011): 63–74.

Liddell Hart, Basil Henry. "Man-in-the-Dark Theory." *Royal Engineers Journal* 33 (1921): 1–22.

Link, Arthur. *Wilson,* vol. 4, *Confusions and Crises, 1915–1916.* Princeton, NJ: Princeton University Press, 1964.

Linn, Brian McAllister. *The Echo of Battle: The Army's Way of War.* Cambridge, MA: Harvard University Press, 2009.

———. *Elvis's Army: Cold War GIs and the Atomic Battlefield.* Cambridge, MA: Harvard University Press, 2016.

Lock-Pullan, Richard. "An Inward-Looking Time: The United States Army, 1973–1976." *Journal of Military History* 67, 2 (April 2003): 483–511.

Ludendorff, Erich. *My War Memories: 1914–1918.* London: Hutchinson, 1919.

Luttwak, Edward, and Daniel Horowitz. *The Israeli Army.* New York: Harper-Collins, 1975.

Lynn, John A. *Battle: A History of Combat and Culture, from Ancient Greece to Modern America.* Oxford: Westview Press, 2003.

MacArthur, Douglas. *Reminiscences* [1964]. Annapolis, MD: Blue Jacket Books, 2001.

Manchester, William. *American Caesar: Douglas MacArthur 1880–1964.* Boston: Little, Brown, 1978.

Mansel, Philip. *Paris between Empires: Monarchy and Revolution 1814–1852.* New York: St. Martin's Press, 2003.

Mansoor, Peter J. *The GI Offensive in Europe: The Triumph of American Infantry Divisions.* Lawrence: University Press of Kansas, 1999.

Marcus, Raphael D. *Israel's Long War with Hizballah: Military Innovation and Adaptation under Fire.* Washington, DC: Georgetown University Press, 2018.

———. "Military Innovation and Tactical Adaptation in the Israel-Hizbullah Conflict: The Institutionalization of Lesson-Learning in the IDF." *Journal of Strategic Studies* 38, 4 (2015): 500–528.

Martin, Frederick. *The Statesman's Yearbook 1868.* London: Palgrave Macmillan, 1868.

Matthews, Matt M. *We Were Caught Unprepared: The 2006 Hezbollah-Israeli War.* Fort Leavenworth, KS: Combat Studies Institute Press, 2008.

McNeill, William H. *The Pursuit of Power: Technology, Armed Force, and Society since A.D. 1000.* Chicago: University of Chicago Press, 1984.

McPherson, James M. *Battle Cry of Freedom: The Civil War Era.* New York: Oxford University Press, 2003.

Miller, John, Jr., Owen J. Curroll, and Margret E. Tackley. *Korea: 1951–1953*. Reprint ed. Washington, DC: Center of Military History, 1997.

Millett, Allan R., Peter Maslowski, and William B. Feis. *For the Common Defense: A Military History of the United States from 1607 to 2012*. New York: Free Press, 2012.

Mofaz, Shaul. "Operation Defensive Shield: Lessons and Aftermath." Washington Institute for Near East Policy, 18 June 2002. https://www.washingtoninstitute. org/policy-analysis/view/operation-defensive-shield-lessons-and-aftermath.

Moltke, Helmuth. *The Franco-German War of 1870–71* [1893]. Auckland, NZ: Pickle Partners, 2013.

Morris, Benny. *1948: A History of the First Arab-Israeli War*. New Haven, CT: Yale University Press, 2008.

———. *Righteous Victims: A History of the Zionist-Arab Conflict, 1881–1998*. Reprint ed. New York: Vintage Books, 2011.

Murland, Jerry. *Aristocrats Go to War: Uncovering the Zillebeke Cemetery*. Barnsley, UK: Pen & Sword, 2010.

Murray, Williamson, and MacGregor Knox, eds. *The Dynamics of Military Revolution, 1300–2050*. New York: Cambridge University Press, 2001.

Murray, Williamson, and Allan R. Millett, eds. *Military Effectiveness*, vol. 1, *The First World War*. New ed. New York: Cambridge University Press, 2010.

———. *Military Effectiveness*, vol. 2, *The Interwar Period*. New ed. New York: Cambridge University Press, 2010.

———. *Military Effectiveness*, vol. 3, *The Second World War*. New ed. New York: Cambridge University Press, 2010.

Murray, Williamson, and Kevin M. Woods. *The Iran-Iraq War: A Military and Strategic History*. Cambridge: Cambridge University Press, 2014.

Nagel, Jacob, and Jonathan Schanzer. *Assessing Israel's Iron Dome Missile Defense System*. Washington, DC: FDD, 2019.

Naor, Mordechai. *Ha'Hagana*. Tel Aviv: IDF, 1985.

Nerguizian, Aram. *The Military Balance in a Shattered Levant: Conventional Forces, Asymmetric Warfare, and the Struggle for Syria*. Washington, DC: CSIS, 2015.

Ney, Virgil. *Evolution of the U.S. Army Division, 1939–1968*. Fort Belvoir, VA: US Army, 1969.

Nicholson, Helen. *Medieval Warfare: Theory and Practice of War in Europe, 300–1500*. New York: Palgrave, 2003.

Odom, William O. *After the Trenches: The Transformation of the U.S. Army, 1918–1939*. College Station: Texas A&M Press, 1999.

Ohl, John Kennedy. *Minuteman: The Military Career of General Robert S. Beightler*. Boulder, CO: Lynne Rienner, 2001.

Oren, Michael B. *Six Days of War: June 1967 and the Making of the Modern Middle East*. New York: Presidio, 2003.

Orr, Ori. *These Are My Brothers: A Dramatic Story of Heroism during the Yom Kippur War*. Tel Aviv: Contento, 2003.

O'Ryan, John F. *The Story of the 27th Division* [1921]. London: Franklin Classics, 2018.

Ostovar, Afshon. *Vanguard of the Imam*. New York: Oxford University Press, 2016.

Otel, Eran. "Turn on the Light, Extinguish the Fire: Israel's New Way of War." *War on the Rocks*, 19 January 2022.

Overy, Richard. *Russia's War: A History of the Soviet Effort, 1941–1945*. Rev. ed. New York: Penguin Books, 1998.

Paret, Peter, ed. *The Makers of Modern Strategy from Machiavelli to the Nuclear Age*. Princeton, NJ: Princeton University Press, 1986.

Parker, Geoffrey, ed. *The Cambridge Illustrated History of Warfare*. New York: Cambridge University Press, 1995.

Parker, James. "The Militia Act of 1903." *North American Review* 177, 561 (August 1903): 278–287.

Parsons, Laila. *The Commander: Fawzi al-Qawuqji and the Fight for Arab Independence 1914–1948*. New York: Hill & Wang, 2016.

Peri, Yoram. *Generals in the Cabinet Room: How the Military Shapes Israeli Policy*. Washington DC: United States Institute of Peace Press, 2006.

Perlinger, Arie. "The Changing Nature of the Israeli Reserve Forces." *Armed Forces and Society* 37, 2 (December 2009): 216–238.

Pershing, John J. *My Experiences in the World War*. New York: Frederick A. Stokes, 1931.

Pollack, Kenneth M. *Arabs at War: Military Effectiveness, 1948–1991*. Lincoln, NE: Bison Books, 2004.

———. *Armies of Sand: The Past, Present, and Future of Arab Military Effectiveness*. New York: Oxford University Press, 2018.

Powell, Colin L. *My American Journey*. New York: Ballantine Books, 2010.

Pressfield, Steven. *The Lion's Gate: On the Front Lines of the Six Day War*. New York: Sentinel, 2014.

Proctor, H. G. *The Iron Division: National Guard of Pennsylvania in the World War*. Philadelphia: John C. Winston, 1919.

Rabin, Yitzhak. *The Rabin Memoirs*. Expanded ed. Berkeley: University of California Press, 1997.

Rabinovich, Abraham. *The Battle for Jerusalem: An Unintended Conquest*. 50th anniversary ed. Middleton, DE: Jewish Publication Society, 2017.

———. *The Yom Kippur War: The Epic Encounter that Transformed the Middle East*. Rev. and updated ed. New York: Schocken, 2007.

RAND Corporation. *From Cast Lead to Protective Edge: Lessons from Israel's Wars in Gaza*. Washington, DC: RAND, 2017.

———. *The Future of Warfare in 2030*. Washington, DC: RAND, 2020.

Rauch, Steven J. *The Campaign of 1812*. Washington, DC: US Army Center of Military History, 2013.

Rearden, Steven L. *History of the Office of the Secretary of Defense: The Formative Years, 1947–1950*. Washington, DC: US Government Printing Office, 1984.

Reese, Roger R. *The Imperial Russian Army in Peace, War, and Revolution, 1856–1917.* Lawrence: University Press of Kansas, 2019.

———. *The Soviet Military Experience: A History of the Soviet Army, 1917–1991.* New York: Routledge, 2002.

Reilly, Henry J. *Americans All; the Rainbow at War: Official History of the 42nd Rainbow Division in the World War.* New York: FJ Heer, 1936.

Ricks, Thomas. *The Generals.* New York: Penguin Books, 2012.

Ridgway, Matthew. *The Korean War: How We Met the Challenge; How All-Out Asian War Was Averted; Why MacArthur Was Dismissed; Why Today's War Objectives Must Be Limited.* New York: Doubleday, 1967.

Rodman, David. *Combined Arms Warfare in Israeli Military History: From the War of Independence to Operation Protective Edge.* Brighton, UK: Sussex Academic Press, 2019.

———. "A Tale of Two Fronts: Israeli Military Performance during the Early Days of the 1973 Yom Kippur War." *Journal of Military History* 82, 1 (January 2018): 208–218.

Rommel, Erwin. *Infantry Attacks* [1935]. Barnsley, UK: Greenhill Books, 1990.

Roosevelt, Theodore. *An Autobiography by Theodore Roosevelt* [1923]. New York: Astounding Stories, 2017.

Ross, Steven T. *From Flintlock to Rifle: Infantry Tactics, 1740–1866.* London: Frank Cass, 1996.

Rostker, Bernard D. *I Want You! The Evolution of the All-Volunteer Force.* Washington, DC: RAND Corporation, 2006.

Rothenberg, Gunther E. *The Anatomy of the Israeli Army.* London: B. T. Batsford, 1979.

———. *The Art of Warfare in the Age of Napoleon.* Bloomington: Indiana University Press, 1981.

Rottman, Gordon. *Korean War Order of Battle: United States, United Nations, and Communist Ground, Naval, and Air Forces, 1950–1953.* Westport, CT: Praeger, 2002.

Russell, William H. *The British Expedition to the Crimea* [1858]. Rev. ed. New York: Routledge & Sons, 1877.

Rutenberg, Amy. *Rough Draft: Cold War Military Manpower Policy and the Origins of the Vietnam-Era Draft Resistance.* Ithaca, NY: Cornell University Press, 2019.

Sachar, Howard M. *A History of Israel: From the Rise of Zionism to Our Time.* New York: Knopf, 2007.

Sakal, Emanuel. *Soldier in the Sinai: A General's Account of the Yom Kippur War,* trans. Moshe Tlamim. Lexington: University Press of Kentucky, 2014.

Samuels, Chad. "Connecting the Battlespace." *Armor and Mobility,* May 2010, 4–6.

Sassoon, Siegfried. *Memoirs of an Infantry Officer* [1930]. Safety Harbor, FL: Simon Publications, 2010.

Scales, Robert H., Jr. *Certain Victory.* London: Brassey's, 1994.

Scharre, Paul. *Army of None: Autonomous Weapons and the Future of War.* New York: W. W. Norton, 2018.

Schiff, Zeev. *A History of the Israeli Army, 1874 to the Present: Israel's Foremost Military Expert Tells the Story of the World's Best Citizen Army.* New York: Macmillan, 1985.

Schwarzkopf, Norman. *It Doesn't Take a Hero: The Autobiography of General Norman Schwarzkopf.* New York: Bantam Books, 1992.

Segev, Tom. *One Palestine, Complete: Jews and Arabs under the British Mandate.* New York: Owl Books, 2001.

Sellers, Terry L., Gregory Fontenot, E. J. Degen, and David Tohn. "On Point: The United States Army in Operation Iraqi Freedom." *Naval War College Review* 59, 2 (2006): article 14.

Setzekorn, Eric B. *The U.S. Army Campaigns of World War I: Joining the Great War, April 1917–April 1918.* Washington, DC: US Department of the Army, 2017.

Shamir, Eitan. *Transforming Command: The Pursuit of Mission Command in the U.S., British, and Israeli Armies.* Stanford, CA: Stanford University Press, 2011.

Shapira, Anita. *Israel: A History.* Waltham, MA: Brandeis University Press, 2012.
———. *Land and Power: The Zionist Resort to Force, 1881–1948.* Stanford, CA: Stanford University Press, 1999.

Sharon, Ariel. *Warrior: An Autobiography.* 2nd ed. New York: Simon & Schuster, 2002.

Shindler, Colin. *A History of Modern Israel.* New York: Cambridge University Press, 2008.

Showalter, Dennis. "The Prussian Landwehr and Its Critics, 1813–1819." *Central European History* 3 :(1971) 1 ,4–33.
———. *Tannenberg Clash of Empires, 1914.* Washington, DC: Brassey's, 2004.
———. *The Wars of German Unification.* 2nd ed. New York: Bloomsbury Academic, 2015.

Silberman, Neil. *A Prophet from amongst You: The Life of Yigael Yadin.* Boston: Addison-Wesley, 1993.

Smythe, Donald. *Pershing: General of the Armies.* Bloomington: Indiana University Press, 2007.

Solka, Michael, and Darko Pavlovic. *German Armies 1870–71.* Vol. 1. London: Opsrey, 2004.

Sorely, Lewis, ed. *Press On! Selected Works of General Donn A. Starry.* Fort Leavenworth, KS: Combat Studies Institute Press, 2009.
———. *Thunderbolt: From the Battle of the Bulge to Vietnam and Beyond; General Creighton Abrams and the Army of His Times.* New York: Simon & Schuster, 1992.

Stanton, Shelby, and Russell F. Weigley. *World War II Order of Battle: An Encyclopedic Reference to U.S. Army Ground Forces from Battalion through Division, 1939–1946.* Mechanicsburg, PA: Stackpole Books, 2006.

Starr, Kevin. *Embattled Dreams: California in War and Peace, 1940–1950.* New York: Oxford University Press, 2003.

The Statesman's Yearbook 1914. London: Macmillan, 1914.

Stewart, Richard W., ed. *American Military History,* vol. 1, *The United States Army and the Forging of a Nation, 1775–1917.* Washington, DC: US Army Center of Military History, 2009.

———. *American Military History,* vol. 2, *The United States Army in a Global Era, 1917–2008.* Washington, DC: US Army Center of Military History, 2010.

Stone, David R. *The Russian Army in the Great War: The Eastern Front, 1914–1917.* Lawrence: University Press of Kansas, 2015.

Stotler, Mark A. *George C. Marshall: Soldier-Statesman of the American Century.* Boston: Twayne, 1989.

Strachan, Hew. *The First World War.* New York: Penguin Books, 2003.

———, ed. *The Oxford Illustrated History of the First World War.* 2nd ed. New York: Oxford University Press, 2014.

Summers Lowe, Miranda. "The Gradual Shift to an Operational Reserve: Reserve Component Mobilizations in the 1990s." *Military Review,* May 2019.

Swain, Richard M. *"Lucky War": Third Army in Desert Storm.* Fort Leavenworth, KS: Combat Studies Institute, 2011.

———, ed. *Select Papers of General William E. DePuy.* Fort Leavenworth, KS: US Army Command and General Staff College, 1995.

Tabatabai, Ariane M. *No Conquest, No Defeat: Iran's National Security Strategy.* New York: Oxford University Press, 2020.

Taylor, Maxwell D. *Swords and Plowshares: A Distinguished Soldier, Statesman, and Presidential Advisor Tells His Story.* New York: W. W. Norton, 1972.

Taylor, William A. *Every Citizen a Soldier: The Campaign for Universal Military Training after World War II.* College Station: Texas A&M University Press, 2014.

Thomas, Nigel F. *German Army in World War I 1917–18.* Oxford: Osprey, 2004.

Trauschweizer, Ingo. *The Cold War U.S. Army: Building Deterrence for Limited War.* Lawrence: University Press of Kansas, 2008.

Tuchman, Barbara W. *The Guns of August: The Outbreak of World War I.* New York: Random House, 1989.

Upton, Emory. *The Armies of Asia and Europe.* London: Griffin, 1878.

Van Creveld, Martin. *Command in War.* Cambridge, MA: Harvard University Press, 1985.

———. *Moshe Dayan.* London: Weidenfeld & Nicolson, 2004.

———. "The Second Lebanon War: A Re-assessment," *Infinity Journal* 1, 3 (Summer 2011): 4–7.

———. *The Sword and the Olive: A Critical History of the Israeli Defense Force.* New York: Public Affairs, 2008.

———. *Technology and War: From 2000 B.C. to the Present.* Rev. and expanded ed. New York: Free Press, 1991.

Ventresco, Fiorello. "Loyalty and Dissent: Italian Reservists in America during World War I." *Italian American* 4, 1 (Fall/Winter 1978): 93–122.

Von Luck, Hans. *Panzer Commander: The Memoirs of Colonel Hans Von Luck.* New York: Dell Books, 1989.

Von Schlieffen, Alfred. "The Schlieffen Plan" [1905]. Reprinted in Gerhard Ritter, *Der Schlieffenplan: Kritik eines Mythos* [The Schlieffen Plan: Analysis of a myth]. Munich: Oldenbourg, 1956, 145–160.

Waldron, William H. *The Infantry Soldier's Handbook: The Classic World War I Training Manual* [1917]. New York: Lyons, 2000.

Walker, Fred. *From Texas to Rome with General Fred L. Walker: Fighting World War II and the Italian Campaign with the 36th Infantry Division, as Seen through the Eyes of Its Commanding General* [1969]. El Dorado Hills, CA: Savas, 2014.

Walker, Wallace Earl. "Comparing Army Reserve Forces: A Tale of Multiple Ironies, Conflicting Realities, and More Certain Prospects." *Armed Forces and Society* 18, 3 (1992): 303–322.

Ward, Steven R. *Immortal: A Military History of Iran and Its Armed Forces.* Washington, DC: Georgetown University Press, 2009.

Watling, Jack, and Nick Reynolds. "Ukraine at War: Paving the Road from Survival to Victory." *RUSI*, 4 July 2022.

Wawro, Geoffrey. *The Franco-Prussian War: The German Conquest of France in 1870–1871.* New York: Cambridge University Press, 2003.

———. *A Mad Catastrophe: The Outbreak of World War I and the Collapse of the Habsburg Empire.* New York: Basic Books, 2014.

———. *Sons of Freedom: The Forgotten American Soldiers Who Defeated Germany in World War I.* New York: Basic Books, 2018.

———. *Warfare and Society in Europe, 1792–1914.* New York: Routledge, 2003.

Weaver, Michael E. *Guard Wars: The 28th Infantry Division in World War II.* Bloomington: Indiana University Press, 2010.

Weber, Claude. "The French Military Reserve: Real or Abstract Force." *Armed Forces and Society* 37, 2 (2011): 321–340.

Weber, Eugen. *Peasants into Frenchmen.* Stanford, CA: Stanford University Press, 1976.

Weigley, Russell F. *The American Way of War: A History of United States Military Strategy and Policy.* Bloomington: Indiana University Press, 1977.

Weinberg, Gerhard L. *A World at Arms: A Global History of World War II.* New York: Cambridge University Press, 1994.

Weitz, Richard. *The Reserve Policies of Nations: A Comparative Analysis.* Carlisle, PA: Strategic Studies Institute, 2014.

Weller, Jac. "Israeli Armor: Lessons from the Six-Day War." *Military Review*, November 1971.

Westlake, Ray, and Mike Chappell. *British Territorial Units 1914–18.* Oxford: Osprey, 2013.

Williams, H. H. "Art. VI.—Remarks by Raja Radhakanta Deva, on Art." *Journal Royal Asiatic Society* 16 (January 1860): 209–222.

Williams, Louis. *Israel Defense Forces: A People's Army.* Tel Aviv: Israeli Ministry of Defense, 1989.

Wilson, John B. *Maneuver and Firepower: The Evolution of Divisions and Separate Brigades.* Washington, DC: US Army Center of Military History, 1998.

Winter, Denis. *Death's Men: Soldiers of the Great War.* New York: Penguin, 2014.

Wise, Terence. *Medieval European Armies.* Oxford: Osprey, 2012.

Wright, Robert K. *The Massachusetts Militia: A Bibliographic Study.* Washington, DC: National Guard Bureau, 1986.

Yermiya, Dov. *My War Diary: Lebanon, June 5–July 1, 1982*, trans. Hillel Schenker. Jerusalem: Mifras, 1983.

Young, Peter. *The British Army: 1642–1970.* London: William Kimber, 1967.

Zorn, E. L. "Israel's Quest for Satellite Intelligence." *Studies in Intelligence* 10 (Winter–Spring 2001): 33–38.

Dissertations and Theses

Brady, James T. "Ready to Serve? The 48th, 155th, and 256th Brigades and the Roundout Concept during Operations Desert Shield and Desert Storm." M.A. thesis, US Army Command and General Staff College, 2007.

De Soet, Jeannine V. "Defence Reviews in Times of Economic Turmoil: British and German Reserve Forces in Transformation (2010–2015/1970–1979)." Ph.D. diss., King's College, 2019.

Jones, David A. "Pinchbeck Regulars? The Role and Organisation of the Territorial Army, 1919–1940." Ph.D. diss., Oxford University, 2016.

Ostovar, Afshon. "Guardians of the Islamic Revolution Ideology, Politics, and the Development of Military Power in Iran (1979–2009)." Ph.D. diss., University of Michigan, 2009.

Sherwood, Ash. "The Training Aspect of Reserve Battalion Combat Readiness." M.A. thesis, US Army Command and General Staff College, 1983.

Abrams, Creighton, 89
Active Defense concept (United States),
   90–91, 92–94
Adan, Avraham, 147
Affiliate Program (United States), 91
Afghanistan, 104–105, 106–107
Agreement for Strategic Cooperation, 157
AirLand Battle (United States), 95–96,
   97, 100–101
Aisne-Marne offensive (World War I), 49
Allon, Yigal, 116, 118
American Revolution, 2–3
Amitai, Eliezer, 139
Arab League, 120
Arab Legion, 120–121
Arab Revolt, 116
Army National Guard (ARNG) (United
   States)
   Affiliate Program and, 91
   AirLand Battle and, 95–96, 97, 100–101
   Associated Unit Program of, 112
   Bold Shift Program of, 103
   challenges of, 70, 73, 77, 81–82, 83, 93,
      100, 108, 109
   deployment timelines of, 84, 111–112
   Desert Strike exercise and, 85
   downsizing of, 101–102
   draft dodgers in, 79
   Enhanced Brigades program of, 103
   Fifth Infantry (Mechanized) Division
      of, 89
   First Cavalry of, 99
   Fortieth division of, 74, 75–76
   Forty-Eighth Infantry (Georgia) of,
      100–101, 106
   Forty-Fifth division of, 74, 75
   Forty-First Infantry Brigade (Oregon)
      of, 89

   Forty-Ninth Armored (Texas) of, 83,
      102–103
   Forty-Third division of, 74
   4.0 initiative of, 111
   improvements to, 77
   investment into, 82, 97
   Korean War and, 75–76
   Kosovo mission and, 103
   mission of, 81
   mobilization exercise of, 92
   New Look strategy and, 78
   155th Armored (Mississippi) division
      of, 100
   as Operational Reserve, 78–86,
      101–112
   Operation Spartan Shield and, 111
   origin of, 66
   Pentomic structure of, 81
   Persian Gulf War and, 98–101
   readiness of, 70–71, 82, 92, 93, 100, 112
   recruitment to, 86, 92, 105
   reestablishment of, 69
   reorganization of, 84–85
   responsiveness of, 67–68
   restrictions to, 107
   Roundout Program and, 89, 91
   Second Brigade Combat Team (BCT)
      (Pennsylvania) of, 106
   Seventh Infantry Division of, 89
   shortages of, 81–82, 86–87
   statistics of, 70–71, 84
   Strategic Reserve Force (STRAF)
      program and, 79
   structure of, 109
   Third Infantry Division of, 106
   Thirty-Second Infantry (Wisconsin)
      of, 83
   training of, 74, 79–81, 85, 91–92, 97, 103

Army National Guard (ARNG) (United States), *continued*
Twenty-Eight division of, 74
Twenty-Fifth Infantry Division of, 89
Twenty-Fourth division of, 75
Twenty-Fourth Infantry of, 99
Twenty-Ninth Brigade (Hawaii) of, 89
Twenty-Ninth Infantry Division (Maryland and Virginia) of, 111
256th Infantry Brigade (Louisiana) of, 89, 100
278th Armored Cavalry Regiment (Tennessee) of, 111
Vietnam War and, 85–86
wages in, 109
weaponry of, 82, 97, 108–109
See also National Guard (NG) (United States)
Army Reorganization Plan (United States), 50
Ashkenazi, Gabriel "Gabi," 183
Aspin, Les, 100
Associated Unit Program (United States), 112
Auftragstaktik (Germany), 23
Austria, 12
Austro-Hungarian Empire, 11, 17, 18, 19, 196
Axis of Resistance (Iran), 157

Barak, Ehud, 163, 165, 167
Bar Lev, Chaim, 142–143
Bar Lev Line, 142
Battle of Gravelotte, 14
Battle of Jenin, 198
Battle of Königgrätz, 12
Begin, Menachem, 156
Beightler, Robert, 61
Beirut, 158–159
Ben-Anat, Shuki, 188
Ben-Ari, Uri, 140
Ben-Gurion, David, 120, 121, 122, 128
Berlin Crisis, 82–83, 84
Boer War, 20
Bold Shift Program (United States), 103
Bonaparte, Napoleon, 3, 4
Bradley, Omar, 65, 67

breech-loading rifle, 7–8
Britain. *See* United Kingdom
British Expeditionary Force (BEF), 19–20, 29–30
British Mandate, 114, 115
Brown, Harold, 94
Brucker, Wilber, 80
Budget Control Act (BCA) of 2011, 108
Bush, George H. W., 99
Bush, George W., 104

cadre approach, 113, 194, 197
Campaign between the Wars (Israel), 187
Camp David Accords, 157
Canada, 19
Carter, Jimmy, 94
Casey, George, 106
CENTCOM (US Central Command), 99, 104
Central Intelligence Agency (CIA) (United States), 69
chassepot rifles, 12, 14
Cheney, Dick, 99, 101
China, 34
Civil War (United States), 6
Coffman, Edward, 51
Cohen, William, 102
Cold War, 33, 66–71, 78
Collingwood, R. G., 191
Collins, J. Lawton, 71
conscription
abandonment or curtailment of, 32, 35, 36
in France, 26–27
in Germany, 31
in Poland, 36
in Russia, 35
in South Korea, 36
in Sweden, 36
in the United Kingdom, 35
in the United States, 35, 57, 77, 85–86, 87
Continental Army (United States), 40–41
Craig, Malin, 55
Crimean War, 6–7
Crossword 2000 (Israel Defense Forces), 166

Dayan, Moshe, 118, 127–129, 130, 140, 147
Defense Service Law (Israel), 122–123
Department of Defense (DOD) (United States)
   Army National Guard (ARNG) decisions by, 81–82
   decisions of, 68–69, 96, 107
   reforms from, 84–85
   rotation policy of, 71
   tensions with, 102
DePuy, William, 89–90, 91
Desert Strike exercise (United States), 85
Dick, Charles, 39
Dick Act (United States), 39–40
Dori, Yaakov, 122
draft. *See* conscription
Dreyse needle rifle, 7–8
Duncan, Stephen, 99

Egypt
   casualties of, 139
   Israel *versus*, 128–132, 142
   raids from, 127
   Six-Day War and, 136–137
   weaponry of, 142, 152
   Yom Kippur War and, 145–149
Eisenhower, Dwight D., 78
Eitan, Rafael, 152
Eizenkot, Gadi, 185, 188
Elazar, David, 143, 145
Enhanced Brigades program (United States), 103
Eshkol, Levi, 137, 138
expanding torrent, 24

Field Corps (Haganah), 117
Field Manual (FM) 3–0 (United States), 110
Field Manual (FM) 100–5 (United States), 83, 90, 93
Field Service Regulation (FSR) (United States), 51–52
First Intifada, 36, 162–163, 164
Flexible Response (United States), 83
Ford, Gerald, 94
Forrestal, James, 67, 68

France
   British Expeditionary Force (BEF) *versus*, 19–20
   chassepot of, 12
   conscription in, 26–27
   Germany *versus*, 26, 27–28
   Maginot Line and, 26, 27
   military modernization in, 26
   military personnel statistics of, 11, 12, 13, 14, 18
   military policies of, 13
   military practices in, 10
   military training in, 13, 27–28
   National Guard (NG) of, 3
   North Atlantic Treaty Organization (NATO) and, 70
   Prussia *versus*, 3–4, 8, 13–14
   reserve system in, 13, 14, 19, 26–27, 28, 196
   Third Republic in, 14
   weaponry of, 12
   in World War I, 26–27
Franco-Austrian War, 6
Franco-Prussian War, 11
French Lebel rifle, 16
French Revolution, 2–3

Gadna (Haganah), 117
Galinka, Shmuel, 131
Gallant, Yoav, 182–183
Gantz, Benny, 184
Garrison, Lindley, 41
Gates, Robert, 107
Gates, Thomas S., Jr., 87
Gaza, 162–163, 174, 186
Gemayel, Bashir, 158
General Staff (Prussia), 8–9
Germany
   assault troop detachments of, 23
   Auftragstaktik of, 23
   cadre system of, 193
   conscription in, 31
   France *versus*, 26, 27–28
   Landwehr militia of, 21–22
   military innovations in, 23
   military personnel statistics of, 18, 30
   military training in, 21, 22, 31

Germany, *continued*
  reserve system of, 21, 193
  Soviet Union *versus*, 31
  Third Reserve Division of, 22
  United Kingdom *versus*, 20
  weaponry of, 23
global positioning systems (GPS), 33
GLONASS, 33
Goder, Shmuel, 131
Gorman, Paul, 91
Government Accountability Office
    (GAO) (United States), 93, 97
Great Britain. *See* United Kingdom
Great Depression, 54
Green, Roy, 80
ground radar systems, 33
Guderian, Heinz, 24, 31
Guerard, John, 80
Gur, Mordechai "Motta," 140, 152, 154

Haganah, 114–115, 116, 117, 119, 120. *See
    also* Israeli Defense Forces (IDF)
Halevi, Herzl, 189
Halutz, Dan, 177–178
Hamas, 162–163, 174, 182, 186, 187, 188
Hay, James, 41
helicopters, 108–109
Hirsch, Gal, 176, 181
Hitler, Adolf, 31
Hizballah, 159, 166, 175–176, 177, 179,
    180, 188
Hodges, Ben, 109
Holland, William, 101
Home Guard (Haganah), 117
Howard, Michael, 1, 25
Hudelson, Daniel, 74, 75

immigration, 19, 114
infantry fighting vehicle (IFV), 34
intelligence, surveillance, and
    reconnaissance (ISR) technology, 33
Iran, 157, 182
Iran-Iraq War, 166
Iraq, 166
Iraq War, 104–105, 106–107
Irgun, 119
ISIS, 108, 109

Islamic Revolutionary Guards Corps
    (IRGC), 182
Israel
  attacks to, 175–176
  cadre system of, 113, 197
  casualties of, 175
  defense spending by, 126, 143–144, 153,
    159, 160, 167, 185, 188
  economic conditions of, 137–138, 149,
    159, 174
  Egypt *versus*, 127, 136–139, 142
  Haganah of, 114–115, 116, 117, 119, 120
  immigration to, 127
  Jordan *versus*, 127, 139–141
  Keshet (Rainbow) Plan of, 177
  Lebanon *versus*, 157–158
  Likud of, 155
  major operations of, 187
  National Water Carrier Project of, 136
  Operation Defensive Shield and, 172
  Peace Now movement in, 156
  political activism in, 155–156
  readiness crisis of, 127–128, 152–157,
    169, 198
  reserve system of, 36, 37, 113
  Suez Crisis and, 128–132
  Syria *versus*, 141
  television influence in, 156
  "There Is a Limit" movement of,
    159–160
  threats to, 113
  War of Independence and, 118–122
  Yishuv of, 114, 115, 118–122
  Yom Kippur War and, 145–149
  See also Israeli Defense Forces (IDF)
Israel Defense Forces (IDF)
  absenteeism in, 168
  absent without leave (AWOL) in, 172
  air power of, 177–178
  Alexandroni Brigade of, 178–179
  building of, 122–128
  Carmeli Brigade of, 179, 181
  casualties of, 130, 149, 154, 175, 179
  challenges of, 126–127, 134, 156–157,
    159, 160
  command structure of, 180–181
  conscript standards of, 155

costs of, 160–161, 167, 184
Crossword 2000 of, 166
decline consequences to, 170–182
decline of, 157–165, 166, 174, 198
decline reversal of, 182–190
defense imports of, 184
demographics of, 123
as distracted and demoralized, 165–170
education of, 127
as elite reserve, 132–136
expansion of, 135, 152–153
failures of, 180
Fifth Infantry Brigade of, 140, 172, 173, 174
Fifty-Fifth Paratrooper Brigade of, 140
First Golani Infantry of, 129, 172–173
551st Brigade of, 178
Forty-Fifth Armored Brigade of, 140
foundation of, 114–118
401st Armored Brigade of, 178
409th Paratrooper Brigade, 158
Fourth Brigade of, 130–131, 140
gender roles in, 123
ground unit categories of, 135–136
immigration and, 127
importance of, 164–165
infantry units of, 135–136
Kadesh operation of, 128–129
Keshet (Rainbow) Plan of, 177
legal obstacles of, 183
losses of, 151–152
major operations of, 187
military doctrine of, 165
Ninety-Eighth Parachute Division of, 176, 178, 180, 185
Ninety-First Division of, 176, 178–180
Ninth Infantry Brigade of, 129, 130, 140
143rd Armored Division of, 146, 147
146th Armored Division of, 146, 147
162nd Armored Division of, 146, 147, 176, 178, 180
overview of, 149–150, 190, 197
personnel benefits in, 169
personnel challenges of, 155, 162, 163–164, 189
personnel costs of, 153

personnel standards of, 135
policy changes to, 152–153
practices and policies of, 125–126
readiness of, 127–128, 152–157, 163, 169, 185, 189, 198
reforms to, 165–166
reorganization of, 121, 124
reserve of, 123, 124–126, 136–141, 142–150
resistance in, 171–172
resupply challenges of, 179–180
Second Intifada and, 170–182
Seventh Armor Brigade of, 129, 136–137
Seventy-Seventh Ugdah of, 129
Six-Day War and, 136–141
Sixteenth Infantry Brigade of, 139
Sixtieth Armor Brigade of, 137
size and order of battle of, 133
Smart Shooter of, 199
statistics of, 154
structure of, 121
Suez Crisis and, 128–132
Tenth Armored Brigade of, 140
Tenth Infantry Brigade of, 129, 130–131
Thirty-Eighth Ugdah of, 129, 130
Thirty-Seventh Armored Brigade of, 128, 140
Thirty-Seventh Mechanized Brigade of, 131
Thirty-Sixth Armored Division of, 147, 176, 178
threats to, 151
300th Infantry Brigade of, 181
340th Armored Division, 173
366th Reserve Armored Division of, 176, 178, 179
Totality of the Tank and, 143
training of, 123–125, 134–135, 137, 142–143, 144, 146, 154–155, 160, 170, 175, 181–182, 183, 185–186, 190, 197
transformation of, 152
transportation of, 134, 155
Twenty-Seventh Infantry Brigade of, 128, 129
202nd Parachute Battalion of, 129

Israel Defense Forces (IDF), *continued*
  210th division of, 146, 147
  Ugdah Peled of, 140
  victories of, 120, 136–141
  wages for, 126, 172
  weaknesses of, 130
  weaponry of, 128, 132, 143, 152, 158,
    161–162, 167, 184, 188–189
  Yom Kippur War and, 145–149
  See also Haganah
Israeli Air Force (IAF), 121, 133–134, 136,
  138, 144, 152, 153, 161
Italy, 18, 19, 30, 196

Jandal, Abu, 173
Japan, 30, 74
Javelin antitank missile, 103–104
Jenin refugee camp, 172
Johnson, Lyndon, 85
Joint Chiefs of Staff (JCS) (United
  States), 69, 74, 78
Joint Readiness Training Center (JRTC)
  (United States), 95
Jomini, Antoine-Henri, 7
Jordan, 127, 139–141

Kadavy, Timothy, 110
Kadesh operation (Israel), 128–129
Kasserine Pass, 90
Keegan, John, 25–26, 198–199
Kennedy, John F., 82, 83
Keshet (Rainbow) Plan (Israel), 177
Khomeini, Ruhollah, 157
Khrushchev, Nikita, 82–83
Kiesling, Eugenia, 25, 28
Knesset (Israel), 155, 168, 183, 186
Kochavi, Aviv, 188–189
Korean War, 38, 71–76, 79
Kosovo mission (United States), 103
Krumper system (Prussia), 4
Kuwait, 111

Labor Zionists, 114
Laird, Melvin, 88
Landwehr militia, 3, 4, 6, 7, 8, 10, 12, 13,
  21–22
Laskov, Chaim, 132

Lawrence, A. W., 117
Lebanon, 157–158, 159, 160, 180, 181–182,
  197
Lebanon War, 151–152, 176, 198
Liddell Hart, B. H., 24
Likud (Israel), 155
limited war, preparation for, 83–84
Lipkin-Shahak, Amnon, 165, 169
loitering munitions, 199

M2 Bradley IFV, 34
M-16 rifle, 33
MacArthur, Douglas, 44, 54, 71
machine guns, 17
Maginot Line, 26, 27
Maklef, Mordechai, 122
Mann, William, 47
Mansoor, Peter, 65
March, Peyton, 50
Marshall, George, 55, 56, 61, 65–67, 68
Marshall, S. L. A., 123
Martin, Charles, 47
Maxim, Hiram, 17
Maxim machine gun, 17
McNair, Lesley, 47, 59–61, 62
McNamara, Robert, 83, 84
McNeill, William, 16
Meuse-Argonne offensive (World War I),
  49
military
  costs regarding, 36
  developments in, 24
  formations of, 16
  incentives for, 35–36
  missions of, 5
  reserve systems of, 1
  subdivisions in, 16
  See also specific countries
Militia Act of 1792 (United States), 3, 39
Milley, Mark, 77, 110–111
mission-essential tasks (METs) (United
  States), 98
Mofaz, Shaul, 169–170, 172
Montgomery, Sonny, 99, 101
Mor, Uzi, 147
Multi-Domain Battle (Multi-Domain
  Operations) (United States), 110

Nabi Musi festival, 114
Napoleon Bonaparte, 3, 4
Nasser, Gamal Abdel, 128, 136, 144
National Commission on the Future of
    the Army (NCFA) (United States),
    107
National Defense Act of 1916 (United
    States), 41
National Defense Act of 1920 (United
    States), 51
National Defense Strategy (United
    States), 110
National Guard (NG) (France), 3
National Guard (NG) (United States)
    activation of, 38
    Air National Guard (ANG) of, 66
    in Aisne-Marne offensive, 49
    Americal Division of, 63
    assessment of, 60–61
    birth of, 39–42
    casualties of, 45, 48, 49, 65, 75
    challenges of, 44–45, 49–50, 52, 56, 58,
        81–82
    Cold War and, 66–71, 78
    composition of, 58
    criticism of, 79
    decline of, 50
    defense spending for, 54
    deployment timeline of, 46, 64, 72
    education of, 57–58
    Executive Order 8244 and, 57
    Fortieth division of, 63, 74, 75–76
    Forty-Fifth division of, 65, 75
    Forty-Second (Rainbow Division)
        division of, 44, 45, 49
    Forty-Seventh division of, 73
    Forty-Third division of, 63, 71, 74
    ineligibility challenges of, 41–42
    interwar years of, 50–56
    Korean War and, 71–76
    leadership of, 51, 61–62
    Meuse-Argonne offensive of, 49
    mission structure of, 81
    mobilization of, 41–42, 58
    New Look strategy and, 78
    Ninety-Third division of, 44
    One Army policy of, 59–60

    as Operational Reserve, 78–86
    organization of, 44
    as Organized Militia, 40
    overview of, 20–21
    Pentomic structure of, 81
    readiness of, 30, 39–40, 51, 53, 55,
        70–71
    reorganization of, 38, 59, 66
    replacements in, 43
    Selective Service Act of 1940 and, 59
    statistics of, 43, 54, 55, 69, 70–71, 106
    Thirty-First division of, 73
    Thirty-Fourth division of, 63–65
    Thirty-Second division of, 63
    Thirty-Seventh division of, 63
    Thirty-Sixth division of, 65
    training for, 39–41, 42–43, 44, 52–53,
        56, 58–59, 68–69, 74, 75, 77–78,
        79–81, 107
    transportation of, 54–55
    Twenty-Eighth division of, 71, 74
    Twenty-Ninth division of, 65
    Twenty-Seventh division of, 47, 49
    Twenty-Sixth (Yankee) division of, 45,
        49
    usage of, 36
    weaponry of, 59
    in World War I, 42–50
    in World War II, 57–66
    See also Army National Guard
        (ARNG)
National Guard Association (NGA)
    (United States), 39
National Guard Association of the United
    States (NGAUS), 50, 54, 68, 69, 75,
    79
nationalism, 4
National Security Act of 1947 (United
    States), 69
National Security Council (NSC) (United
    States), 69
National Training Center (NTC) (United
    States), 91
National Water Carrier Project (Israel),
    136
Nelson, Bill, 105
New Look Strategy (United States), 78

Nixon, Richard, 87
noncommissioned officers (NCOs), 10, 124
North Atlantic Treaty Organization (NATO), 70, 88
nuclear arms, 78

officer candidate school (OCS) (United States), 80
Offset Strategy (United States), 94–95
Olmert, Ehud, 176
One Army policy (United States), 59–60
Operation Accountability (Israel), 175
Operational Reserve, 78–86, 101–112
Operation Breaking Dawn (Israel), 187
Operation Cast Lead (Israel), 187
Operation Defensive Shield (Israel), 172
Operation Desert Storm (United States), 92
Operation Grapes of Wrath (Israel), 175
Operation Guardian of the Walls (Israel), 187
Operation Litani (Israel), 158
Operation Peace for Galilee (Israel), 151, 159
Operation Pillar of Defense (Israel), 187
Operation Protective Edge (Israel), 187
Operation Shield and Arrow (Israel), 187
Operation Spartan Shield (United States), 111
Opposing Force (United States), 91
Organized Militia (United States), 40
Organized Reserve (US Army Reserve) (United States), 51
O'Ryan, John, 47

Palestine, 114, 115, 163, 174, 175
Palestine Liberation Organization (PLO), 157–158
Palestinian Arabs, 116, 118–122
Palestinian Authority (PA), 170
Palestinian Islamic Jihad, 182, 186, 187
Palmach (Haganah), 117–118
Pasha, Abdul Rahman Azzam, 120
Patton, George, 65
Peace Now movement (Israel), 156
Peled, Elad, 140

Pentomic structure, 81
Peres, Shimon, 159
Pershing, John J., 42, 45, 46–47, 52
Persian Gulf War, 34, 98–101, 162, 165, 166
Poland, 36, 111
precision guidance, 33
precision-guided munitions (PGMs), 143
Prussia
    army elements of, 7
    Austria *versus,* 12
    challenges of, 5
    defense spending in, 10–11
    economy of, 5–6, 10–11
    France *versus,* 3–4, 8, 13–14
    General Staff of, 8–9
    generation model statistics of, 7
    Krumper system of, 4
    Landwehr militia of, 3, 4, 6, 7, 8, 10, 13
    leadership in, 7, 8–9
    literacy in, 9–10
    military benefits of, 6
    military personnel statistics of, 11, 12
    noncommissioned officers (NCOs) in, 10
    part-time soldier policies within, 6
    political climate of, 6
    railroad in, 8, 11, 12
    recruitment practices of, 6
    reserve systems of, 1, 7, 14
    telegraph use in, 9, 11
    training tactics in, 9–10
    victories of, 1
    weaponry of, 7

Rabin, Yitzhak, 132, 135–136, 138
Radford, Arthur, 78
radio controllers, 33
railroad, 8, 11, 12
Reagan, Ronald, 95, 96–97
Reckord, Milton, 62
Reorganized Objective Army Divisions (ROAD) (United States), 84, 85
Reserve Enlistment Program (REP) (United States), 85
Reserve Militia (United States), 40
Reserve Officers' Training Corps (ROTC) (United States), 80

reserve systems, 1–2, 18, 25, 32–37. *See also specific countries*
Ridgway, Matthew, 73
Rogers, Bernard W., 97
Roosevelt, Franklin D., 57, 65–66
Roosevelt, Theodore, 38, 39
Root, Elihu, 39
Roundout Program (United States), 89, 91, 96
Rumsfeld, Donald, 94
Russia
  conscription abandonment in, 35
  France *versus*, 3
  GLONASS of, 33
  military personnel statistics of, 11, 18
  readiness challenges of, 30
  reserve systems of, 14, 19
  Ukraine *versus*, 37, 111, 198, 199–200
  See also Soviet Union
Russia-Ukraine war, 37, 111, 198, 199–200

Sadat, Anwar, 144–145
Sadeh, Yitzhak, 117–118
Schwarzkopf, Norman, 99
Second Intifada, 36, 151–152, 170–182
Selective Service Act of 1940 (United States), 59
Selective Service Act of 1948 (United States), 67
Selective Service Act of 1967 (United States), 85–86
Serbia, 18
Shamir, Yitzhak, 163
Sharon, Ariel, 137, 147, 158, 160
Shomron, Dan, 161–162, 164
Six-Day War, 136–141
Skills Qualification Test (United States), 91, 97
Smart Shooter, 199
Somalia, 111
South America, immigration to, 19
South Korea, 36
Soviet Union
  BMP-1 infantry fighting vehicle (IFV) of, 34
  Germany *versus*, 31
  military expansion of, 87, 90, 94

military improvements in, 31, 34–35
reserve system of, 196
United States *versus*, 82–83
weaponry of, 34, 36, 87–88, 90
See also Russia
Special Night Squads (SNS) (Israel), 116–117
Special Operations Forces (United States), 108
Special Reserve (Britain), 15
Stalin, Joseph, 76
Starry, Don, 91
Stern Gang, 119
Stimson, Henry L., 40, 59
Strategic Reserve Force (STRAF) program (United States), 79
Suez Crisis, 128–132
Sullivan, Gordon, 102
Sweden, 36
Syria, 36–37, 111, 141, 152, 157, 182

Taft, William Howard, 40
Tal, Israel, 132, 134, 136–137, 143, 146
Tal, Yiftah Ron, 175
Tankersley, Will, 86
tanks, 33, 55, 87–88, 90, 132, 143. *See also* weaponry
Task Force Smith (Korean War) (United States), 71, 90
Taylor, Maxwell, 79
telegraph, 9, 11
Territorial Army (Britain), 15–16, 28–29
"There Is a Limit" movement (Israel), 159–160
Third Republic, 14
Third Reserve Division (Germany), 22
Tnufa plan, 188
Total Force Policy (TFP) (United States), 88–89, 98–101
Totality of the Tank (Israel), 143
TRADOC (US Army Training and Doctrine Command), 89–90, 91
training, military
  Active Defense concept and, 90–91
  AirLand Battle, 95, 97
  of Army National Guard (ARNG), 74, 79–81, 85, 91–92, 97, 103

training, military, *continued*
  challenges regarding, 192–193
  developments in, 25
  extended reserve, 194
  for firearms, 5
  in France, 13, 27–28
  in Germany, 21, 22, 31
  of Israel Defense Forces (IDF),
      123–125, 134–135, 137, 142–143, 144,
      146, 154–155, 160, 170, 175, 181–182,
      183, 185–186, 190, 197
  limitations of, 2, 37
  for mission-essential tasks (METs), 98
  for National Guard (United States),
      39–41, 42–43, 52–53, 56, 58–59,
      68–69, 74, 75, 77–78, 79–81, 107
  National Training Center (NTC) for,
      91
  physical fitness, 5, 22
  in Prussia, 9–10
  for reserve systems, 1
  restrictions to, 19
  technology, 25
  in United Kingdom, 15, 29
  in the United States, 15, 52–53,
      196–197
  universal military training (UMT)
      program (United States), 66–67
transportation, 24, 54–55, 134, 155
trauma, military, 26
Treaty of Versailles, 31
Truman, Harry, 66, 69–70, 71, 73
Truman Doctrine (United States), 69–70
Tzur, Tzvi, 132

Ukraine, 37, 111, 198, 199–200
United Kingdom
  British Expeditionary Force (BEF) of,
      19–20, 29–30
  conscription abandonment in, 35
  doctrine of, 29
  Germany *versus*, 20
  military improvements in, 31
  military personnel statistics of, 11, 18,
      28–29
  military training in, 15, 29
  Palestinian control by, 115

reserve system of, 14–15
  Special Reserve of, 15
  Territorial Army of, 15–16, 28–29
  volunteer soldiers of, 2
United States
  American Revolution and, 2–3
  Army mission of, 70
  Army organization of, 40, 51, 55
  Army Reorganization Plan of, 50
  Civil War, 6
  Cold War and, 196
  conscription abandonment in, 35, 77
  Continental Army plan of, 40–41
  defense spending by, 57, 70, 83, 87, 94,
      95, 96, 97, 101, 106, 108
  Dick Act of, 39–40
  draft of, 57, 87
  economic conditions of, 69, 95
  Field Service Regulation (FSR) of,
      51–52
  France *versus*, 45
  Great Depression in, 54
  immigration to, 19
  Joint Chiefs of Staff (JCS) of, 69, 74
  M-113 armored personnel carrier
      (APC) of, 34
  military earnings in, 36
  military improvements in, 31–32, 34
  military organization of, 42
  military personnel statistics of, 40, 42,
      66
  military reorganization of, 66
  military training in, 15, 52–53, 196–197
  Militia Act of 1792, 3, 39
  National Defense Act of 1916 of, 41
  National Defense Act of 1920 of, 51
  National Security Act of 1947 of, 69
  National Security Council (NSC) of,
      69
  New Look strategy of, 78
  open-warfare doctrine of, 45
  Organized Reserve of, 51
  reserve system of, 14–15, 20–21, 37
  Selective Service Act of 1940 of, 59
  Selective Service Act of 1948 of, 67
  Selective Service Act of 1967, 85–86
  Soviet Union *versus*, 82–83

universal military training (UMT)
  program of, 66–67
  volunteer soldiers of, 2
  weaponry of, 55, 103–104
  in World War I, 193, 196
  See also specific entities
universal military training (UMT)
  program (United States), 66–67
unmanned aerial vehicles (UAVs), 151
US Army
  AirLand Battle of, 95–96, 97, 100–101
  challenges of, 108
  doctrine of, 23
  Field Manual (FM) 100–5 of, 83, 90, 93
  incentives of, 36
  mission of, 70
  organization of, 34, 40, 51, 55
  population of, 42
  schools of, 52
  statistics of, 105
  structure of, 51, 81
  training of, 196–197
  See also Army National Guard
    (ARNG) (United States); National
    Guard (United States)
US Army Reserve (Organized Reserve)
  (United States), 51, 84
US Army Training and Doctrine
  Command (TRADOC), 89–90, 91
US Central Command (CENTCOM),
  99, 104

Van Creveld, Martin, 164
Vietnam War, 85–86
Villa, Pancho, 41
von Moltke, Helmuth, 8, 14
von Seeckt, Hans, 30–31
Vuono, Carl, 99

Walker, Fred, 62, 63
Walsh, Ellard, 68
War Department (United States), 40–41,
  42, 43, 50, 62–63, 67
War of Attrition, 142–143
War of Independence (Israel), 118–122
War Powers Act of 1973 (United States),
  99

Warsaw Pact, 95
weaponry
  AirLand Battle and, 95–96
  AK-47 rifle, 33
  of Army National Guard (ARNG), 82,
    97, 108–109
  breech-loading rifle, 7–8
  chassepot, 12
  in the Cold War, 33
  developments in, 6, 16, 24, 33, 34,
    103–104, 199
  Dreyse needle rifle, 7–8
  of Egypt, 142, 152
  of France, 12
  French Lebel rifle, 16
  frontage coverage of, 34
  of Germany, 23
  GPS for, 33
  of Israel Defense Forces (IDF), 128,
    132, 143, 152, 158, 161–162, 167, 184,
    188–189
  of Israeli Air Force (IAF), 144, 153,
    161
  Javelin antitank missile, 103–104
  M-16 rifle, 33
  machine guns, 17
  Maxim machine gun, 17
  of the National Guard (United States),
    59
  policies regarding, 5
  precision-guided munitions (PGMs),
    143
  of Prussia, 7
  Smart Shooter, 199
  of the Soviet Union, 34, 36, 87–88,
    90
  of Syria, 152
  tanks, 87–88, 90, 132, 143
  of the United States, 55, 103–104
  Winchester repeater rifle, 16
  in World War I, 17, 192
  in World War II, 33
West Bank, 162–163, 186
Westmoreland, William, 85
Wickersham, George W., 40
William I (king), 7
Wilson, Charles, 78–79

Wilson, Woodrow, 40
Winchester repeater rifle, 16
Wingate, Charles Orde, 116
World War I
    Aisne-Marne offensive of, 49
    France in, 26–27
    Meuse-Argonne offensive of, 49
    National Guard (United States) in,
        42–50
    reserve systems in, 18, 193
    stalemate of, 24
    statistics regarding, 17
    trauma from, 26
    weaponry in, 17, 192
World War II, 32, 33, 57–66

Ya'alon, Moshe "Bogie," 174
Yadin, Yigael, 120, 122, 125, 127
Yishuv, 114, 115, 118–122
Yoffe, Avraham, 138
Yom Kippur War, 90, 143, 145–149, 156

Zaluzhnyi, Valerii, 200
Zuckerman, Erez, 179

Printed in the USA
CPSIA information can be obtained
at www.ICGtesting.com
LVHW052205141223
766376LV00016B/404/J